Getting Started with Visual Studio 2026

Master the New Era of Visual Studio, AI, and Productivity

Gerald Versluis

Apress®

Getting Started with Visual Studio 2026: Master the New Era of Visual Studio, AI, and Productivity

Gerald Versluis
HULSBERG, Limburg, The Netherlands

ISBN-13 (pbk): 979-8-8688-2690-0
https://doi.org/10.1007/979-8-8688-2691-7

ISBN-13 (electronic): 979-8-8688-2691-7

Managing Director, Apress Media LLC: Welmoed Spahr
Acquisitions Editor: Ryan Byrnes
Editorial Assistant: Gryffin Winkler

Cover designed by eStudioCalamar

Distributed to the book trade worldwide by Springer Science+Business Media New York, 1 New York Plaza, New York, NY 10004. Phone 1-800-SPRINGER, fax (201) 348-4505, e-mail orders-ny@springer-sbm.com, or visit www.springeronline.com. Apress Media, LLC is a Delaware LLC and the sole member (owner) is Springer Science + Business Media Finance Inc (SSBM Finance Inc). SSBM Finance Inc is a **Delaware** corporation.

For information on translations, please e-mail booktranslations@springernature.com; for reprint, paperback, or audio rights, please e-mail bookpermissions@springernature.com.

Apress titles may be purchased in bulk for academic, corporate, or promotional use. eBook versions and licenses are also available for most titles. For more information, reference our Print and eBook Bulk Sales web page at http://www.apress.com/bulk-sales.

Any source code or other supplementary material referenced by the author in this book is available to readers on GitHub. For more detailed information, please visit https://www.apress.com/gp/services/source-code.

If disposing of this product, please recycle the paper

To Oliver and Victor,

who remind me that the most important things in life

are not in the debugger, the terminal, or the backlog…

But in the middle of a very poorly planned Pokémon Go hunt.

Table of Contents

About the Author

Gerald Versluis is a software engineer at Microsoft on the .NET MAUI team, building the cross-platform framework that lets developers target iOS, Android, macOS, and Windows with C# and .NET. He is deeply invested in AI-powered developer tooling and how it is changing the way we build software.

Beyond his day job, Gerald is an active voice in the .NET community—through his YouTube channel, his blog, and public speaking at events internationally.

When he's not writing code, he's apparently writing books.

About the Technical Reviewer

Codrina Merigo is an international speaker, mentor, and coding coach with a long-standing passion for mobile apps and AI. With 13 years of experience in web development with Xamarin.Forms and MAUI, she currently works as a digital product manager, managing mobile apps that have recently migrated to MAUI. Codrina is especially passionate about UX and UI. She speaks at 10–12 conferences per year about MAUI and AI and is a mentor with the .NET Foundation.

Acknowledgments

Writing a book is never a solo project, and this one is no exception. I would like to thank my editors at Apress, Ryan and Sriram, for their guidance and the opportunity to write this book.

I am especially grateful to Rachel, a friend and colleague from the Visual Studio Copilot team, for contributing the foreword and for her insights into the real-world ways developers use this IDE every day. Thanks also to Codrina, the technical editor, for catching the places where I got too excited about the new features and forgot to explain them clearly.

On the personal side, this book would not have happened without the support of my partner, Laurie, for putting up with late nights, half-finished explanations of "this cool new Copilot thing," and the occasional debugging session that crept into family time. And to Oliver and Victor, who kept me grounded in the most important things in life: the latest brain rot, songs that will be forever stuck in my head rent free, and the critical reminder that even the smoothest IDE can't fix a missing LEGO piece.

Finally, to all the readers: thank you for spending time with Visual Studio 2026 and with this book. If anything in here makes your daily development feel a little smoother, faster, or just a bit more fun, that is all I ever hoped for.

Foreword

What does it mean to be a programmer? In the 1940s, computers filled entire rooms, and programming meant physically rewiring cables, flipping switches, and spending days reconfiguring changes. The program was the hardware. By the 1950s, it was punch cards: you typed your logic, handed a deck to an operator, and came back hours later, often with more errors to fix. In the 1980s, the PC put the machine on your desk, and the IDE started actively helping you write, flagging errors as you typed. Each shift made it more seamless to transform our ideas into working solutions.

The nature of the job has changed more than once, and Visual Studio has changed with it. It is changing again now, with AI and the power of natural language bringing the machine closer to understanding us than ever before. Adapting to the latest technologies has always been one of the most exciting things about working in this industry. And if the uncertainty feels familiar, it should. We have been here before.

As a former software engineer and current Product Manager for Visual Studio Copilot, here is what I have noticed: the best developers are the ones who continually pick up new tools, approaching the latest innovations with curiosity and a willingness to learn and adapt. Development is headed in a direction where the programming language will matter increasingly less. This is not something I fully understood when studying Computer Science in college, where the curriculum centered on theory and programming concepts rather than any particular language. What I have come to appreciate since then is that what matters more than the languages themselves are the tools we choose and how we use them. Copilot is now my primary way of writing code, not occasionally, not as a shortcut, but as the default. And Visual Studio 2026 is built for exactly that reality. It embraces where development is right now, and it is designed to keep pace with wherever it goes next.

The person who wrote this book understands that better than most. Gerald Versluis is a senior software engineer at Microsoft on the .NET MAUI team, with a decade of experience building across the .NET and Visual Studio ecosystem, and is one of the most trusted educators in the space. When I first joined Microsoft, Gerald was one of the first people to welcome me. I remember it clearly because we were not even on the same team at the time, yet there he was, carving out time for me before some of my own teammates even had. He had no obligation to, but he just did.

Someone new had arrived, he knew what it was like to be new, and that was enough. That was the beginning of a friendship that has now spanned more than five years, and I have watched him do versions of that same thing, over and over, for the community he has built around him. It is telling that the person who wrote this book is someone who reaches out to strangers because he wants them to feel less alone in a new place. Just as he reached out to welcome me when I was new, he is doing the same for all of you now, welcoming you to Visual Studio 2026.

You might reasonably wonder whether a book is worth reading when new things are being announced tomorrow, next week, next month. Here is what I can tell you: the future of development is already here, and Gerald has written the guide you need to meet it. He does not just explain the features. He shares the detailed context you need to make informed decisions, from what specs to look for in a new machine, to navigating version upgrades, to getting the most out of the latest AI-assisted features throughout the IDE. The practical, real-world examples of how to bring the various parts of Visual Studio together are what make this book shine. As a Visual Studio developer adapting to the AI era himself, Gerald presents scenarios that could not be more relevant. This is the book I wish I had when I started my career, and it is the book I am so glad to have now.

If there is anyone who knows this community and what developers need to stay ahead, it is Gerald. By the end of this book, you will be well equipped for the next era of development. And if you find yourself wanting more, Gerald's community of over 100,000 subscribers on YouTube awaits you. So what does it mean to be a programmer today? And how does Visual Studio meet the moment? You will find answers to both questions in these pages.

Rachel Kang
Product Manager, Visual Studio Copilot

Introduction

Now more than ever, Visual Studio is changing the way we work by putting AI right where developers need it most. It is no longer just an editor, a debugger, or a project system; it is becoming an active partner in the development process, helping you think through problems, write code faster, debug smarter, and move from idea to implementation with far less friction. That shift is a big deal, and Visual Studio 2026 is one of the clearest signs yet that the IDE is evolving into something much more powerful than a place to type code.

For a while, using Visual Studio 2022 in 2026 started to feel a little awkward, not because it stopped working, but because the pace of change in development has picked up so much that the old release cycle could no longer keep up. Visual Studio 2026 feels like Microsoft's answer to that reality: faster updates, more continuous improvement, and an IDE that is evolving at the same speed as the tools and practices around it.

What makes this release exciting is that it does not abandon the foundations developers already trust. Visual Studio still gives you the familiar core tools: Solution Explorer, the debugger, source control, the error list, and all the structure that makes large-scale development manageable, but now those tools are wrapped in a (much!) faster, cleaner-looking, more intelligent experience. You get the stability and depth of a classic IDE, plus the speed and assistance modern developers expect.

For me, that combination is exactly what makes Visual Studio 2026 worth paying attention to. It feels like the IDE has evolved right alongside the pace of modern development. Copilot is not sitting off to the side as a novelty; it is showing up in the flow of your work. Agents are helping with bigger tasks. The interface is more responsive. The whole environment feels designed to keep you moving instead of slowing you down.

This book is your guide to making the most of that experience. We will start with installation and configuration, move through the updated interface and project system, and then dive into debugging, source control, DevOps, and the AI-powered features that are changing how developers work every day. The goal is simple: to help you understand not just what Visual Studio 2026 can do, but how to use it effectively in real projects.

If you are upgrading from Visual Studio 2022, returning after some time away, or coming from another editor and want to understand what makes Visual Studio special, this book will walk you through it step by step. By the time you finish, you should feel confident in the IDE, comfortable with its new rhythm, and ready for Visual Studio 2026 today and for what comes next.

CHAPTER 1

Welcome to Visual Studio 2026

If you've been developing with Visual Studio 2022, you're probably familiar with those moments when you're waiting for your solution to load, watching the build spinner, or dealing with that slightly sluggish feeling when navigating through large code bases. Well, I've got good news for you. Visual Studio 2026 isn't just another incremental update; it's Microsoft's answer to the performance and productivity challenges that have been nagging developers for years.

What makes Visual Studio 2026 truly exciting is how Microsoft has fundamentally shifted their approach. Instead of treating AI as a nice-to-have add-on, they've woven GitHub Copilot and intelligent assistance directly into the fabric of your daily development workflow. This isn't about getting better autocomplete suggestions (though those are great too!). We're talking about an Integrated Development Environment (IDE) that can plan and execute multi-file refactoring tasks, analyze performance bottlenecks with real data, and even help you debug issues by examining build outputs and test failures.

The release also introduces something that should make your IT department happy: a predictable monthly update schedule through two channels—Insiders for you, early adopters, who want the latest and greatest, and Stable for teams that need battle-tested reliability. This means you won't have to wait years for significant improvements, but you also won't be forced into disruptive upgrades that break your workflow.

Speed That You'll Actually Notice

Let's talk about performance, because this is where Visual Studio 2026 really shines. At least, this is the first thing I immediately noticed. If you've ever found yourself grabbing coffee while waiting for a large solution to load, you're going to appreciate what

© Gerald Versluis 2026
G. Versluis, *Getting Started with Visual Studio 2026*, https://doi.org/10.1007/979-8-8688-2691-7_1

Microsoft has done here. They've systematically tackled the bottlenecks that eat away at your productivity throughout the day: solution loading, code navigation, compilation, and debugging startup times. Just starting Visual Studio 2026 and loading a solution already feels much faster and snappier.

The numbers are impressive. Early testing shows startup performance improvements of up to 30% for .NET 10 solutions compared to Visual Studio 2022 with .NET 9 projects, and these gains are particularly noticeable if you're working with large enterprise code bases. And it is not just features that have improved. Visual Studio 2026 is also the fastest version of the IDE ever shipped. Load times are now on par with VS Code, meaning you no longer have to choose between a lightweight experience and a fully capable one.

But here's what's really clever about their approach: they've redesigned solution loading to prioritize the projects and files you're most likely to work with first. This means you can start coding before your entire solution has finished loading, which is a game-changer if you're working with those massive solutions that seem to have a life of their own.

You know how Visual Studio 2022 introduced build acceleration features but made them optional? Well, in 2026, Microsoft has refined and expanded these features, making them work much more efficiently with SDK-style .NET projects. The incremental build optimizations can reduce your build times significantly, which means less time staring at progress bars and more time actually solving problems.

AI That Really Works for You

In the age of AI, here's where Visual Studio 2026 gets really interesting. If you've used GitHub Copilot in other editors, you might think you know what AI-assisted development looks like. But what Microsoft has built into Visual Studio 2026 goes way beyond smart autocomplete.

The standout feature is Agent Mode, and once you try it, you'll wonder how you ever managed complex refactoring tasks without it. Instead of manually planning and executing changes across multiple files, you can describe what you want to accomplish in natural language, and Agent Mode will create a plan, implement the changes, run tests, and even iterate if something doesn't work as expected. I'm talking about requests like "Refactor the authentication system to use OAuth 2.0" or "Add proper error handling throughout the data access layer" and having the AI actually execute a comprehensive solution across your entire code base.

But it gets even better. The Profiler Agent takes AI assistance into performance optimization territory. When you're dealing with performance bottlenecks (and let's face it, we all have those apps that mysteriously slow down over time), the Profiler Agent can analyze your trace data, identify problematic patterns, and suggest specific optimizations based on actual performance data rather than generic advice. It's like having a performance expert looking over your shoulder, but one that never gets impatient when you ask the same question twice. I don't know about you, but I've never particularly enjoyed profiling, and I especially dislike trying to decipher the complex trace results. That is why the new Profiler Agent is such a game-changer for me; it translates a mountain of raw performance data into plain English and actionable fixes.

If your organization has specific requirements around AI models, maybe for compliance reasons or because you prefer certain capabilities, the Bring Your Own Model (BYOM) feature lets you integrate models from OpenAI, Anthropic, Google, or other providers directly into Visual Studio's chat experience. This means you get to keep the familiar interface while using the AI back end that works best for your team's needs.

A Refreshed Visual Experience

You might not think much about Visual Studio's interface until you spend eight hours a day staring at it. Microsoft clearly recognized this and has given Visual Studio 2026 a comprehensive UI refresh that goes beyond just making things look prettier.

The new Fluent UI implementation tackles something that's been bothering developers for years: visual clutter. When you're debugging a complex issue and have multiple windows open, every pixel of screen real estate matters. The updated iconography and typography create better visual hierarchy, making it much easier to scan complex interfaces like Solution Explorer or the debugging windows when you're in the middle of a troubleshooting session.

What I particularly appreciate about the spacing improvements is that they provide breathing room without sacrificing information density. This is especially important if you're working on a laptop or a smaller monitor where every inch counts. The theme system has been completely redesigned too—instead of just offering different colors, you now have fundamentally different approaches to syntax highlighting, UI chrome, and accessibility that are designed to reduce eye strain during those inevitable long coding sessions.

From the first dialog you see when you open Visual Studio to the Options dialog system, a lot of things have been reorganized to make IDE customization more approachable. Whether you're new to Visual Studio or you're someone who has been tweaking settings for years, finding what you need should be much more intuitive. And this is probably only just the beginning!

To get an idea of the new look, please refer to Figure 1-1.

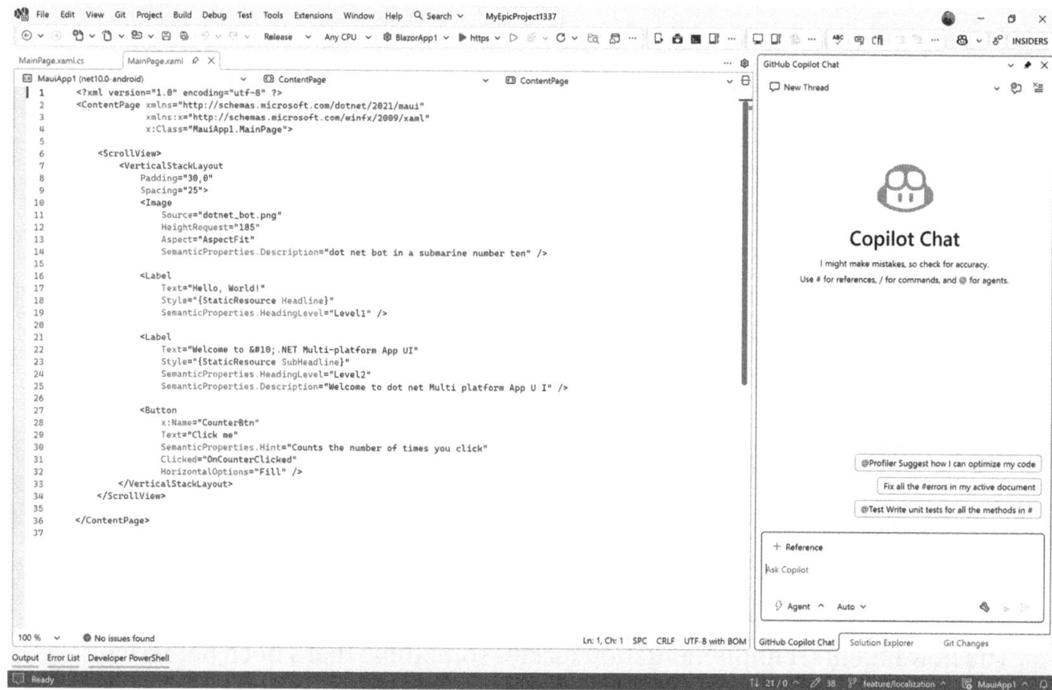

Figure 1-1. Visual Studio 2026 with a new .NET MAUI project open and GitHub Copilot visible. You can see that the UI has a subtle, refreshed, modern look

Ready for the Future: .NET 10 and Modern Development

One of the best things about Visual Studio 2026 is how ready it is for modern development practices. If you're planning to adopt .NET 10 (and you should be), the IDE comes with the newest project templates, IntelliSense, and debugging tools that are optimized for the latest language features and runtime capabilities.

The C# 14 support is comprehensive, with analysis engines that understand and actively suggest usage of new language features like extension members, null-conditional assignment operators, and enhanced pattern matching capabilities. But here's what makes this really useful. The tooling doesn't just recognize these features; it actively suggests refactoring opportunities to modernize your existing code and improve performance.

If you're working with C++, Visual Studio 2026 defaults to C++20 for new projects while providing enhanced support for C++26 features as they become available. The improvements in IntelliSense performance for template-heavy code and concept-based programming are particularly significant if you're working with modern C++ libraries and frameworks.

Updated Release Cadence: Monthly Updates

Here's something that should make both you and your team lead happy: Visual Studio 2026 introduces a monthly update rhythm that's designed to deliver improvements without disrupting your workflow. Instead of waiting years (using Visual Studio 2022 in 2025 did start to feel a bit awkward...) for the next major version to get significant improvements, you'll see incremental but meaningful enhancements that you can adopt when you're ready. Perfect for a world where everything is moving pretty fast.

The Insiders Channel is perfect if you're the type of developer who likes to stay on the cutting edge and help shape the direction of the tools you use. New features get tested here first before flowing to the Stable Channel. But if you're on a team that needs predictable, tested functionality, the Stable Channel gives you access to proven features without the experimental aspects. These release channels replace the current and preview channels. Looking at the naming, I would guess that this has been done to match Visual Studio Code.

What's really clever about this approach is the side-by-side installation capability. You don't have to make an all-or-nothing decision about upgrading. You can install Visual Studio 2026 alongside your existing Visual Studio 2022, selectively migrate projects and workflows as you validate the new environment, and reduce the risk that typically comes with major IDE updates. Or you can even install Visual Studio 2026 Stable and Insiders next to each other.

At the time of writing, the Long-Term Servicing Channel (LTSC) has also been announced, but with little detail. I would suspect this channel will move at a slower cadence and will have a longer support window which is probably to support (bigger) enterprise customers.

Discovering What's New

Because updates are now arriving on a predictable monthly rhythm, keeping track of new features could easily become overwhelming. To help with this, Visual Studio 2026 introduces a proactive "What's New" tab.

Whenever your IDE installs an update and launches for the first time, this document tab opens automatically in your main editor space. Instead of forcing you to hunt down release notes on Microsoft Docs, the tab provides a highly visual, summarized breakdown of the exact features, performance tweaks, and AI improvements added in that specific build. It often includes animated GIFs or quick shortcuts to immediately try out the new settings, making it much easier to digest the monthly improvements without breaking your development flow. (If you accidentally close it, you can always bring it back by going to Help ➤ What's New in the top menu.)

In Figure 1-2, you can see an example of the What's New screen. The contents will probably be different for you since new versions and new features have come out since this book got published.

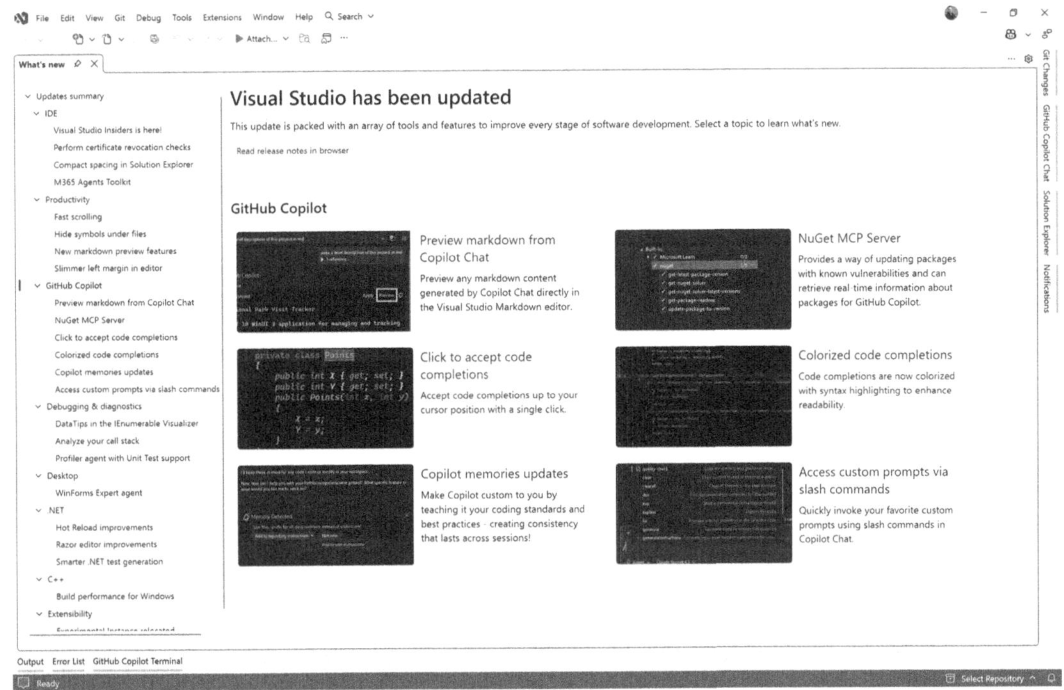

Figure 1-2. *The What's New screen in Visual Studio gives you all the improvements of the latest version at a glance*

Visual Studio 2027, 2028, and Beyond!

Let's go back to what I said just a little earlier: it felt a bit awkward to work with Visual Studio *2022* in *2025*. Luckily, Microsoft is fixing that too!

Visual Studio 2026 also introduces a new "always current" annual rhythm on top of the monthly feature updates. Each November, together with the latest .NET release, your existing installation will roll forward in place to the next major version (e.g., Visual Studio 2026 seamlessly becoming Visual Studio 2027) without disrupting your environment or breaking your build tools. Your configured SDKs, compilers, and workloads remain available after the annual update, so you get the latest IDE features and AI improvements while your projects continue to build as before, with the option for enterprises to pin to a one-year Long-Term Servicing Channel if they need extra stability.

While this book is focused on Visual Studio 2026 and all the new things this release brings, the majority should also be applicable on coming versions. But as Visual Studio is now kicking into this new gear, things might be moving a little bit faster!

Your Extensions? Just Work!

One of the many great features of Visual Studio has always been the extensibility. Everyone can write valuable extensions for Visual Studio. However, this has also always been one of the biggest pain points with major version upgrades. You know the drill: you upgrade the IDE, and suddenly half your essential tools don't work anymore. Microsoft has addressed this head-on in Visual Studio 2026 with backward compatibility for Visual Studio 2022 extensions.

The extension migration system automatically identifies compatible tools from your Visual Studio 2022 installation and offers to transfer them during setup. For extensions that use the standard VSIX packaging format, this migration is seamless and requires no action from you. Some more complex extensions like ReSharper have developed migration assistants to ensure continuity across versions.

This compatibility removes one of the traditional barriers to IDE adoption in enterprise environments, where teams often delay upgrades until essential extensions have been validated. With Visual Studio 2026, most of your tools will work immediately, letting you focus on evaluating the new features and gaining productivity immediately, rather than dealing with workflow disruptions.

Making the Move: Migration Without Losing Productivity

The path from Visual Studio 2022 to Visual Studio 2026 has been designed to minimize friction while maximizing the benefits you'll get from the upgrade. The installer can automatically detect and migrate your settings, extensions, and project configurations, making the transition as smooth as possible. This is assuming that you are on Visual Studio 2022 right now. It is being said that (some) migration is possible for older project types and older Visual Studio versions, but your mileage may vary.

If you're managing multiple developers on your team, the .vsconfig file system lets you standardize installations across team members, ensuring everyone has the same workloads and components configured. This configuration-as-code approach simplifies onboarding new team members and maintains consistency across your development environment.

The migration process preserves your customizations—keyboard shortcuts, window layouts, and debugging configurations—recognizing that these personal optimizations are crucial for maintaining your productivity during the transition. Early adopters report that the familiar feel of their customized environment, combined with the performance improvements, creates an immediate positive impact on their daily development experience.

Just to share a little bit of my personal experience: I did not notice a thing moving from Visual Studio 2022 to Visual Studio 2026, at least not in terms of migration. Things just worked. My settings and preferences were all there, no extra effort needed. I hope it will be the same for you!

To be prepared, please find the Migration Checklist from Visual Studio 2022 in Appendix B.

What This Means for Your Development Future

Visual Studio 2026 positions itself as more than just an upgrade to your existing workflow—it's a platform for the next generation of software development practices. The deep AI integration, performance optimizations, and modern language support create an environment where you can take on more complex challenges while maintaining the productivity and reliability you depend on.

The monthly update rhythm ensures that Visual Studio 2026 will continue evolving rapidly, incorporating feedback from developers like you and staying current with the fast-moving landscape of modern development technologies. This creates a development environment that grows with you rather than requiring those disruptive periodic major transitions we've all experienced.

For you and your team, Visual Studio 2026 offers immediate benefits in performance and AI assistance while establishing a foundation for long-term adoption of emerging development practices and technologies. The side-by-side installation capability and extension compatibility reduce the risks traditionally associated with major tooling changes, making it practical to begin your migration and validation process without disrupting your current project deliveries.

In the next chapter, we'll dive into the actual installation and configuration process, walking through how to get Visual Studio 2026 set up on your machine and configured for your specific development needs.

Summary

In this chapter, you've got your first glimpse of Visual Studio 2026, a major leap forward in both performance and developer productivity. Microsoft has reengineered the IDE to address long-standing pain points like sluggish solution loading and slow builds, delivering noticeably faster startup and navigation, especially for large projects. The integration of AI is now deeply woven into the workflow, with features like Agent Mode and Profiler Agent enabling natural language-driven refactoring and intelligent performance analysis, while also supporting custom AI models for organizational flexibility. The user interface has been modernized with a refreshed Fluent UI, improved accessibility, and new theme options to reduce eye strain. Visual Studio 2026 is fully prepared for .NET 10 and the latest C# and C++ features, offering smart suggestions and seamless migration from previous versions, including backward compatibility for most extensions. With a new monthly update cadence, side-by-side installations, and a focus on frictionless migration, this release positions Visual Studio as a future-ready platform designed to evolve rapidly with your development needs.

In the next chapter, we will start looking at actually installing Visual Studio 2026 on your machine!

CHAPTER 2

Installing and Configuring Visual Studio 2026

In the previous chapter, you have learned what Visual Studio 2026 has to offer you, time to experience it for yourself.

Getting Visual Studio 2026 up and running on your machine is more straightforward than you might expect, especially if you've been through this process with previous versions. Microsoft has learned from years of feedback and has streamlined the installation experience significantly. In this chapter, we'll walk through the entire process from downloading the installer to getting your first project open, and we'll cover how to migrate smoothly from Visual Studio 2022 if you're upgrading.

System Requirements

Before we dive into the installation steps, let's talk about what hardware you'll actually need. At the time of writing, Microsoft states that Visual Studio 2026 requires a minimum of 4 GB of RAM, but recommends 16 GB for typical professional solutions and works best with 64 GB RAM. You'll need at least a quad-core processor (16 cores or more is ideal) and anywhere from 20 to 50 GB of disk space for a typical installation, depending on which workloads you choose. The absolute minimum is Windows 10 version 1909, though Visual Studio 2026 runs best on Windows 11. Both x64 and ARM64 processors are supported. 32-bit (or ARM32) systems are **not** supported.

Before you go out and start buying new hardware: while the documentation mentions that Visual Studio 2026 "works best" with 64 GB of RAM and 16 cores, you definitely don't need a supercomputer to get started. Those are optimal specs for absolutely massive enterprise solutions with dozens of projects and continuous background analysis running. For most developers working on real-world projects,

© Gerald Versluis 2026

G. Versluis, *Getting Started with Visual Studio 2026*, https://doi.org/10.1007/979-8-8688-2691-7_2

16 GB of RAM and a modern quad-core processor will give you a perfectly good experience. That said, if you're planning to use the AI features heavily—especially Agent Mode working across multiple files—more RAM will make things noticeably smoother. So if you were looking for an excuse to buy new toys anyway...

Keep in mind that system requirements can change as Microsoft refines Visual Studio 2026 through its monthly updates. For the most current specifications, always check the official documentation at **https://learn.microsoft.com/visualstudio/ releases/vs18/vs-system-requirements**.

Understanding Your Installation Options

The first decision you'll make is which edition of Visual Studio 2026 to install. Microsoft offers three main editions, and your choice depends on your needs and budget. The Community edition is free and fully featured for individual developers, students, and open-source contributors. Any individual developer can use Visual Studio Community to create their own free or paid apps without restrictions.

For organizations, the licensing is more specific. If you're a small organization (fewer than 250 PCs and less than $1 million USD in annual revenue), up to five users can use Visual Studio Community. However, if you're an enterprise organization (defined as having more than 250 PCs or more than $1 million USD in annual revenue that we've just mentioned), you cannot use the Community edition except for specific scenarios like open source projects, academic research, or classroom learning. In those cases, you'll need Professional or Enterprise licenses for your team. I am in no way authorized to offer any legal advice, so if you have any doubts, be sure to check online sources or directly with your Microsoft representative.

Throughout this book, I'll be using Visual Studio Community edition for all examples and walkthroughs. This ensures that everything you see here is freely available to you as an individual developer, student, or small team member. You won't encounter any features that require paid licenses, making this book accessible regardless of your budget. All the core functionality we'll explore, from AI-powered development with Copilot to debugging and profiling, works identically across all editions, so you're not missing out on any of the learning experience.

Lastly, don't worry about making the wrong decision; I think you'll mostly get the same version of Visual Studio anyway, and features are unlocked based on the license that is attached to the account that you log in with.

Side-by-Side Installations

Not necessarily new to Visual Studio 2026, but still very convenient is that you can install it side-by-side with Visual Studio 2022 without any conflicts. This means you don't have to commit to a complete migration on day one—you can keep your existing VS 2022 installation running while you validate the new version with your projects. This side-by-side capability has been a game-changer for teams who want to adopt new tools gradually rather than forcing everyone to switch at once.

The last choice you are presented with is between the Stable Channel and the Insiders Channel. If you're reading this book, you're probably interested in staying current with the latest features, which makes the Insiders Channel worth considering for at least one machine in your environment. The Insiders build gets monthly feature updates first and helps you prepare for what's coming to the Stable Channel. That said, for production work where stability is paramount, stick with the Stable Channel until you've validated new features on your Insiders installation. The good news here is: the side-by-side installations also work for the different channels of Visual Studio 2026, so why not both?

Downloading and Installation

Getting started is as simple as heading to the Visual Studio download page and selecting your edition. Microsoft provides a small bootstrapper file (around 1–3 MB) that downloads when you click the download button. This bootstrapper is what starts the actual installation process, and that will download many more gigabytes.

In an attempt to not have this book be outdated by the time you read this, I'm not going to provide you with the exact details of where the download button is. Instead, I will just tell you to go to `https://visualstudio.microsoft.com/`, and you will be able to figure it out yourself, I'm sure. Double-check to download Visual Studio, not Visual Studio Code. If you are interested in the Insiders channel, you can go to `https://visualstudio.microsoft.com/insiders/` instead. As mentioned, you can install those side-by-side at a later point in time if that's what you want.

After you have downloaded the pre-installer, just double-click to start it, and you will be greeted by a small dialog window. Please note that by continuing, you agree to the Microsoft License Terms and Privacy Statement. Make sure to read and understand that (I'm obligated to tell you this, but also, I'm just a book, so I can't tell you what to do), accept it, and the process will then continue to download and launch the actual installer. This installer is a separate application that manages all your Visual Studio installations, updates, and modifications. If you already have Visual Studio 2022 installed, you'll see it listed in the installer alongside your new Visual Studio 2026 installation once it's complete.

Note   Make sure to run the installer with administrator rights on the machine.

In this case, we're going to assume that this is a first installation for Visual Studio 2026 in which case you will automatically be presented with a screen that lets you choose the so-called workloads to install. Please have a look at Figure 2-1 for reference.

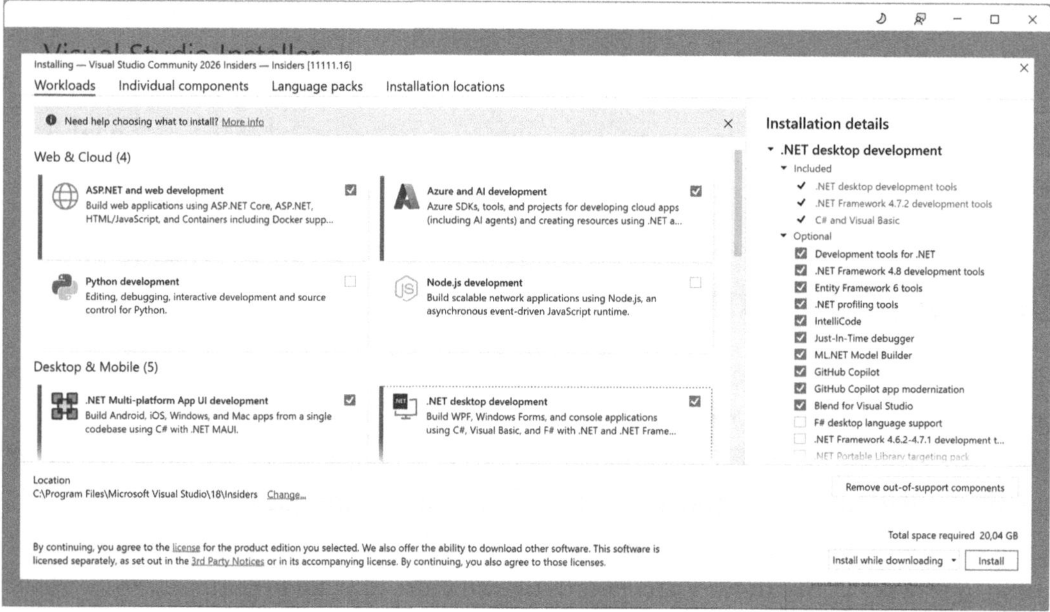

Figure 2-1. *The Visual Studio Installer showing the different workloads that are available for installation*

Before I go into the different workload options, let me first make a quick note about migrating from Visual Studio 2022. If a Visual Studio 2022 installation is detected by the Visual Studio Installer at the time you start the installation of Visual Studio 2026, the installer will come up with a screen that helps you with a migration should you want that. Have a look at Figure 2-2.

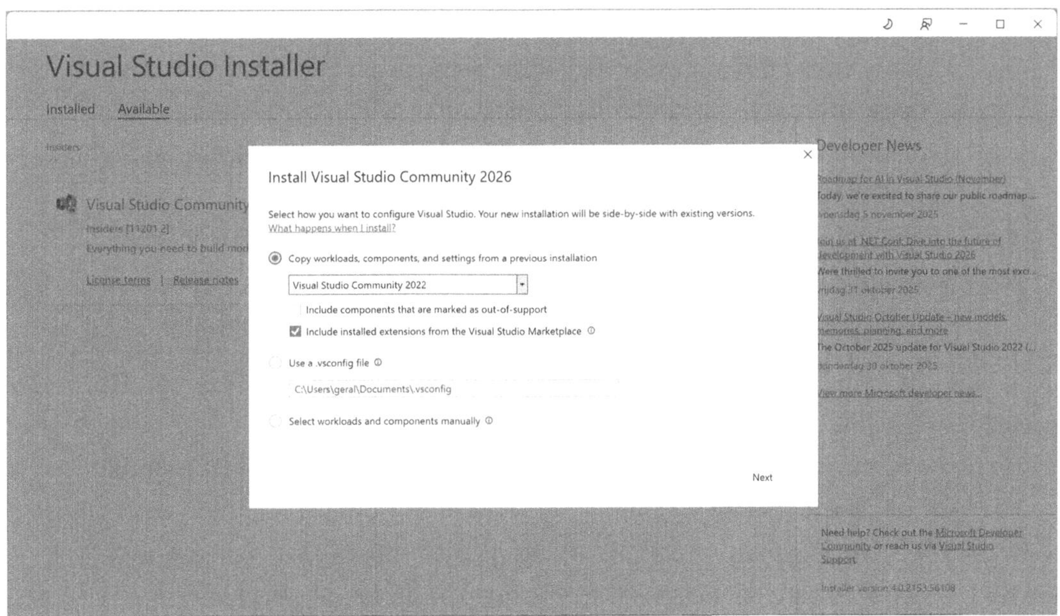

Figure 2-2. *The Visual Studio Installer showing the migration options from Visual Studio 2022 to Visual Studio 2026*

If you chose the first option: Migrate my installation from this product version, you can migrate your Visual Studio 2022 configuration to copy workloads, SDKs, toolsets, and components that are already installed for that instance. This migration option makes it incredibly easy to get up and running with a familiar configuration. In the drop-down, you can also select other versions of Visual Studio that were detected.

When choosing this option, you also have check boxes to steer some behavior for the migration.

- Include out-of-support-items in the Visual Studio Installer: Over time, Microsoft deprecates certain older components, SDKs, or tools (e.g., older unsupported versions of the .NET framework or legacy Azure tooling). By default, the installer will *not* migrate these unsupported items to keep your new VS 2026 installation clean, secure, and modern. However, if you are maintaining a legacy application that strictly relies on one of these older, out-of-support components, you must check this box to ensure they are carried over to your new installation.

- Include installed extensions from the Visual Studio Marketplace:
  This is one of the most loved features of the migration process. If you
  check this box, the installer will look at all the third-party extensions
  you have installed in Visual Studio 2022 (like custom themes,
  productivity tools, or syntax highlighters) and automatically attempt
  to download and install their Visual Studio 2026-compatible versions
  from the Marketplace. This saves you from having to manually search
  for and reinstall your favorite tools one by one after the upgrade.

The second option lets you import a `.vsconfig` file, if your team has standardized on specific workloads.

In case you are not familiar with a `.vsconfig` file, a `.vsconfig` file is a simple JSON file that lists the specific Visual Studio workloads, components, and extensions to be installed, helping teams and individuals quickly standardize development environments. For more details, see the official documentation: **https:// learn.microsoft.com/visualstudio/install/import-export-installation- configurations**.

And finally, you can choose to start fresh with the last option: Do not migrate my existing installation. If you choose this one, you will be brought to the screen that you've seen in Figure 2-1. With that, let's learn about the different workloads.

Choosing Your Workloads Wisely

Here's where the installation process gets interesting and, honestly, where you can save yourself considerable disk space and future headaches by thinking carefully about what you actually need.

Visual Studio organizes its features into workloads. A workload is a collection of tools and components grouped by development scenario. The workload system is designed to prevent you from installing everything and wasting disk space on tools you'll never use. This modular approach was also already available in Visual Studio 2022.

You don't have to get your workload selection perfect on the first try. You can always go back into the Visual Studio Installer later and add or remove workloads through the Modify option on the Visual Studio instance you want to modify. This flexibility means you can start light and add capabilities as you need them rather than front-loading a 50 GB installation.

Let's go through the most common workloads and when you'd want each one.

ASP.NET and Web Development

For ASP.NET and web development, you'll want the "ASP.NET and web development" workload, which gives you everything needed for building web applications with Blazor, ASP.NET Core, and modern JavaScript frameworks. This workload has become significantly more capable in Visual Studio 2026, with improved support for Blazor Hybrid scenarios and better JavaScript/TypeScript tooling.

.NET Desktop Development

If you're building desktop applications, the ".NET desktop development" workload covers Windows Forms, WPF, and console applications targeting .NET 10. This is your bread-and-butter workload for traditional Windows desktop development. The "Desktop development with C++" workload is essential if you're working with C++ projects, and it includes the latest C++20 and C++26 language features.

.NET Multi-platform App UI (.NET MAUI)

For mobile and cross-platform development, my favorite workload, the ".NET Multi-platform App UI (.NET MAUI)" workload, is what you need. This lets you build applications for Android, iOS, macOS, and Windows from a single code base using C# and XAML. Visual Studio 2026 has made significant improvements to the MAUI tooling, particularly around Hot Reload and the visual previewer.

Azure and AI Development

The "Azure and AI development" workload is essential if you're deploying to Microsoft Azure or using Azure services like App Service, Functions, or Container Apps. It includes Azure SDK tools, emulators for local testing, and deployment integrations that make publishing to Azure straightforward.

Visual Studio Extension Development

We've already mentioned them a couple of times: Visual Studio extensions. Maybe you want to develop your own; in that case, the "Visual Studio extension development" workload is what you need. You only need this if you're building your own extensions or customizing Visual Studio's behavior, but if that's something you do, this workload provides the templates and debugging tools to make extension development much more manageable.

Other Notable Workloads

While the workloads described above cover the majority of modern .NET and cloud scenarios, the Visual Studio Installer includes several others tailored to specific domains. If you are building games, you will find dedicated workloads for Game development with Unity and Game development with C++. For low-level systems programming, the Desktop development with C++ and Linux and embedded development with C++ workloads provide world-class compilers, CMake support, and remote debugging tools. There are also specialized workloads for Python development, Node.js development, and Data storage and processing (which installs the SQL Server Data Tools). You don't need to memorize these; just know that if you step into a new technology stack in the future, Visual Studio likely has a pre-configured workload waiting for you.

Individual Components and Language Packs

Beyond workloads, the Visual Studio Installer lets you drill down into individual components if you need something specific that isn't included in the standard workload bundles. You'll find this in the "Individual components" tab of the installer. Most developers won't need to touch this section, but it's useful when you need something like a specific SDK version or a niche build tool.

The "Language packs" tab lets you install Visual Studio's interface in languages other than English. If you're working on a multinational team or prefer to use Visual Studio in your native language, you can select additional language packs here. Each language pack adds about 500 MB to your installation size, so only install what you'll actually use.

One thing worth mentioning in the individual components section is the various .NET SDK versions. Visual Studio 2026 includes .NET 10 by default, but if you're maintaining older projects, you might need .NET 8 or .NET 9 SDKs as well. You can install multiple SDK versions side-by-side without any conflicts, which is incredibly useful for maintaining legacy applications while building new ones on the latest framework.

Note   While this book is about Visual Studio and not .NET, I do want to call out
the Standard-Term Support (STS) and Long-Term Support (LTS) cycle of .NET really
quickly. Every even version (8, 10, 12, etc.) is an LTS version. This means that you
get three years of support. The odd-numbered STS versions give you two years
of support. There are some wild stories about LTS versions being more stable,
which is untrue. Everything that goes into an STS version also goes into an LTS
version and goes through the same quality checks, etc. For more information, see
`https://dotnet.microsoft.com/platform/support/policy`.

For .NET MAUI, the standard STS/LTS does not apply. Every version of .NET MAUI
is supported for 18 months. This is due to the third-party dependencies. For more
information on that, see `https://dotnet.microsoft.com/platform/
support/policy/maui`.

Here again, don't worry too much about not selecting all the required components
and maybe forgetting something you will need later. After Visual Studio is installed and
you open a project that needs additional bits, Visual Studio is very good at telling you
what those bits are and offering to install them for you. Additionally, some workloads,
like the .NET MAUI one, will need some subsequent installation of dependencies like the
Android SDK(s). Also, for this, Visual Studio will guide you the way.

Personally, I have rarely had the need to select individual components; installing the
workloads that I needed typically gives me everything I need. So, if you are new to this
and a bit overwhelmed with all the options, choose one or more workloads that seem to
describe what you want to focus on and start from there.

Installation Progress and What Happens Behind the Scenes

You are almost about to hit the Install button and experience the power of Visual
Studio 2026 on your machine, but before you do, let's explore some last things on the
installation screen. I've added it for your reference again in Figure 2-3.

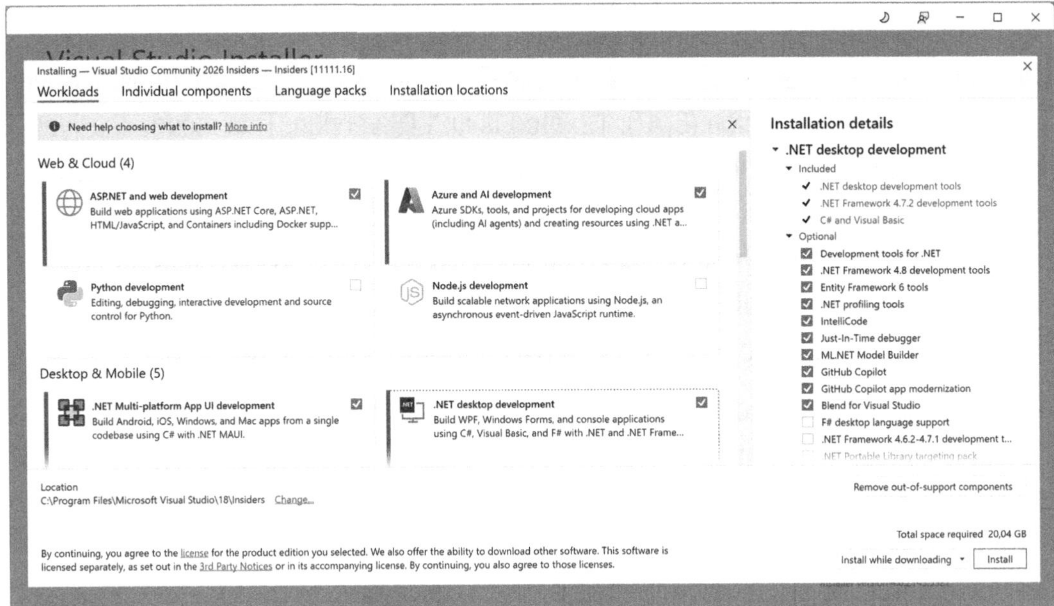

Figure 2-3. *Workload selection screen for Visual Studio 2026*

First, have a look just below the workload selection which takes up most of the screen. There you will see Location. If you want, you can customize the location on disk where Visual Studio will be installed. Typically, you should not have to do this unless you want to maybe put it on a separate disk that has more space. Another scenario where I did use it was to do a side-by-side installation.

At the same height as the install location but more to the right, you will see "Total space required." If you are being mindful about the disk space you are using, keep an eye on that portion of the screen. As you select workloads and components, you will see the required disk space requirement for your selection.

In that same area, you will notice a little drop-down that says: Install while downloading. If you expand it, there is another option that says: Download all, then install. If you have an unreliable internet connection or your connection has lower bandwidth, this might be a good option to use. Please note that Microsoft indicates that the files downloaded are specific to your machine and installation; these are not suitable for transfer to another computer. More on that we will see a little later when we talk about offline installations.

Once you've selected your desired workloads, language packs, and other components, you are ready to click the Install button, and Visual Studio begins downloading and installing the components you've chosen. The installer shows you a progress screen with details about what's being downloaded and installed. Depending on your internet connection and the number of workloads you've selected, this process can take anywhere from 15 minutes to a couple of hours, depending on the specifications of your machine and mostly the available speed of your internet connection. Have a look at the installation progress screen in Figure 2-4.

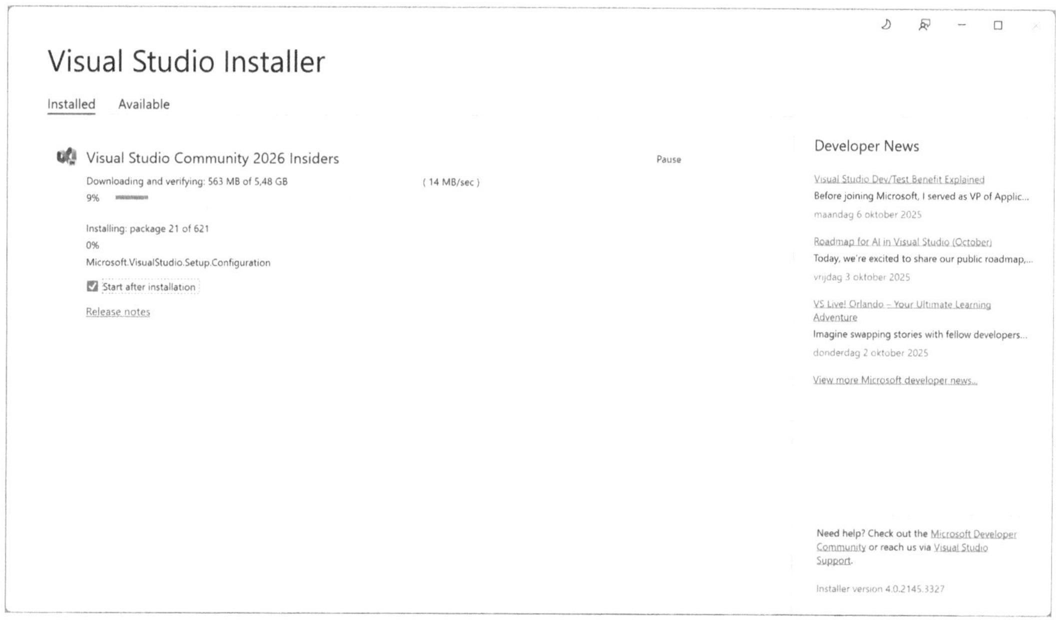

Figure 2-4. *The Visual Studio Installer showing the installation progress of installing Visual Studio Community 2026 Insiders on my machine*

On the right of this screen, you can find the latest news about Visual Studio and related products, so while you are waiting, you will have something to read. Or, just stay here while the installation is progressing, and learn some other things about the installation process.

And don't worry! The installer is smart about handling interruptions. If your installation gets interrupted by a network issue or you need to restart your computer, the Visual Studio Installer will resume where it left off rather than starting over. This resilience is particularly valuable when you're installing large workloads over a slower connection.

Offline Installation for Restricted Environments

Not every development environment has reliable internet access. Maybe you're working in a secure facility with restricted network access, or perhaps you need to install Visual Studio on multiple machines and don't want to download gigabytes of data repeatedly. For these scenarios, Visual Studio supports offline installation through network layouts.

Creating a network layout involves downloading all the Visual Studio installation files to a local directory or network share using the command line. You can do this by opening a command-line window (press the Windows key+R, type cmd, and hit Enter), navigating to the folder where you downloaded the pre-installer, and running a command like `vs_enterprise.exe --layout c:\VSLayout` to download everything needed for offline installation to the VSLayout folder on your C:\ drive. This creates a complete installation package that can be used to install Visual Studio without internet access. The `vs_enterprise.exe` file is the Visual Studio Installer pre-installer we downloaded earlier.

Note   Running this command will download ALL options of Visual Studio and will take a long time. There are options to only download selected options; for more details, please refer to the official documentation: `https://learn.microsoft.com/visualstudio/install/create-an-offline-installation-of-visual-studio`.

Once you've created the layout, you can install it on offline machines using the `--noWeb` parameter to ensure the installer doesn't try to reach the internet. This approach is particularly popular in enterprise environments where IT departments maintain centralized software deployment systems. A sample installation command could look like: `c:\localVSlayout\vs_enterprise.exe --noWeb --add Microsoft.VisualStudio.Workload.ManagedDesktop --add Microsoft.VisualStudio.Workload.NetWeb –includeOptional`

Speaking of enterprise environments, in those cases, the `.vsconfig` file plays a crucial role in offline scenarios too. You can export a configuration file that specifies exactly which workloads and components should be included in your layout, ensuring consistency across your organization. When you create a layout using `--config c:\myconfig.vsconfig`, only the components specified in that file are downloaded. And as you might remember from a little earlier, you can also import a `.vsconfig` file through the Visual Studio Installer to use.

Configuration Files: Standardizing Your Team's Setup

Speaking of `.vsconfig` files, let's talk about how these can simplify your team's onboarding process. A `.vsconfig` file is a JSON file that specifies which workloads, components, and extensions should be installed. The easiest way to get a `.vsconfig` file is by installing Visual Studio; configure it as you want it to be for your whole team or company, and then you can export the config file from your current Visual Studio installation. When you then share that with your team, they can import it to get exactly the same development environment you have. Have a look at Figure 2-5 which shows where to find this option in the Visual Studio Installer.

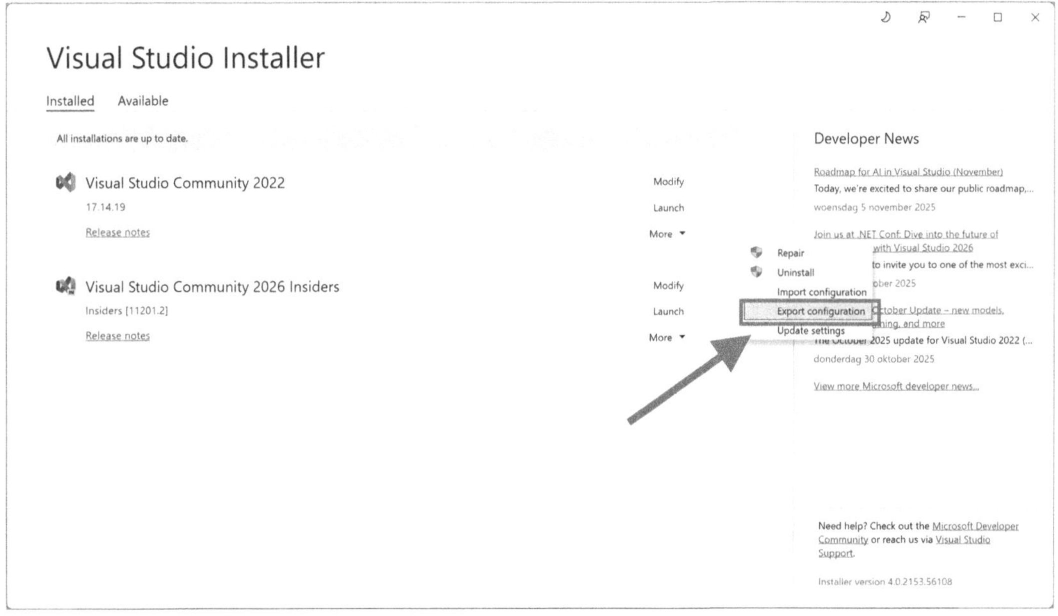

Figure 2-5. *Export a .vsconfig file from the Visual Studio Installer*

In the Visual Studio Installer, you click More ➤ Export Configuration on the Visual Studio installation where you want to export the configuration from. Choose where to save the file, and review which workloads and components will be included. The resulting file is just a few kilobytes and can be committed to your source control repository alongside your solution.

What makes `.vsconfig` files even more powerful is Visual Studio's automatic detection feature. If you place a `.vsconfig` file in your application solution's root directory, Visual Studio will automatically detect missing components when someone opens the solution and prompt them to install what they need. This eliminates the "it works on my machine" problem caused by missing workloads or SDKs. While Visual Studio does a good job detecting this itself, this might be a good idea if you have some more or less common components that you need for your project and want to make sure Visual Studio gets them right. More information about this feature can be found here: `https://learn.microsoft.com/visualstudio/install/import-export-installation-configurations`.

To give you an idea of what a `.vsconfig` file looks like, have a look at Listing 2-1.

Listing 2-1. A simple .vsconfig file

```
{
  "version": "1.0",
  "components": [
    "Microsoft.VisualStudio.Workload.ManagedDesktop",
    "Microsoft.VisualStudio.Workload.NetWeb",
    "Microsoft.VisualStudio.Workload.Azure",
    "Microsoft.VisualStudio.Component.NuGet"
  ]
}
```

Please note there are some caveats when using this for extensions that need to be installed for Visual Studio: `https://learn.microsoft.com/visualstudio/install/import-export-installation-configurations#extensions`.

First Launch: Initial Configuration and Sign-In

For this chapter (and this book mostly), I will assume that you are going to do a clean installation. The migration options should mostly be self-explanatory, and because of the countless different configurations out there, it's impossible to describe all the different paths. Even more so, when you do go through the migration path, your existing account will probably already be logged in, and the initial configuration that we're going to talk about here might actually be (partly) skipped. So, if you're reading this and going through a migration, things might be a bit different for you and probably for the best.

When Visual Studio 2026 launches for the first time after installation, you'll be greeted with a welcome experience that walks you through some initial configuration choices. The first thing Visual Studio will ask is whether you want to sign in with your Microsoft or GitHub account. You will also find the option to create a new account. In Figure 2-6, you can see what this screen looks like.

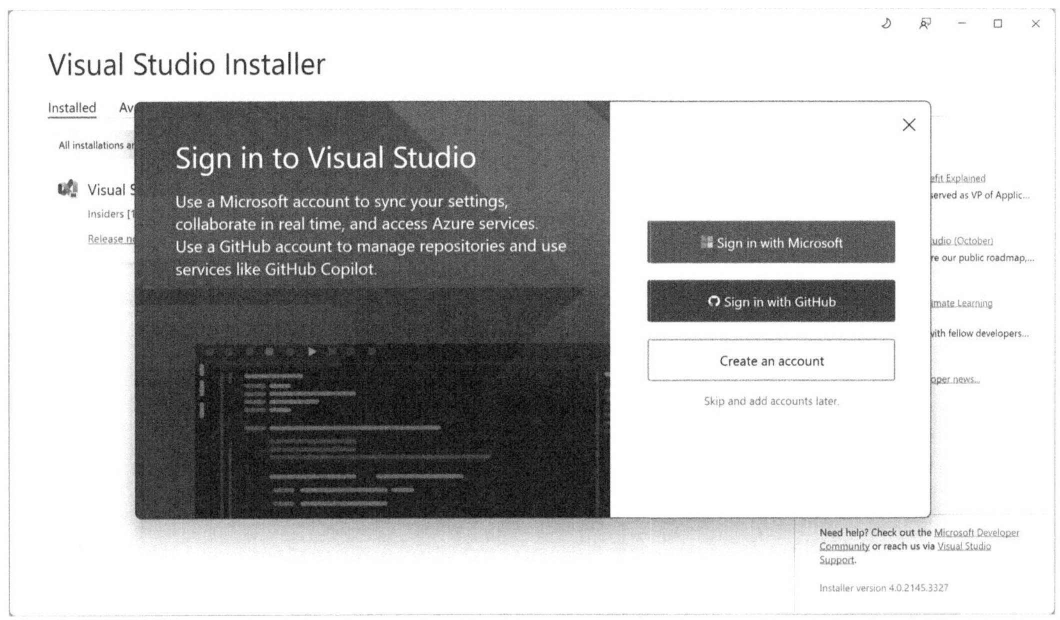

Figure 2-6. *Visual Studio 2026 welcome screen with several options: sign in with a Microsoft or GitHub account, create an account, or skip and add accounts later*

Signing in isn't strictly required for the Community edition. Arguably, the most important "feature" that logging in will grant you is the license you or your company has bought will be applied, and that then upgrades your Visual Studio Community to a higher tier and unlocks more features. However, logging in with the Community edition still unlocks several valuable features.

When you sign in, Visual Studio can sync your settings across machines, which is incredibly convenient if you work on multiple computers. Your theme preferences, keyboard shortcuts, window layouts, and even your Copilot settings can follow you from machine to machine automatically. This settings sync works through your Microsoft account's cloud storage and happens transparently in the background.

Signing in also enables Azure authentication for development scenarios. If you're building applications that connect to Azure services, Visual Studio can use your signed-in account for local development authentication without requiring you to manage separate service principals or connection strings.

If you really want to, you can continue without logging in, but personally, I think having an account provides so much benefit, such as seamless settings synchronization, instant access to GitHub Copilot, and hassle-free Azure authentication, that I highly recommend you take a moment to sign in.

After signing in (or choosing to continue without an account), Visual Studio will ask you to choose a color theme and development settings profile. The theme options include Light, Blue, Dark, and several new tinted themes that were introduced in Visual Studio 2026. Take a moment to pick one that feels comfortable for your eyes, because you'll be staring at it for hours. As mentioned before, if you have used Visual Studio before and you logged into your account, chances are that you won't see any of this, and your settings are automatically synced for you!

You will also be presented with a screen that lets you choose your primary development profile. Think of this as telling Visual Studio what kind of developer you are. This choice influences your keyboard shortcuts, window layouts, and which tool windows are visible right from the start, setting up your environment for C#, C++, web, or other workflows. Don't worry if you're not sure which to pick; you can always tweak or fully customize everything later using Tools ➤ Options or through the Import and Export Settings Wizard.

Migrating Projects from Visual Studio 2022

Now that you have Visual Studio 2026 installed and configured, let's talk about moving your existing projects over from Visual Studio 2022. The good news is that for most project types, this is remarkably painless. Visual Studio 2026 can open projects created in Visual Studio 2022 directly, without requiring any conversion in many cases. You might notice that a version number is updated in your `sln` file, but that's about it. While on the topic of solution files, a quick note: for Visual Studio 2026, the default format for solution files has been switched to `slnx`.

For projects targeting .NET 9 or earlier, you can simply open your solution in Visual Studio 2026, and everything should work as you are used to. The solution and project files are compatible across versions, and Visual Studio 2026 knows how to work with older target frameworks. You don't need to upgrade your projects to .NET 10 immediately; you can continue developing .NET 8 or .NET 9 projects in Visual Studio 2026 while you plan your framework upgrade. The update for Visual Studio is completely separate from any framework version your project is targeting.

When you *are* ready to upgrade your projects to .NET 10, Visual Studio 2026 makes the process easier and smarter than ever. The .NET Upgrade Assistant is now a fully integrated, stable part of Visual, and is available directly from Solution Explorer. You simply right-click your project and select "Upgrade" to open a guided wizard that walks you through each step.

What's even more impressive is that, in recent versions, Upgrade Assistant is enhanced with AI features powered by GitHub Copilot, known as the GitHub Copilot app modernization chat agent. The upgrade process analyzes your project structure, reviews dependencies, suggests targeted code changes, and can even automatically fix or refactor outdated APIs for .NET 10 (and beyond in the future), all within a single streamlined workflow. You stay in control every step of the way, validating or rolling back any changes as needed. A full coverage of the Upgrade Assistant is outside of this scope for this book, but please find more information here: `https://learn.microsoft.com/dotnet/core/porting/upgrade-assistant-overview`.

Extension Migration and Compatibility

Already briefly mentioned earlier: extensions and how they just migrate without any effort. Microsoft redesigned the extension compatibility system so that most VS 2022 extensions work in VS 2026 without modification. This backward compatibility eliminates the traditional painful transition period where you're waiting for extension authors to update their tools.

When you install Visual Studio 2026, the installer can automatically migrate your extensions from Visual Studio 2022. During the installation process, you'll see an option to "Include installed extensions from the Visual Studio Marketplace"; make sure this is checked if you want your extensions to come along. For most extensions, this migration happens seamlessly, and they'll be available immediately when you launch Visual Studio 2026.

Some extensions, particularly those with more complex installation requirements, use a migration assistant to handle the transition. ReSharper is a notable example. JetBrains created a Migration Assistant extension that bridges the gap between VS 2022 and VS 2026. If you use ReSharper, you'll install the Migration Assistant in VS 2022, then when you upgrade to VS 2026, it guides you through installing ReSharper in the new version.

If you're not sure about that one extension you had installed, you can always check your extension status in the Extension Manager (Extensions ➤ Manage Extensions) after the Visual Studio 2026 installation. This shows you which extensions are installed, which have updates available, and which might have compatibility issues. If an extension isn't working properly, checking here should be your first troubleshooting step.

Customizing Your Environment

With Visual Studio 2026 installed and your projects migrated, you'll want to spend a few minutes customizing the environment to match your workflow. It might very well be that all your settings have synced perfectly from your previous installation, but it never hurts to double-check, and maybe you'll even discover new options that were added!

The Options dialog (Tools ➤ Options) is where you'll find most customization settings, and Visual Studio 2026 has reorganized this dialog to make it more navigable. You can search for specific settings using the search box at the top rather than hunting through category trees. Another thing you'll immediately notice is that the Options are not a modal dialog anymore, but rather a screen-filling tab in the main window which makes it much easier to navigate. Have a look at Figure 2-7 to see what it looks like. I recognize the text might be a bit small to read depending on what you're reading this book on, but that is not really important in this case; I just wanted to give you an idea of the new layout.

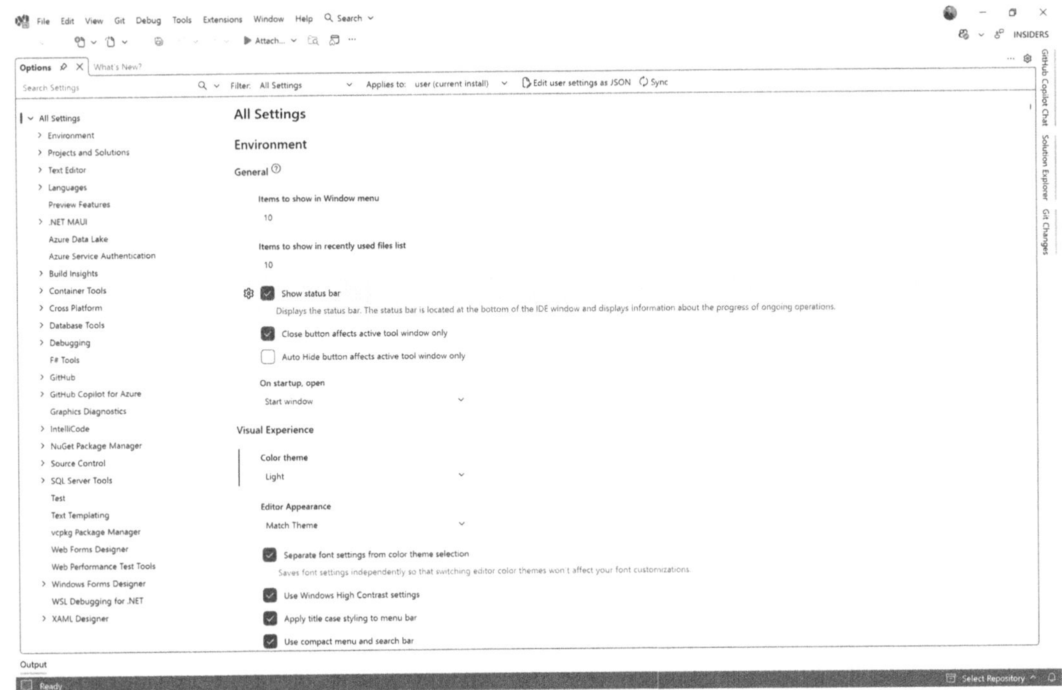

Figure 2-7. *The new Options window design in Visual Studio 2026*

Keyboard shortcuts are one of the most personal aspects of your development environment. If you're coming from Visual Studio 2022 and chose to migrate your settings, your keyboard shortcuts should already be configured. If you're setting up fresh or want to explore new options, check Tools ➤ Options ➤ Environment ➤ More Settings ➤ Keyboard. You can search for commands, see their current key bindings, and assign new ones.

Window layouts can make a huge difference in your productivity, especially if you frequently switch between different types of tasks. Visual Studio lets you save and load custom window layouts through Window ➤ Save Window Layout. You might create one layout for coding with minimal tool windows visible, another for debugging with all the diagnostic windows arranged just right, and a third for code reviews. You can switch between these layouts with keyboard shortcuts you assign or through the same menu, but now: Window ➤ Apply Window Layout and choose a previously saved layout.

The fonts and colors settings control every aspect of Visual Studio's text rendering, from the editor to the output windows. You'll find these under Tools ➤ Options ➤ Environment ➤ More Settings ➤ Fonts and Colors. While the default settings are well-chosen, many developers like to customize their syntax coloring scheme or switch to a different programming font. Popular choices include Cascadia Code (which supports ligatures), JetBrains Mono, and Fira Code.

With that out of the way, let's see if we can actually get something to compile.

Verifying Your Installation

Before you dive into serious development work, it's worth spending a few minutes verifying that your Visual Studio 2026 installation is working correctly. The easiest way to do this is to create a simple test project in your primary development area.

Create a new project (File ➤ New ➤ Project), and select a simple template for your technology stack—maybe an ASP.NET Core Web App if you do web development or a Console App if you're focused on back-end services. Build the project and run it with F5 to make sure the debugger attaches correctly and your application launches. This simple test can reveal issues with SDK installation, firewall settings, or missing components before you start working on your actual projects.

Maybe you want to check that Copilot is working if you have a Copilot subscription. You should see the Copilot icon in the title bar and be able to open the Copilot Chat window. Try asking Copilot a simple question about your code to verify the AI features are connected and working properly.

If you migrated projects from Visual Studio 2022, open one of your existing solutions and make sure it loads cleanly without errors. Build the solution and run any tests to verify that everything works as expected in the new environment. This is also a good time to check that any custom build scripts or deployment configurations still function correctly.

Troubleshooting Common Installation Issues

I'm an optimistic person, so I will assume all went well and everything is working! In the off case it didn't, let's explore some things that might have gone wrong and how to go about it. Please keep in mind that this book is about introducing you to Visual Studio

2026 and not necessarily about troubleshooting your installation, so if you run into real issues, you might want to turn to your favorite search engine or Copilot for more in-depth help.

If you feel that something is an issue with the Visual Studio product, go to the Help menu inside of Visual Studio, and then choose Provide Feedback and Report a Problem. That will make sure its routed to the right team for follow up.

If your installation failed partway through, the Visual Studio Installer usually provides a detailed error log that you can review. These logs are verbose but often contain the specific error that caused the failure. Look through those and extract any information that might be useful, and start searching for that on the internet.

One common issue is insufficient disk space. Remember that Visual Studio 2026 can require 20–50 GB, depending on your workload selection, and you need some overhead beyond that for temp files during installation. If you're running low on disk space, consider installing on a different drive or clearing space before trying again.

Network connectivity problems can interrupt downloads and cause installation failures. If you're on an unreliable connection, consider using the "Download all, then install" feature in the Visual Studio Installer that we learned about earlier. This downloads all the necessary files before starting the installation, so network interruptions during the install phase won't cause problems.

Extension compatibility issues usually manifest after installation when Visual Studio won't start or crashes on launch. If this happens, try launching Visual Studio in safe mode using `devenv.exe /safemode` from the command line. Safe mode disables extensions, letting you start Visual Studio and troubleshoot which extension is causing the problem.

If something appears to have gone wrong, you can always go back into the Visual Studio Installer, find the installation that you want to look into, and select the More menu, followed by Repair. This will reinstall that instance of Visual Studio.

For more help and resources, please have a look at the official Microsoft Learn documentation: `https://learn.microsoft.com/troubleshoot/developer/visualstudio/installation/troubleshoot-installation-issues`.

What's Next

With Visual Studio 2026 installed, configured, and verified, you're ready to start exploring the modernized IDE. In the next chapter, we'll walk through the updated user interface and all the productivity features that make Visual Studio 2026 such a powerful development environment. You'll learn how to navigate efficiently, customize your workflow, and leverage the new features that will make you more productive every day.

The time you've invested in getting your installation right will pay dividends as you work. A well-configured development environment doesn't just save you minutes here and there—it fundamentally changes how you approach your work and removes friction from your creative process. Now let's put that environment to work.

CHAPTER 3

Navigating the Updated IDE

Now that you've got Visual Studio 2026 installed and configured, it's time to actually work with it. The IDE has received a comprehensive visual and functional refresh, and understanding how to navigate the updated interface will save you hours of frustration and help you work faster from day one. Whether you're brand new to Visual Studio or you've been using it for years, this chapter will show you where everything lives, what's new in the UI, and how to leverage the productivity features that make Visual Studio 2026 such a powerful development environment.

Understanding the Default Layout

If you have used Visual Studio before, then what follows next here might not be accurate to you, and honestly, it's been a while since I have seen the default layout of Visual Studio. But to make sure that everyone can read this book, even newcomers to Visual Studio, let's have a look at the default layout that comes out of the box with a fresh installation.

When you first open Visual Studio 2026, you're greeted with a thoughtfully organized workspace designed to keep everything you need within easy reach. At the center of your screen is the main area which typically is your code/text area. This is probably (hopefully?) where you'll spend most of your time writing code, viewing files, and working with designers. The tabs for your open files appear along the top by default, though you can move them to the left or right side if that works better for your workflow.

On the right side of the IDE, you'll initially find Copilot Chat. This is your way to interact with GitHub Copilot; we will learn more about that in Chapter 8, so I will not go into it too much right now. If you're not logged in, it will suggest that you do, and if you are logged in, you will get some suggestions on what you can do with Copilot.

At the bottom of Copilot Chat, you will see a couple of tabs. The first and arguably most important one is the Solution Explorer. This is your file and project navigator, where you can browse your solution structure, search for files, and manage your project hierarchy.

Recently, there has been some discussion if the Solution Explorer should be on the left, like VS Code has, and probably to make room for GitHub Copilot on the right. Maybe by the time you're reading this book, this has changed. For now, the Solution Explorer is on the right.

The last tab you see here out of the box is the Git Changes. This is where you find the integrated source control functionality in Visual Studio 2026. Depending on what you currently have opened, you can create a Git repository, see the currently made changes in an existing Git repository, push, pull, navigate into diff views, and much more.

I could probably fill an entire book with all the different windows and panes that you can find in Visual Studio, and they can all dock on the right, left, top, or bottom, but these are the ones that you see when you first start Visual Studio 2026, at least at the time of writing. Have a look at Figure 3-1 to see an overview of the Visual Studio window with all the components highlighted. Some like the toolbar and status bar, which we will learn about a little later.

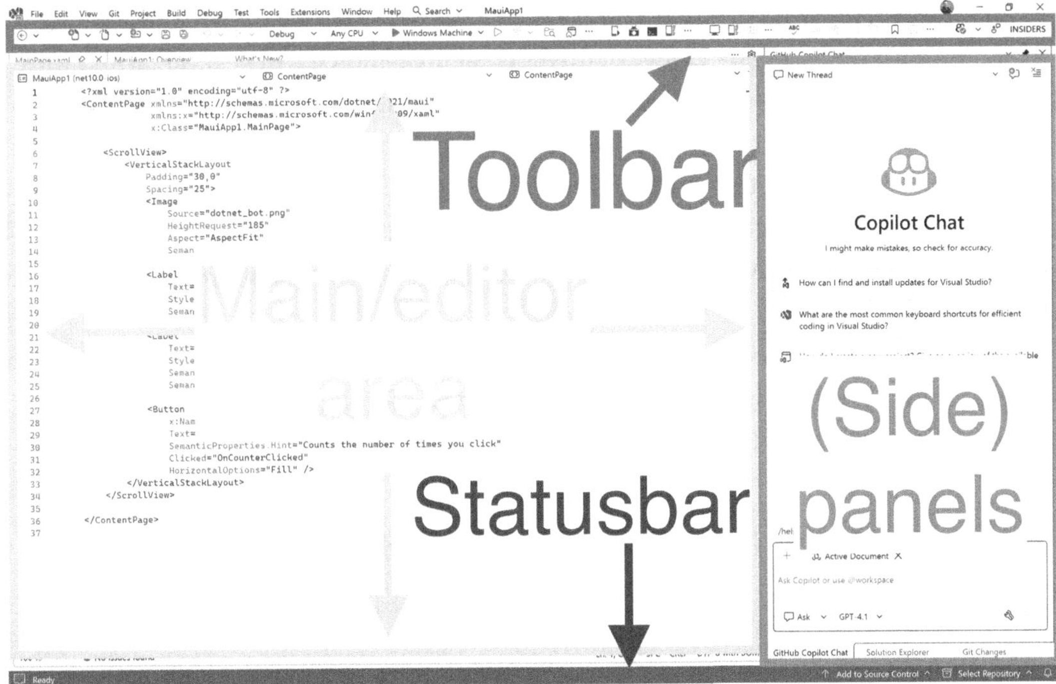

Figure 3-1. *Visual Studio 2026 default layout. In the top (red), there is the toolbar. Below it on the left (green), there is the main area where the code/text editor is. To the right of that (pink), there are the side panels which currently show Copilot Chat, but underneath, the tabs for Solution Explorer and Git Changes can be seen. And across the bottom (blue) is the status bar*

Another notable one I do want to point out is the Properties window. Whenever you open the properties of any file or other object (for instance, if you right-click and choose Properties on something), you'll typically also see the Properties window here, which displays context-sensitive properties for whatever you've selected in the editor or designer.

The bottom portion of the IDE, not shown in the above screenshot, is reserved for informational and diagnostic windows. The Error List shows build errors, warnings, and messages in real time. The Output window displays detailed build logs, package manager output, and other diagnostic information. These windows typically only pop up whenever you need them, for instance, when you start compiling your code or when you start a debugging session. This is also true for other windows; you'll see some things show up or be hidden depending on the context of your current work. In case you are missing something, you can go to the View menu and find the window you're missing to bring it back up.

On the left side, whenever you start working with the user interface (UI), you might see the Toolbox docked (especially useful for designers and UI work), along with other tool windows you've chosen to keep accessible. The beauty of Visual Studio's layout system is that everything can be moved, docked, floated, or hidden based on your preferences. And even better, the IDE remembers your choices between sessions and even across different machines if you've enabled settings sync. You can even drag panels out of the main window and onto a secondary window if that makes you more productive!

Depending on your preferences and the way you work, you will find certain things more or less important in the layout. However, I do want to call out two things specifically, just because I think they are things you will probably use a lot.

The Toolbar: Your Quick Access to Development Commands

Along the top of Visual Studio, just below the menu bar, you'll find the main toolbar, a collection of icons that provide quick access to frequently used commands. The toolbar adapts based on what you're working on and what context you're in, but certain buttons remain constant. One toolbar that deserves special attention is the Debug Toolbar, which becomes particularly important when you're testing and troubleshooting your code. When you start a debugging session by pressing F5 or clicking the Start Debugging button, the Debug Toolbar appears with controls for stepping through your code. The primary stepping commands you'll use are Step Over (F10), which executes the next line of code without stepping into function calls, and Step Into (F11), which lets you drill down into function calls to debug them step by step. You can also use Step Out (Shift+F11) to exit a function when you've finished examining it and want to return to the calling code. These stepping commands, combined with breakpoints that pause execution at specific lines, form the core of your debugging workflow. Chances are that you will use the shortcut keys for most things, but it's still good to know where certain actions are in the toolbar. In Figure 3-2, you can see two partial screenshots of the Visual Studio toolbar. On the left, you can see the run menu for a .NET MAUI project where you can select the target platform to run on. And on the right, you can see the debug toolbar with a button to pause the debugging session, stop the debugging session, or to step into, out of, etc., breakpoints in your code.

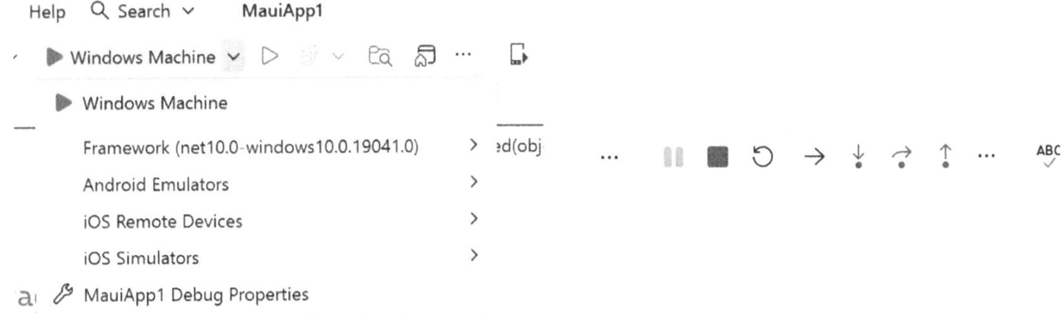

Figure 3-2. *Two partial toolbar screenshots. On the left: the run menu, selecting a platform to start a debug session. On the right: the debug toolbar with buttons to stop the debugging session and step through breakpoints*

The Status Bar: Your Development Status at a Glance

The status bar runs along the very bottom of the Visual Studio window and provides real-time information about your development environment and project state. The status bar is divided into several regions that display different types of information. We'll learn more about those in a second.

But maybe more importantly: the status bar also displays progress indicators when you're building your solution, downloading packages, or performing other long-running operations. Color coding in the status bar provides quick visual feedback: when you're actively debugging, the status bar turns orange; when your solution is loaded, it's blue; when the IDE is idle, it appears in its default color. This simple visual indicator helps you stay aware of your IDE's state without having to look elsewhere. For developers working in large solutions, the status bar is also where you'll see animation indicators showing that background processes like IntelliSense indexing or source control sync are happening.

In Figure 3-3, you can see some different states of the status bar. Behind number 1, you can see the orange color which indicates that you are in a debug session. The purple/blue background color behind number 2 indicates that your code is compiling. The gray one behind number 3 is the default color for when you're just working in your code base. Number 4 shows you that the status bar gives you all kinds of useful information, like here, where it shows you that the NuGet packages have been restored for a project. And the status bar in number 5 shows you the right side of the status bar where there are some interactive buttons to work with the configured source control for the opened code base.

Figure 3-3. *The Visual Studio status bar displaying various states: (1) Ready state in orange, (2) active build process in blue, (3–4) Ready state with project restoration details showing file path and completion time, and (5) source control options for version management*

The code editor window, depending on the context, has a little "status bar" of its own, if you will. At the bottom of the file with the code you have opened, there is a bar with information about this file. On the left, you can select the zoom factor of the editor. Next to that, there is an indicator that shows you if there are any errors and/or warnings in this file.

In the bottom right, you'll see the cursor position; the line and column number of where your cursor currently sits in the editor, displayed as a unified `line:column` format. Clicking this information opens the Go To Line dialog, letting you quickly jump to any line in your current file. You will also find indicators to tell you what indentation this file uses, what line endings, and what character encoding this file has. In Figure 3-4, you can see the code editor's "status bar."

Figure 3-4. *The code editor "status bar"*

The Copilot Chat Pane: Your AI-Powered Assistant

One of the most transformative additions to Visual Studio 2026 is the integrated GitHub Copilot Chat pane. If it's not showing for you by default when you read this, or you close it, you can access it through View ➤ GitHub Copilot Chat or by clicking the Copilot icon in the toolbar in the top-right. The Copilot Chat pane typically docks on the right side of your screen, alongside other tool windows, and provides a conversational interface where you can ask coding questions in natural language and receive AI-powered responses. I won't go into too much detail here; we will learn more about this and other AI integrations in Chapter 8.

Fresh Fluent UI: Modern Design That Actually Helps

The first thing you'll notice when you launch Visual Studio 2026 is the refreshed Fluent UI design. This isn't just a cosmetic update; Microsoft has fundamentally rethought how the interface supports your workflow. The new design language brings cleaner lines, more generous whitespace, and improved visual hierarchy that makes it easier to scan complex interfaces and find what you need quickly.

Typography has been upgraded throughout the IDE with crisper, more readable fonts that scale better across different monitor resolutions and DPI settings. Icon design has been completely modernized with a consistent visual language that makes it easier to recognize tools and commands at a glance. The spacing between UI elements has been carefully tuned to reduce visual clutter without sacrificing the information density that professional developers need.

Accessibility improvements are woven throughout the updated interface. High-contrast themes have been refined, screen reader support has been enhanced, and keyboard navigation has been improved across the entire IDE. These changes benefit everyone, not just users with specific accessibility needs. Better contrast and clearer visual hierarchy reduce eye strain during long coding sessions and help you maintain focus when working with complex code bases.

The active region styling is a subtle but powerful addition. Visual Studio now highlights the currently active areas of the UI, making it immediately obvious which window or panel has focus. This might seem like a small detail, but when you're rapidly switching between the editor, debugger, and various tool windows, these visual cues help you stay oriented without consciously thinking about where your attention should be. Figure 3-5 demonstrates the redesigned Visual Studio 2026 interface, showcasing the streamlined menu bar, contemporary icon design, and the updated tab layout for managing project files.

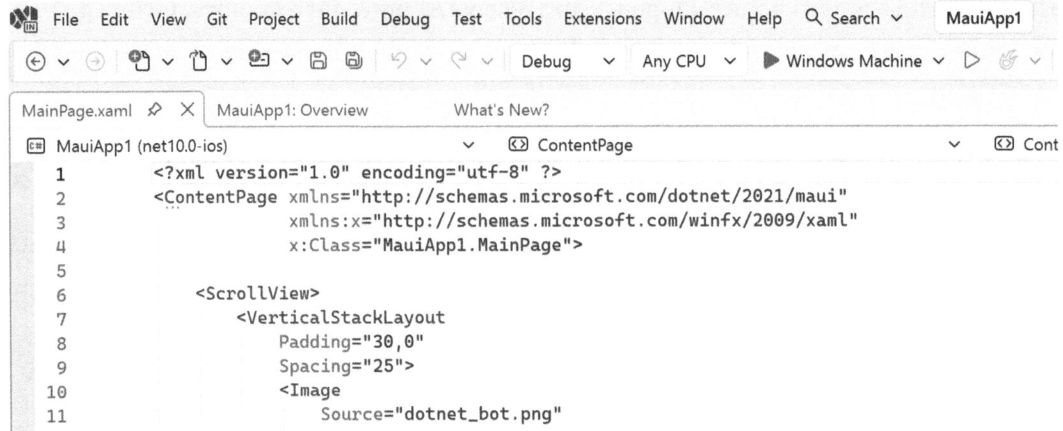

Figure 3-5. *Close-up of the top-left corner of the Visual Studio 2026 window. Here, you can clearly see the new tab design, modern-looking icons, and clear typography that this new version has to offer*

Theming: Make Visual Studio Yours

Visual Studio 2026 expands your ability to personalize the IDE's appearance. In addition to the classic Light and Dark themes, you now have access to 11 new tinted themes with cool-sounding names like Bubblegum (a pink theme), Icy Mint (light blue), Juicy Plum (purple), and more. But here's where it gets interesting: you can now set different themes for the editor and the surrounding IDE independently. In Figure 3-6, you can see Visual Studio 2026 with the Bubblegum theme, and the code editor has a separate dark, extra contrast appearance.

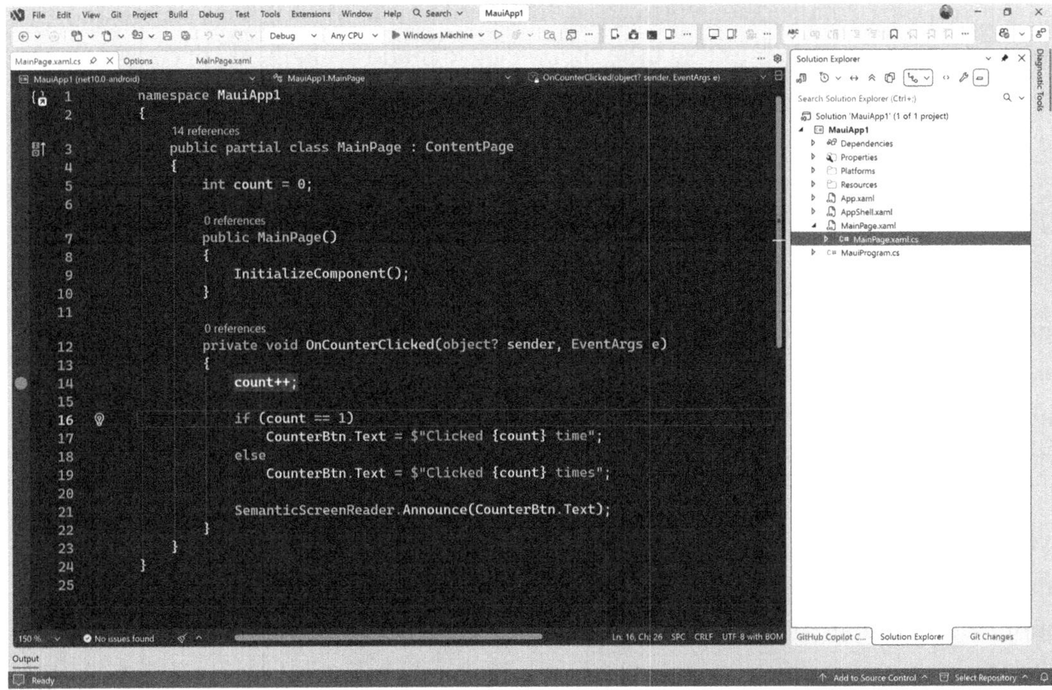

Figure 3-6. *Visual Studio with the Bubblegum theme and the code editor has a separate dark, high-contrast appearance*

This separation means you could have a high-contrast dark theme in your code editor for maximum readability while keeping the rest of the IDE in a lighter, less intense theme that's easier on your eyes during design work or when reviewing documentation. To access this, you'll navigate to Tools ➤ Options ➤ Environment ➤ Visual Experience, where you'll find the new Editor Appearance setting that can either match your overall theme or be customized separately. You can also reach this from the Tools ➤ Theme and Tools ➤ Editor Appearance menus, respectively.

The theme system has been designed to preserve your other customizations when you switch themes. Your font settings, custom colors for specific syntax elements, and icon choices all persist across theme changes, so you're not starting from scratch every time you want to try a different look. This makes it practical to experiment with different themes to find what works best for your eyes and your environment.

Creating and sharing custom themes has also gotten easier. The modernized settings interface lets you export your complete visual configuration, including your chosen theme, custom colors, and editor preferences, making it simple to maintain consistency across multiple machines or share your preferred setup with team members.

And on top of that, you can also go to the Visual Studio Marketplace online and choose from custom themes that other people have made available or, of course, create your own and publish that!

Enhanced Search: Finding What You Need, Fast

Search in Visual Studio 2026 has been completely reimagined, and if you've ever wasted time hunting for a file, type, or method in a large code base, you're going to love these improvements. The new All-In-One Search, accessible with Ctrl+Shift+P (for Feature Search or Ctrl+P, for Code Search), combines file search, code search, and feature search into a single, lightning-fast interface.

What makes this search truly powerful is the AI-powered "Did You Mean" feature. When Copilot detects that you might have mistyped a search term or that there's a better match than what you're seeing, it suggests alternatives. This works especially well with public GitHub repositories and is being expanded to support private code bases in future updates. You can enable or disable this feature in Tools ➤ Options ➤ GitHub ➤ Copilot ➤ Search. By default, this setting is on.

File exclusion is another game-changer for search productivity. You can now configure glob patterns to exclude specific files or directories from your search results entirely. This is incredibly useful for filtering out generated code, node_modules folders, or build artifacts that clutter your results. Configure this in Tools ➤ Options ➤ Environment ➤ Search, where you'll find the new "Enable search exclusions" section. Here you can add patterns of files and paths that should be excluded from search.

The search interface itself can now be docked as a persistent window or used as a pop-up. Whatever fits your workflow better. When you're searching within the Text Visualizer during debugging (more on that in Chapter 5), you can press Ctrl+F to bring up Quick Find directly within long strings, with highlighting that makes it easy to spot patterns, errors, or specific values. Hold Ctrl while searching, and the search UI becomes transparent, so you never lose sight of the content underneath. It's these little things that make all the difference.

In Figure 3-7, you can see the code editor with the top-right Quick Find (Ctrl+F) to find (or replace) something in the current file quickly, and under that is All-In-One Search that you can use to find code across the whole code base or a feature within Visual Studio.

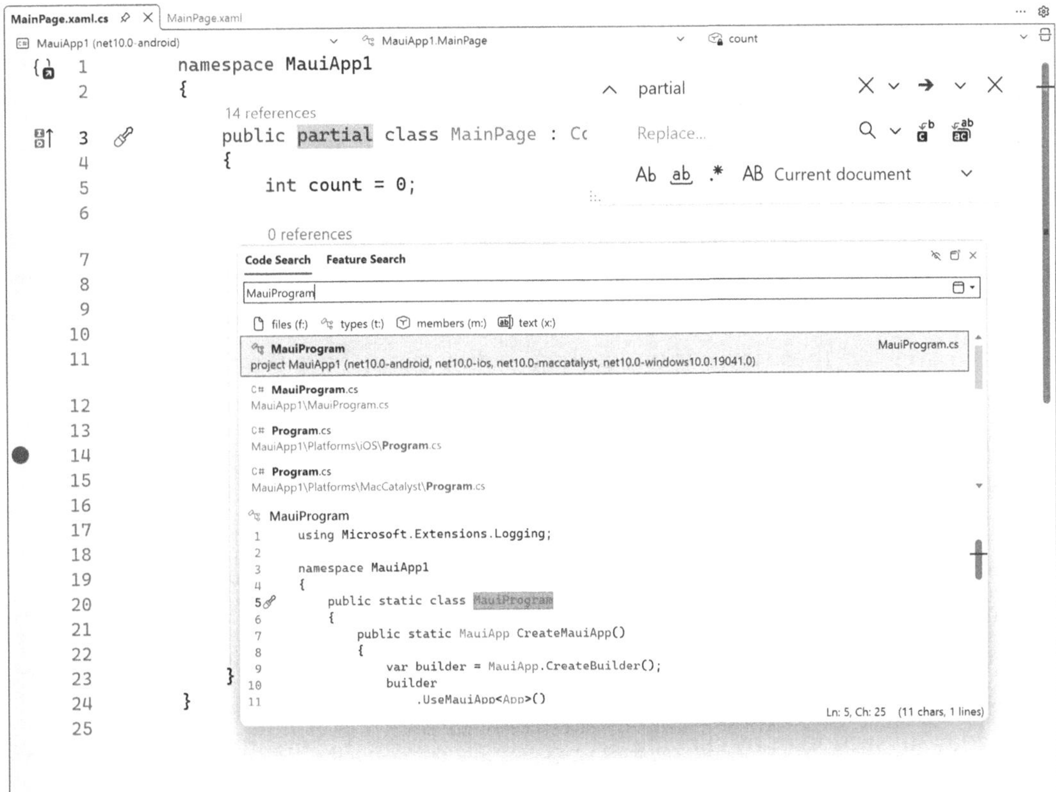

Figure 3-7. *A code editor showing Quick Find in the top-right and the All-in-One Search in the middle*

Smarter Navigation and Productivity Shortcuts

Visual Studio 2026 has harmonized its keyboard shortcuts with popular editors like VS Code, making it easier to switch between tools without constantly retraining your muscle memory. Ctrl+W now closes the current tab (in addition to the existing Ctrl+F4), and Ctrl+P opens Code Search alongside its traditional Ctrl+T shortcut. These additions don't replace your existing shortcuts; they work alongside them, giving you more options for how you want to work.

Window management has been refined to make docking and floating operations smoother and more intuitive. You can quickly restore a tool window to its last known docked location by holding Ctrl and double-clicking the window's title bar: this toggles the window between docked and floating states. When dragging windows to dock them, the guide diamond appears to show you exactly where the window will land, with shaded areas indicating the docking location.

Custom window layouts are now easier to create and manage. You can save up to ten different layout configurations and switch between them instantly using Ctrl+Alt+1 through Ctrl+Alt+0. This is perfect for creating specialized layouts for different tasks: one for coding with minimal distractions, another for debugging with all diagnostic windows visible, and a third for code reviews with side-by-side file comparisons. You will find the options to manage these layouts under the Window menu. Save Window Layout allows you to save the layout by specifying a name, Apply Window Layout lets you apply a previously saved layout (or you can use one of the previously mentioned shortcut keys), and with Manage Window Layouts, you can manage the order and rename or delete existing layouts.

Tab management has been enhanced with vertical tab support, letting you place document tabs along the left or right side of the editor instead of just across the top. This is especially useful on widescreen or ultra-wide monitors where vertical space is at a premium. You can configure this in Tools ➤ Options ➤ Environment ➤ Tabs and find the Tab layout section or by clicking the cogwheel icon on the far-right side of the editor tab bar and selecting one of the options like Place Tabs on the Left. It's a little bit hidden, so please refer to Figure 3-8 which shows you where the icon is exactly.

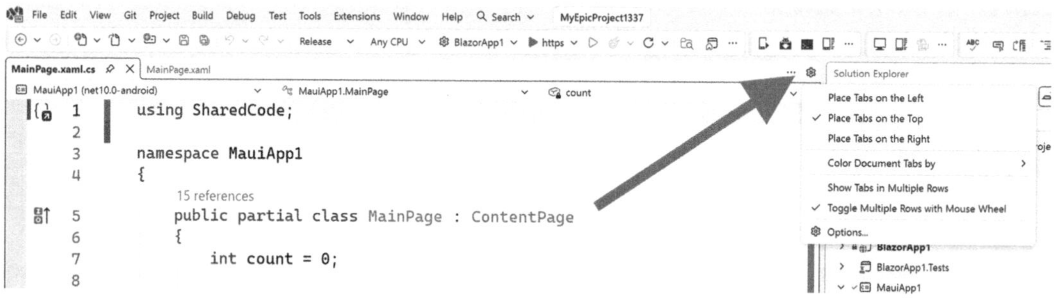

Figure 3-8. *The arrow points out the cogwheel icon that holds some tab layout options*

In the Options screen or under the cogwheel, you will also find configuration options to color documents, allow the tabs to show on multiple rows, and some other options you can play with to suit your needs. Figure 3-9 shows you the tabs configured to be shown on the left. At the top, two of them are pinned.

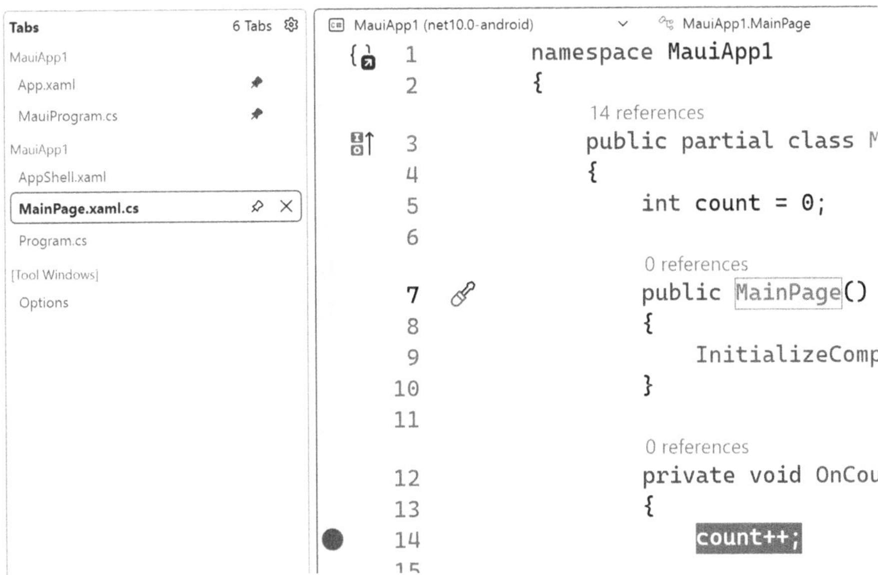

Figure 3-9. *The tabs configured to show on the left instead of on top of the document*

Solution Explorer: Your Command Center

Solution Explorer remains one of the most essential tools in Visual Studio, and in 2026, it's faster and more capable than ever. The incremental loading system means your project tree appears almost instantly, even in massive solutions with hundreds of projects. As soon as you open a solution, you can start working. Solution Explorer now loads and indexes files in the background without blocking your workflow. I typically work on the .NET MAUI code base which is a rather large and complex one, and I have definitely been noticing (and loving!) the improvement in this area.

The file system mirroring has been enhanced to reflect changes immediately. When you add, delete, or reorganize files in Windows Explorer or through Git operations, Solution Explorer updates in real time without requiring manual refresh. This bidirectional sync ensures that what you see in Solution Explorer always matches your actual file structure.

Multi-select operations make bulk file management much more efficient. You can select multiple files or entire folders, then drag them to reorganize your project structure, batch rename files, or perform group operations like include/exclude from the project or stage for Git commit. The instant expansion and collapse of folder hierarchies handles even solutions with thousands of files smoothly, without the lag that plagued earlier versions.

File preview is smarter in Visual Studio 2026. Single-clicking a file shows a preview in a temporary tab (indicated by the tab being aligned to the right as opposed to the left where the permanent tabs are), while double-clicking opens it in a permanent tab. The preview tab management prevents you from accidentally cluttering your workspace with dozens of open files when you're just browsing through code. You can search within Solution Explorer using Ctrl+; to instantly filter your file tree by name, making it easy to find files even in deeply nested folder structures.

In Figure 3-10, you can see the Solution Explorer while searching for "App". You can see not only the files and folders that match but also dependencies and potentially other objects that are shown in the Solution Explorer that match the search term.

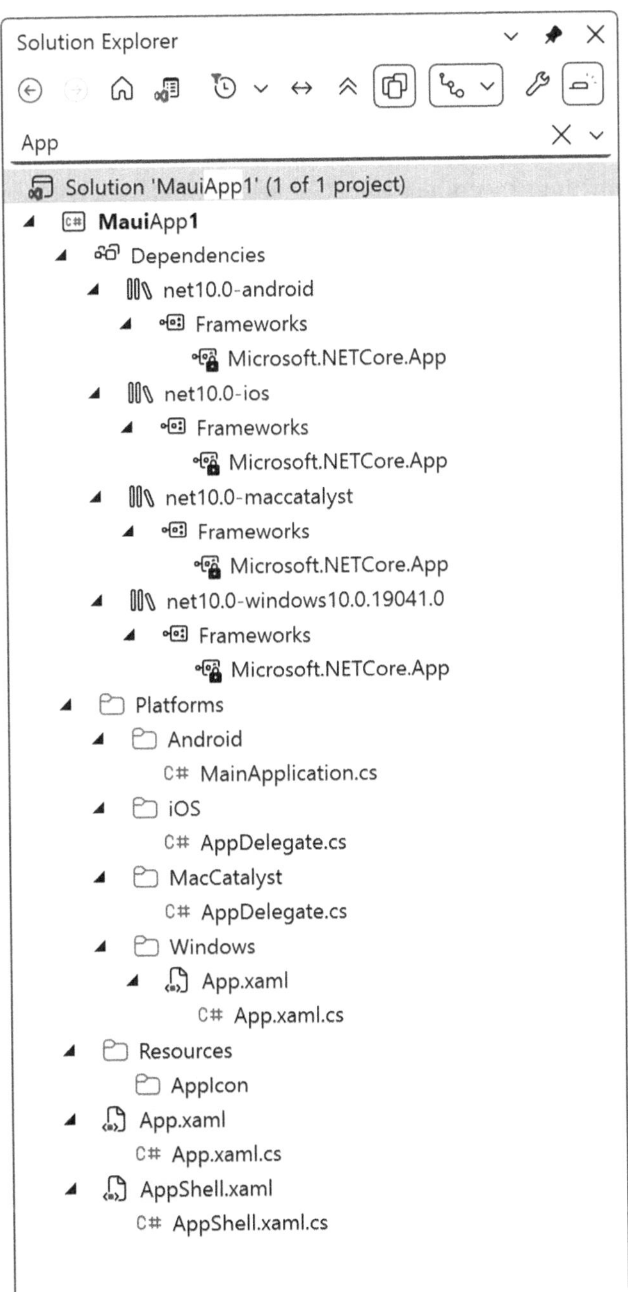

Figure 3-10. *Solution Explorer showing the search results for "App"*

Error List: More Than Just Errors

The Error List in Visual Studio 2026 has evolved from a graveyard for build failures into a powerful diagnostic and navigation tool. The enhanced filtering system lets you break down errors and warnings by code, project, severity, or status, with new filter tokens that let you focus on exactly what matters. For example, you can filter to show only errors from your code (excluding third-party libraries) or only warnings introduced in the last build.

Column customization gives you control over what information is displayed. Right-click any column header to show or hide columns, and drag headers to reorder them based on your workflow. You can sort by any column and hold Shift while clicking additional column headers to apply multi-level sorting. This makes it easy to group related issues together for efficient fixing.

The search functionality within Error List helps you quickly locate specific errors or patterns across large lists of build messages. Type in the search box and Error List filters to show only entries matching your search terms across all visible columns. This is particularly useful when you're tracking down specific compiler warnings or trying to understand error patterns across your solution. In Figure 3-11, you can see how the Output window is filtered using the search box in the top-right. Other ways to filter information are through the errors, warnings, and messages buttons just above the grid view to filter only on that specific type of entry.

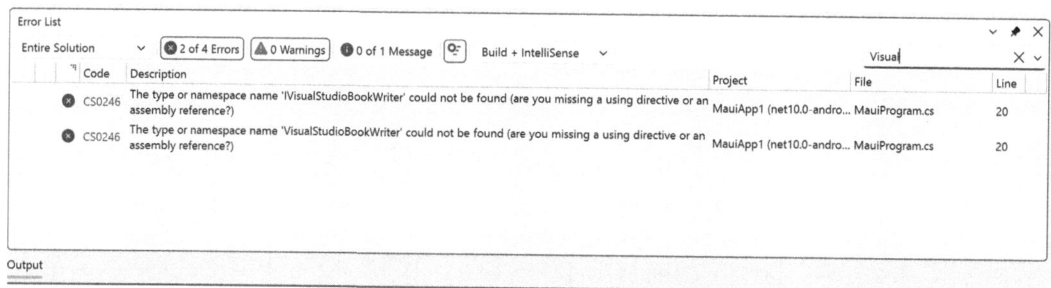

Figure 3-11. *Filtering the Output window*

Clicking any error takes you directly to the relevant line of code, and the Error List can be kept visible as a compact panel or docked to float over your workflow without taking up too much screen space. The integration with IntelliSense means you see both build-time errors and real-time code analysis warnings in a single unified view.

Modern Settings Experience

We've already touched on it briefly in the last chapter, but the legacy Tools > Options dialog is gone, replaced by a modern settings interface that's faster to navigate and easier to customize. The new settings experience uses the Fluent UI design language, with improved organization, real-time search, and better persistence across sessions.

The search functionality in the settings panel is context-aware and instant. Start typing what you're looking for like "keyboard" or "theme", and the settings interface filters to show only relevant options. You can bookmark frequently accessed settings for one-click access, and the interface supports JSON editing for advanced customizations.

In Figure 3-12, you can see how the Options screen is filtered to show everything that has to do with git. At the top, just under the tab bar, you can see the search box, but also settings to influence the scope of these settings, edit the settings as a JSON file, and sync the settings with the cloud.

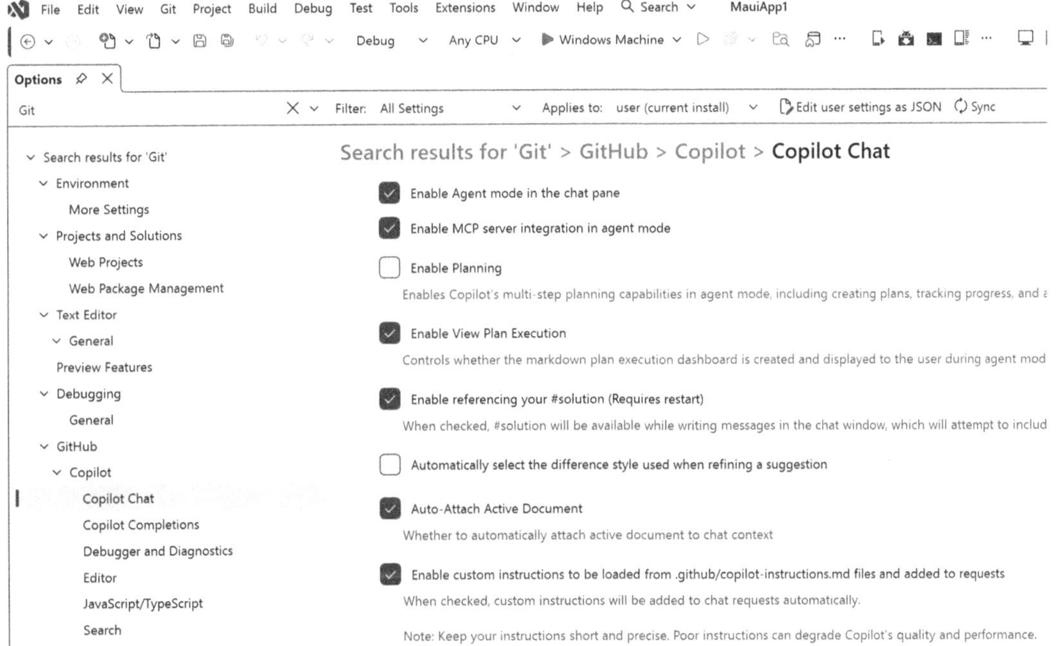

Figure 3-12. *The Options screen filtered to show all settings that have to do with git*

Cloud sync for settings means your preferences, keyboard shortcuts, theme choices, and extension configurations follow you across devices automatically. This works through your Microsoft account and happens transparently in the background. You can selectively choose which settings sync and which remain machine-specific.

Extension management is now integrated into the main settings interface, making it easier to install, update, and configure extensions without hunting through multiple dialogs. The centralized registration system means extensions can expose their settings in a consistent way, and you can see all extension-related configuration in one place.

Productivity Features That Add Up

Visual Studio 2026 includes dozens of smaller productivity improvements that individually seem minor but collectively make a huge difference in your daily workflow. Fast scrolling lets you hold Alt while scrolling with the mouse wheel to move through large files, vertically and horizontally, much more quickly. Perfect for reviewing code or reading documentation. You can adjust the fast-scrolling sensitivity in Tools ➤ Options ➤ Text Editor ➤ Advanced.

The editor's bottom margin has been upgraded to be more informative and interactive. Line, column, and character position are now unified into a single display, and clicking it opens the Go To Line dialog for faster navigation. When working with multiple selections, you'll see total counts for selections, characters, and lines; hovering over the selection margin reveals detailed information per selection.

Markdown preview and Mermaid chart rendering are now built directly into the IDE. If you haven't used it before, Mermaid is a popular text-based diagramming tool that lets you generate flowcharts, sequence diagrams, Gantt charts, and more using simple Markdown-like code. You can visualize flowcharts, sequence diagrams, and other Mermaid charts in Markdown files, either by writing the syntax yourself or having Copilot generate it for you. This makes architecture documentation and workflow visualization much more accessible without leaving Visual Studio. In Figure 3-13, you can see a Markdown file on the left and on the right the rendered preview including a complex Mermaid chart.

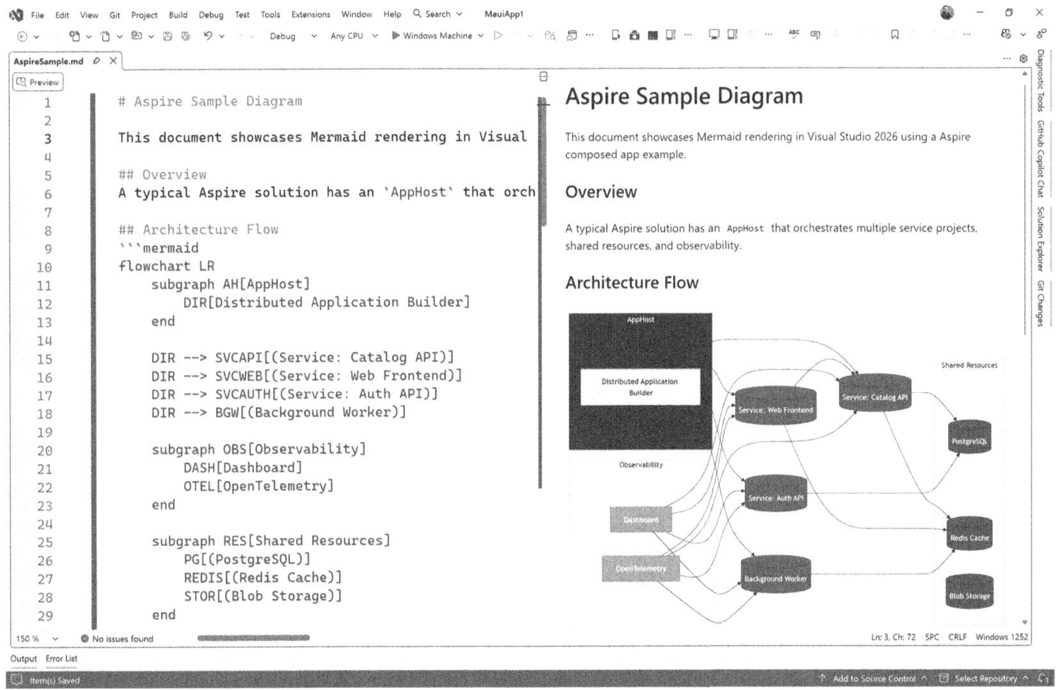

Figure 3-13. *Markdown files with Mermaid charts can now be previewed from inside Visual Studio 2026*

Code search in Copilot Chat has been enhanced to provide more relevant results by leveraging remote indexes of your code base. This means Copilot can retrieve better code snippets related to behaviors, concepts, or functionality you describe in natural language, even if the code isn't currently open in your editor.

Summary

Visual Studio 2026's updated IDE represents a thoughtful evolution that balances modern design with the power and flexibility developers need. Understanding the default layout helps you know where to find tools quickly, while the Fluent UI refresh reduces visual clutter and improves accessibility without sacrificing information density. The expanded theming system with 11 new tinted themes and independent editor appearance settings lets you create a workspace that's comfortable for long coding sessions.

Enhanced search capabilities, including All-In-One Search, AI-powered "Did You Mean" suggestions, and customizable file exclusions, dramatically reduce the time spent hunting for files, types, and symbols in large code bases. Harmonized keyboard shortcuts with VS Code and improved window management make it easier to work efficiently, whether you're switching from other tools or optimizing your existing Visual Studio workflow.

Solution Explorer and Error List improvements bring real performance gains through incremental loading, instant file system sync, enhanced filtering, and smarter navigation. The modernized settings experience with real-time search, cloud sync, and integrated extension management makes customization faster and more accessible.

Dozens of smaller productivity enhancements, from fast scrolling to enhanced bottom margins to built-in Mermaid rendering, add up to an IDE that feels noticeably more responsive and pleasant to use every day.

In the next chapter, we'll dive into project management and Solution Explorer in more depth, exploring how Visual Studio 2026's enhanced organization tools help you manage large solutions, work with multiple projects efficiently, and keep your code base maintainable as it grows.

CHAPTER 4

Project Management and Solution Explorer

Working with large code bases can be overwhelming. Hundreds of projects, nested folders, complex dependencies, and files scattered across multiple levels of hierarchy can turn what should be a straightforward development session into a navigation nightmare. Visual Studio 2026 recognizes this challenge and gives you powerful tools to organize, filter, and manage your solutions at scale. Whether you're building a monorepo with dozens of interdependent services, maintaining a legacy application with layers of complexity, or working on a smaller project that's growing, this chapter shows you how to keep everything organized and accessible.

Understanding Solution Explorer and Your Project Structure

Before we dive into advanced organization techniques, it's important to understand how Visual Studio structures your code. Solution Explorer is your command center for project management. It's where you see and interact with your entire solution's hierarchy. Unlike your file system explorer, Solution Explorer is primarily a virtual representation of your project structure, which means you have tremendous flexibility in how you organize what you see and work with.

At the top level sits your solution file. Which, by the way, in Visual Studio 2026 is now an `.slnx` file by default (though legacy `.sln` files are still fully supported). This XML-based solution file acts as a container for all your projects and is much more concise and human-readable than the older format. The `.slnx` format also reduces merge conflicts when working with version control, making it especially valuable for teams. Below the solution level are your individual projects; each project represents a compilable unit that produces a specific output, whether that's a DLL, EXE, NuGet package, or something else. Within each project are your files, depending on the type of project, those can be (but are not limited to) C# classes, C++ files, HTML files, JavaScript source, XAML files, configuration files, dependencies, and everything else that makes up your project.

Note   If you have existing solutions using the older `.sln` format, you can easily migrate them to `.slnx` using the dotnet CLI command `dotnet sln migrate` or by right-clicking your solution in Solution Explorer in Visual Studio and selecting "Save Solution As," then choosing "XML Solution File (*.slnx)". All functionality remains identical; it's simply a modernized format that's cleaner and easier to work with.

Solution Explorer itself lives on the right side of the Visual Studio window by default, though you can move it anywhere you prefer. The icons tell you what you're looking at: folder icons for directories, project icons that vary by project type, and file icons that indicate file type. The search functionality in Solution Explorer lets you quickly narrow down this tree to find exactly what you're looking for, even in enormous repositories.

Have a look at Figure 4-1; it shows different types of nodes that you can encounter in the Solution Explorer. It would be impossible to show them all, but this is a good overview of the typical things you will find.

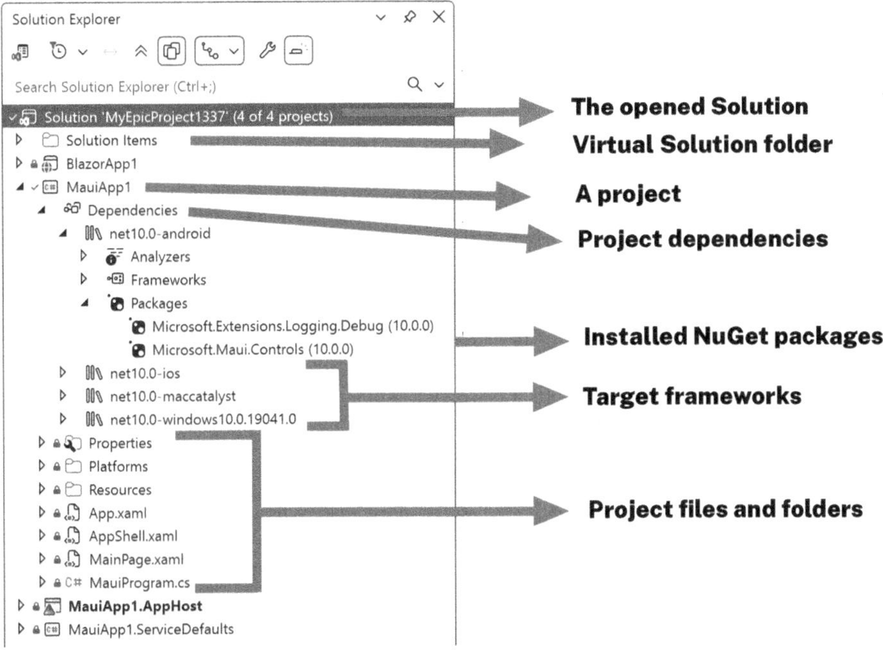

Figure 4-1. *Overview of the Solution Explorer with all the different nodes*

I think the descriptions should be pretty self-explanatory; let me add a couple of notes. The target frameworks are not always there. If a project only targets a single framework, which is most common, then under Dependencies, you will see the Analyzers, Frameworks, and Packages directly. If a project does target multiple frameworks, then each target can have different analyzers, frameworks, and packages; that is why those nodes are then repeated for each target.

An example of a multi-targeted project is a .NET MAUI (Multi-platform App UI) project. This is a project that lets you build cross-platform apps for iOS, Android, macOS, and Windows from a single project. However, as you still need to cater to multiple target platforms, you need to *multi-target* your project.

You might not always see the Solution Items, but they are very useful; let's learn about those in the next section.

Organizing with Solution Folders: Virtual Organization Without File System Constraints

One of the most powerful organizational tools in Visual Studio is the Solution Folder, a purely virtual container that helps you group and organize projects without any impact on your actual file system. Solution Folders are what you need when you have many projects that logically belong together but physically live in different directories on disk.

Creating a Solution Folder is straightforward: right-click on your solution node in Solution Explorer and select Add ➤ New Solution Folder, or use the Project menu and choose Add New Solution Folder. You can nest these folders as deeply as you want, creating logical groupings like Frontend, Backend, Services, Tests, or however your architecture is organized. What I typically use it for is to also include the README file of the project so that it's also visible from within Visual Studio and not just the repository, and now with full Markdown support, this shows up nicely as well!

The beauty of Solution Folders is that they're virtual. Moving a project into a Solution Folder doesn't move the actual project files on disk. This means you can organize your Visual Studio view however makes sense for your team, independent of how your files are arranged in Windows Explorer or your Git repository. For example, you could group test projects together in Solution Folders even though they're physically scattered across different directories.

Visual Studio 2026 has improved Solution Folder operations. When organizing large solutions, you can now bulk expand and collapse folder hierarchies much more efficiently. Right-click any folder and select "Collapse All Descendants" to quickly tidy up deeply nested structures. Conversely, expanding a folder now shows its contents instantly, no more waiting for Visual Studio to load thousands of nested items.

In Figure 4-2, you can see the Solution Items folder right under the Solution node.

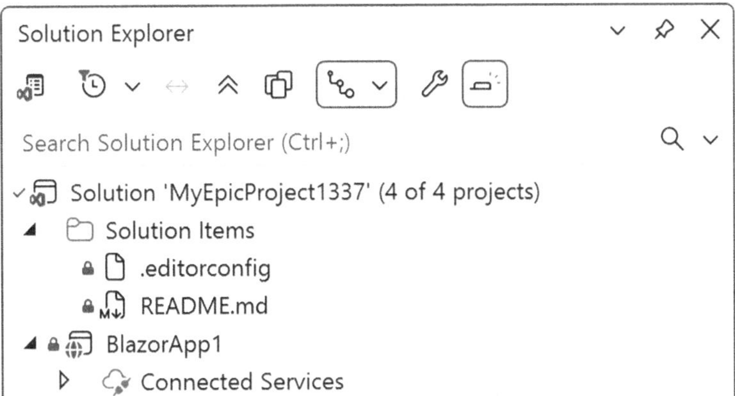

Figure 4-2. *The Solution Explorer with a Solution Items folder that has the repository's README and .editorconfig file*

Filtering and Scoping: Focus on What Matters

When you're working on a specific feature or bug fix, the last thing you want is Visual Studio spending time loading and analyzing hundreds of projects you're not even touching. Visual Studio 2026 introduces filtering and scoping capabilities that let you narrow down what's loaded and visible, dramatically improving performance and reducing cognitive load.

Solution Filters (`.slnf` files) are one of the most valuable improvements for large code bases. A Solution Filter is a subset of projects from your main solution, defined in a separate file that you can check into source control and share with your team. When you open a `.slnf` file instead of the solution file, Visual Studio loads only the projects you've specified, which can reduce load times from minutes to seconds.

The good news is that Solution Filters work seamlessly with both the classic `.sln` and the newer `.slnx` file formats. Whether your solution uses the legacy text-based format or the new XML-based `.slnx` format, filters work the same way and provide the same performance benefits. However, if you migrate your solution from `.sln` to `.slnx`, you'll need to update your filter files to reference the new `.slnx` file; otherwise, the filter will continue trying to open the old `.sln` file.

To create a Solution Filter, open your solution, load only the projects you need, then right-click the solution node, and select "Save as Solution Filter". A dialog appears asking where to save the `.slnf` file. A good practice is to keep it in your repository alongside your solution file. You can now create multiple filters for different teams or workflows: one for front-end work, one for back-end services, one for the data layer, etc.

This approach is particularly powerful in monorepos where different teams work on different parts of the code base. Instead of requiring everyone to load every project, you can distribute team-specific filter files that each team checks out and uses. A front-end team might use `Frontend.slnf` that loads web UI and API projects, while a backend team uses `Backend.slnf` that loads services and database projects.

Have a look at Figure 4-3. Notice how there are two projects unloaded in the Solution Explorer, the ones that have to do with Aspire. If you then do File ➤ Save Solution As Filter… You will get a save dialog that lets you save the .slnf file.

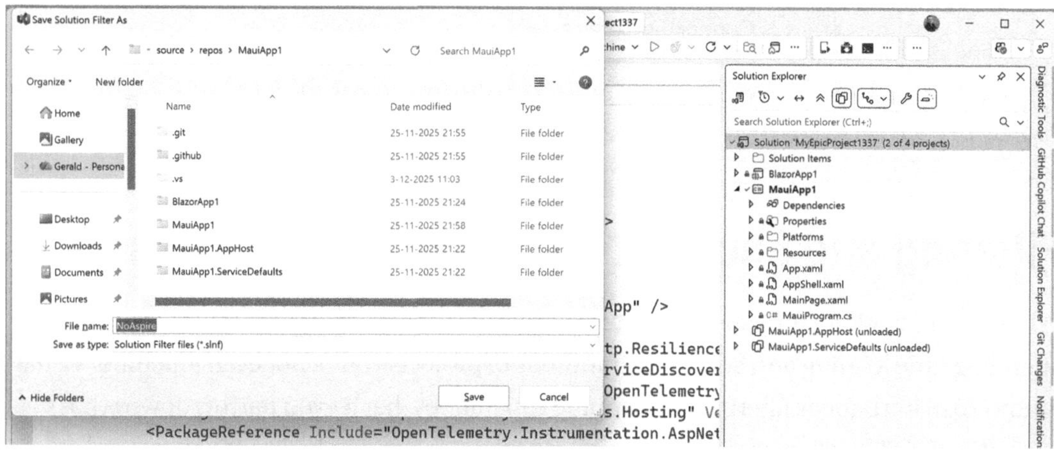

Figure 4-3. *Saving a solution filter (.slnf) file. On the right, the two Aspire projects are unloaded; saving a slnf file will hide these projects by default*

Managing Project Dependencies: Understanding Build Order

When you have multiple projects that depend on each other, Visual Studio needs to understand the dependency chain to build them in the correct order. Project dependencies ensure that if Project A depends on Project B, Visual Studio builds Project B first, so Project A has everything it needs.

In Visual Studio 2026, managing project dependencies has been further improved. Right-click on your solution node in Solution Explorer, and select "Project Build Dependencies" from the context menu; note that this is now a solution-level menu option rather than a project-level option. This opens the Project Dependencies dialog where you can see all your projects and explicitly specify which projects other projects depend on. In Figure 4-4, you can see the Project Build Dependencies dialog.

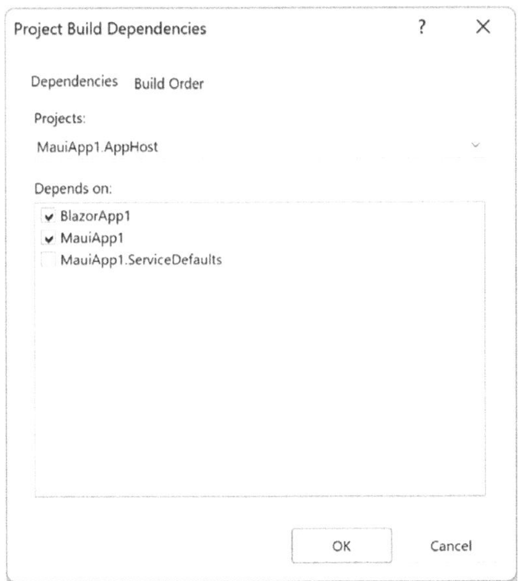

Figure 4-4. *On the left, the Dependencies tab which shows the dependencies of the selected project. On the right, determined by the dependencies, the determined build order of the projects for the solution*

The Dependencies tab lets you select any project and check boxes next to the projects it depends on. The Build Order tab shows you the logical build order that Visual Studio will use to compile your solution. Keep in mind that Visual Studio also optimizes by building multiple projects in parallel whenever possible, so the actual build process may differ from the logical order depending on which dependencies can safely build concurrently.

It's worth noting that for modern project types using .NET, project-to-project references (which you add by right-clicking References and selecting "Add Reference") automatically create dependency relationships and are generally preferred over manually setting build dependencies. However, understanding build dependencies is still important when you have projects that need to build first for reasons other than a direct reference. For example, when one project generates build tasks used by another.

Tip   Something that is not very widely known is that you can drag-and-drop one project on the other in the Solution Explorer, and that will add a reference from the dragged project to the project where you drop it on. Now you have learned a new party trick to show off to your colleagues!

Visual Studio 2026 can sometimes automatically detect and suggest missing project references through its enhanced analyzer. If you're getting build errors that suggest circular dependencies or missing project references, the Error List and quick fix suggestions can help you resolve these issues directly.

Advanced Organization: Multi-project Launch Profiles

When you're working with solutions that have multiple interdependent services or components, you often need to start several projects at once during debugging. Visual Studio 2026 improves this experience with multi-project launch profiles.

Rather than manually selecting multiple startup projects every time you open your solution, you can save launch profiles that specify exactly which projects should start when you press F5 and whether each should be debugged or just run. To set this up, right-click your solution in Solution Explorer and select "Configure Startup Projects".

In the dialog that appears, select "Multiple startup projects", and then choose the action for each project: "Start" (launch with debugging), "Start without debugging," or "None" (don't launch). You can reorder projects using the up and down arrows to control the launch sequence.

Visual Studio 2026 has added the ability to save and switch between multiple launch profiles. This is perfect when you have different scenarios: maybe you have one profile for local development that starts your web server and database, another for testing a specific microservice in isolation, and a third for performance profiling work. The multi-project launch profile feature saves your configuration, so switching between scenarios is as simple as selecting a different profile.

In Figure 4-5, you can see the dialog when you select the Configure Startup Projects option. Here, you can create different launch profiles which allow you to start projects together and configured to run in a debug session or not, etc.

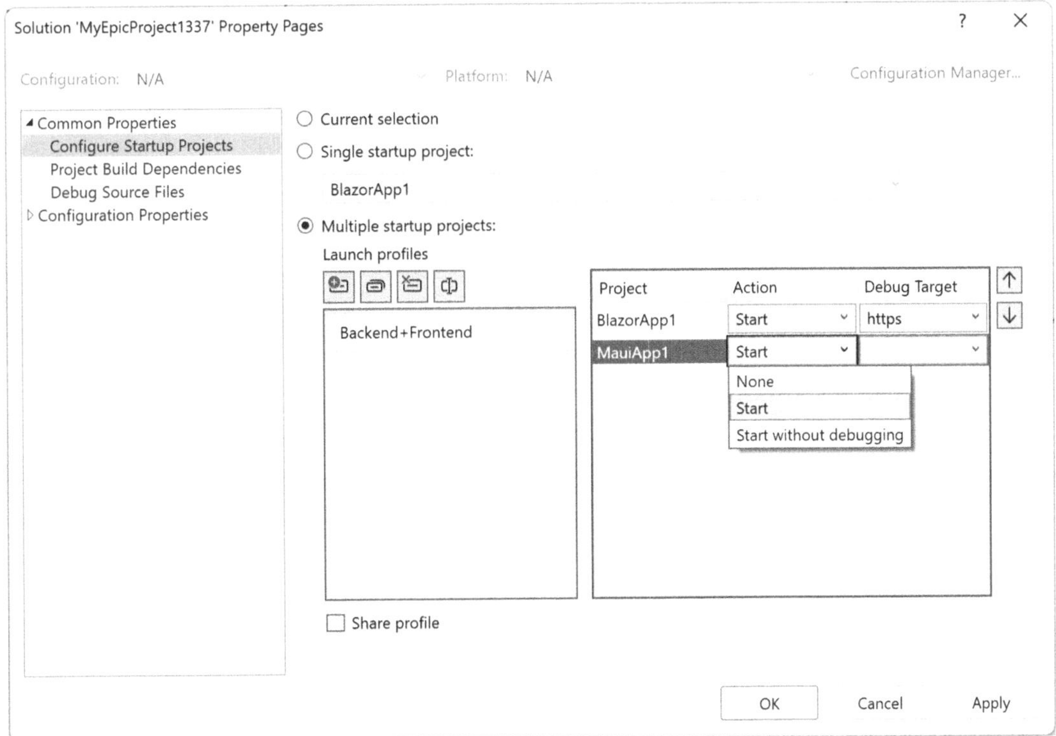

Figure 4-5. *Solution Property Pages dialog opened on the Configure Startup Projects pane where you can define one or more launch profiles*

While not really a comparable feature, another way to manage the startup of your application landscape is by using Aspire. Aspire is a .NET product, but its use goes far beyond the .NET ecosystem. You can use it to describe your application landscape in code which includes but is not limited to: JavaScript-based projects, Python projects, AI models, databases, proxies, and much, much more. Aspire is a topic that can very easily fill a book by itself. We will touch on it a little bit more in Chapter 10, but otherwise, it is out of scope for this book as it has little to do with Visual Studio itself.

Search and Navigation Within Large Solutions

As your solution grows, finding the specific file, class, or method you need becomes increasingly challenging. Visual Studio 2026's enhanced search capabilities make this manageable, even in repositories with thousands of files.

The All-In-One Search we discussed in Chapter 3 takes on even more power in the context of large solutions. Press Ctrl+Shift+P to open the search interface, and you can now scope your search to "Current Project" or "Entire Solution" using drop-down options. The search remembers your scope preference, so if you typically work within your current project, you won't accidentally get thousands of irrelevant results from the entire solution.

Search scoping works across different search types too. File search, symbol search, and code search all support scoping, and you can even set different scopes for different search types. For example, you might scope file search to the current project but code search to the entire solution, depending on what you're looking for.

Within Solution Explorer itself, the search box lets you filter the tree by file name instantly. Type a few characters and the tree collapses to show only matching files. If you need to drill down into deeply nested folders to find something, Solution Explorer search saves you from endless clicking.

Quick Add functionality lets you rapidly add files and folders to your project without navigating through templates. Just right-click your project, select "Add > New Item" or press Ctrl+Shift+A, and type a file name directly. You can even create nested folder structures in one operation by using forward slashes in the file name—for example, typing `Utilities/Helpers/StringUtils.cs` creates the complete folder hierarchy and file in one step!

Note   If you just see the regular Add Item dialog, find the Show Compact View in the bottom left. This dialog remembers the last form it was shown in and uses that when you press Ctrl+Shift+A or do Add ➤ New Item from the context menu. For more information, see `https://learn.microsoft.com/visualstudio/ide/use-solution-explorer?view=visualstudio#the-quick-add-dialog`.

The dialog that makes this all possible can be seen in Figure 4-6.

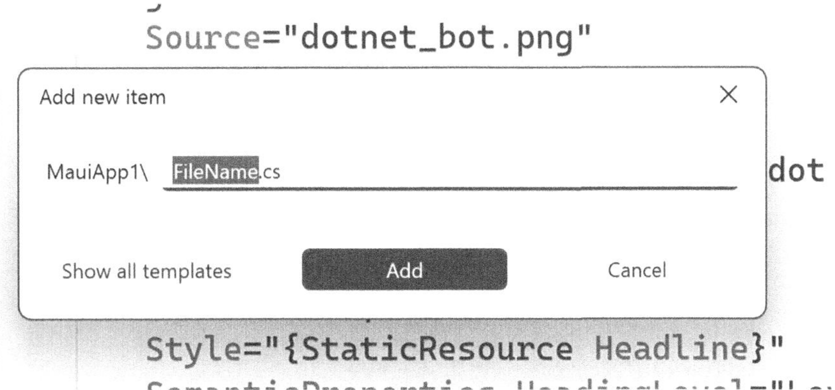

Figure 4-6. *Add new item dialog that allows you to enter just a file name or path and will create that file for you in the specified location*

Still Powerful: Multi-select Operations and Bulk Actions

Solution Explorer in Visual Studio 2026 lets you work with multiple files and projects simultaneously, which saves enormous amounts of time when you need to organize or modify groups of items.

You can select multiple files by holding Ctrl and clicking, or Shift+click to select ranges, just like you're probably used to from the File Explorer on Windows. Once selected, you can drag the entire group to move them together, right-click to get a context menu with bulk operations, or delete them all at once. This is especially useful when reorganizing file structures or moving related files into Solution Folders.

Batch renaming is now more accessible too. Select multiple files, right-click, and use the rename context menu option to rename them in batch. Patterns and variables are supported for advanced scenarios. This might seem like a small feature, but when you're refactoring a large code base and need to rename dozens of related files, it becomes invaluable.

The drag-and-drop operations have been refined in Visual Studio 2026 to be more intuitive and reliable. You can now drag projects into Solution Folders, drag files between projects, and even drag entire folders to reorganize your project structure. Visual Studio shows you a preview of where the items will land before you release the mouse button, reducing mistakes.

In Figure 4-7, you can see a multi-select drag and drop operation happening in the Solution Explorer.

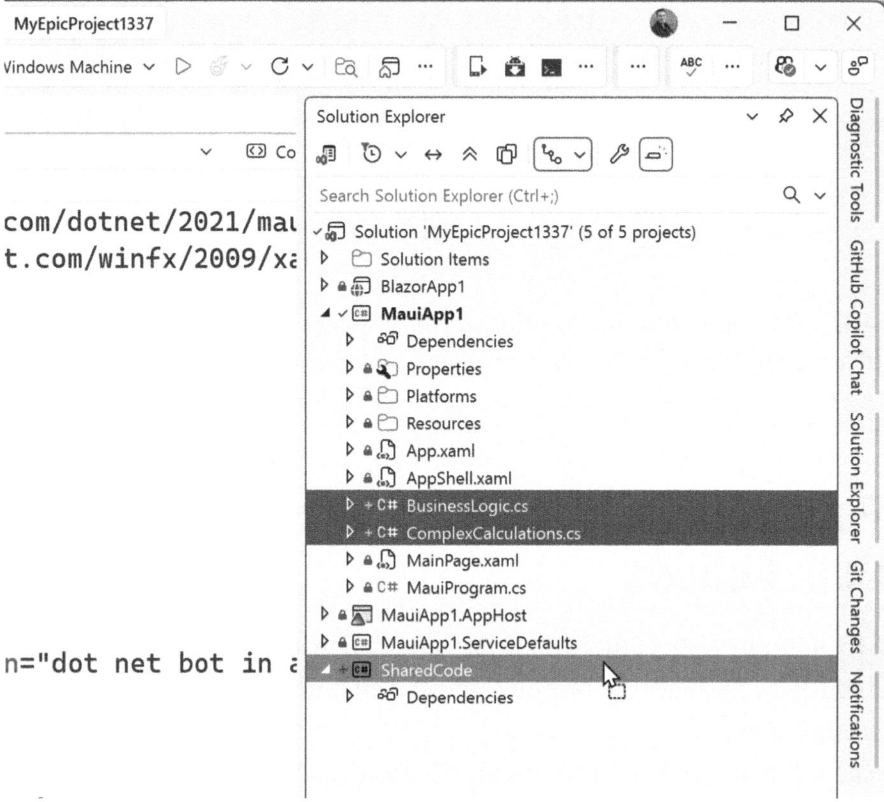

Figure 4-7. *Multiple files are being dragged from one project to the other*

Folder View: Working Without Solutions

Not every code base fits neatly into Visual Studio's traditional solution and project structure. Monorepos, CMake-based projects, Node.js applications, Python scripts alongside C# services, or any mixed-language workspace can feel awkward when forced into a solution file. Visual Studio 2026 recognizes this reality and offers Folder View as a flexible alternative to working with solution files.

Opening a Folder View is straightforward: go to File ➤ Open Folder and select any directory on your machine. Or, if you have a solution already open, you can very easily switch between Folder View and Solution view with the shortcut button at the top of the

Solution Explorer. Visual Studio immediately scans that folder and all its subdirectories, displaying the complete directory tree in Solution Explorer. Unlike Solution Explorer's project-centric view, Folder View shows your actual file system structure: folders, files, symbolic links, and everything else exactly as it exists on disk. This directness is powerful when you're working with code bases that don't follow .NET project conventions or when you're maintaining infrastructure-as-code, configuration files, documentation, and code all in the same repository.

The integration with everything we have learned so far is seamless. Full-text search works across all files in the folder. Git integration shows status, branches, and commit history. IntelliSense works for supported file types: C#, C++, JavaScript, TypeScript, Python, XML, JSON, YAML, and many others. You can edit, refactor, and build code exactly as you would in a solution-based workflow, without the overhead of maintaining solution files or project structure.

One of the most practical uses for Folder View is working with monorepos, large repositories containing multiple independent services or libraries. A typical monorepo might have a structure like `services/auth`, `services/api`, `services/billing`, `frontend/web`, `frontend/mobile`, `infrastructure/terraform`, all in one repository. Rather than creating a massive solution file that includes every project, you can open the entire folder and navigate fluidly between different services. And maybe each subset has its own `slnf` file. The search and navigation tools remain lightning-fast because Visual Studio isn't trying to load and parse hundreds of projects; it's just working with files and their content.

Figure 4-8 shows the same solution we have seen so far, but now with the Folder View enabled.

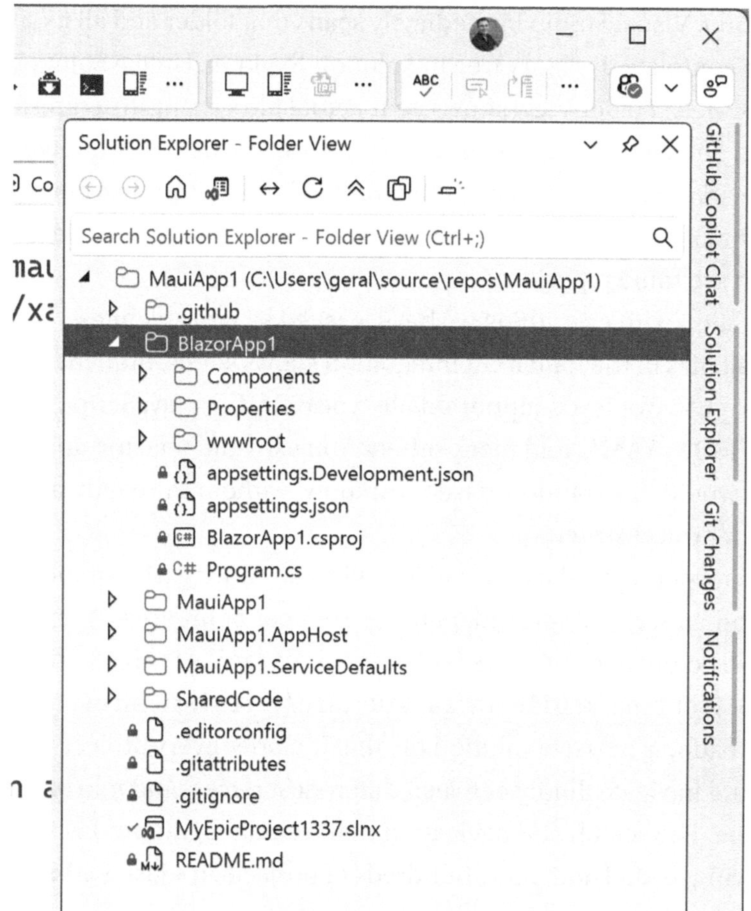

Figure 4-8. *Solution Explorer showing the Folder View*

Performance Considerations: Large Solution Best Practices

Managing performance in large solutions requires intentional decisions. Visual Studio 2026 has made many improvements, but following a few best practices will help you get the most out of your IDE.

First, use Solution Filters for common development scenarios. If your solution has 150 projects but you typically only work on 15 of them, create `.slnf` files that load just those 15. This dramatically reduces load times, memory usage, and build times while you're focused on specific work.

Second, disable extensions you don't actively use. Some extensions hook into project loading and can slow things down significantly in large solutions. Go to Extensions ➤ Manage Extensions, and disable extensions that aren't essential for your current work.

Third, configure your solution to use incremental builds where possible. In large solutions, clean rebuilds can take a long time. Visual Studio's incremental build system only rebuilds projects that have changed and their dependents, which is typically much faster. Make sure your build configuration isn't forcing full rebuilds unnecessarily.

Fourth, consider using search exclusions to prevent Visual Studio from indexing files you don't need to search. We've seen how to do this back in Chapter 3. Generated code, build artifacts, package dependencies, and vendor directories can all be excluded, making both search and general IDE responsiveness faster.

Finally, keep your solution structure relatively organized. While Solution Folders are virtual and don't affect the file system, having a logical structure makes navigation much easier and helps you think about your project organization. Deeply nested folder structures (50+ levels) can become unwieldy regardless of how fast your IDE is.

Historically, developers reaching for a lightweight, instant-load experience would default to opening VS Code. With Visual Studio 2026, that dynamic has changed. Thanks to massive under-the-hood optimizations to the project loading and indexing systems, Visual Studio 2026 load times are now virtually on par with VS Code. Whether you are opening a massive `.slnx` file or just opening a folder directly, the IDE becomes responsive almost instantly, letting you get straight to coding without the traditional "loading projects" coffee break.

At the time of writing, there are also some preview features (enabled by default, find them under Tools ➤ Options ➤ Preview Features) that help optimize Visual Studio's speed.

Summary

Project management in Visual Studio 2026 gives you powerful tools to handle solutions of any size. Solution Folders provide a virtual organization independent of your file system, letting you group projects logically without moving actual files. Solution Filters (`.slnf` files) let you load subsets of your solution for dramatically faster load and build times, perfect for large code bases and distributed teams.

Scoping and filtering features, from narrowing Solution Explorer to specific folders to excluding files from search results, help you focus on what matters and reduce cognitive load. Project dependencies and multi-project launch profiles ensure that complex multi-service architectures are built in the correct order and start cleanly during debugging.

Enhanced multi-select operations, bulk actions, and Quick Add functionality make organizing and reorganizing files efficient, even when you're working with hundreds of items. Performance best practices, using Solution Filters, disabling unnecessary extensions, configuring incremental builds, and excluding generated files from search, ensure that even enterprise-scale code bases remain responsive and pleasant to work with.

In the next chapter, we'll shift focus to the actual code editing experience. You'll learn how Visual Studio 2026's improved IntelliSense, refactoring tools, and debugging capabilities help you write better code faster while maintaining the quality and reliability your projects demand.

CHAPTER 5

Editing, Refactoring, and Debugging

If you've spent any time coding, you know that the real magic (and sometimes the real frustration) happens in the moments between writing, fixing, and understanding what your code is actually doing. Visual Studio 2026 raises the bar in these areas, marrying best-in-class coding assistance and diagnostics with AI-powered insight, all while making sure new users aren't left behind. In this chapter, you'll learn everything from smarter IntelliSense to next-generation debugging, with plenty of practical context along the way.

Understanding the Editing Foundation

Before diving into what's new in 2026, let's establish the fundamentals that make Visual Studio a productive coding environment. At its core, the editor is where you spend most of your time: writing code, reading existing implementations, and understanding complex systems. Visual Studio's editing experience is built on two core technologies that work together seamlessly: the Roslyn compiler platform (which provides deep code understanding) and IntelliSense (which surfaces that understanding as you type).

IntelliSense is your code completion engine. As you type a class name, method, or variable, Visual Studio watches what you're writing and offers intelligent suggestions. Press Ctrl+Space to trigger the completion list manually, or let it appear automatically, usually when you type a dot or a space after a variable reference or assignment. Select a suggestion with the arrow keys or mouse cursor, and press Enter or Tab to accept it. This saves countless keystrokes and prevents typos, but more importantly, it teaches you what's available in your libraries and APIs without requiring you to memorize method signatures. Not just the available members show up in the list, but if the library author

© Gerald Versluis 2026

G. Versluis, *Getting Started with Visual Studio 2026*, https://doi.org/10.1007/979-8-8688-2691-7_5

did their job right, IntelliSense will also be filled with relevant documentation. For newcomers, IntelliSense is often the first feature you learn to love about using an IDE.

In Figure 5-1, you can see IntelliSense in action where it suggests the potential methods available in the `builder.Services` object. You can see the suggested list in the middle drop-down; on the far right, you can see the API documentation for the selected method in the IntelliSense drop-down.

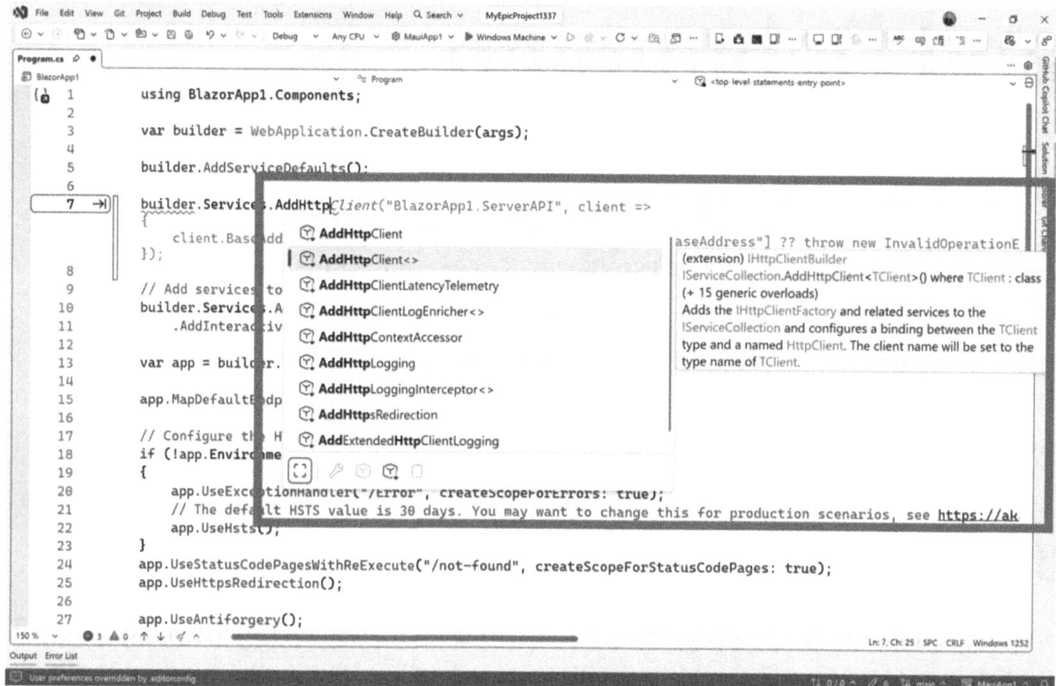

Figure 5-1. *IntelliSense showing suggestions for the code being implemented*

IntelliSense Improvements in Visual Studio 2026

Visual Studio 2026 brings targeted improvements to IntelliSense, particularly for specific scenarios where you'll notice immediate productivity gains.

Razor, Blazor, and HTML IntelliSense

If you're working with Razor and Blazor, you'll notice significantly better support. Improved Razor IntelliSense now provides accurate completion suggestions for `@bind:event` values. When using two-way data binding with custom events (e.g., `@bind="Value"` or `@bind:event="oninput"`), the editor autocompletes valid event names like `oninput` or `onchange`.

HTML snippets like typing `div` + Tab to expand a `<div>` block now appear consistently in Razor files, where they previously sometimes failed to show up. Autocomplete for hyphenated attributes and component parameters (e.g., `data-*` attributes or Blazor component parameters with dashes) is now more robust.

Control Over IntelliSense Appearance and Behavior

One of the most practical improvements is granular control over when and how IntelliSense appears. You can now configure whether suggestions appear automatically or only after you pause typing, giving you the ability to reduce distractions if you prefer a quieter editing experience. You can also partially accept Copilot suggestions; if a suggestion includes more than you want, accept just the portion you need rather than accepting the entire completion and editing afterward.

These settings are found at Tools ➤ Options ➤ Text Editor ➤ Code Completions in Visual Studio 2026 (note that this location changed from the VS 2022 path). Depending on what behavior you want to tweak, you can enable or disable things like Copilot Completions, Copilot Next Edit Suggestions, or IntelliCode and choose the Copilot model that you want to use for these suggestions. More on this you will find in Chapter 8 when we dive into the AI-powered development.

In Figure 5-2, in the highlighted box, you can see some grayed-out text (starting at `WeatherForecastService` on line 7). This text, also known as "ghost text," is a Copilot suggestion. You can press Tab to accept. In this example, it's only a couple of lines, but this can also be complete blocks of code that are relevant to what you are trying to do.

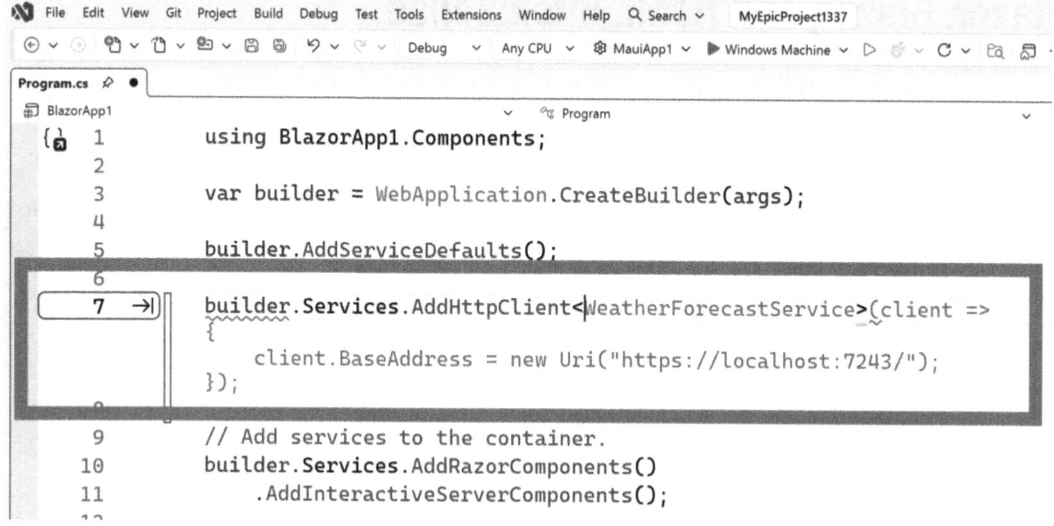

Figure 5-2. *Copilot Completion being suggested through ghost text*

Adaptive Paste: Code That Automatically Fits Your Project

One of the most practical improvements for everyday coding is Adaptive Paste, of course, powered by Copilot. Anyone who codes has experienced this: you find a useful code snippet online or in another project, copy it, paste it into your file (of course, after verifying the licensing allows it), and spend the next five minutes fixing variable names, adding imports, adjusting formatting, and translating terminology to match your project's conventions.

Adaptive paste eliminates this friction. When you paste code into a file, Copilot analyzes the context and automatically adapts the pasted code to fit your file. This means

- Variable and method names are adjusted to follow your project's naming patterns

- Import statements are added or updated automatically; this already happened but has been improved

- Code formatting is applied to match your configured style rules

- Type names are updated if your project uses different naming

- Comments are adjusted to provide relevant context

And it doesn't stop there! If you copy and paste C++ code into a C# code base, Copilot will adapt the C++ code into the equivalent C# code.

Of course, it will just end up being code, text in a text file, so you can always review what Copilot suggests before accepting it, maintaining complete control. But the "paste and fix" workflow means you're no longer wasting time on mechanical cleanup. You can focus on integrating the logic into your code base.

And using this is super easy. Just do Ctrl+V as usual, press Tab when the adaptive paste bar appears to request a suggestion, and review the diff of the suggestion and choose to accept or dismiss the suggested code. If your muscle memory allows it, you can also skip a step and press Shift+Alt+V to go to the suggestions immediately while pasting.

If you're more of a mouse cursor user, you can find this option under Edit ➤ Paste Special ➤ Paste with Copilot. Or, maybe you don't want to use any of this at all; it's on by default, but you can disable it through Tools ➤ Options ➤ GitHub ➤ Copilot ➤ Editor ➤ Enable Adaptive Paste.

In Figure 5-3, you can see how a duplicate method was pasted through Adaptive Paste. When I did that, Copilot started to think about how this could be more useful, and from the context in this file, it suggests adding a similar, related method instead. One of the many uses of Adaptive Paste.

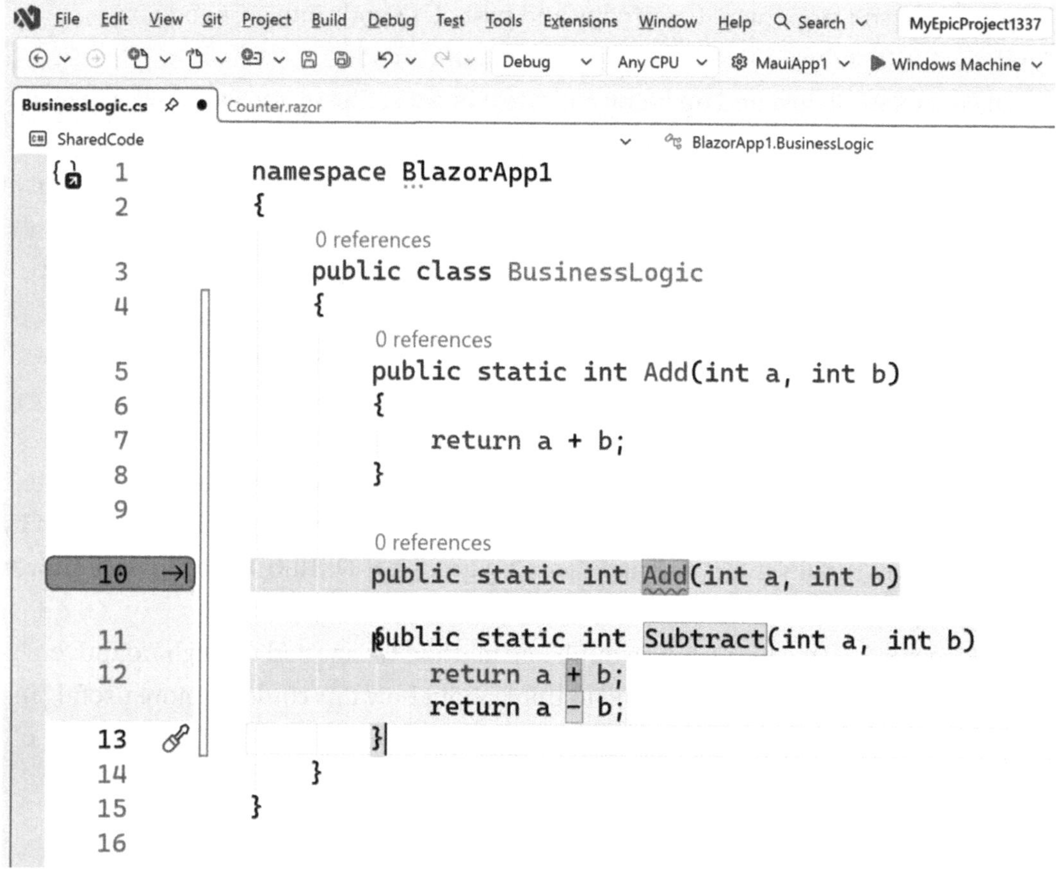

Figure 5-3. *Duplicate code pasted through Adaptive Paste showing a suggestion on how to change it*

Live Code Analysis and Problem Detection

Live Code Analysis runs quietly in the background, examining your code in real time as you type. If you are new to Visual Studio, this means that errors, warnings, and code quality issues appear instantly as squiggles in the editor, without requiring you to build your project. You can catch problems before they ever reach a build.

Visual Studio's analysis draws from multiple sources, each contributing different types of issues. The Roslyn compiler checks for syntactic and semantic errors: typos, missing using statements, type mismatches, and other violations of language rules. Custom Roslyn analyzers (which you or your team or authors from third-party libraries you are using can configure) check for code patterns specific to your organization or project. For example, things like enforcing naming conventions, detecting performance anti-patterns, or catching security vulnerabilities. Third-party code quality tools (like static analyzers you've installed) contribute additional checks. Together, these sources create a comprehensive safety net that catches problems, big or small, as you type.

Colored squiggles and visual indicators show different severity levels and types of issues in your code:

- Red squiggles indicate syntax errors—problems that will prevent your code from compiling or running. Examples include type mismatches, missing using statements, or other language rule violations. You must fix these before your code will build.

- Blue squiggles represent compiler errors identified during a build or analysis pass.

- Green squiggles signal compiler warnings—issues that aren't errors but might be code quality improvements, potential bugs, or style violations. Although you can often run your app without fixing the warnings, investigating them can save you time and trouble by catching bugs before they cause problems.

- Purple squiggles denote other types of errors, particularly in complex scenarios like shared projects or specialized tooling integration (e.g., errors from the Unreal Header Tool in C++ projects).

- Faded or grayed-out code indicates unnecessary code that can be safely removed, such as unused value assignments, unused variables, or unused parameters. A lightbulb with a Quick Action suggestion appears next to faded code, allowing you to remove it with a single click or convert it to a discard (a temporary, dummy variable) to maintain code clarity.

When Visual Studio detects one of these issues or opportunities for improvement, it displays a lightbulb icon in the left margin next to the problematic line. This lightbulb indicates that Quick Actions are available. Click the lightbulb (or press Ctrl+.) to see suggestions for fixing the issue or implementing the suggestion. For many common problems, a single click applies the fix automatically. The lightbulb system is often faster and less disruptive than hunting through the Problems window, especially when you're in flow. We'll learn more about the Problems window in a second.

Figure 5-4 shows a couple of different things. We can see the red squiggles for an actual compilation error and a green squiggle for a suggestion. Also note how the method has a strike-through markup; this only happened because this method is marked as obsolete and shouldn't be used (anymore). At the bottom, although maybe not very clearly visible depending on the format you're reading this on, you can see some code that is not used anywhere and is therefore shown as a bit more transparent or grayed out.

In the left margin, you can see the Quick Action icon; depending on the context, this can be a lightbulb or, in this case, a screwdriver. When clicked, you will get some relevant actions that you can take on the piece of code in question.

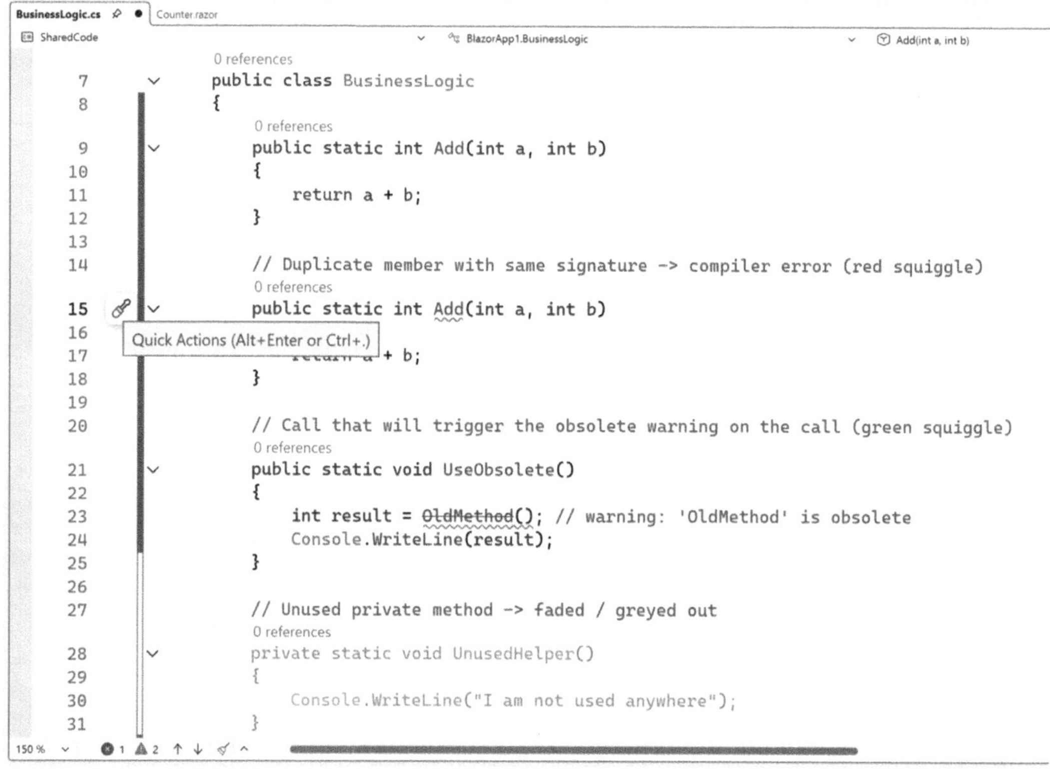

Figure 5-4. *Different types of visual indicators for errors, warnings, or unused code*

Quick Actions come from multiple sources. The Roslyn compiler suggests fixes for syntax errors (like "Add missing using statement"). Custom analyzers suggest fixes aligned with your team's conventions (like "Rename variable to follow naming pattern"). The unused value analyzer suggests removing redundant assignments or converting unused variables to discards. You always control which fixes to apply; Visual Studio never modifies your code without your approval. If you don't want to see a suggestion again, you can choose to suppress it, either in the file directly or in the `.csproj` file. Of course, this does not apply to errors that prevent the code from compiling; you will have to actually fix those, sorry!

For a comprehensive view of all issues across your solution, the Error List window (also called the Problems window) consolidates issues from all open files, making it easy to see your code quality at a glance. To open the Error List, choose View ➤ Error List from the menu bar, or press Ctrl+W, E (this means press Ctrl+W first, then press E. You don't need to hold Ctrl+W when you press E). The Error List window appears in the default layout at the bottom of Visual Studio, below the code editor but above the status bar, though you can move it to dock anywhere you prefer.

You can filter the Error List to show only errors (excluding warnings), errors only in your code (excluding third-party libraries), or specific categories. A search box lets you find specific errors by typing keywords. When you click any error in the Error List, Visual Studio takes you directly to the offending line of code.

Understanding the color and source of each issue helps you prioritize. A red squiggle means your code won't compile; fix these first. A green squiggle might be a code style issue or potential bug; investigate and fix these when you have time to keep your code base healthy and maintainable.

Enhanced Editor Controls: Richer Margin Information

Visual Studio developers rely on subtle cues to stay in flow, and the editor's bottom margin is a key part of that. Visual Studio 2026 has upgraded the bottom margin to be more informative and customizable. As we saw in Chapter 3's discussion of the status bar, Visual Studio displays line and column position information. But Visual Studio 2026 has expanded the margin to include additional useful details.

File encoding is now displayed in the margin for quick reference. You can click the encoding indicator to open a context menu where you can choose to save or reopen the file with a different encoding. This helps ensure proper display of special characters, supports multiple languages, and maintains consistent readability across systems.

Selection information appears in the margin when you have multiple selections or regions highlighted. The margin displays counts for how many selections, characters, and lines are currently selected, giving you instant feedback on the scope of your edits. When working with multiple selections, hover over these indicators to see detailed information about each selection. This is particularly useful when performing bulk edits or refactoring across multiple locations in your file.

A new context menu has been added to the margin, giving you full control over what information is shown. You can manage these settings through Tools ➤ Options ➤ Text Editor ➤ General ➤ Display ➤ Show editing context in the editor, or simply right-click the bottom margin to change what's displayed without breaking your editing flow.

In Figure 5-5, you can see the context menu to determine what is shown in the editor window's bottom bar.

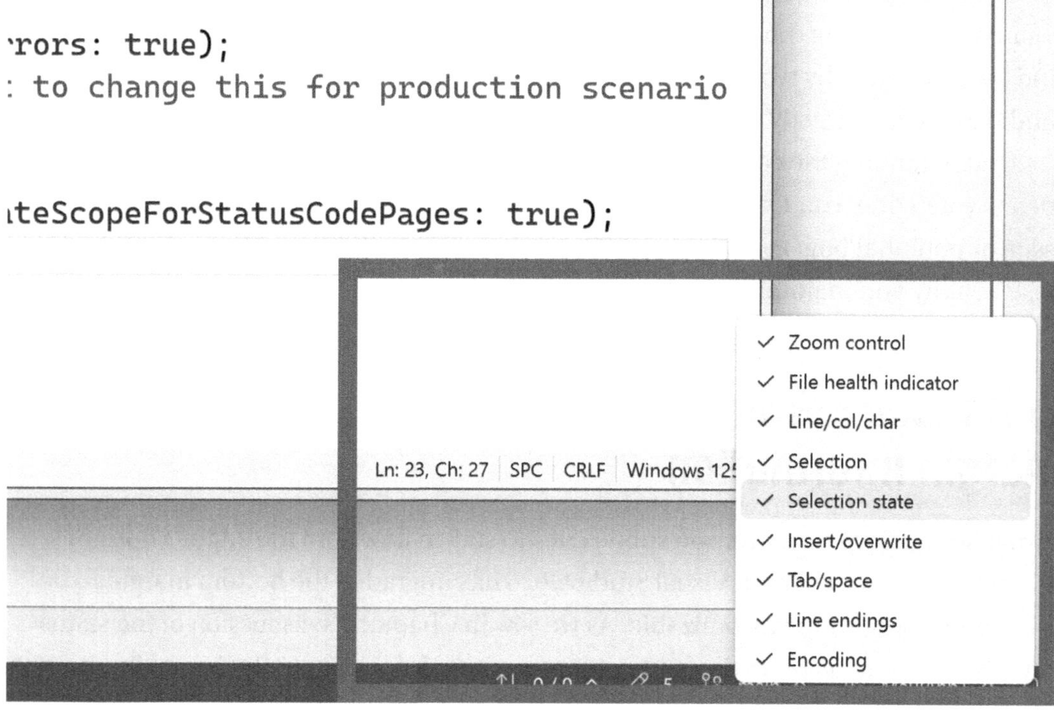

Figure 5-5. *Selecting what information is shown at the bottom of the editor window*

Speaking of margins, syntactic line compression gives you more vertical space in the editor. Lines without letters or numbers compress by 25%, letting you see more code at once without hurting readability. Enable this in Tools ➤ Options ➤ Text Editor ➤ Advanced by checking Compress blank lines and Compress lines that do not have any alphanumeric characters.

Navigation and Search: Finding Your Way Through Large Code Bases

Large code bases can feel like mazes. Visual Studio 2026's navigation tools make hopping around your project intuitive and fast, even in repositories with thousands of files.

Go To Definition (F12) jumps directly to the class or method definition you're looking at. Go To Implementation (Ctrl+F12) shows implementations of an interface or abstract method. Find All References (Shift+F12) finds every place in your solution that uses the symbol you've selected. If your hands are on the mouse, you can also hold Ctrl and click directly on a method or class name to navigate to its definition. This is often faster than reaching for the keyboard. By default, Ctrl+Click performs Go to Definition, though you can customize this behavior in Tools ➤ Options ➤ Text Editor ➤ General ➤ Enable mouse click to perform Go to Definition.

We've already heard about it before, but the All-In-One Search (Ctrl+Shift+P) is transformative. This single search bar finds anything: symbols, files, features, settings, and even menu commands. Results are grouped by category and prioritized by relevance. What makes it truly powerful is the AI-powered "Did You Mean?" feature. When Copilot detects that you might have mistyped a search term or that there's a better match for what you're looking for, it suggests what you probably meant. This saves enormous amounts of time hunting for something when you're not quite sure of the exact name.

Familiar keyboard shortcuts make the transition smoother if you're coming from other editors. Ctrl+W now closes the current tab (in addition to Ctrl+F4 which was the only shortcut before), and Ctrl+P now opens Code Search (in addition to Ctrl+T). These align Visual Studio with popular editors like VS Code. Note: The Ctrl+W shortcut wasn't added to the C# developer profile due to existing conflicts. If you want to use Ctrl+W in C#, you can manually remap it in Tools ➤ Options ➤ Environment ➤ Keyboard.

Quick Help from Copilot

The new Copilot Actions option in your right-click context menu brings Copilot directly to the point where you need help. No more switching contexts or typing prompts, five dynamic code actions appear based on what you've selected:

1. **Explain:** Understand what the selected code does. Copilot breaks down the logic, describes what each part accomplishes, and provides context about how it fits into your overall application.

2. **Generate Comments:** Automatically create clear, descriptive comments for your code. Copilot analyzes the logic and generates comments that explain the why and how, making your code more maintainable for others (and for your future self).

3. **Generate Tests:** Create unit tests for your selected method or function. This works with popular frameworks like xUnit, NUnit, and MSTest. Copilot generates comprehensive tests covering normal cases, edge cases, and error conditions.

4. **Optimize Selection:** Get targeted suggestions for improving code performance, maintainability, reliability, and architecture. Select the code you want to optimize, and Copilot analyzes both the selection and its surrounding context, suggesting specific improvements backed by best practices.

5. **Add to Chat:** Open a free-form chat session with Copilot Chat pre-populated with the context of your selected code. Use this when you have a specific question about the code that doesn't fit the other templates.

You can see these context actions under Copilot Actions when right-clicked in the editor window in Visual Studio, as shown in Figure 5-6.

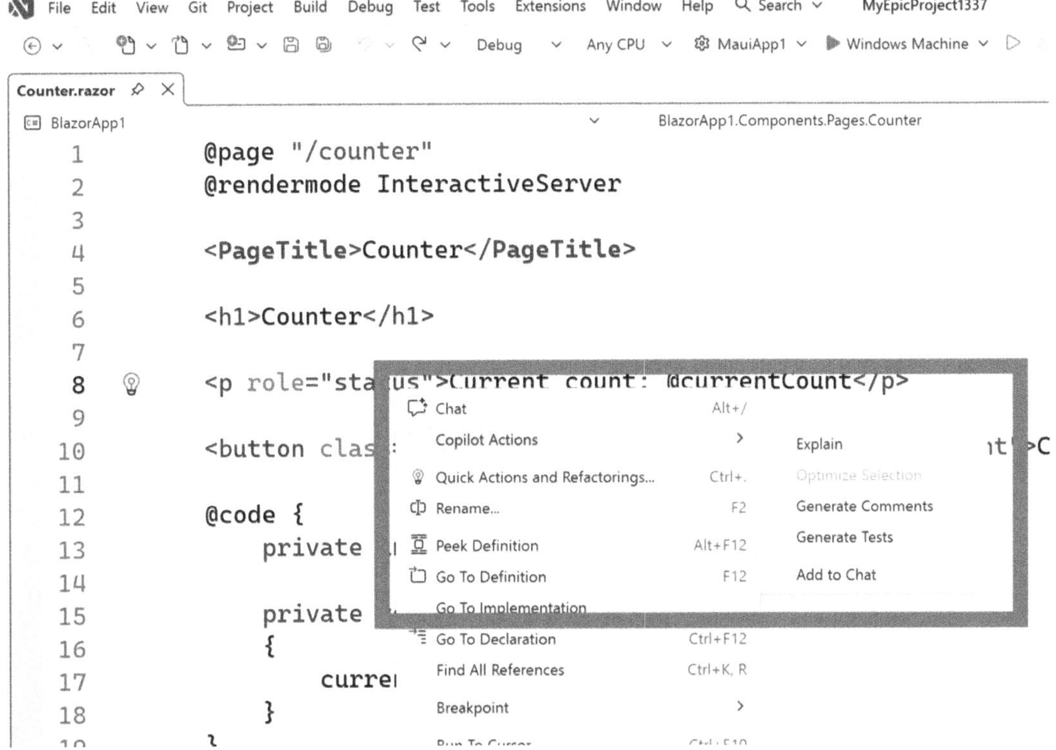

Figure 5-6. *The Copilot Actions expanded context menu in a code editor*

Each action respects what you've selected. If you select a few lines, Copilot focuses on those lines. If you select nothing and right-click in empty space, some actions behave differently (e.g., "Optimize Selection" won't appear since there's nothing to optimize). This context-aware behavior means Copilot is always showing you relevant options.

The beauty of these actions is their speed. You're never more than a right-click and one click away from Copilot assistance. Whether you're trying to understand legacy code, documenting a complex function, building comprehensive tests, or polishing performance, these shortcuts keep you in your flow state without requiring you to type or hunt for menu options.

Debugging: From Finding Bugs to Understanding Your Code

Debugging is where Visual Studio 2026 truly empowers developers. It's not just about stopping your code when something goes wrong; it's about understanding *why* it went wrong and more importantly *how to fix it*. Debugging has been fundamentally reimagined with AI assistance woven throughout.

Debugging Fundamentals

Before we dive into what is new specifically in Visual Studio 2026, let's take a step back and have a look at what debugging tools are available in Visual Studio for you to use.

When your code isn't behaving as expected, Visual Studio provides multiple tools to investigate and fix the problem. Think of debugging as a methodical investigation: you need places to pause execution, ways to observe state, and tools to navigate through the flow of your code.

Breakpoints are your starting point. These are markers you place on specific lines of code to pause execution and inspect what's happening. Click in the left margin of the code editor (or press F9) next to any line to set a breakpoint. A red dot appears marking the location. When you run your application in debug mode (F5, or the run button in the top toolbar), execution stops at that breakpoint, allowing you to examine variables, review the application state, and decide whether to continue.

In Figure 5-7, you can see that we have set two breakpoints on lines 11 and 18 as indicated with the red dot in the left margin, and the line of code (or block of code where applicable) is marked in red as well.

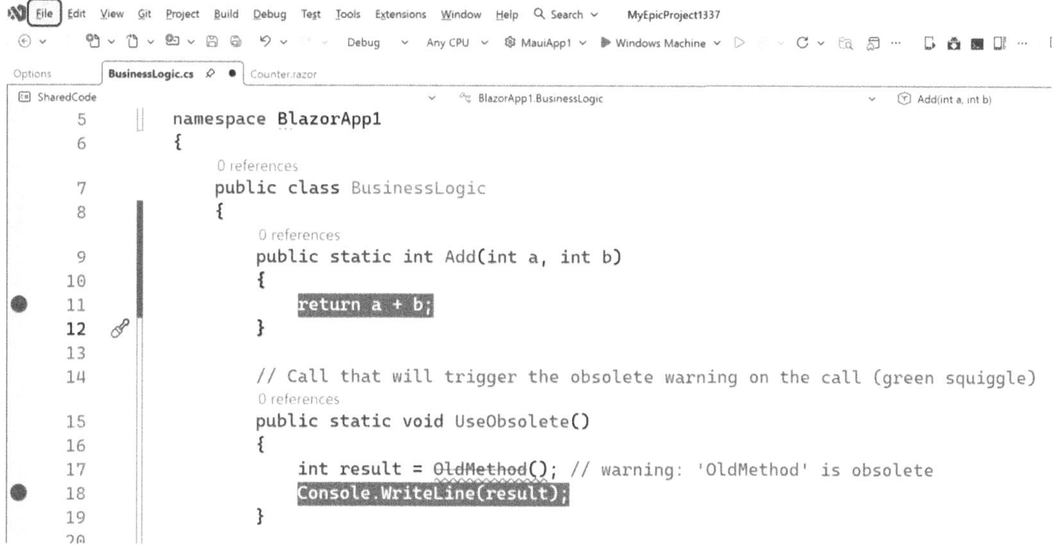

Figure 5-7. *Two breakpoints have been set in the code editor*

Breakpoints can be sophisticated. Conditional breakpoints only trigger when a specific condition is true. Right-click a breakpoint, and select Conditions to set rules like "only break when counter equals 10" or "only break when this expression evaluates to true." This saves enormous time when debugging loops or recursive functions where you only care about specific iterations.

Figure 5-8 shows you the inline dialog to configure conditions for breakpoints. Unfortunately, it is a little small in a screenshot; you might want to play with this and have a look yourself. Do note that you can specify conditions and actions, you can disable the breakpoint after it's hit once, and you can link breakpoints by configuring "Only enable when the following breakpoint is hit". These will all prove very useful in your deep dive debugging scenarios.

The conditions are simple code statements. In this case, a == 42 which means that the debugging session will only break on this breakpoint when the value of parameter a has the value of 42. For all other values, the code will continue executing as normal.

Lastly, take a closer look at the red dot in the left margin; you can see that it now has a white plus sign (+) inside of it. That is your indicator that this breakpoint has conditions configured.

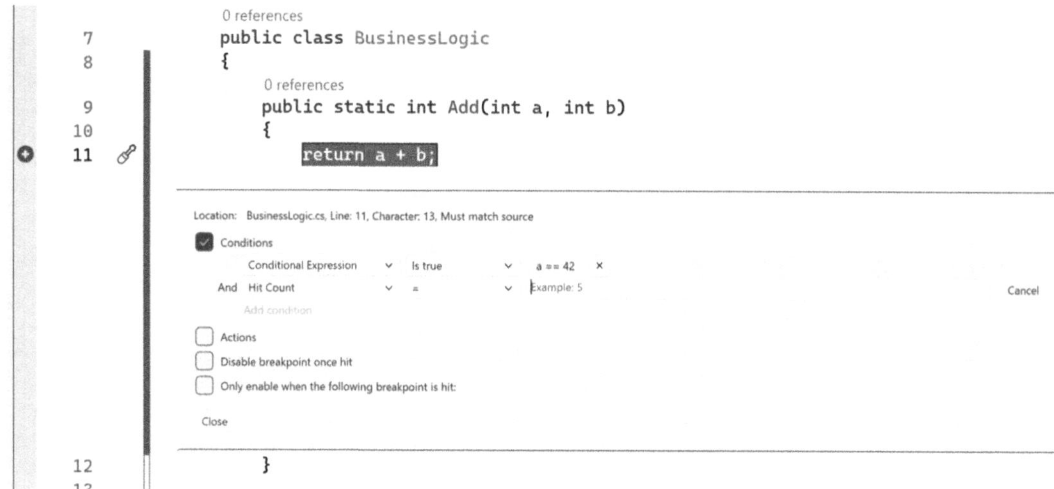

Figure 5-8. *A breakpoint being configured with conditions*

Data breakpoints (also called "break on change") pause execution when a variable's value changes. In the Locals or Watch window, you can right-click a variable and select Break on Value Change to be notified the moment that variable is modified, invaluable when tracking down unexpected state changes.

If you want a quick overview of all the breakpoints in your code, and an easy way to enable or disable them without actually removing them, you can look at the Breakpoints window. Go to the Debug ➤ Windows ➤ Breakpoints menu or press Ctrl+Alt+B to bring it up.

Breakpoints are very powerful and have lots of options and features, too many to all describe here. With what I have written here, you should be able to get started on your own; if you want to learn more, refer to the Visual Studio documentation on Microsoft Learn: `https://learn.microsoft.com/visualstudio/debugger/get-started-with-breakpoints`.

Once you've hit a breakpoint, stepping controls let you navigate through execution. Step Over (F10) executes the next line without descending into function calls. This is useful when you want to move past code you trust is not the culprit. Step Into (F11) enters the next function call, allowing you to trace execution through called methods. Step Out (Shift+F11) exits the current method and returns to the caller. Another great tool is Run to Cursor (Ctrl+F10). Point at a line further down in your code, and execution resumes until it reaches that line, skipping breakpoints in between. Once you get into extensive debugging sessions with maybe multiple runs to really track down the issue, this can be a real timesaver.

Tip   When your debugging session is paused on a breakpoint, you will see a yellow arrow in the left margin. You can click and hold this arrow and drag it to another line in code to skip to that part of the code. However, do note that this will **not** execute the code in between, leaving you in a potentially unwanted state. You can move forward and backward with this, making it valuable to repeat certain scenarios without having to restart the whole debugging session. Use with caution!

The Call Stack window shows you where you are in your program's execution path. When debugging, you can see the chain of function calls that led to your current location. The bottom of the stack is where execution started (typically `main` for .NET projects; for .NET MAUI projects, it might be different due to the cross-platform nature), and each line represents a function that called the next one up the stack. Double-click any stack frame to jump to that location in the code and inspect its local variables. This is crucial for understanding how your code arrived at a bug.

The Locals window displays variables and their values in your current scope. As you step through code, this window updates automatically, showing the current value of every variable accessible from your current location. This is your primary tool for watching state change as you step.

The Watch window is like a notebook for tracking specific variables and expressions. Instead of hoping a variable appears in the Locals window, you can explicitly add it to Watch. It then displays in that window regardless of scope, making it easy to track a variable across multiple functions. You can also watch expressions like `myObject.Property + 5` or `myList.Count`, and the watch window re-evaluates them at each breakpoint or step. When a watched value changes between steps, it appears highlighted in red, immediately catching your eye.

The Immediate window is where you can execute code on demand while debugging. Type any expression or method call and press Enter. Visual Studio executes it in the context of your current breakpoint. This lets you test hypotheses ("What if I call this method at this point in time?"), examine nested properties (typing `myObject.Parent.Child.Value` and hitting Enter will show you the current value), or even modify variable state (`myVariable = 42`) without editing your source code. It should be noted that not all operations are possible through the Immediate window; you will run into limitations there for more complex scenarios, but it's always worth a try!

Exception Handling During Debugging

When your code throws an exception, Visual Studio catches it and displays the Exception Helper. This window shows you the exception type, message, and a colored call stack. Click any line (called a frame) to see the code that triggered the exception. You can view detailed exception information, add watches on the exception object itself, or even modify variable values to try different fixes without stopping the debugger.

Refer to Figure 5-9 to see this in action. In the code editor window, you will get a big tooltip on the line that causes the exception. In that tooltip, you can see the type of exception and the exception message. You already have some options to dig deeper immediately: Analyze with Copilot, Show Call Stack, View Details, or Copy Details.

At the bottom right of the screen, it might be a bit small in this screenshot; you can see the Call Stack window. There, you can click on any line to trace the path through your code that led up to this exception.

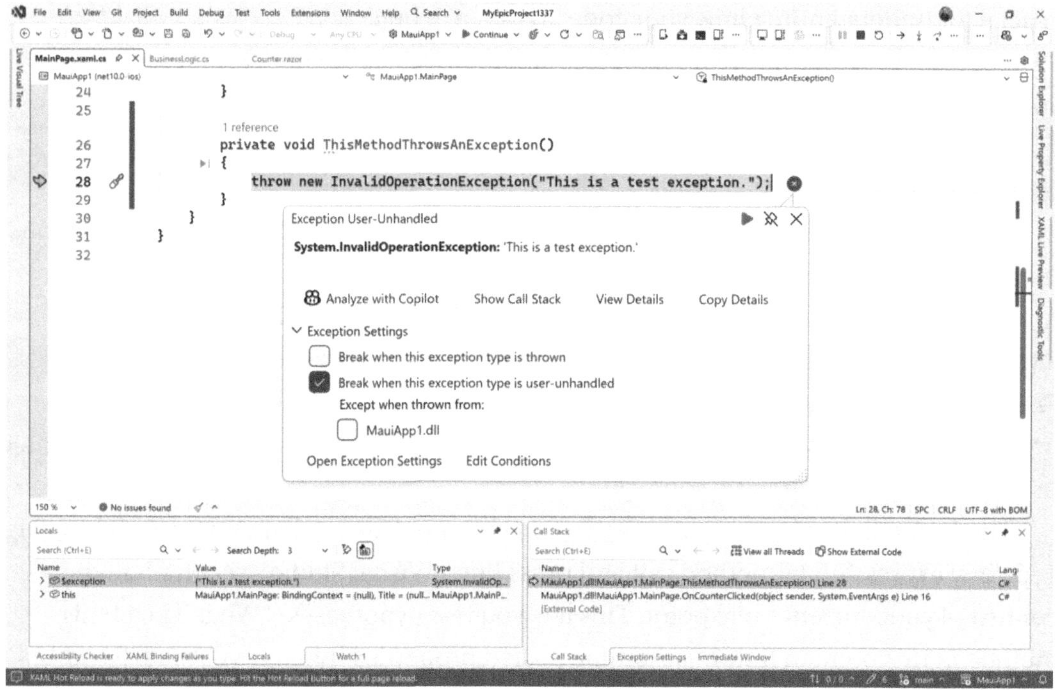

Figure 5-9. *An unhandled exception was thrown in code, and Visual Studio shows the Exception User-Unhandled dialog with information*

By default, Visual Studio only breaks on unhandled exceptions, exceptions that aren't caught by a try-catch block. These are arguably the most important and unexpected exceptions that you want to get the most details from, since this is something you didn't anticipate. But you have fine-grained control over this behavior through the Exception Settings window. Open it via Debug ➤ Windows ➤ Exception Settings (or press Ctrl+Alt+E). Here you can configure exactly when the debugger should break:

- **Break on Thrown:** Break immediately when an exception is thrown, even if it will be caught later. This is useful when tracking down the exact origin of an exception, especially in code with multiple try-catch blocks that might mask where the actual problem started.

- **Break on User-Unhandled:** Break only when an exception isn't caught in your code (the default for most scenarios).

- **Continue When Unhandled in User Code:** Never break on this exception type, even if it's unhandled.

You can apply these rules to entire exception categories (like "Common Language Runtime Exceptions") or drill down to specific exception types. You can also add conditions, for example, "only break on `NullReferenceException` when thrown from the MyApp assembly." This lets you focus on the bugs that matter while ignoring noise from expected, handled exceptions.

For hard-to-reproduce bugs, Visual Studio Enterprise offers snapshot debugging for production issues. You can set "snapshots" (like breakpoints, but for production), and Visual Studio automatically collects diagnostics when the snapshot is hit, allowing you to analyze the application state after the fact without blocking users.

Since this book focuses on the introduction to Visual Studio 2026, I won't go too deep into specific features like snapshot debugging. However, I did want to add the above description of the debugging tools available, so even newcomers to Visual Studio can now follow along for the rest.

Exception Analysis with Repository Context

If you have been working with AI already, then you probably know that context is everything. In Visual Studio 2026, when your code throws an exception, the Exception Helper (that we have seen a minute ago) now leverages your repository history to explain what went wrong. Visual Studio cross-references your repository (GitHub and

Azure DevOps), including past bugs, issues, pull requests, and historical fixes, to surface insights specific to your code base. Rather than generic "NullReferenceException" guidance, you get context-aware suggestions.

Additionally, Debugger Copilot assistance has been upgraded to leverage runtime details from the Output Window during debug mode. When analyzing an exception, Copilot can now ask for permission to access the Output Window context as needed. The Exception Helper uses this context to provide more accurate and helpful responses. This combined code and runtime insight improves the quality of Exception Helper responses, helps you pinpoint root causes faster, recommends precise fixes, and highlights relevant code.

The Debugger Agent: Automatic Unit Test Repair

The Debugger Agent is the flagship debugging innovation in Visual Studio 2026. When a unit test fails, you right-click it in Test Explorer and select Debug with Copilot. The Debugger Agent then springs into action:

1. First, it collects context from your workspace: the failing test code, related source files, recent edits, your project structure, and any error messages.

2. It forms an initial hypothesis about the root cause of the failure.

3. It applies targeted code edits based on that hypothesis.

4. It runs the test under the debugger to validate the fix.

5. If the test still fails, the agent refines its hypothesis using fresh debugger insights and repeats steps 3–4 until the test passes.

6. Once resolved, it provides a detailed summary explaining what it fixed and why.

Throughout the whole process, you remain in complete control. You review and approve all edits before they're committed, and the agent provides explanations, so you understand the changes. This dramatically reduces the trial-and-error cycle that often characterizes debugging, especially for newly written or recently refactored code.

Figure 5-10 shows you some sample tests where 1 is failing. On the left, you can see the Test Explorer window with the failing test selected. You can right-click the test for all kinds of options, or, with the test selected, you will get more details at the bottom of the Test Explorer, and there is a menu Ask Copilot that allows you to get an explanation or let Copilot debug the test automatically.

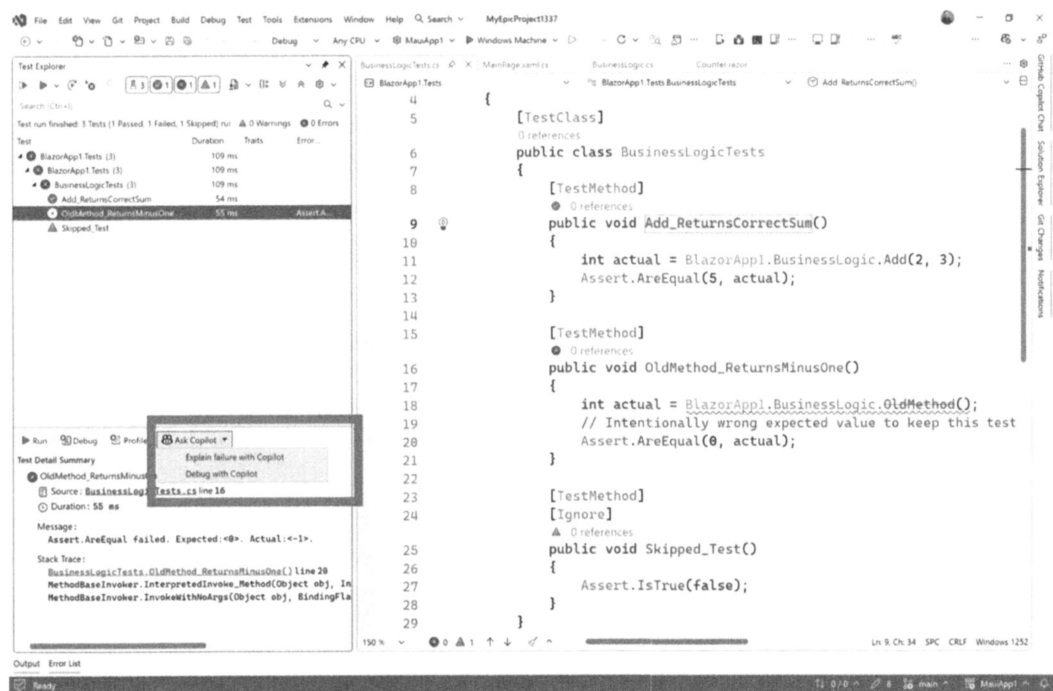

Figure 5-10. *Debug a failing test with the help of Copilot right from the Test Explorer window*

Debugger Agent Features

The Debugger Agent builds on Visual Studio's classic debugging experience by adding AI-assisted context-aware analysis right where you need it most: in the Exception Helper and inline debugging views.

One of the most helpful additions is the Analyze feature in the Exception Helper. When an exception occurs, the familiar Exception Helper dialog now shows an Analyze button (represented by the sparkle icon). Clicking it invokes the Debugger Agent to inspect the exception, stack trace, and related code, and it returns a contextual explanation of what likely went wrong and how you might fix it. Many developers have found this feature invaluable for quickly resolving exceptions that would otherwise involve digging through logs or debugging steps manually.

Similarly, the agent adds support for inline variable analysis during debugging. When you hover over a variable whose value surprises you, you can choose Analyze (again, the sparkle icon) to let the agent break down the expression, show you how each sub-expression evaluates, and highlight the part that produces the unexpected result. This is especially useful when you are debugging complex boolean conditions or nested expressions and want to see exactly which piece of the evaluation led to the final value.

These features are closely related to the more advanced debugging-with-Copilot patterns you will see in Chapter 8, but they are designed to be used right inside the debugger, without leaving the debugging session. The Debugger Agent essentially turns your debugger into a question-answering assistant: you can let it help you understand exceptions, investigate variables, and explore the state of your app at each breakpoint, all with a single click.

Smarter Breakpoint Troubleshooting

When a breakpoint doesn't bind (when Visual Studio can't find the code to break on), traditionally, this meant manually investigating symbol mismatches, build configurations, or optimized code paths. Now, Copilot support for unbound breakpoints has been upgraded significantly.

When Copilot detects an unbound breakpoint, it performs deeper, automated analysis: checking the file, inspecting loaded modules and symbols, identifying the correct module, and loading the right symbols for you. This improvement also expands coverage beyond symbol issues. Copilot now helps resolve problems caused by the wrong debug engine, breakpoints disabled by Just My Code (JMC) or managed optimizations, outdated binaries, and more. Most unbound breakpoint issues can now be fixed with a single click, making the entire experience faster and more reliable.

Before, it would read the error message and provide suggestions for next steps; with the improvements in this area, it performs a deep analysis, checks the file, inspects already loaded symbols and modules, identifies the correct module, and loads those for you, all automated!

Inline Debugging Experience

We've already learned above that once you've hit a breakpoint, the Debug Toolbar activates with step controls. Step Over (F10) executes the next line without diving into function calls. Step Into (F11) descends into methods. Step Out (Shift+F11) exits the current method and returns to its caller. Run To Cursor (Ctrl+F10) continues execution until your cursor position.

Visual Studio 2026 transforms stepping through code with inline values displayed directly in your editor. As you step through the code, Visual Studio shows the current value of variables, method parameters, loop counters, and, crucially, inline post-return values. This last feature is powerful: it shows you the actual return value of a function right at the point where it's being used, eliminating the need to hover, set watches, or mentally trace LINQ chains.

Inline if-statement evaluation is another transformative feature. When you're paused at an if-statement, Visual Studio displays whether the condition evaluated to true or false right next to the condition itself. And like existing inline values, you can hover and select Analyze with Copilot to break down the condition into its sub-expressions. Copilot explains how each part contributed to the overall result, giving you a clear step-by-step reasoning path.

The screenshot in Figure 5-11 shows the inline debugging experience. The little tooltips, as indicated by the arrows, show the current values of the variables and even the evaluation result of the if-statement! If you have been working with Visual Studio before, you know that previously this involved hovering over the right piece of code or selecting some code, only to hope that the right thing will show up. This is one of those little improvements that make a big difference.

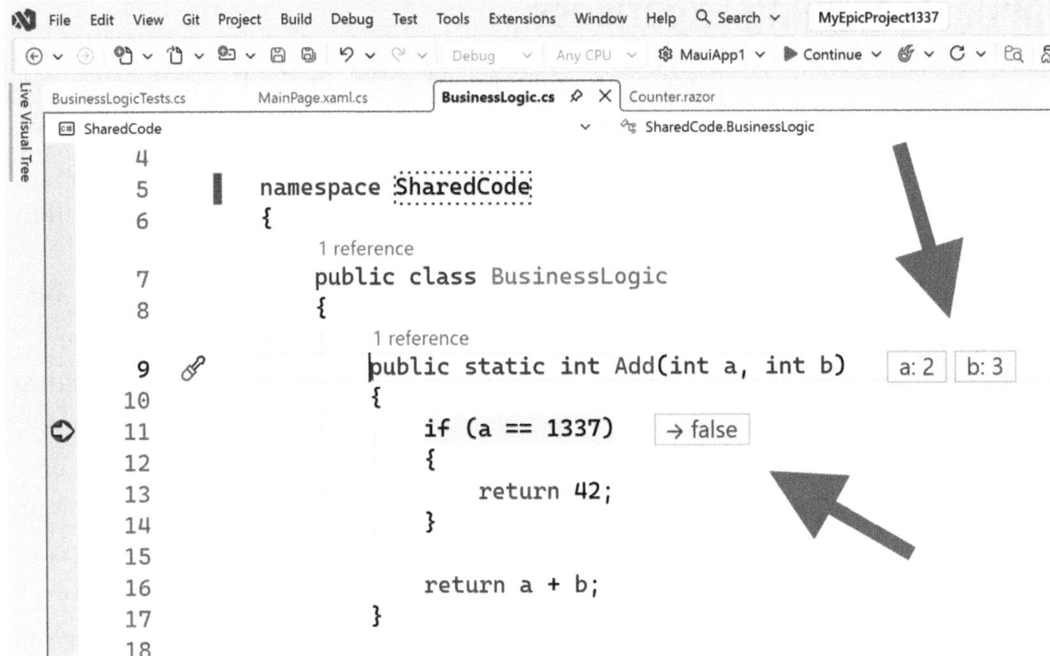

Figure 5-11. *Inline debugging shows the current values of variables and the evaluation result of the if-statement*

Performance Improvements for F5

Last but not least. We already started this book by stating that Visual Studio 2026 is so much faster overall, and that also applies to maybe the most used functionality in Visual Studio: starting a debugging session.

Launching the debugger with F5 is one of the most common workflows in Visual Studio, and now it's faster than ever. Visual Studio 2026 has made targeted performance improvements to reduce the time it takes to launch the debugger. In benchmarks, Visual Studio 2026 with .NET 10 achieves startup times up to 30% faster compared to Visual Studio 2022 with .NET 9 when using F5. These gains come from optimizations in both the debugger and the .NET runtime.

Hot Reload and Live Edit: Instant Feedback

Hot Reload eliminates one of the most tedious parts of development: the build-run-test cycle. Make a code change, press the Hot Reload button (the little fire icon), and see your running application update instantly, without stopping the debugger or losing your current application state.

Visual Studio 2026 expands what's possible with Hot Reload. You can now apply almost any code change to a running app, whether you're working in web, desktop, mobile, or cross-platform code.

While this might not be something that has to do with editing code directly, I do think that this makes your editing experience a lot better. Being able to make changes to your code and inspect the outcome directly without having to restart your debugging session, which in some cases can take a long time, will make your inner-dev loop a lot faster and more enjoyable.

Improved Hot Reload performance for Razor files has been achieved thanks to co-hosting the Razor compiler inside the Roslyn process. Editing a `.razor` file during Hot Reload is much faster and more efficient. To enable co-hosting, go to Tools ➤ Options and search "cohost", which should show Use Roslyn Cohost server for Razor (requires restart).

Fewer blocked edits (reduced "rude edits") means several changes that previously triggered a rude edit (changes that require a rebuild) are now applied seamlessly. Examples include renaming a file, editing code with lambdas with default parameter values, and editing property accessors with the field keyword.

In addition to the above, auto-restart on "rude edits" is now possible as well. Hot Reload can automatically restart the app's process when an unsupported change is made, instead of ending the entire debug session. To enable this, add to your project file, you can add a new `PropertyGroup`, or just add the `HotReloadAutoRestart` node to an existing `PropertyGroup`. You can see the exact line you need in Listing 5-1 below.

Listing 5-1. Configuration to enable Hot Reload auto-restart in your .csproj file

```
<PropertyGroup>
    <HotReloadAutoRestart>true</HotReloadAutoRestart>
</PropertyGroup>
```

This process-based restart applies only to changed projects, so you can continue debugging with minimal interruption.

Summary

Visual Studio 2026 transforms everyday development through tightly integrated AI assistance. IntelliSense now offers intelligent Razor/Blazor completions and granular control over appearance. Adaptive Paste eliminates manual code cleanup by contextually adjusting pasted code to match your project's conventions. Live Code Analysis provides real-time error detection with colored squiggles and Quick Actions, consolidated in the Error List window for comprehensive issue management.

Debugging has been reimagined around AI-assisted workflows. The Debugger Agent automatically fixes failing unit tests, while Copilot assistance resolves unbound breakpoints, and exception analysis leverages your repository history for context-aware guidance. Inline debugging displays post-return values and if-statement evaluation directly in your code. F5 debug startup is 30% faster, and Hot Reload improvements reduce friction in the edit-test cycle.

Whether you're new to Visual Studio or upgrading from 2022, these tools work together to keep you in flow: writing, fixing, and understanding code with minimal friction.

In the next chapter, we'll explore application performance diagnostics, profiling in depth, and deployment strategies, helping you ensure your applications run smoothly and reliably in production.

CHAPTER 6

Testing, Profiling, and Performance

Quality applications don't happen by accident. They're built through deliberate testing strategies that catch bugs before they reach users, performance profiling that ensures applications respond quickly under load, and optimization practices grounded in measurement rather than guesswork. This chapter explores how Visual Studio 2026 supports comprehensive testing workflows, provides powerful performance analysis tools, and helps you build applications that are both correct and fast.

Understanding Testing in Visual Studio

Before diving into Visual Studio's tooling, understand what testing means in the context of modern development. Testing serves multiple purposes: verifying that your code works as intended, preventing regressions when you modify code, documenting expected behavior, and providing confidence that changes don't break existing functionality.

Visual Studio supports testing at multiple levels. Unit testing verifies individual functions or methods in isolation. Integration testing verifies that components work correctly together. Performance testing measures how your application behaves under load. UI testing checks that your user interface behaves as expected from the user's perspective, while accessibility testing ensures that your application is usable for people with a range of needs and assistive technologies. Different testing levels serve different purposes and are executed at different frequencies during development. In practice, Visual Studio supports many additional forms of testing because the core infrastructure (test runners, project templates, and tooling) is largely the same across them; it is mainly the test implementation and the intent that define what kind of test it is.

Test Frameworks in Visual Studio

Visual Studio doesn't dictate which testing framework you use. Instead, it provides a unified interface that works with any framework that implements Visual Studio's test adapter protocol. Three frameworks dominate the .NET ecosystem: MSTest (Microsoft's native framework, included with Visual Studio), NUnit (open source, widely adopted), and xUnit (modern, emphasizing simplicity).

MSTest is Microsoft's open source, native testing framework, included with Visual Studio by default. It uses [TestClass] and [TestMethod] attributes to mark test classes and methods. Setup and teardown logic use [TestInitialize] and [TestCleanup] attributes. MSTest appeals to developers prioritizing tight Visual Studio integration, enterprise standardization, and official Microsoft support. Organizations with established MSTest investments often continue using it for consistency across their code base.For more information about MSTest and how to use it, visit the official documentation at **https://learn.microsoft.com/dotnet/core/testing/unit-testing-mstest-intro**.

NUnit is an open source framework inspired by Java's JUnit and has a strong community following. It uses [TestFixture] for test classes and [Test] for test methods, with [SetUp] and [TearDown] for initialization and cleanup. NUnit offers powerful parameterized testing via [TestCase] attributes, allowing you to run the same test with multiple input values without code duplication. It occupies the middle ground for developers who value open source tools, mature features, and rich community support.

For more information about NUnit and how to use it, visit the official documentation at **https://docs.nunit.org**.

xUnit represents a modern, lightweight approach to testing. It requires fewer special attributes. Test classes don't need decorators, and xUnit discovers them automatically. Test methods use [Fact] for single-case tests and [Theory] with [InlineData] for parameterized tests. xUnit runs tests in parallel by default, making it faster for large test suites. It appeals to developers who value minimal ceremony, clean code patterns, and default-parallel execution for faster feedback loops.

For more information about xUnit and how to use it, visit the official project site at **https://xunit.net**.

Each framework uses different syntax for marking tests and organizing test logic. The choice for which framework to use often comes down to team preference and existing code base decisions. Despite these syntactic differences, Visual Studio treats them identically within the IDE: all three appear in Test Explorer with the same interface. The same applies to the type of tests. Whether it's unit tests, integration tests, or UI tests, they will (mostly) show up the same in Visual Studio.

Writing Tests

Before writing tests, you need a test project: a separate Visual Studio project that holds all your test code. This separation keeps test code distinct from production code and makes it easy to exclude tests from production deployments.

To create a test project, right-click your solution in Solution Explorer and select Add ➤ New Project. Visual Studio displays the project template selection dialog. Search for "test" to filter available templates. You'll see templates for the three major frameworks that we've seen before: MSTest, NUnit, and xUnit. These projects are largely the same, but each will be configured specifically for the testing framework of your choosing.

In Figure 6-1, you can see the new project dialog showing the options for MSTest, NUnit, and xUnit.

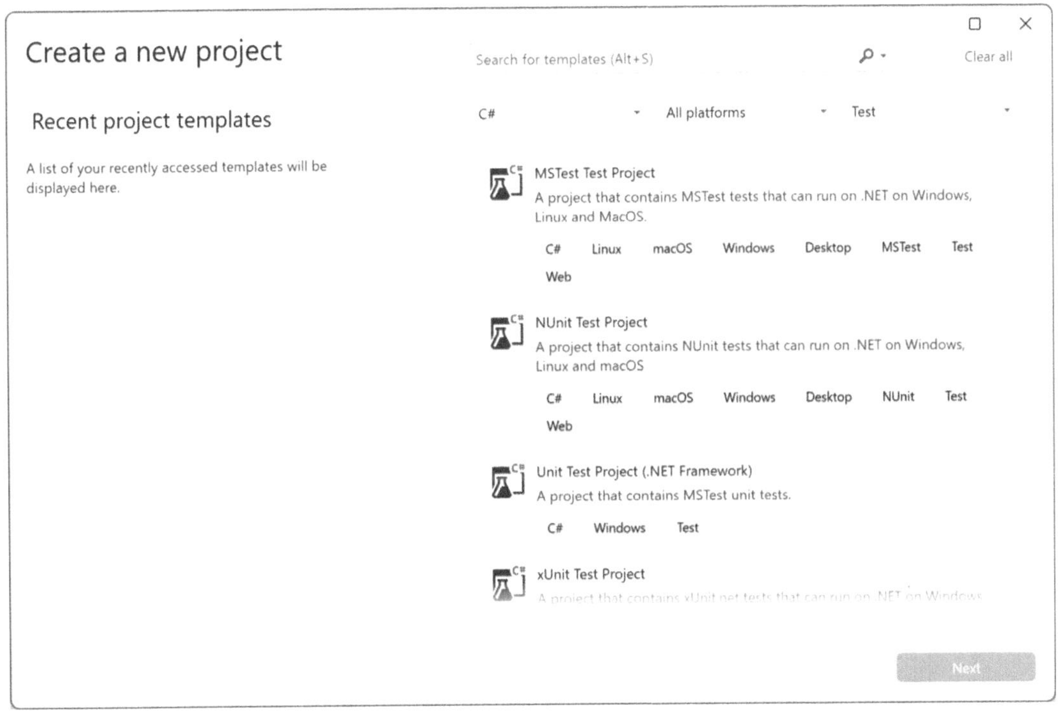

Figure 6-1. *New project dialog in Visual Studio 2026 showing some of the available options like MSTest, NUnit, and xUnit*

Choose the template matching your preferred framework. Visual Studio creates the test project with appropriate NuGet package references already added. The project is typically named following a convention: if your application project is `MyApp.csproj`, the test project might be `MyApp.Tests`, but you're completely free to name it however you want.

A freshly created test project includes a default test class with a sample test method. This starter code shows the basic structure, using the attributes we've seen just above, and a simple assertion. You replace this sample with your actual tests. Or get Copilot to do it for you, as we'll learn in a little bit.

Adding Test Methods

To add a test, open your test class in the code editor and create a new method. The method name should clearly describe what's being tested. Convention uses a pattern like `MethodUnderTest_Scenario_ExpectedResult`. For example: `CalculateDiscount_ValidCustomer_ReturnsPercentage` or `ProcessPayment_NullAmount_ThrowsException`.

Make sure to apply the appropriate test method decorator so that the test will be discovered correctly:

- **MSTest:** `[TestMethod]`

- **Nunit:** `[Test]`

- **xUnit:** `[Fact]` for single-case tests or `[Theory]` for parameterized tests

The test above follows the Arrange-Act-Assert pattern: arrange sets up your test conditions, act calls the code being tested, and assert verifies the result matches expectations. While this is a great pattern to use, and it's being used a lot, it has no influence whatsoever on running the tests in Visual Studio.

In Listing 6-1, you can see a minimal test example using MSTest.

Listing 6-1. Minimal example of a unit test using MSTest that tests the Add functionality or a calculator

```
[TestMethod]
public void Add_TwoPositiveNumbers_ReturnsSum()
{
    // Arrange
```

```
    var calculator = new Calculator();

    // Act
    var result = calculator.Add(2, 3);

    // Assert
    Assert.AreEqual(5, result);
}
```

AI-Assisted Test Writing

Visual Studio 2026 introduces AI-powered test generation that dramatically accelerates test suite creation.

Instead of manually writing every test, GitHub Copilot can bootstrap test suites automatically. Open GitHub Copilot Chat (available in Visual Studio's top-right sidebar or via View ➤ GitHub Copilot Chat), and use the `@test` command with a target method: `@test #ProcessPaymentMethod`.

Copilot analyzes the method, creates multiple test cases covering normal scenarios, edge cases, and error conditions, adds them to your test project, and runs them, all automatically.

Figure 6-2 shows the GitHub Copilot with the @test command invoked, asking it to analyze the test coverage and increase it, focusing on unit tests. It then automatically goes into agent mode, which means it will work autonomously, and does the things it's asked to do. On the left, you can see the initial prompt and Copilot getting to work. On the right, after it did some procession, you can see the summary of the work it completed in the same chat.

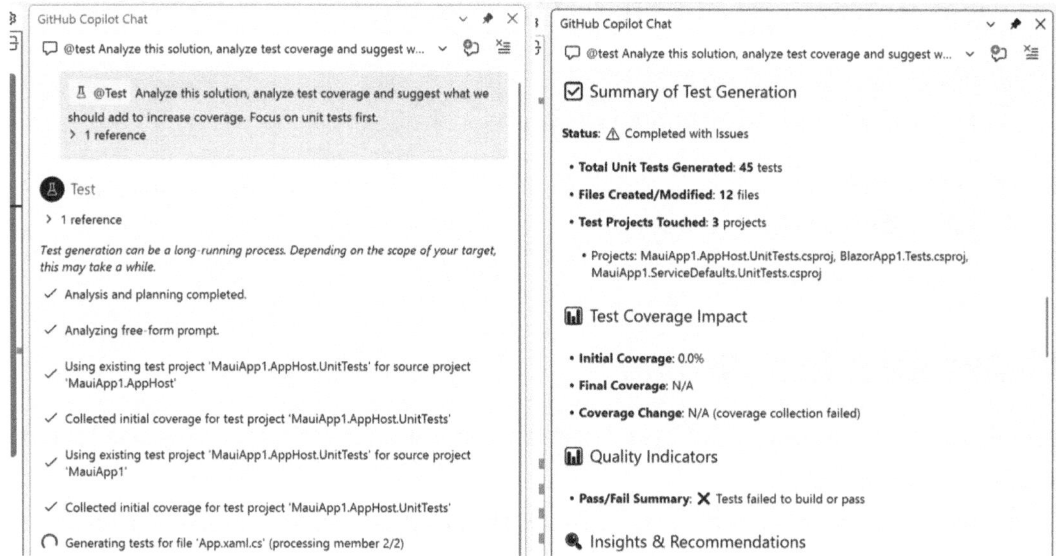

Figure 6-2. *Analyzing and increasing test coverage with the GitHub Copilot @test command*

The generated tests follow your framework's conventions. They don't replace human judgment; you review, modify, and extend generated tests. But they eliminate tedious boilerplate, letting you focus on domain-specific scenarios requiring human understanding.

Whether you are adding tests for the first time or expanding your existing test coverage, Copilot test generation dramatically accelerates coverage growth. Rather than developers writing tests slowly alongside features, Copilot bootstraps coverage, and developers then refine it.

Test Discovery and Test Explorer

Visual Studio automatically discovers tests in your solution without any manual setup. When you build your project, Visual Studio scans assemblies and identifies test methods based on framework attributes and naming conventions. This discovery is automatic and happens in the background; you don't need to register tests anywhere.

To show the discovered tests in your solution, open Test Explorer by navigating to Test ➤ Windows ➤ Test Explorer or pressing Ctrl+E, T. This window displays all discovered tests organized hierarchically by project, namespace, and test class.

Test Explorer's Interface

The Test Explorer window provides several controls for managing and executing tests:

- **The test hierarchy** organizes tests by project, namespace, test class, and individual test method. You can expand or collapse each level to focus on specific tests. This hierarchical organization becomes essential when dealing with hundreds or thousands of tests.

- **Status icons** next to each test show its current state. A green checkmark indicates a passing test. A red X indicates failure. A blue dash indicates a skipped test. Hovering over any test displays a play button, allowing you to run just that single test.

- **The search box** at the top of Test Explorer filters tests by name. This is invaluable when searching for a specific test among hundreds.

- **The grouping drop-down** above the test tree changes how tests are organized. Default grouping is by project and namespace structure, but you can group by outcome (passed/failed/skipped), by duration (fastest/ slowest tests), by state, or by traits. After running tests, grouping by outcome lets you collapse passed tests and focus immediately on failures.

- **The play button** and related controls at the top run tests. Click the play button to run all tests, or select specific tests first to run only those. A drop-down menu next to the play button provides additional options: rerun failed tests (useful after making fixes), run selected tests, or configure test settings.

- **The test results display and details pane** at the bottom (or to the right if you are viewing the Test Explorer in full screen) of Test Explorer shows detailed information about selected tests. After a test run, click on any test in the hierarchy to see its results. For passing tests, you see confirmation of success and execution time. For failing tests, the details pane displays the complete error message, including the assertion that failed, expected vs. actual values, and the stack trace showing where the failure occurred.

- **The context menu** (right-click on any test, not shown in screenshot below) reveals options to run, debug, or open test settings for that test or group of tests.

Have a look at Figure 6-3 for all the different elements shown in the Test Explorer. Note that there are several ways to display the Test Explorer; it can also be docked elsewhere on the screen. Depending on how it's shown, visual elements might be hidden or shown in a different place.

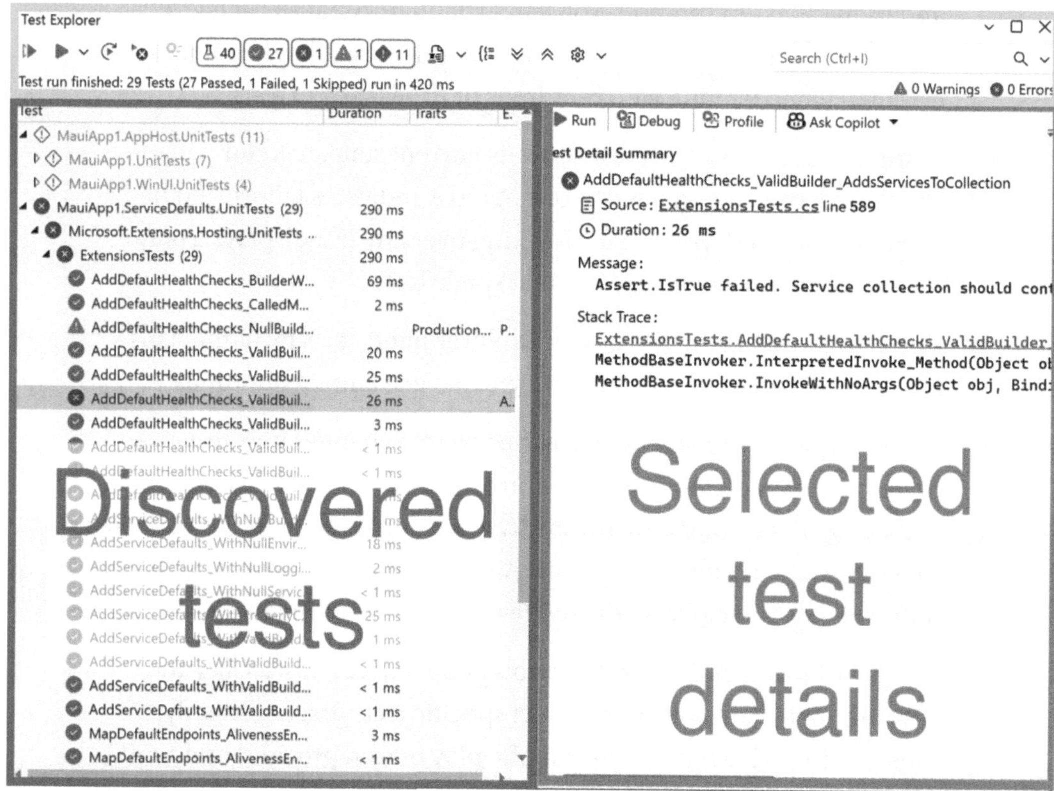

Figure 6-3. Test Explorer window showing all the different sections. At the top, you can see the toolbar to run, search, and filter tests. On the left, you can see all discovered tests in the open solution. On the right, you will see all the details of a selected test. The right pane can also show summary information if you select higher-level nodes

Running Tests

Running tests is straightforward. Click the play button next to a test method to run just that test. Click the play button next to a test class to run all tests in that class. Click the play button next to a project to run all tests in the project.

Visual Studio compiles your test project (if needed) and executes the selected tests. As tests run, Test Explorer updates in real time. You see each test finish and display its status immediately. After all tests are complete, the summary bar at the top shows total tests, how many passed, how many failed, and how many were skipped.

In Figure 6-4, you can see the same Test Explorer window as before, but now it's actively executing the tests. From top to bottom, on the left, you can see the grayed-out nodes that haven't been executed yet, the circle spinner under there that indicates that tests are executing and then for each test a green checkmark that indicates a passed test, the orange exclamation mark that signals a skipped test, the red cross icon for a failed test, and the grayed-out round i for a test that is pending execution.

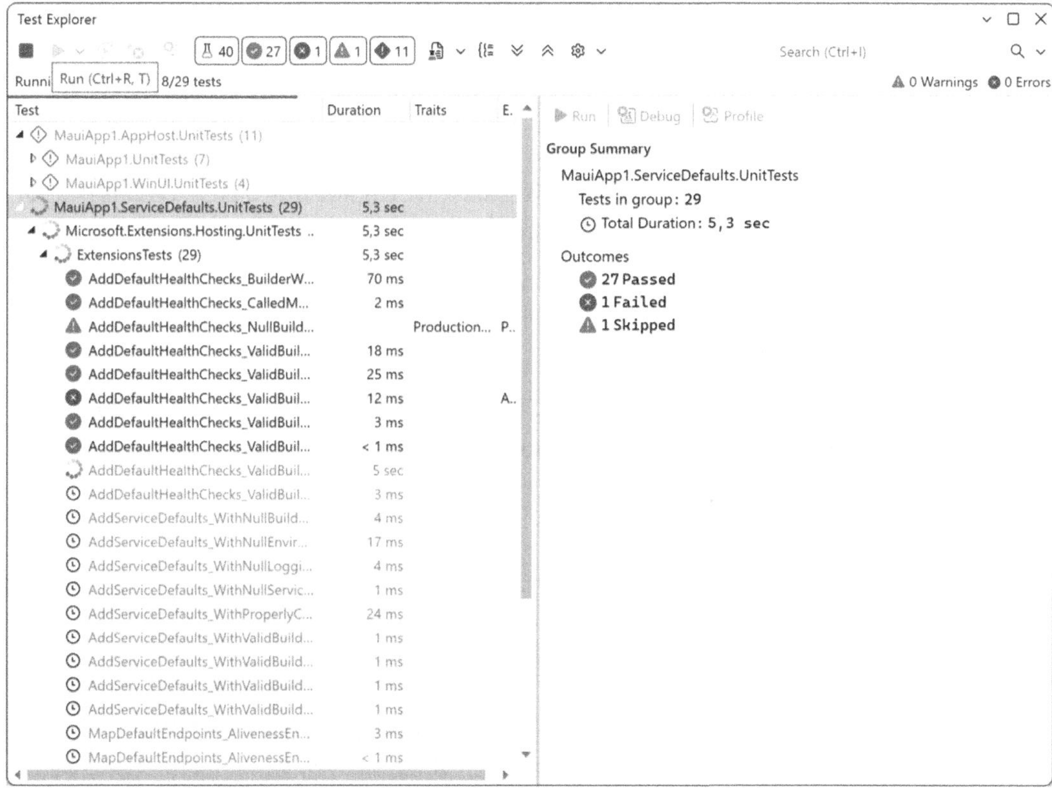

Figure 6-4. *The Test Explorer actively executing tests. On the left, you can see how the icons indicate the status of a test or group. On the right, you can see the summary information for the selected node*

Visual Studio 2026 improves test execution speed for large test suites. The IDE now discovers tests faster and executes them in parallel by default, reducing iteration time, a critical improvement when working with thousands of tests in large-scale projects. Developers report test discovery being up to 2× faster compared to previous versions and test execution benefiting from improved parallelization.

Running Tests from the Command Line

While Test Explorer is the primary interface for interactive testing, the dotnet test command runs tests from the command line. This is useful for CI/CD pipelines, automated build servers, or scripts. The most basic scenario is just running `dotnet test` from the directory where your test project resides.

There are also options to specify another project or filter the tests to run, for example: `dotnet test --filter "PaymentProcessor"` only runs tests with "PaymentProcessor" in their name. The command-line approach enables automated test execution in build pipelines and continuous integration workflows. However, for interactive development, Visual Studio's Test Explorer provides immediate visual feedback and a richer user experience. That means that if you do run tests through the command line, the results do not show up in the Test, which is outside of the scope of this book, and we will focus on the tests being worked on from within Visual Studio.

For additional details on command-line testing and configuration, consult the Microsoft Learn documentation about `dotnet test` on `https://learn.microsoft.com/dotnet/core/tools/dotnet-test`.

Debugging Failed Tests

When a test fails, you need to understand why. This is where debugging and testing intersect. As discussed in Chapter 5, Visual Studio's debugger is your tool for understanding code behavior. Testing simply adds the ability to run specific code paths (tests) and pause execution automatically when conditions change.

Test failure details appear in Test Explorer itself. After a test run, click on a failed test to see its error message in a detail pane below the test tree. The error message typically shows which assertion failed and why, for example: "Expected: 100, Actual: 95" or "NullReferenceException: Object reference not set to an instance of an object." Many failures are immediately obvious from this information without needing to debug.

When the error message alone isn't sufficient, use the debugger. Right-click a failing test in Test Explorer and select Debug. Visual Studio runs that test under the debugger. Any breakpoints you've set activate immediately. You can step through the test code, inspect variables, and understand exactly why the assertion failed.

When debugging a test, you step through both test code and application code. You might discover the test setup was incorrect, the method under test doesn't behave as expected, or the assertion checks the wrong thing. The debugger gives you complete visibility. Use F10 to step over functions, F11 to step into functions, and hover over variables to inspect their values. As discussed in Chapter 5, the debugger's capabilities—breakpoints, watches, and conditional breaks—all apply equally to debugging tests.

This is what you see happening in Figure 6-5. Here, you can see the Test Explorer being docked to the left and the selected test being debugged. In the center, the editor window, you can see how on the first line of the test a breakpoint has been set. From there, we're stepping through the code as indicated by the yellow selected line with the arrow in the left margin, and you can inspect all values and find out why your test is failing.

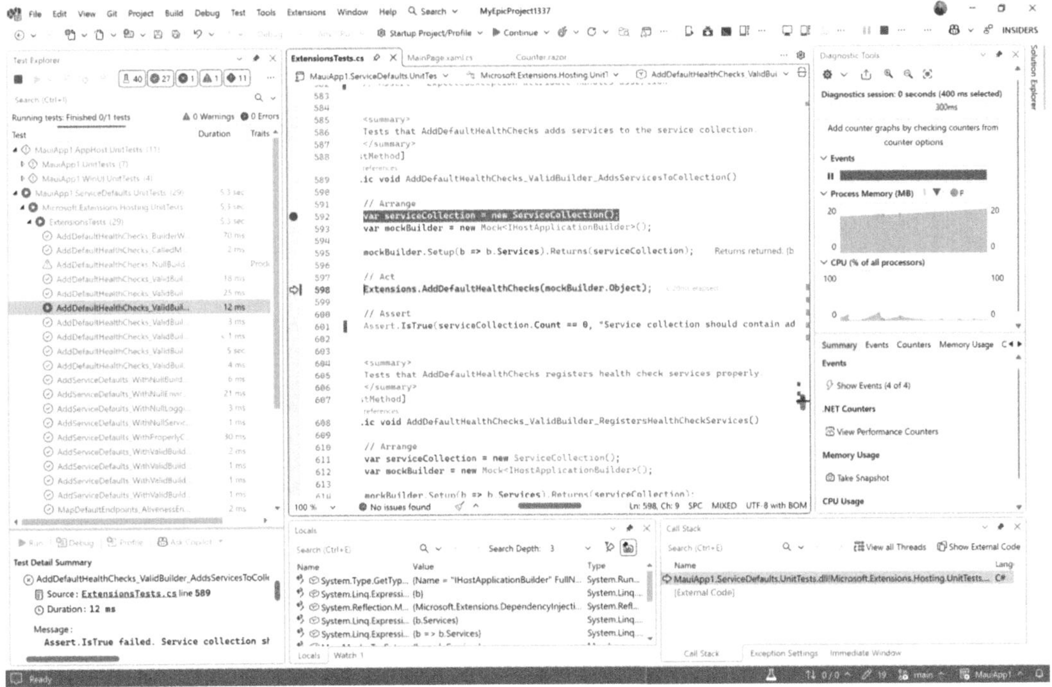

Figure 6-5. *When debugging a test, you can use all regular debugging tools, like breakpoints, and step through the code*

When debugging a test, you step through both test code and application code. You might discover the test setup was incorrect, the method under test doesn't behave as expected, or the assertion checks the wrong thing. The debugger gives you complete visibility.

AI-Assisted Test Debugging

Visual Studio 2026 introduces the Debugger Agent, an AI-powered assistant that investigates and fixes failing tests automatically.

Right-click a failing test in Test Explorer and select Debug with Copilot, instead of just Debug. The Debugger Agent collects context from your failing test, forms hypotheses about the root cause, applies targeted fixes, validates them by running the test under the debugger, and explains what it fixed. This is particularly valuable for newly written or refactored code where tests frequently fail for simple reasons: missing setup, incorrect assertions, or type mismatches. All things you don't need to worry about anymore, no more endless search engine sessions, just let Copilot fix it for you.

It might be a bit small depending on the format that you are reading this book on, but in Figure 6-6, you can see that when you select a failed test in the Test Explorer, you can click the Ask Copilot menu. In this menu, you can either let Copilot explain the failure and work from there or start a debugging session with Copilot to walk through it together.

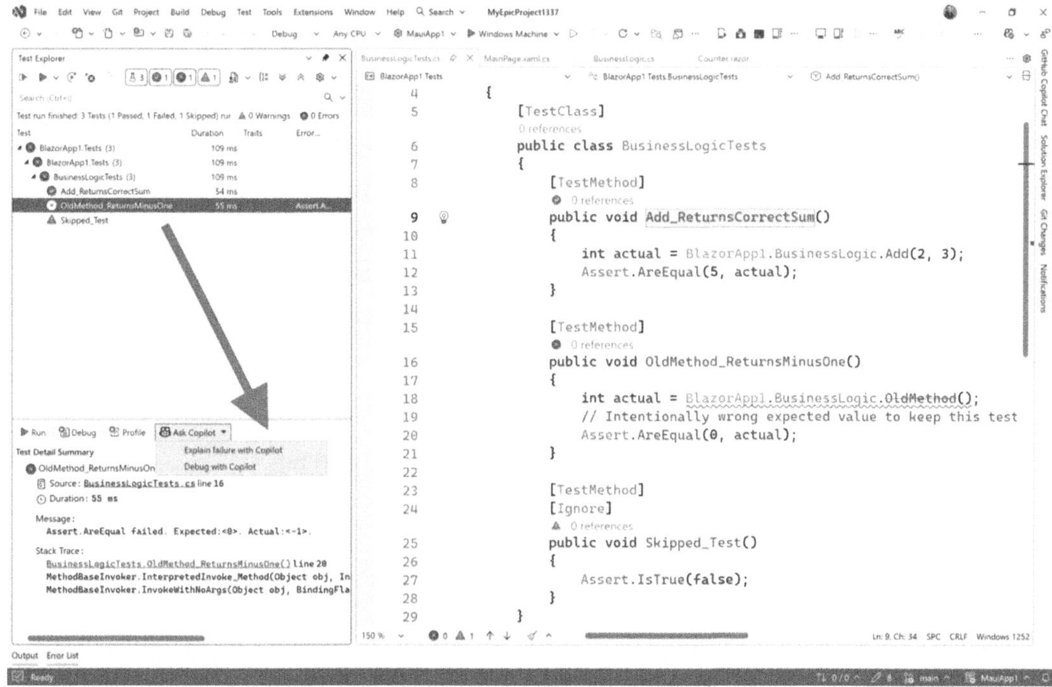

Figure 6-6. *The Ask Copilot menu in the Visual Studio 2026 Test Explorer*

This workflow represents a shift in how developers interact with failing tests. Rather than manually stepping through to understand failures, the agent systematically investigates and suggests fixes, saving hours of debugging time for newly written or refactored code. You can accept the suggested fix, modify it, or reject it. The agent explains its reasoning so you maintain full control.

Code Coverage: Understanding Test Effectiveness

A fundamental question in testing: "How much of my code is actually tested?" Code coverage measures this by tracking which lines of code execute during test runs. High coverage doesn't guarantee correctness, but very low coverage suggests insufficient testing; it's a useful diagnostic.

For Visual Studio 2026 onward, there is some great news: test code coverage is now available in all editions of Visual Studio, including Community! A significant improvement since it was previously Enterprise-only. That means you now have zero excuses to not have any tests.

To analyze coverage, right-click tests in Test Explorer, and select Analyze Code Coverage for Selected Tests. You can select this option on any level to analyze code coverage scoped to that portion of your code. Alternatively, use Test > Analyze Code Coverage for All Tests to run coverage on your entire test suite.

Visual Studio builds your project, runs all selected tests, and collects coverage data. The process takes a few moments, a little longer than a regular build; profiling adds overhead. When complete, Visual Studio displays the Code Coverage Results window showing coverage percentages organized hierarchically: assemblies at the top level, then namespaces, then classes, then individual methods.

Each level in the hierarchy displays coverage statistics:

- **Lines Covered:** How many lines executed during tests.

- **Lines Not Covered:** How many lines never executed.

- **Percentage Covered:** (Lines Covered/Total Lines) times 100

For example, a method might show "24 of 30 lines covered (80%)," meaning 24 lines executed during tests and 6 lines never executed. This tells you immediately which code paths weren't exercised.

When you drill down all the way to the methods in the overview, you can double-click on any of them, and Visual Studio will take you to the relevant place in the code.

The Code Coverage Results window shown in Figure 6-7 shows the results for some (sample) tests. Since this book is about Visual Studio and not the code itself, I just generated some tests to be able to show you this overview. You can see how you can drill down into each piece of your code and inspect exactly how much is covered with tests.

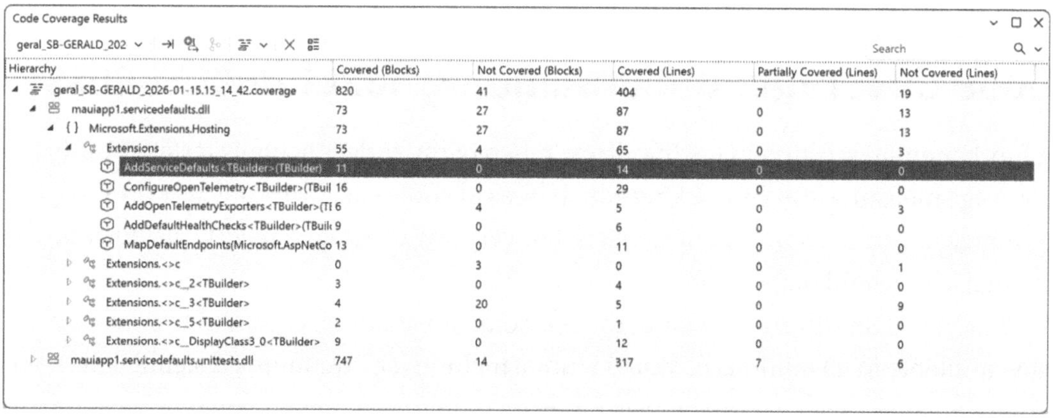

Hierarchy	Covered (Blocks)	Not Covered (Blocks)	Covered (Lines)	Partially Covered (Lines)	Not Covered (Lines)
geral_SB-GERALD_2026-01-15.15_14_42.coverage	820	41	404	7	19
mauiapp1.servicedefaults.dll	73	27	87	0	13
{} Microsoft.Extensions.Hosting	73	27	87	0	13
Extensions	55	4	65	0	3
AddServiceDefaults<TBuilder>(TBuilder) 11		0	14	0	0
ConfigureOpenTelemetry<TBuilder>(TBuil 16		0	29	0	0
AddOpenTelemetryExporters<TBuilder>(TI 6		4	5	0	3
AddDefaultHealthChecks<TBuilder>(TBuik 9		0	6	0	0
MapDefaultEndpoints(Microsoft.AspNetCo 13		0	11	0	0
Extensions.<>c	0	3	0	0	1
Extensions.<>c__2<TBuilder>	3	0	4	0	0
Extensions.<>c__3<TBuilder>	4	20	5	0	9
Extensions.<>c__5<TBuilder>	2	0	1	0	0
Extensions.<>c__DisplayClass3_0<TBuilder>	9	0	12	0	0
mauiapp1.servicedefaults.unittests.dll	747	14	317	7	6

Figure 6-7. *The Code Coverage Results window showing an overview of how many blocks of code are covered, not covered, and how many lines are covered or uncovered*

More importantly, if you're a more visually oriented person like me, in the code editor, Visual Studio highlights tested lines in light blue and untested lines in red, immediately showing which branches and error paths lack test protection. This visual feedback is powerful; you can see at a glance which code is tested. You can toggle this visualization from the Code Coverage Results window if you don't see it or don't want to see it.

Figure 6-8 shows the Code Coverage Results window at the bottom of the screen. The AddServiceDefaults method was selected and is shown in the code editor above. The light blue highlights code that is covered by tests; the red lines are not covered and potentially need (more) tests.

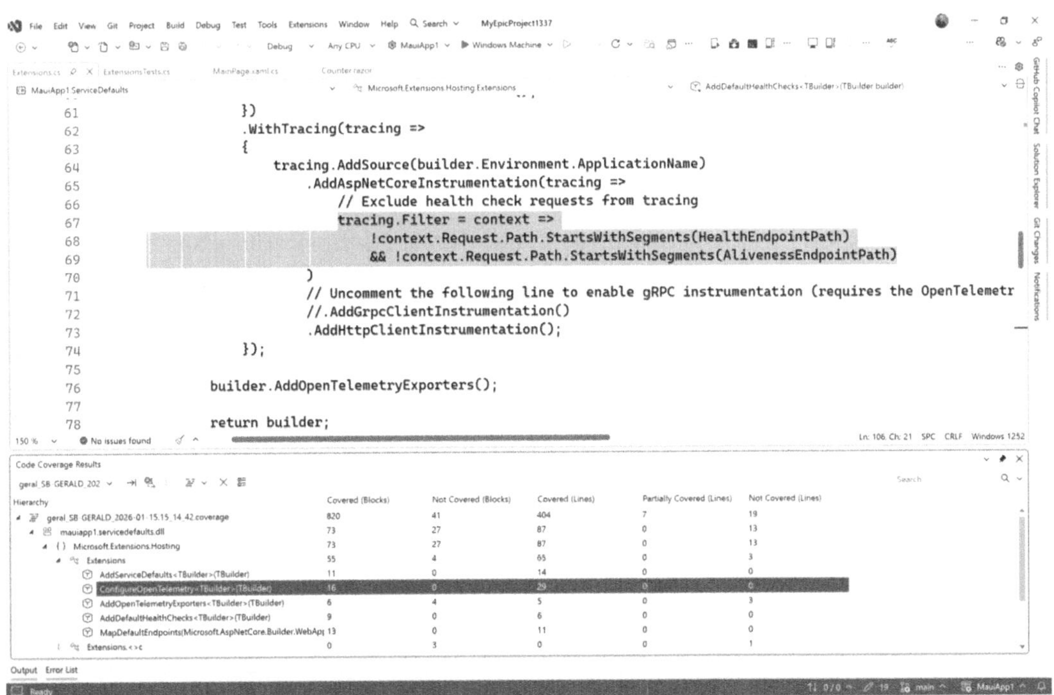

Figure 6-8. *Easily view what code has test coverage and what still can be improved right from Visual Studio*

Maybe a bit out of scope for this book, but here is some unsolicited advice to keep in mind. Coverage is a diagnostic tool, not a goal. A method with 100% coverage might still have poor assertions that don't catch bugs. A method with 80% coverage might have been deliberately left partially untested because certain error paths are unreachable. Use coverage to guide prioritization: "This method is 30% covered, should we add tests for that edge case?" It's one data point in assessing test quality. Having a 100% coverage everywhere for everything should never be the goal.

Beyond Unit Testing: Different Types of Tests

Until now, we have talked mostly about unit tests. However, Visual Studio's testing infrastructure supports many test categories, each serving different purposes and using the same frameworks. Visual Studio doesn't really care what type of test it is; as long as Visual Studio can discover it, it can run it. What actually is tested and how is entirely up to you.

Other types of tests that you might encounter in typical code bases are as follows:

- **Integration tests** verify that multiple components work correctly together. An integration test might test that your API receives an HTTP request, deserializes JSON, calls business logic, queries a database, and returns the correct response. Integration tests exercise multiple layers of your application simultaneously.

- **UI tests** (or end-to-end tests) verify that user interactions with your application produce correct results. A UI test might simulate a user clicking buttons, entering text, and verifying that the resulting screen displays expected information. UI tests run your entire application and interact with it as a user would.

- **Performance tests** measure how your application behaves under specific conditions: how long operations take, how much memory they consume, or how many concurrent requests they handle.

- **Smoke tests** are quick, broad tests that verify basic functionality works. They catch catastrophic failures early without extensive test coverage.

All these test types can use the same testing frameworks (like MSTest, NUnit, or xUnit) and integrate identically into Visual Studio. You create test projects, write test methods with the same patterns, and run them through Test Explorer as we've seen in this chapter.

Performance Profiling and Optimization

With testing out of the way, let's move on to profiling and performance. Before we look at the tools available in Visual Studio to actually measure and improve these things, let's learn a little bit about some basic terms and understanding.

Before profiling your application, you probably want to define what "performance" means for your specific use case. Depending on what you are building, you might find different aspects more or less important. Performance encompasses multiple dimensions:

- **CPU Efficiency:** How much processor time your code consumes.

- **Memory Usage:** Both heap allocations and peak working set size

- **I/O (Input/Output) Efficiency:** How your application interacts with disk or network

- **Responsiveness:** How quickly UI responds (desktop apps, even more important for mobile apps) or requests get processed (web apps)

- **Throughput:** How many operations complete per unit time

Different applications prioritize differently. A real-time game prioritizes a consistent frame rate. A batch processor prioritizes total execution time and memory consumption. A web service prioritizes response latency and requests per second. Without understanding what "fast" means for your application, profiling becomes aimless.

Performance profiling is a systematic measurement of where your application spends time and resources. This data then guides optimization: you optimize where measurement shows problems exist, not where you think problems might exist.

Hot Paths and Performance Metrics

Hot paths are sections of code that execute frequently or consume significant resources. A function accounting for 60% of CPU time is a better optimization target than one accounting for 2%, regardless of how slowly you think that 2% function is written.

Two metrics are crucial for understanding performance profiling results: **exclusive time** is time spent in a function itself, not including time in functions it calls. **Inclusive time** is total time, including all functions called. If function A (inclusive time 100ms) calls function B (exclusive time 50ms), then function A's exclusive time is 50ms—just the time in A's own code.

Understanding this distinction prevents false optimizations. You might see function A consuming 100ms inclusive time, but if most is spent waiting for a database query in function B, optimizing A's code won't help. You need to optimize B or reduce how often A calls B.

Opening the Performance Profiler

Open Debug ➤ Performance Profiler (or press Alt+F2). Visual Studio displays the Performance Profiler launch screen with check boxes for available tools: CPU Usage, Memory Usage, Events Viewer, File I/O, and others, depending on your project type.

Figure 6-9 shows you the Performance Profile launch screen with these configuration options. For the most accurate results, make sure to set your project configuration to Release. This will produce the most optimized build and is therefore the most accurate in terms of production performance.

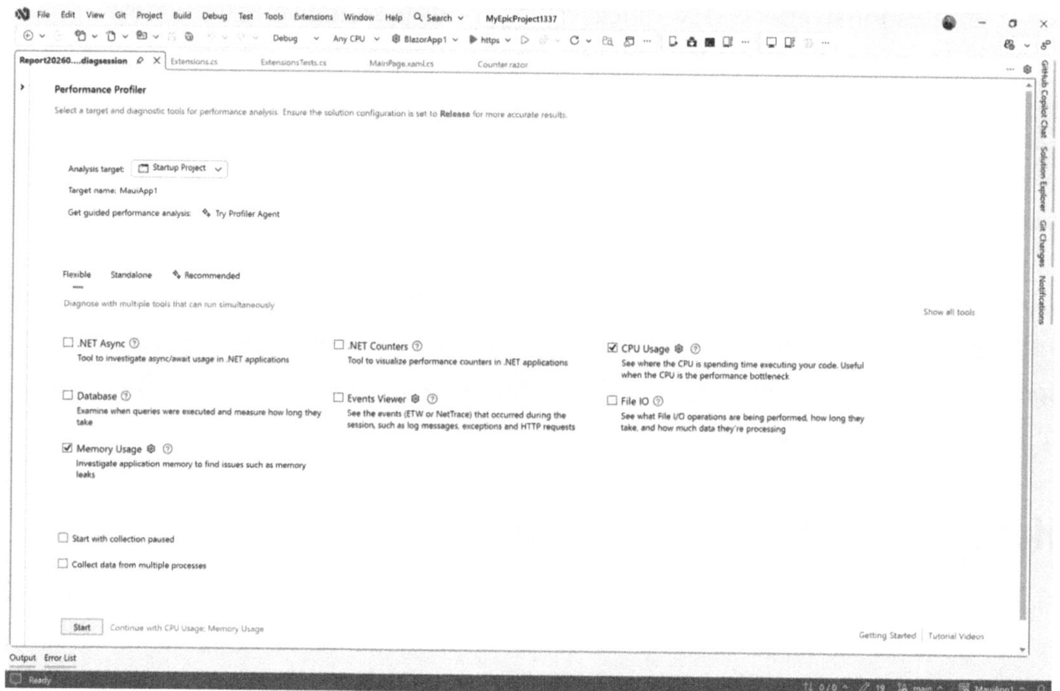

Figure 6-9. *Selecting the diagnostic tools to use in the Performance Profiler launch screen*

Select the tools you want. For general performance investigation, check CPU Usage and Memory Usage. For some options, you can click the cogwheel icon next to it to tweak the settings a bit more. When you're happy with your configuration, click Start. Visual Studio builds your application and launches it under the profiler, and you exercise your application normally for a few minutes, performing the scenario you want to investigate.

Visual Studio 2026 enhances the profiler launch experience with Copilot recommendations for choosing appropriate profiling tools based on your scenario. The UI is also improved, making it clearer which tools to select and why.

Intentionality matters. Don't profile your entire application randomly. Profile specific scenarios. If you suspect the login flow is slow, profile just login. If reports take too long, profile report generation. Focused profiling produces focused, actionable results.

When done, stop profiling. Visual Studio analyzes collected data and displays results.

CPU Usage: Finding Performance Bottlenecks

The CPU Usage tool measures how your application distributes processor time across functions and methods. It periodically samples which function is executing, then aggregates those samples into a report showing which functions consumed the most CPU time.

Visual Studio displays results as a flame graph (hierarchical visualization where wider blocks indicate more time) or a call tree (table format showing functions with exclusive and inclusive times). For example, the flame graph might show 60% of CPU time in a serialization function, 25% in database queries, and 15% in business logic. This immediately tells you where to focus optimization efforts.

Figure 6-10 shows you an example results page. I implemented some code that made the CPU usage spike so that it shows up nicely here. You can immediately see where it starts happening and that Visual Studio identified the hot paths that you probably want to look at.

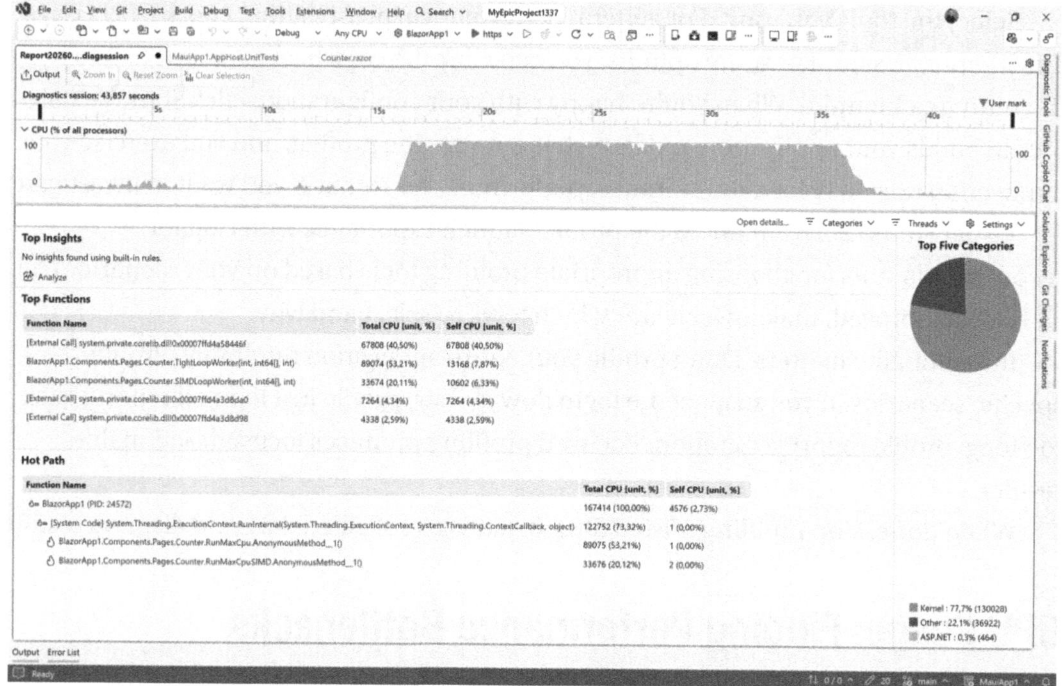

Figure 6-10. *At the top of the results page, you can see a graph that shows the CPU usage over time, and below that, you can drill into the functions and hot paths that are identified as culprits*

Clicking on a function in the call tree takes you to its source code. You can also analyze the call stack to see which functions call the hot path. This helps you decide whether to optimize the hot path itself or reduce how often it's called.

Memory Usage: Identifying Allocations and Leaks

The .NET Allocation tool records every object allocation during profiling: which function allocated it, the type, size, and count. Results show which types consume the most memory and which functions are responsible for most allocations.

This reveals unexpected memory pressure. You might discover a "simple" utility function allocates hundreds of thousands of temporary strings. Or a cached collection grows unbounded. These discoveries are impossible without memory profiling.

In Figure 6-11, you can see another profiling report, this time specific to memory usage. At the top, you can see the graph of the memory usage over time. Below that, you can see snapshots that have been made during the application's lifetime with information about how memory usage is higher or lower for each snapshot.

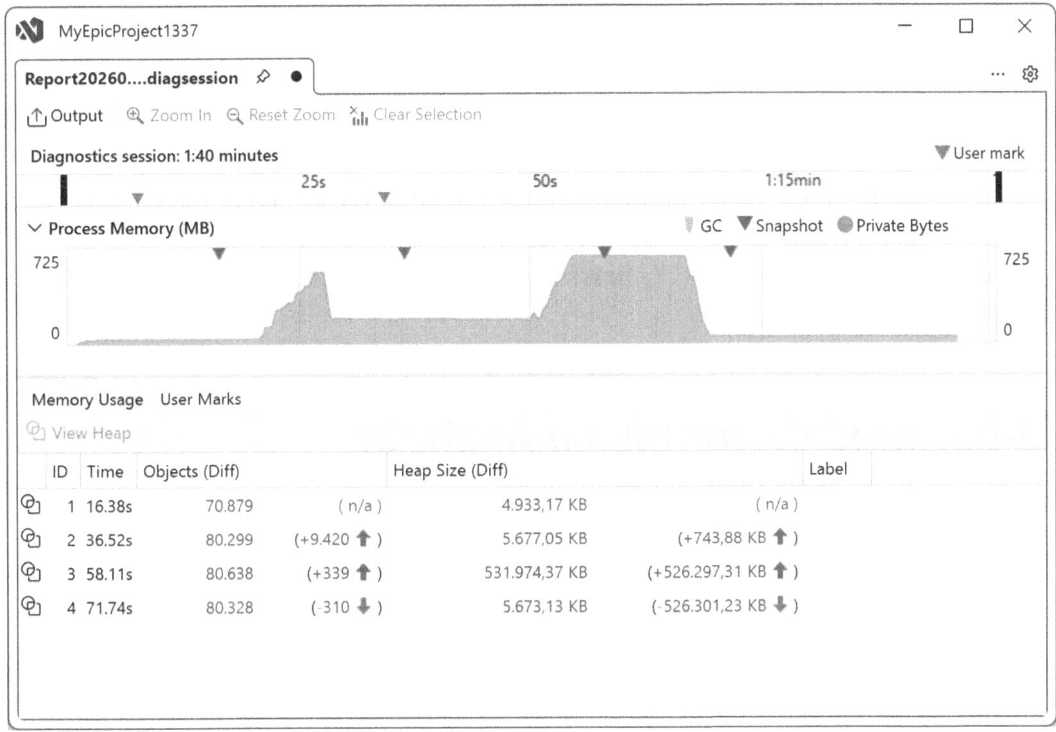

Figure 6-11. *A Visual Studio diagnostics report showing real-time memory profiling data with a timeline graph of process memory usage and a detailed snapshot table tracking objects and heap size changes*

Visual Studio 2026 enhances memory profiling with Copilot assistance for zero-length array allocations, a subtle performance issue where arrays are allocated with no capacity. When Copilot detects this pattern, it provides guidance, helping you determine whether it's intentional or an optimization opportunity. This AI-powered analysis surfaces performance problems that would otherwise require deep expertise to identify.

Additional Profiling Tools

The Events Viewer captures runtime events: exceptions, logs, HTTP requests, and performance markers, giving you a timeline of application behavior. The File I/O tool tracks disk access patterns: how frequently your code reads and writes files, which files are accessed most, and how long operations take.

These tools diagnose unexpected latency. If your app feels sluggish but CPU and memory look fine, the problem might be hundreds of unnecessary disk reads or network requests. These tools surface that immediately.

Visual Studio 2026 expanded profiling support to C++ developers. CMake projects now receive full support for CPU Usage, File I/O, and Events Viewer tools, a significant improvement, making performance debugging accessible to game developers and high-performance computing workloads. Previously, C++ performance profiling required additional setup; now it's integrated into the same unified profiler interface.

For comprehensive information on profiling tools, see **Overview of the profiling tools** on Microsoft Learn: `https://learn.microsoft.com/visualstudio/profiling/profiling-feature-tour`.

AI-Powered Performance Analysis with the Profiler Agent

Visual Studio 2026 introduces the Profiler Agent, an AI-powered assistant that automates performance analysis and optimization workflows.

Performance optimization typically follows a familiar but tedious workflow: identify that something is slow, attach profiling tools, collect data, interpret results, propose changes, test, and repeat. The Profiler Agent is Copilot applied to this entire cycle, automating much of the busywork so you can focus on understanding and fixing actual performance problems.

The Profiler Agent was originally introduced in Visual Studio 2026, but due to strong customer demand, it was also brought back to Visual Studio 2022 as well. That means you might already have worked with it, or you are able to work with it even if you don't want to upgrade to Visual Studio 2026 (yet). If you haven't heard of this feature before, let's first learn what the Profiler Agent is all about.

Rather than you manually running the profiler, interpreting results, testing fixes, and re-profiling, the agent handles this systematically. Open GitHub Copilot Chat and ask your performance question with the `@profiler` tag. For example: "@profiler Why is my app slow?".

The above is what we will look at next, but you might also find some buttons that lead to this Profiler Agent elsewhere. For example, in Figure 6-10, there is also an Analyze button (on the left in the middle right under Top Insights) to be seen that feeds the data directly into Copilot for analysis. Wherever you see a button with a sparkle icon, you know this will go to AI; it seems that sparkles are now the universal icon for Copilots and AI tools.

The Profiler Agent then follows a systematic workflow:

1. **Running Your Application Under the Profiler:** Collecting detailed CPU, memory, and runtime behavior data using Visual Studio's built-in, existing profiling tools

2. **Analyzing the Data:** Identifying bottlenecks, hot code paths, and expensive operations, rather than making you manually parse flame graphs and call trees

3. **Cross-Referencing Your Code:** Understanding the context of performance issues by examining the actual code paths identified in the trace

4. **Proposing Optimizations:** Suggesting specific, actionable improvements backed by real performance data rather than guesswork

5. **Implementing and Validating:** Automatically applying suggested changes, re-running benchmarks, and measuring the performance delta so you see exactly how much improvement you've achieved

While this whole process uses existing tools and practices that have been available in Visual Studio for a long time, this is fundamentally different from manual profiling where you collect data, stare at it, form a hypothesis, make a change, and hope it helped. The agent follows a systematic workflow: establish a baseline, analyze results, propose fixes, validate improvements, and provide metrics. I don't know about you, but while I think performance is *very* important, it's not my favorite part of the software development cycle to optimize this. So being able to pass this off to Copilot is a very welcome improvement for me!

In the screenshot in Figure 6-12, you can see how I asked Copilot, using the `@Profiler` command, to profile my Blazor project. Without me having to do anything, it launched the project; I clicked around and stopped the process, and again, without doing anything, it picked up the results and started analyzing. One of the things it did do was create a benchmark project and run that as part of this as well.

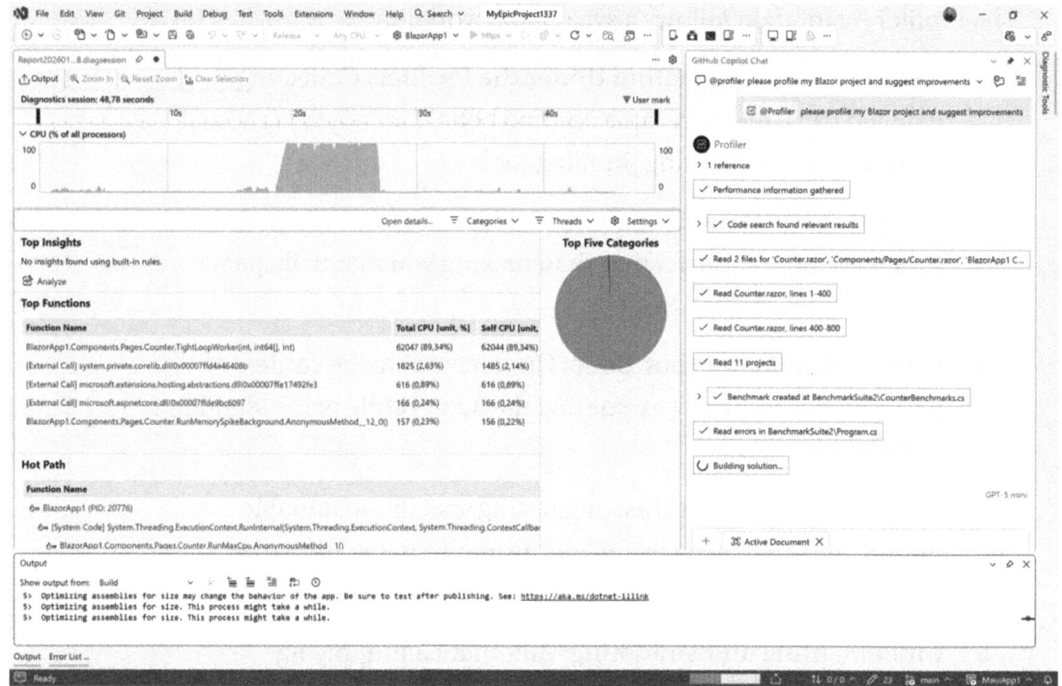

Figure 6-12. Using the @Profiler command in GitHub Copilot

This iterative loop is fundamentally different from manual profiling. You're not left interpreting graphs and forming theories: the agent handles hypothesis formation and validation. This is particularly valuable for large-scale projects where performance complexity makes manual analysis time-consuming.

Profiler Agent for ASP.NET Applications

For ASP.NET applications, the Profiler Agent now uses .NET Counters to provide deeper insights beyond CPU and memory.

- **Project Trait Detection:** Intelligent analysis of your application architecture to surface relevant performance issues

- **Counters-Driven Analysis:** Analysis of framework-level metrics (HTTP request counts, exception rates, garbage collection statistics) to identify infrastructure bottlenecks

- **End-to-End Insights:** Complete visibility from request entry through database queries and back to response

This reveals where latency in your application actually originates, often surprising developers who expected CPU to be the bottleneck but discover database queries are the real issue.

CodeLens Integration for Benchmark Optimization

CodeLens is a Visual Studio feature that displays contextual information directly in your code editor above methods and classes. CodeLens shows things like the number of references to a method, recent code changes, or test status. In Visual Studio 2026, CodeLens has been extended to surface performance optimization opportunities.

When you write benchmarks using BenchmarkDotNet, Visual Studio 2026 surfaces optimization shortcuts directly in your editor via CodeLens decorations. Above benchmark methods, you'll see "Optimize Allocations with Copilot". Click it, and the Profiler Agent analyzes your benchmark, identifies memory allocation inefficiencies, and suggests fixes, all without manually launching the profiler.

This represents a workflow shift. Instead of profiling being a separate activity, it's woven into coding. You write a benchmark, notice CodeLens offering optimization, click it, and get data-backed suggestions immediately.

Performance Optimization in Visual Studio

Once profiling reveals where your application spends time, Visual Studio's tools guide optimization efforts. Common strategies include caching, lazy loading, batching operations, algorithm improvement, parallelization, and data structure optimization. The critical principle: always measure impact using the Performance Profiler before and after changes. Sometimes, optimizations that seem beneficial actually make performance worse due to added complexity or cache effects.

For large-scale projects, Visual Studio Enterprise provides the Performance Profiler's trace comparison feature, allowing you to compare profiling runs between builds. If CPU usage per operation increases between releases, investigate what changed. Some teams integrate continuous performance benchmarks into CI/CD pipelines using Visual Studio's test infrastructure, alerting developers to performance regressions before they accumulate.

The Profiler Agent simplifies this workflow by automating profiling, analysis, and validation cycles. Rather than manually repeating profiling after each optimization attempt, the agent handles the repetitive work, letting you focus on understanding and addressing the performance issues it identifies.

Summary

Testing and profiling are not optional activities; they're central to building applications that work correctly and perform well. Visual Studio provides comprehensive tooling for both.

Create test projects from templates, write test methods using Arrange-Act-Assert patterns, and Visual Studio discovers them automatically in Test Explorer. Copilot accelerates test suite creation by generating comprehensive test cases. The Debugger Agent automatically investigates and fixes failing tests. Test Explorer serves as your command center, running tests efficiently and enabling debugging with the same tools you use for application code.

Code coverage is now available in all Visual Studio editions, providing immediate visual feedback on tested code paths through line-by-line highlighting in the editor.

Performance profiling measures where applications spend time and resources. The Profiler Agent automates profiling and analysis, removing expertise barriers. CodeLens integration surfaces optimization suggestions directly in the editor.

Visual Studio 2026's improvements make testing and profiling naturally integrated into daily workflows. Whether through faster test execution, AI-assisted test generation, or automated performance analysis, these enhancements support building high-quality applications at scale.

In the next chapter, Extensions and Marketplace, we'll explore how Visual Studio 2026's backward-compatible extension model eliminates friction when upgrading between IDE versions. We'll discover popular productivity extensions that enhance testing, profiling, and other workflows and develop best practices for selecting, installing, and managing extensions safely, both individually and at an organizational scale.

CHAPTER 7

Extensions and Marketplace

By now, you have probably noticed that Visual Studio can do quite a lot right out of the box. But here's the thing: the real magic of Visual Studio isn't just what Microsoft built into the core IDE. It's what the community, third-party vendors, and Microsoft's own teams have built on top of it through extensions. These little (and sometimes not so little) add-ons transform Visual Studio from a powerful editor into a personalized development powerhouse tailored exactly to how you work.

In this chapter, we're going to explore the Visual Studio Marketplace, understand how extensions work in Visual Studio 2026, and learn how to find, install, and manage extensions that can genuinely make your life easier. Whether you're looking to boost productivity, improve code quality, collaborate with teammates, or harness AI-powered development tools, there's an extension out there for you. And the great news? Visual Studio 2026 has made working with extensions better than ever before.

Understanding the Visual Studio Marketplace

The Visual Studio Marketplace is your one-stop destination for finding and installing extensions that extend Visual Studio's capabilities. It's not just a repository where extensions sit waiting to be discovered. It's an actively managed, security-conscious ecosystem designed to protect you while giving you access to thousands of tools that enhance your development experience.

When you navigate to the Marketplace, either directly from Visual Studio via the Extension Manager or by visiting marketplace.visualstudio.com, you'll see a carefully organized collection of extensions sorted by category, popularity, rating, and release date. The Marketplace also serves as the extension hub for other tools in the Visual

© Gerald Versluis 2026
G. Versluis, *Getting Started with Visual Studio 2026*, https://doi.org/10.1007/979-8-8688-2691-7_7

Studio family, including Azure DevOps, Azure DevOps Server, and Visual Studio Code, making it a comprehensive resource for the entire Microsoft development ecosystem.

Think of the Marketplace as an app store, but specifically designed for developers. You can browse extensions by category, search for specific functionality, read reviews from other developers who've used them, and see detailed information about what each extension does before you install it. When you find an extension you like, you can install it with just a few clicks, and Visual Studio handles the rest. In most cases, you won't even need to restart the IDE; the extension just appears and starts working.

In Figure 7-1, you can see the online Visual Studio Marketplace.

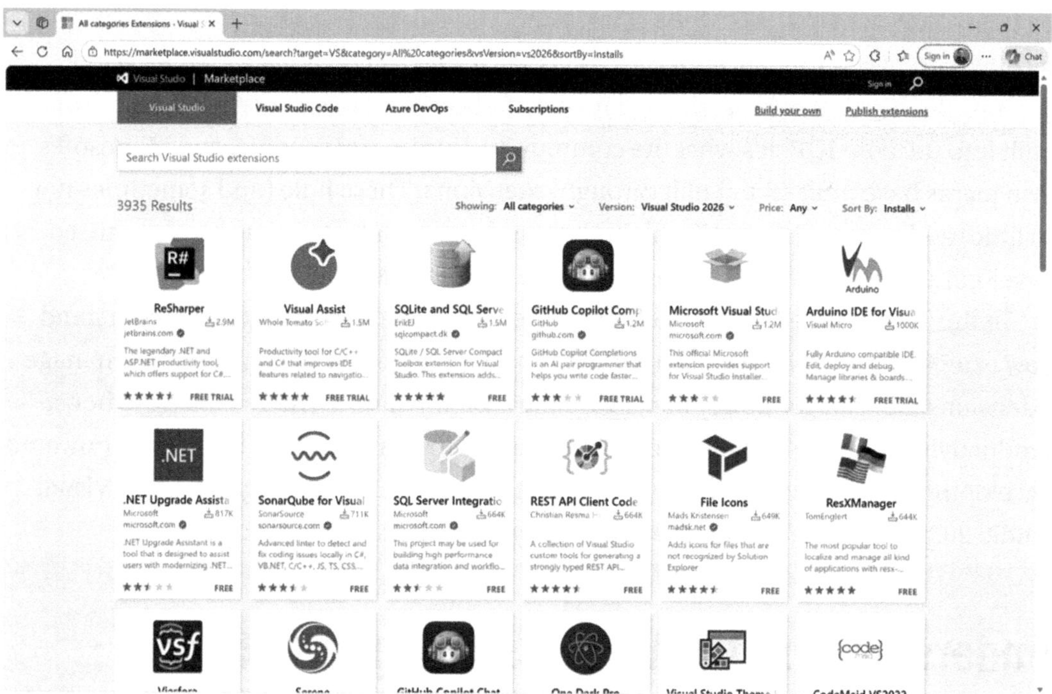

Figure 7-1. *The online Visual Studio Marketplace filtered on extensions for Visual Studio 2026, showing almost 4,000 results*

One important thing to understand about the Marketplace is that it hosts two types of extensions: VSIX-based extensions and MSI-based extensions. VSIX (Visual Studio Integration Extension) is the modern standard format. It's what most extensions use, and it's what the Extension Manager in Visual Studio handles most smoothly. MSI-based extensions use a traditional Windows installer format. They work, but they require more manual management and won't benefit from some of Visual Studio 2026's newer convenience features. Generally speaking, if you're choosing between an MSI and a VSIX version of an extension, go with the VSIX version whenever possible.

One last thing about extensions: while a lot of the extensions are free, there are also paid ones. They usually offer a trial so you can try out what you would be buying. I won't go much into the specifics of this. How an extension handles trials, payment, etc. very much differs between extensions based on how it's implemented.

Extension Compatibility in Visual Studio 2026

Visual Studio 2026 introduces a completely new approach to extension compatibility, and it's a game-changer. Allow me to explain why this matters.

In previous Visual Studio versions, whenever Microsoft released a major new version of the IDE, extension developers had to do significant work to make their extensions compatible with the new version. They'd need to update version numbers, test thoroughly (OK, you should still do that…), and often publish separate builds. This meant that when you upgraded to a new version of Visual Studio, some of your favorite extensions might not work immediately. You'd have to wait for updates, find alternatives, or stick with your old version of Visual Studio.

Not anymore. Visual Studio 2026 uses a new extension compatibility model that's fundamentally different. Instead of targeting specific Visual Studio versions, extensions now target API versions. The key insight here is that Visual Studio 2026 supports API version 17.x, the same API version as Visual Studio 2022. This means that extensions built for Visual Studio 2022 are automatically compatible with Visual Studio 2026. You don't need to wait for extension developers to update anything. Your extensions just work.

If we get a bit more technical about this and look at an extension's installation target in the manifest file, it used to look something like this: `<InstallationTarget Id="Microsoft.VisualStudio.Community" Version="[17.0, 18.0)"/>`.

That upper bound of 18.0 meant the extension was designed for Visual Studio 2022 but not any version after that. In Visual Studio 2026, that upper bound is ignored. The IDE only looks at the lower bound. So if you have an extension built for Visual Studio 2022 with that manifest above, it automatically works in Visual Studio 2026 with zero changes needed.

When Visual Studio 2026 creates new extensions, the manifest looks like this: `<InstallationTarget Id="Microsoft.VisualStudio.Community" Version="[17.0,)"/>`.

See that open-ended upper bound? That means the extension will work with both Visual Studio 2022 and Visual Studio 2026 automatically.

What does this mean for you as a user? When you upgrade to Visual Studio 2026, you can use the installer's "Include installed extensions from the Visual Studio Marketplace" option, and most of your extensions will migrate automatically. When you open Visual Studio 2026 for the first time, around 4,000 extensions are already compatible and ready to use. It's as close to a friction-free upgrade as Visual Studio has ever offered.

However, while the compatibility model makes it so extensions *can* run in Visual Studio 2026, extension developers still recommend testing their extensions on the new version to catch any compatibility bugs. If you find an extension that isn't working properly, report it through the Developer Community portal so the extension author can investigate.

For detailed information about the extension compatibility model and how it benefits your upgrade experience, see the official Microsoft documentation on **Modernizing Visual Studio Extension Compatibility**.

Finding and Installing Extensions

Now that you understand how extensions work in Visual Studio 2026, let's get practical. How do you actually find and install them?

The primary way you'll interact with extensions is through the Extension Manager in Visual Studio itself. You can open it by navigating to Extensions ➤ Manage Extensions in the main menu. Alternatively, if you're like most developers and prefer using the keyboard, then you can use the quick search feature that we've seen before; just press Ctrl+Q and type "extensions," and then select "Manage Extensions" from the results.

Like the Settings screen, the Extension Manager is now also opened as a tab in the main editor space rather than a separate dialog as it was before Visual Studio 2026. You can see an example in Figure 7-2 with the Extension Manager open on the Browse tab.

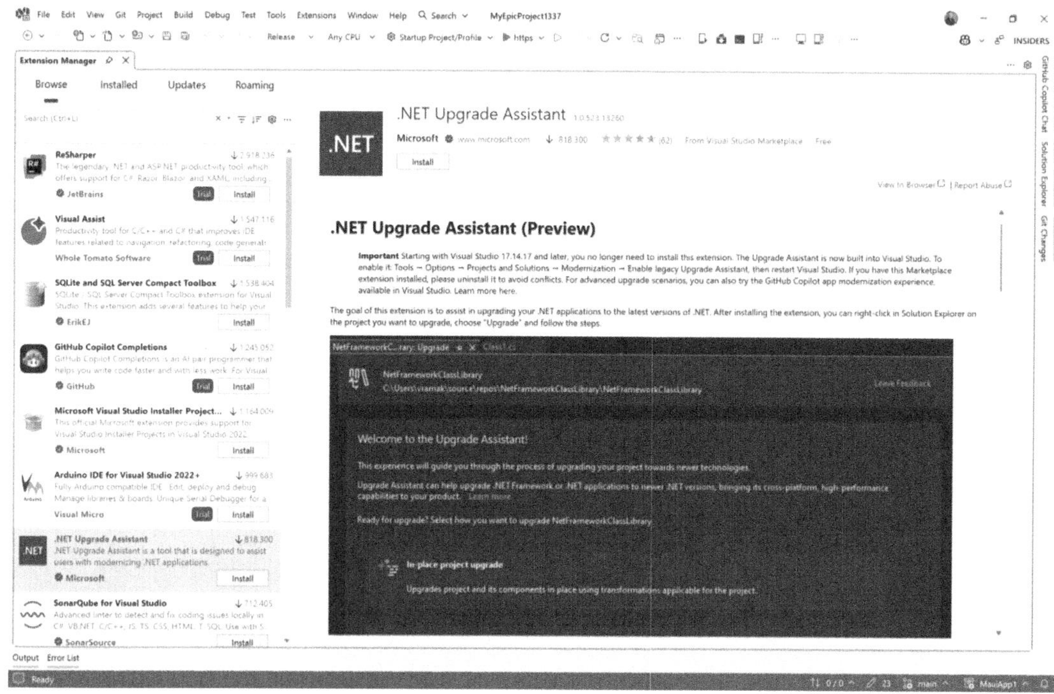

Figure 7-2. *The Extension Manager now opens as a tab in the main editor space rather than a separate dialog in Visual Studio 2026*

The Extension Manager window is organized into several tabs. When you first open it, you'll likely see the Browse tab, which shows extensions available on the Visual Studio Marketplace. You can search for extensions by name, category, or description. Want all the code quality tools? Filter by category. Looking for something specific like a debugger? Search for it. The search box at the top of the window is quite powerful; it understands multiple keywords, so you can search for things like "code formatter" or "AI productivity" and get relevant results.

Each extension in the list, whether that's from search results or just browsing, shows you key information at a glance: the extension icon, its name, the publisher, the rating, the number of downloads, and a brief description. When you find one that interests you, click on it to see the full details page. Here, you'll find more information about what the extension does, screenshots or videos showing it in action, user reviews and ratings, installation requirements, and any dependencies it might need.

Ready to install? Just click the Install button at the top. Visual Studio will download the extension from the Marketplace. Depending on the type of extension, you'll usually see a notification that says something like "Your changes are scheduled. The modifications will begin when Microsoft Visual Studio is closed." This is Visual Studio being smart. For most extensions, it can install them without restarting the IDE, but it might need to restart for some advanced ones. What can also happen is that the Install button will go to a browser window and start a download that you must install manually. If the extension(s) will be installed after closing Visual Studio, you will see a dialog pop up, and that will guide you through the last steps. You can see that in Figure 7-3 which shows the VSIX installer that pops up.

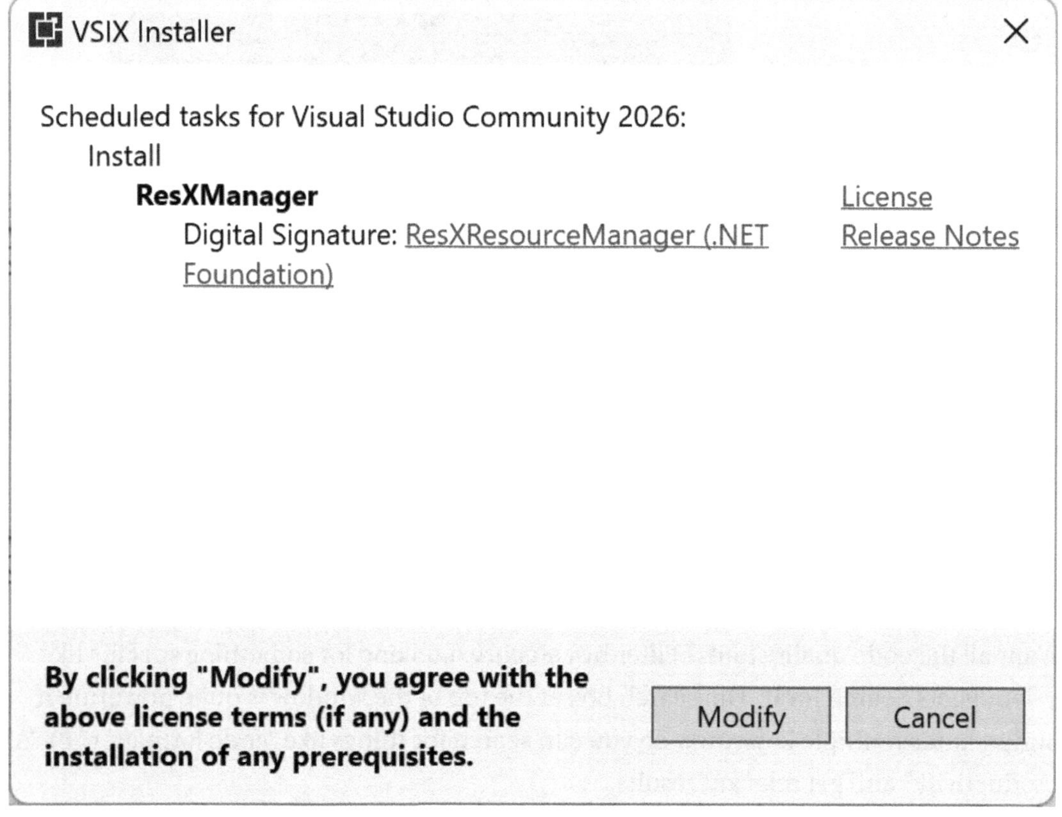

Figure 7-3. *The VSIX installer that popped up after closing Visual Studio. This is needed to finalize the installation of the scheduled extensions that we wanted to install*

Click Modify (granted, a bit of a weird caption), and the installer will complete the installation of your chosen extension(s). After that is finished, start Visual Studio back up, and the extensions are ready to be used!

Tip   When you click Install on an extension but change your mind before you restart Visual Studio, you can go to that extension in the Extension Manager again, and you'll notice the Install button is now a Cancel button. This will cancel the scheduled changes before they happen.

What if you find an extension on the Marketplace website or someone sends you a `.vsix` file directly? You can simply double-click it, and Visual Studio will handle the installation. This is particularly useful if you're working with private or custom extensions that aren't on the public Marketplace. Or also the ones on the Marketplace website that you have to download manually.

Once an extension is installed, take a look at the other tabs in Extension Manager. The Installed tab shows all the extensions you have on your system. The Updates tab shows you extensions that have newer versions available. (We'll talk more about updates in a moment.) The Roaming tab is particularly useful if you use Visual Studio on multiple machines; it shows you extensions you've installed across all your Visual Studio instances, making it easy to keep your development environment consistent.

Navigating Extension Categories and Finding What You Need

The Visual Studio Marketplace has thousands of extensions, which can feel overwhelming. To help you navigate, extensions are organized into three main top-level categories: Controls, Templates, and Tools. Understanding these categories can help you find what you're looking for more quickly.

Controls are reusable UI components and controls that you can integrate into your projects. These include custom controls, components, and UI elements that extend the standard toolbox and provide specialized functionality for specific frameworks or design patterns. Trigger warning: one of the subcategories is still Silverlight.

Templates provide project and code templates that help you quickly get started with new projects. Whether you need templates for ASP.NET applications, WPF projects, Azure solutions, or specialized frameworks, these extensions give you pre-built project structures and boilerplate code that save significant setup time.

Tools is by far the largest category, containing the vast majority of extensions that add functionality to Visual Studio. Tools include numerous subcategories such as Build tools (for compilation and deployment), Coding tools (for productivity and code editing), Security (for code analysis and vulnerability scanning), Performance (for profiling and optimization), Data (for database and data management), Services (for cloud and web services integration), and many others.

Within the Tools category, some of the most popular subcategories include Coding for productivity enhancements like CodeMaid and Roslynator, Programming Languages for language-specific support, Connected Services for integrating cloud services and APIs, and Documentation for generating and managing code documentation. If you're looking for AI-powered extensions, these would fall under the broader Coding sub-category also. A lot of the Microsoft extensions that were here are now directly integrated into Visual Studio. If you are familiar with AI already, another thing you might be expecting to see here would be Model Context Protocol (MCP) servers, a new way for AI tools to access context and tools within Visual Studio, but we'll explore those in depth in Chapter 8 when we cover AI-powered development more thoroughly.

Other valuable Tools subcategories include Security for code quality and vulnerability detection, Services for connecting to cloud platforms and APIs, and Setup & Deployment for build automation and deployment workflows. Extensions like GitLens enhance your Git workflow with powerful repository insights, while Live Share enables real-time collaboration with teammates.

Earlier in this book, in Chapter 3, we touched on the new themes that are provided out of the box; among the extensions, you can find additional themes that match your preferences or accessibility needs.

The beauty of this ecosystem is that if you can think of something that would make development easier, someone has probably built an extension for it. And if they haven't, well, you could build one yourself. A little more on that later.

Managing Your Extensions

Installing extensions is just the beginning. Once you have them installed, you need to manage them thoughtfully. Visual Studio 2026 gives you several tools to do this effectively.

Let's start with the basics: enabling and disabling. Sometimes you'll want to temporarily turn off an extension without uninstalling it completely. Maybe it's conflicting with something, or you just don't need it right now. Depending on what the extension does, it might take up valuable resources in terms of CPU or memory. In the Installed tab of Extension Manager, find the extension, and you'll see a Disable button. Click it, and the extension gets disabled without being removed from your system. Visual Studio might ask to restart, but once it does, the extension won't load. To re-enable it later, just click the Enable button. This is different from uninstalling. Uninstalling completely removes the extension from your system, and you'd need to install it again if you change your mind.

If you're absolutely certain you don't want an extension anymore, you can uninstall it. Keep in mind that you can typically disable VSIX-based extensions without restarting, but some MSI-based extensions might require a restart to uninstall. Visual Studio will let you know if that's the case. Next to the Disable button, you can find the Uninstall button, and that allows you to completely uninstall the extension from your Visual Studio instance.

Actually, that is a good side-step right here. Remember from the earliest chapters where we installed Visual Studio, and I mentioned that you can have multiple Visual Studio versions side-by-side? The extensions can be installed on a per-Visual Studio instance basis. Whenever you install an extension and you see the dialog from Figure 7-3 that we've seen above, and you have multiple Visual Studio installations, you can check or uncheck the Visual Studio instances that you want the extension to be installed on.

Now, about updates. Visual Studio 2026 has made extension updates much more convenient than in the past. By default, extensions update automatically in the background when new versions become available on the Marketplace. The next time you open Visual Studio, the updated extension will be running. This is usually a good thing; you get bug fixes and new features without having to think about it.

However, you might sometimes want more control. Maybe you're in the middle of a critical project, and you don't want any surprises from automatic updates. You can disable automatic updates globally by going to Tools ➤ Options ➤ Environment ➤ Extension Manager and unchecking "Install updates automatically." Or, if you want to disable automatic updates for just one specific extension, you can do that from its details page in Extension Manager, find the cogwheel icon, and then uncheck "Automatically update this extension".

Besides the Browse and Install tabs, you will also find the Updates tab. Under this tab, you will find extensions that have updates that are not installed yet. If you have the above setting on for installing updates automatically, you should never have to be here. However, if you choose to manually update, this is where you can find a handy overview of your extensions that need an update. In Figure 7-4, you can see the Updates tab with 1 pending update.

You can choose to update just one extension at a time by clicking the Update to x.y.z button for that extension, or, just above the list, you see the Update All button to update them all in one go.

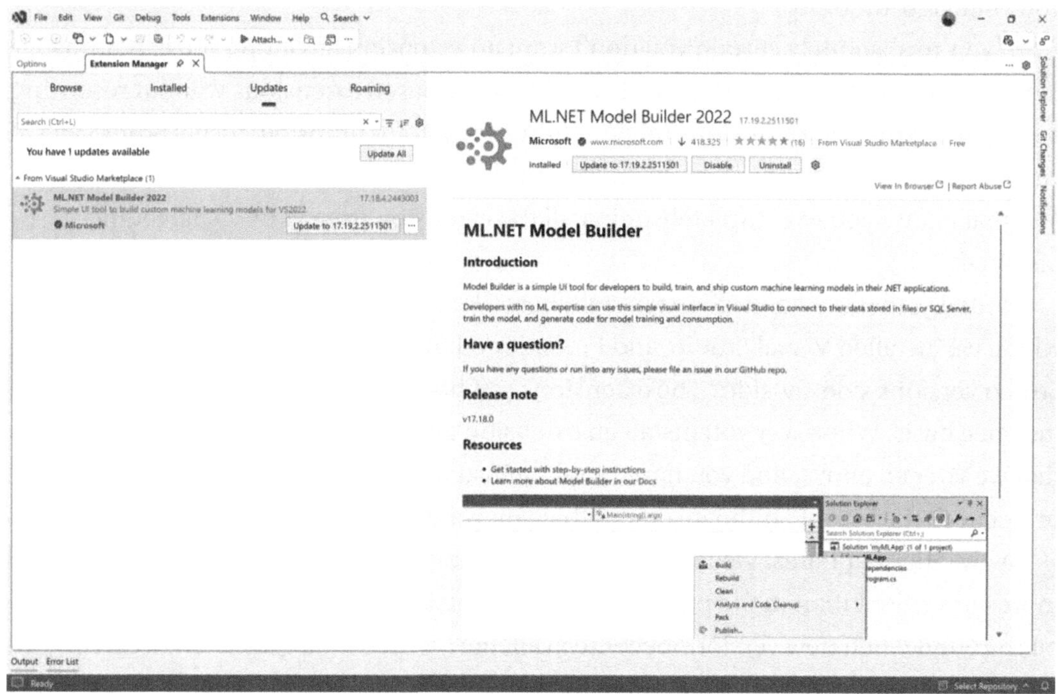

Figure 7-4. *The ML.NET Model Builder 2022 has a pending update as seen in the Extension Manager under the Updates tab*

Lastly, under the Roaming tab, you can find the extensions that roam together with your Microsoft account to every Visual Studio that you log into. This is a cloud-synced list of extensions that will automatically be installed whenever you log into a new Visual Studio instance with your Microsoft account. If you don't want certain extensions to follow you around, but only keep them on this machine for this Visual Studio, go into this tab, find the extension, and under the three dots button, select Stop Roaming.

One more important thing: Visual Studio keeps track of which extensions are enabled and disabled on a per-user basis. If you're running Visual Studio with elevated permissions (as an administrator), you might notice that your per-user extensions don't load. This is actually a security feature. It prevents potentially problematic extensions from running with elevated privileges unless you explicitly want them to. You can change this behavior in Tools ➤ Options ➤ Environment ➤ Extensions by checking "Load per user extensions when running as administrator," but generally, the default behavior is the safe choice.

For comprehensive guidance on finding and managing Visual Studio extensions, see the official Microsoft Learn documentation: `https://learn.microsoft.com/visualstudio/ide/finding-and-using-visual-studio-extensions`.

Managing Extensions in Enterprise Environments

If you're working in a large organization or managing Visual Studio deployments across multiple teams, you might need more control over which extensions are available to developers. Visual Studio 2026 supports enterprise-grade extension management through Group Policy and Microsoft Intune, allowing administrators to apply policies that govern extension behavior across the organization.

IT administrators can use Visual Studio Administrative Templates (ADMX) or the Microsoft Intune settings catalog to configure policies that control which extensions developers can install, disable specific extensions organization-wide, allow only extensions from approved publishers, restrict extensions to specific versions, and manage automatic extension updates. For example, an organization might allow all extensions from Microsoft and GitHub while blocking third-party extensions, or they might create a private marketplace to host internal extensions that meet security and compliance standards.

These policies are particularly useful for organizations that need to maintain security standards, ensure compliance with regulations, protect intellectual property, or maintain consistency across development teams. When policies are configured, developers can still browse the Marketplace, but the Install button will be grayed out for extensions that don't meet the organization's approval criteria.

For detailed information about implementing enterprise extension management, see the official Microsoft Learn documentation on **Configuring policies for enterprise deployments** and **Visual Studio Administrative Templates (ADMX).**

Security: Trust and Protect Your Development Environment

Here's something you might not think about much: security when it comes to extensions. The Visual Studio Marketplace is a curated ecosystem, and Microsoft takes security seriously. Before you install an extension, you should understand the protections in place.

Every extension published to the Visual Studio Marketplace goes through a malware scan. The scan uses multiple antivirus engines to ensure that the extension doesn't contain malicious code. The scan runs not just when an extension is first published, but also each time an extension is updated. Until the scan clears, the extension won't appear on the Marketplace for public use. This is a baseline security measure.

Beyond malware scanning, the Marketplace uses several other security mechanisms. Publishers can become "Verified publishers" by proving domain ownership. If you see a blue checkmark next to a publisher's name, it means the publisher has been verified by the Marketplace. This doesn't mean the publisher is "approved" in some absolute sense, but it does mean they've proven their identity and have a track record on the Marketplace over at least six months. In Figure 7-5, you can see how Mads Kristensen is a verified publisher. The arrow in the screenshot points out the blue verification badge. While this is not 100% fool proof, it should give you some extra trust.

Figure 7-5. *The blue checkmark badge indicates a verified publisher*

The Marketplace also monitors unusual usage patterns. If an extension suddenly starts being downloaded far more frequently than usual, or if usage patterns seem suspicious, the Marketplace team investigates. And if a security vulnerability is discovered in an extension, or if the extension is reported and verified to be malicious, it can be blocklisted and removed from the Marketplace.

One more security layer: the Marketplace automatically scans every newly published extension for secrets. Things like API keys, authentication tokens, or credentials. If secrets are detected, the Marketplace blocks the publication to prevent the extension author from accidentally leaking sensitive information into the public repository.

Finally, every extension published to the Marketplace is digitally signed. When you install an extension, Visual Studio checks this signature to verify the integrity and source of the extension package. This helps ensure that the extension you're installing hasn't been tampered with.

This doesn't mean the Marketplace is 100% risk-free; no system is. But it does mean that the protections in place are solid, and you can generally feel confident installing extensions from the official Marketplace. That said, always review what permissions an extension requests, and if something feels off, trust your instincts. You can report suspicious extensions to Microsoft through the Marketplace.

For more detailed security information about Visual Studio extensions and the Marketplace scanning process, consult the **Visual Studio Marketplace Security Documentation**.

Building Your Own Extensions

By now, you might be thinking: "These extensions are useful, but what if I want to build my own?" And that's a great question. It is absolutely possible to create extensions for Visual Studio 2026. Whether you want to build a small utility for your team, create a specialized tool for a particular workflow, or contribute to the open source ecosystem, the extensibility model in Visual Studio 2026 makes it accessible to any developer with some C# experience and an understanding of the Visual Studio API.

However, building extensions for Visual Studio goes well beyond the scope of this book. Creating production-quality extensions involves understanding the Visual Studio SDK, navigating the VisualStudio.Extensibility model (or the older VSSDK), learning about command definitions, tool windows, menu integrations, and much more. It's a rich and deep topic that deserves its own dedicated resources. If you find yourself interested in extension development, the best place to start is the official **Introduction to Visual Studio Extension Development** documentation on Microsoft Learn. There, you'll find comprehensive guides on the extension architecture, getting started templates, API references, and best practices for publishing to the Marketplace.

For now, as a user of Visual Studio 2026, focus on discovering and using the thousands of extensions already available. Many of them were created by developers like yourself who invested the time to build tools they wanted to use and thought others might benefit from as well.

The New VisualStudio.Extensibility Model

I know, I just said to focus on using extensions and not building them, but just one more note which will also help you understand the performance gains in Visual Studio 2026.

Historically, Visual Studio extensions ran in-process, meaning they ran in the same process as the IDE itself. This was efficient, but it meant that if an extension crashed, it could crash the entire IDE. If an extension hung, it could make the entire IDE unresponsive. Not ideal.

Microsoft has introduced a new extensibility model called `VisualStudio.Extensibility`. This model focuses on extensions that run out-of-process from the IDE. Extensions that follow this model run in their own separate process, so if they crash or hang, they don't take down Visual Studio with them. The IDE remains responsive and stable.

The `VisualStudio.Extensibility` model also introduces hot-loading, which means you don't need to restart Visual Studio to install many extensions anymore. The extension just loads in its own process and appears in the IDE. This is a huge quality-of-life improvement compared to the old model.

The new model uses a Remote UI framework, which allows extensions to display custom tool windows and UI elements that integrate cleanly with Visual Studio's interface. The API is also designed to be more modern and intuitive, with a focus on asynchronous programming patterns that are standard in modern .NET development.

That said, `VisualStudio.Extensibility` is still in preview. It doesn't yet cover all possible extension scenarios. If you're an extension developer and you find that VisualStudio.Extensibility doesn't provide everything you need, you can use it together with the traditional Visual Studio SDK (VSSDK) running in-process to cover any gaps. But the direction is clear: the future of Visual Studio extensions is out-of-process and more stable.

If you're interested in learning more about developing extensions with VisualStudio. Extensibility, the official documentation on Microsoft Learn is a great starting point. The **VisualStudio.Extensibility overview** provides comprehensive guidance on the new model, its architecture, and how to get started building modern extensions. The model is actively being refined based on developer feedback, so if you have ideas about what the extensibility API should support, Microsoft wants to hear from you.

Best Practices for Working with Extensions

Let's wrap up this chapter with some practical best practices for managing your extensions as you work with Visual Studio 2026.

Test extensions on your development environment first. If you're upgrading from Visual Studio 2022 and migrating your extensions, take some time to verify that they're working as expected. Just because an extension is compatible doesn't mean it works perfectly in every scenario. If you find an issue, check the extension's documentation or GitHub repository; you might find a workaround or a notice about the issue.

Don't install extensions you don't need. Extensions are powerful tools, but each one adds a bit of overhead to your IDE's startup time and memory usage. If you've installed an extension but you're not actively using it, disable it or uninstall it. A leaner IDE is often a faster, more responsive IDE.

Keep your extensions updated. While it's tempting to disable automatic updates to "keep things stable," in practice, extension developers are usually releasing updates to fix bugs and improve compatibility. Letting your extensions update automatically is generally the right choice. If an update breaks something, you can always downgrade by installing a previous version (most Marketplace pages let you do this).

Understand extension dependencies. Some extensions depend on other extensions. If you uninstall an extension that another extension depends on, Visual Studio will warn you. Pay attention to these warnings.

For team environments, consider using .vsconfig files to share extensions. If you're working on a team and you want everyone to use the same set of extensions and workloads, Visual Studio supports this through installation configuration files. You can export your current Visual Studio configuration, including installed workloads, components, and Marketplace extensions, to a .vsconfig file directly from the Visual Studio Installer or by right-clicking your solution in Solution Explorer and choosing Add ➤ Installation Configuration File. When team members receive this file, they can import it to ensure their Visual Studio installation matches the team's configuration. Starting with Visual Studio 2022 version 17.10, Marketplace extensions loaded in an instance-wide context can be included in the export. This is particularly useful if your team has specific code quality standards or productivity tools that you want everyone using together, similar to how we covered team settings in Chapter 4 on Project Management and Solution Explorer. For more details on using configuration files, see the official documentation on **Import or export installation configurations.**

Handle incompatible extensions thoughtfully. If you find an extension that isn't working in Visual Studio 2026, check the Marketplace to see if there's an alternative that provides similar functionality. Many popular extension categories have multiple options. If an extension is critical to your workflow and hasn't been updated for VS 2026, file an issue on the extension's GitHub repository (if it's open source), or contact the extension author directly.

Summary

By now, extensions should feel a bit less like mysterious add-ons and more like a natural part of how Visual Studio 2026 works. You have seen how the Marketplace acts as the central hub, how the new compatibility model lets most of your Visual Studio 2022 extensions come along for the ride with almost no friction, and how you can browse, install, update, and remove extensions from the Extension Manager without losing control of your environment. There was also a look behind the scenes at security, from malware scanning to verified publishers, and at the newer `VisualStudio.Extensibility` model that moves extensions out of the process, so they no longer jeopardize the stability of the IDE when they misbehave. Along the way, you picked up some practical habits, like only keeping the extensions you actually use, letting them auto-update in most cases, and using installer configuration files or enterprise policies when you want a team or an entire organization to share a consistent, well-governed setup.

In the next chapter, things get even more interesting because extensions are only part of the story of how Visual Studio 2026 is changing the way you write code. You will dive into AI-powered development: GitHub Copilot, IntelliCode, and the new Agent-style workflows that can refactor or extend entire code bases for you. That is also where MCP servers come in, those Model Context Protocol back ends you briefly met here, so you can see how AI-driven tools securely tap into your code, your tools, and your project context to become real collaborators instead of just smarter autocompletion.

CHAPTER 8

AI-Powered Development

If you've been paying attention so far, you've probably noticed that I've mentioned GitHub Copilot several times throughout this book. That's intentional, because for the first time ever, Microsoft is positioning an IDE as "AI-native," meaning artificial intelligence isn't bolted on as an afterthought; it's woven into the development experience itself. This chapter is where we dive deep into how that actually works in practice, moving beyond the brief mentions we've made in earlier chapters.

The shift is significant. A few years ago, AI assistance in development meant autocomplete that was a bit smarter than before. Now it means you can have an autonomous agent plan and execute multi-file refactoring tasks while you review the results. It means performance analysis doesn't require hours of manual investigation. As we already saw in Chapter 6, the Profiler Agent can suggest optimizations based on actual trace data. And the Test Agent helps you find gaps in your test suite and helps you cover those, with zero code written by you. It means debugging exceptions comes with repository-aware analysis that understands the context of your code base. This isn't science fiction anymore; it's how Visual Studio 2026 actually works.

The exciting part? You're in control. You can choose your AI model, scope what features you use, and decide when to let the AI take the wheel. Let's explore how this works.

Note   *If there is one thing moving faster than the Visual Studio release cycle, it is the evolution of AI. Because GitHub Copilot and the underlying AI models are constantly being updated via the cloud, the exact UI layouts, model names, and specific capabilities you see in this chapter may evolve rapidly. Microsoft is iterating on these tools almost weekly. As you read this chapter, focus less on*

© Gerald Versluis 2026
G. Versluis, *Getting Started with Visual Studio 2026*, https://doi.org/10.1007/979-8-8688-2691-7_8

the exact placement of a button or the specific name of a chat mode, and focus instead on the patterns of AI-assisted development: planning, agent delegation, inline prompting, and context gathering. Those core workflows will remain the foundation of how you develop software in Visual Studio 2026, regardless of how the UI shifts.

Getting Started with GitHub Copilot: Prerequisites and Setup

While GitHub Copilot is only one part of the AI story in Visual Studio, it definitely is the biggest one, by far. When we talk about GitHub Copilot, that can mean a couple of different things, as we will learn in this chapter. So to make sure that you can explore and use everything that is available to us, let's make sure that you are set up correctly.

Before you can use GitHub Copilot and all its AI-powered features in Visual Studio 2026, you'll need to have the right account in place. Here's what you need to know at the time of writing, though please keep in mind, pricing and plans can evolve over time. Check the official GitHub Copilot page at **https://github.com/features/copilot** for the latest information.

Before you can use GitHub Copilot and all its AI-powered features in Visual Studio 2026, you need two things: a GitHub account and a Copilot plan or free entitlement (e.g., Copilot Free, Pro, Business, or Enterprise; offerings may change over time, so always check the official Copilot plans page for the latest details). If you don't have a GitHub account yet, you can create one as part of the Copilot sign-in flow; Visual Studio will open a GitHub page where you can both create the account and activate Copilot, without requiring you to visit github.com separately first.

The easiest way to get started is to invoke any Copilot feature in Visual Studio. For example, opening Copilot Chat or trying to use inline suggestions when you are not signed in. Visual Studio then shows a "Get started with Copilot" or "Get started with Copilot Free" dialog with a Continue with GitHub button. Clicking that button signs you into GitHub (or lets you create an account if needed) and walks you through activating Copilot Free or connecting your existing Copilot subscription; when you complete that flow, you're brought back to Visual Studio with Copilot ready to use.

You can always add additional accounts or manage your currently logged-in accounts through File ➤ Account Settings or by clicking your profile icon in the top-right corner of Visual Studio. In the dialog that comes up, shown in Figure 8-1, you can add additional Microsoft or GitHub accounts.

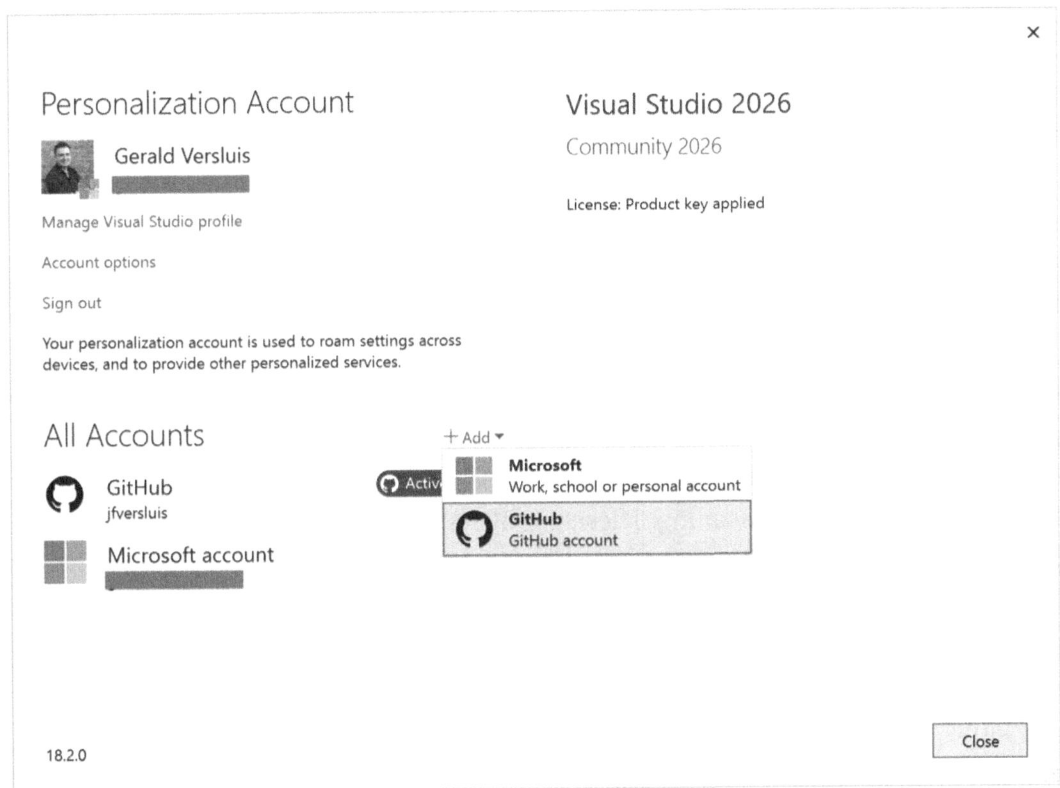

Figure 8-1.   *The Personalization Account dialog where you can add GitHub and Microsoft accounts to use with Visual Studio*

Pricing and Premium Requests

Now for the Copilot subscription itself. GitHub offers several tiers tailored to different needs. The Copilot Free plan provides a generous allowance of code completions and a set number of premium requests per month at no cost, which is perfect if you're learning or want to try Copilot before committing.

For individual developers who need more, Copilot Pro is available for a flat subscription fee and includes unlimited completions along with a significantly higher tier of premium requests. For organizations, Copilot Business and Copilot Enterprise offer team management, SSO, audit logs, and enterprise-grade security features.

Here's where the structure gets interesting: premium requests are used for advanced features like Copilot Chat interactions, Agent Mode, and multi-file editing. But not all models consume premium requests equally. GitHub uses a "model multiplier" system to account for the computational cost of different AI models.

The standard base models typically use a multiplier of zero for paid users, meaning you effectively get unlimited requests when using them. However, when you switch to premium models or cutting-edge reasoning models, each request counts more heavily against your premium request budget.

This means that while you can use the base model freely, switching to a more capable model for Agent Mode or complex chat interactions will consume your monthly premium request allowance much faster. The more advanced reasoning models cost significantly more per request because they involve greater computational overhead for fact-checking and deep reasoning. These modifiers are always visible when you switch to a different model in the GitHub Copilot chat window.

There's also an Auto mode that lets Copilot choose a chat model for you. In Auto mode, Copilot selects from the models that are available to your plan and allowed by your administrators, with the goal of giving you a fast, reliable response while honoring rate limits and capacity constraints. Instead of you manually picking a specific model every time, Auto routes your request to an appropriate model based on availability and service health, skipping models that are temporarily unavailable or exceed your configured multipliers. Over time, Auto is expected to take more task characteristics into account, but today it primarily optimizes for model availability and usage limits rather than trying to "guess" the complexity of each request.

In Figure 8-2, you can see the list of models with the corresponding multipliers listed behind them. Note that these are the models and modifier values at the time of writing; they might have changed by the time you read this. Additionally, you might see more or less options here depending on the plan that you are on and what models are (or are not) allowed by your organization's settings.

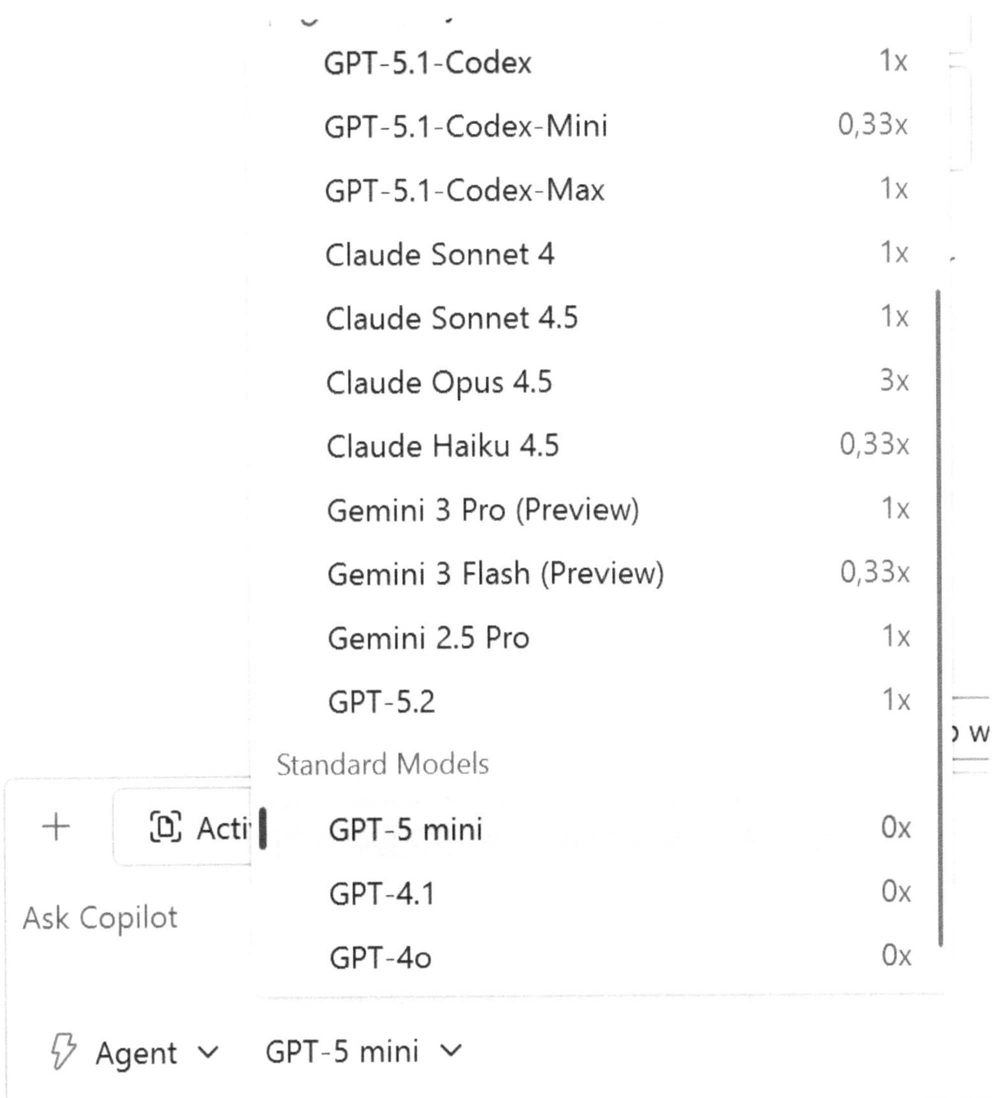

Figure 8-2. *The list of available models for Copilot Agent mode, with the modifiers listed on the right*

We'll learn more about this window and what else you are seeing here in a minute.

If you're primarily using inline code suggestions (ghost text) with the base model, you won't consume many premium requests. But if you're actively using Agent Mode with advanced models or chat features with premium models, your usage will add up faster. Understanding which model you're using is important for planning your spending. Over time, models might become cheaper, and modifiers might change, so keep your eye on the changes there.

To track your current usage and plan accordingly, you can check your Copilot activity directly from Visual Studio. Click the down arrow next to the GitHub Copilot icon in the top-right and select Copilot Usage. That will bring up a dialog that shows you your current plan and usage.

You can see more details on your usage on GitHub.com. Visit your GitHub account settings, navigate to the "Billing and Plans" section, and look for your Copilot usage dashboard. This shows you how many premium requests you've used in the current billing cycle and your current plan tier. For organization administrators, GitHub provides organization-scoped Copilot usage metrics, so they can see how Copilot is being adopted within their organization and which teams are using it most. In larger companies that use GitHub Enterprise, enterprise owners or enterprise admins get an additional, enterprise-wide view with richer reporting across all organizations in the enterprise account, including Copilot license assignments, aggregate usage trends, and policy enforcement. This data helps you make informed decisions about upgrading plans or adjusting how your team uses Copilot. If you're on an organization plan, your admin can grant you access to view these metrics through the GitHub Copilot usage dashboard.

If you're learning, teaching, or maintaining a popular open source project, you can get free access at **`https://github.com/github-copilot/free_for_qualified_developers`**, for instance, if you are a verified student. Check if you might be eligible and how to claim your free access at the link above.

Your Copilot Chat Companion: The Foundation of AI-Assisted Development

Every development session in Visual Studio 2026 with Copilot enabled starts the same way: with access to Copilot Chat, the conversational interface that serves as your primary interaction point with GitHub Copilot. As mentioned, Microsoft positions the 2026 version of Visual Studio as an AI-centric IDE, so when starting Visual Studio now, you will find GitHub Copilot Chat opened by default on the right side. And honestly, once you start using it, you'll wonder how you ever managed without it.

Opening a conversation is effortless. Whether Copilot Chat isn't visible for you or you just want to bring it into focus, you can press Ctrl+\+C or simply click the Copilot icon in the top-right corner of the toolbar. The chat window opens as a familiar conversational interface; you type what you want to accomplish, and Copilot responds with explanations, code suggestions, or direct edits.

What makes Copilot Chat different from just typing your question into a web browser is context. When you open the chat, Copilot knows your current file, your open files, your project structure, and even your build errors. This contextual awareness means your questions get far more relevant answers. Ask "How should I refactor this?" and Copilot understands what "this" is: the code you're looking at right now. That contextual loop creates a feedback system where each response builds on the previous conversation, letting you refine your approach iteratively.

Consider a practical scenario. You're building an ecommerce API endpoint that processes customer orders. You want it to handle various payment methods, validate input, and log transactions. Rather than writing everything from scratch, you could open Copilot Chat and ask: "I need to create an endpoint that accepts order data, validates customer payment method, and logs the transaction. What's a good structure?" Copilot analyzes your current project structure, sees what libraries you're using, and suggests an implementation that fits naturally with your existing code patterns. You can then ask follow-up questions: "How should I handle payment failures?" or "What logging should I add for compliance?" Each answer builds on the conversation and your actual code base context.

The conversation history persists within your Visual Studio session. If you close Copilot Chat and reopen it later, you'll see your previous conversations, making it easy to pick up where you left off. And because Copilot understands the evolution of your conversation, it can reference earlier context. You might ask, "What did you suggest before about error handling?" and it will recall and build on previous recommendations.

Of course, the above is a very simplified version of the truth. There is much more nuance in here; by just prompting one-liners, you're unlikely to get the results that you want. I could write an entire book just on working effectively with AI, but that's a bit outside of scope for now. In the next chapter, you will find some guidance and tools, but for a great experience, you might want to educate yourself a bit more beyond this.

In Figure 8-3, you can see the anatomy of the GitHub Copilot Chat window. I have numbered and colored the different sections for easier reference.

1. **Red:** At the top, you can open a drop-down with previous chats/sessions and revisit it to pick up where you left off. On the right of that, you can see a button to start a new chat and a button to delete the current thread.

2. **Green:** The bulk of the screen is where you will find the chat messages, both from yourself and Copilot. This has all the code, Copilot's "thoughts," and things it considered while making decisions. You can also see what tools it called, etc.

3. **Pink:** Right underneath the chat messages, you can see suggestions for follow-up questions that you can use.

4. **Blue:** With the plus button, you can add additional context for Copilot. This can be a variety of things: files in your code base, the whole solution, classes, methods, Output Window logs, MCP prompts or resources, an image, etc. Right next to that, you can see what is currently attached for the message to be sent. In this case, the Active Document.

5. **Purple:** The box where you can enter your message/prompt. At the bottom, you can set the mode: Ask or Agent and the model to be used. On the bottom-right, you can select the MCP tools that should be used for this prompt and the send button.

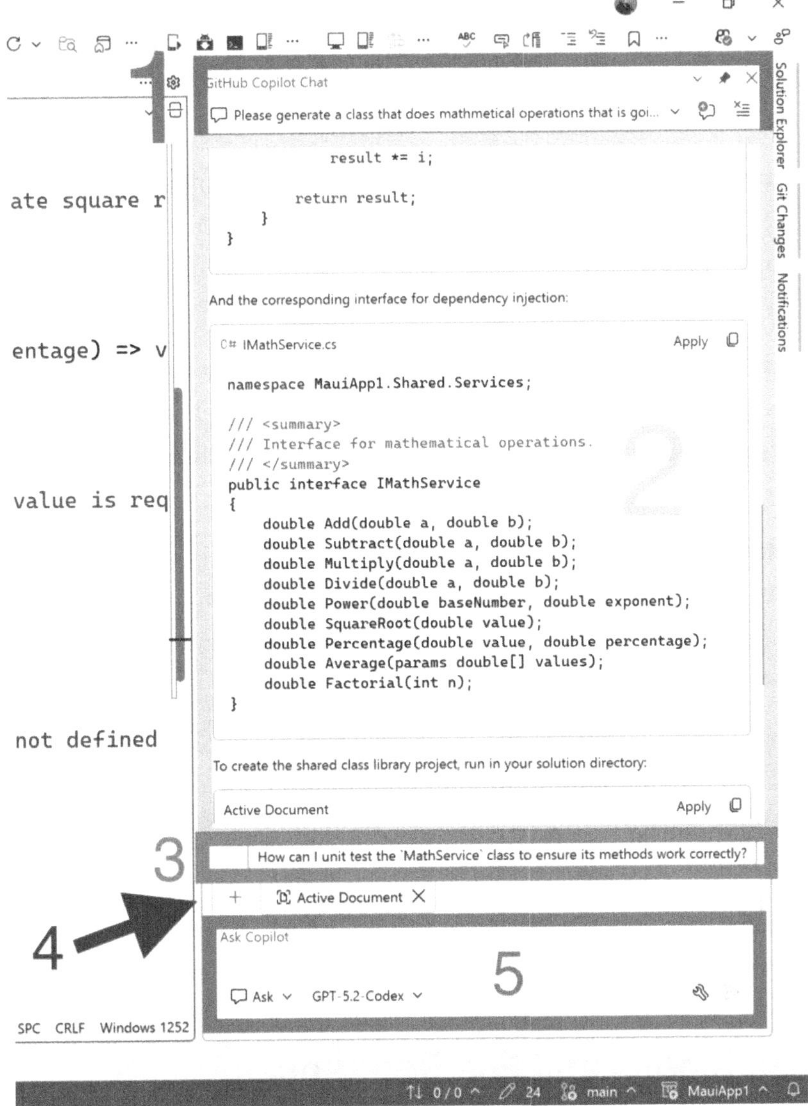

Figure 8-3. *The anatomy of the GitHub Copilot chat window*

Copilot Everywhere: Beyond the Chat Window

It's easy to think of GitHub Copilot as just a chat panel on the right side of your screen, but in Visual Studio 2026, AI is woven into the fabric of the IDE. You don't always have to go to Copilot; Copilot comes to you exactly where you are working:

- **Fix with Copilot**: When you get a red squiggle or build error, you no longer have to copy-paste the error into a search engine. Hovering over the error provides a "Fix with Copilot" option that analyzes the specific context of your broken code and offers an inline fix.

- **Inline Documentation**: Need to document a complex method? Simply type /// above a C# method, and Copilot will generate comprehensive XML documentation based on what the code actually does.

- **Source Control**: As we will see a bit more in Chapter 10, Copilot lives in the Git Changes window, generating accurate commit messages and providing preemptive PR reviews before you even push your code.

- **Feature Search**: If you don't know where a setting is in Visual Studio, pressing Ctrl+Q for the All-In-One search allows you to search for IDE features using natural language; Copilot translates your intent into the correct IDE menu option.

- **Inline Variable Debugging**: While paused at a breakpoint, hovering over complex objects allows Copilot to analyze the state of your variables and explain *why* a variable holds a certain value based on the previous execution path.

Some of these we have already seen, some we will see in what's still coming in this book, but just to illustrate that Copilot is an integral part of Visual Studio 2026.

Interaction Modes and File References

When you're asking Copilot for help, you have a few different interaction modes available. The default "Ask" mode is what we've been discussing: conversational help where Copilot provides explanations and suggestions. But there's more to discover as you get comfortable with the tool.

One of the most underrated features for quick questions is simply typing in the chat window without any specific mode. Ask Copilot about a language feature ("What's the difference between struct and class in C#?"), request explanations of concepts ("Explain dependency injection"), or ask for best practices ("What's the best way to handle cancellation tokens?"). These rapid-fire conversations keep you in flow because you don't have to leave the IDE or break your coding rhythm.

For more complex needs, you can reference files directly in your chat. Type `#filename` to bring specific files into context, or use `#errors` to include all build errors in your conversation. This scoping is powerful because sometimes you want to keep the conversation focused. If you're dealing with a compilation error and you ask Copilot for help, including `#errors` in your message gives Copilot exactly what it needs to understand the problem without cluttering the conversation with unrelated code.

Code Completion Features

Code completion has evolved significantly in Visual Studio 2026, and you'll see this in action immediately as you type. The most obvious manifestation is ghost text suggestions, those dimmed suggestions that appear at your cursor position as you code. As you type a function signature, Copilot suggests the body. As you start a loop, it predicts the iteration pattern. These suggestions are contextual to your project, so if you're using a specific library or following a pattern you've established elsewhere in the code base, Copilot learns that and suggests accordingly.

You don't have to accept entire suggestions. If Copilot suggests a full method but you only want the first few lines, use Ctrl+Right arrow to accept word-by-word, or Tab to move line-by-line through the suggestion. This granular acceptance means you're not forced into an all-or-nothing choice every time.

GitHub Copilot provides two kinds of inline suggestions in Visual Studio: traditional code completions (ghost text) and Next Edit Suggestions (NES). Completions help you finish the code you're currently typing at the cursor, while NES predicts where your next edit is likely to be, even if that's in a different part of the file, and proposes that change in place. As you refactor a class, for example, NES might detect that after renaming a method, you'll probably need to update its call sites and surface those edits directly where they should be applied. Both kinds of inline suggestions appear in the editor and can be accepted with familiar shortcuts such as Tab or word-by-word acceptance, so the experience feels cohesive even though the underlying behavior is different.

While Ask mode in Copilot Chat does not make any changes to code for you, it can, of course, make suggestions. Whenever you see a code block, you have the power to copy and paste it, or there are some context buttons to make your life easier and insert it directly at your cursor.

In Figure 8-4, you can see Copilot in Ask mode suggesting a new class.

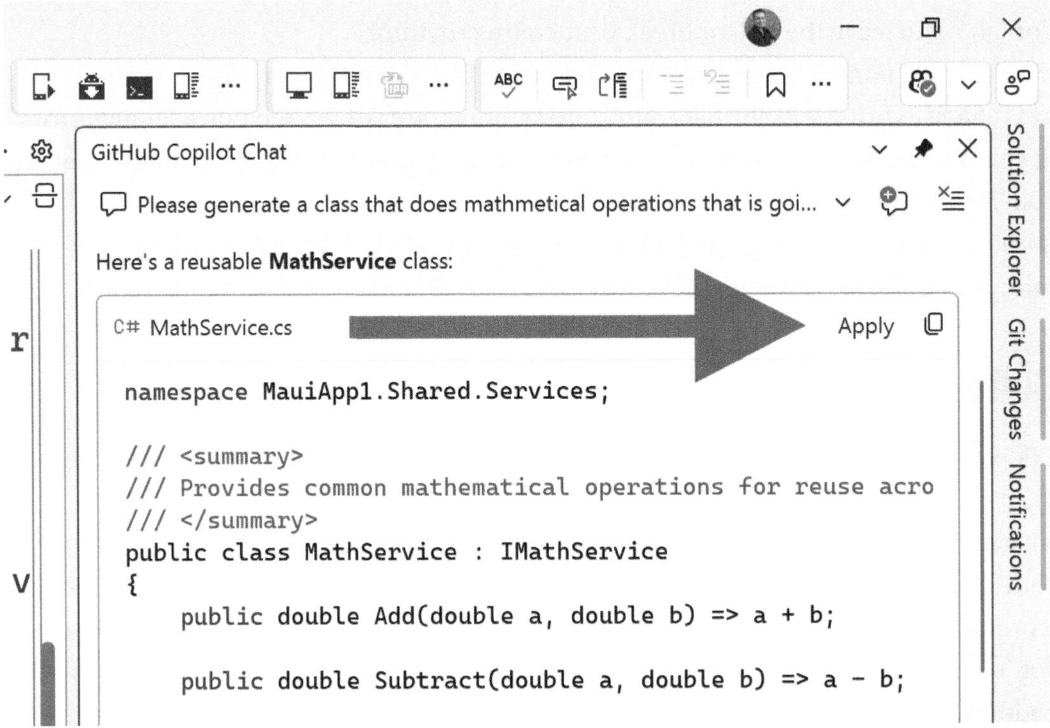

Figure 8-4. *The buttons to apply the suggested piece of code or copy it can be seen on top of a code block in Copilot chat with Ask mode*

However, if you want Copilot to be of *real* help, Agent mode is what you want to look at.

Agent Mode: Let Your AI Pair Programmer Take the Wheel

If Copilot Chat in Ask mode is your conversational assistant, Agent Mode is your autonomous pair programmer. This is where things get genuinely remarkable, and it's also where the rubber really meets the road in terms of productivity gains. Agent Mode is available through the Copilot Chat interface, and accessing it is straightforward: click the "Ask" button in the Copilot Chat window to expand the mode selector, then choose "Agent."

Here's what makes Agent Mode fundamentally different from regular chat. When you submit a request in Agent Mode, Copilot doesn't just suggest code: it plans, executes, and validates changes across multiple files autonomously. You describe what you want done at a high level ("Refactor the authentication system to use OAuth 2.0 instead of username/password"), and Agent Mode goes to work. It creates a plan (optionally, enable through Tools ➤ Options ➤ GitHub ➤ Copilot ➤ Copilot Chat, and check Enable Planning), applies the changes, runs tests, encounters problems, self-corrects, and iterates until the task is complete. As mentioned before, it all starts with the ability to craft good prompts and have supporting instructions and skills, but once you know how to work with it, it is very powerful!

Figure 8-5 shows Copilot Chat using Agent mode where it has been asked to implement code and then add tests and run them and refine them until they all pass. You can see that whenever it calls a command or tool, it will ask for permission. But you also have options to always allow the command or just for this session.

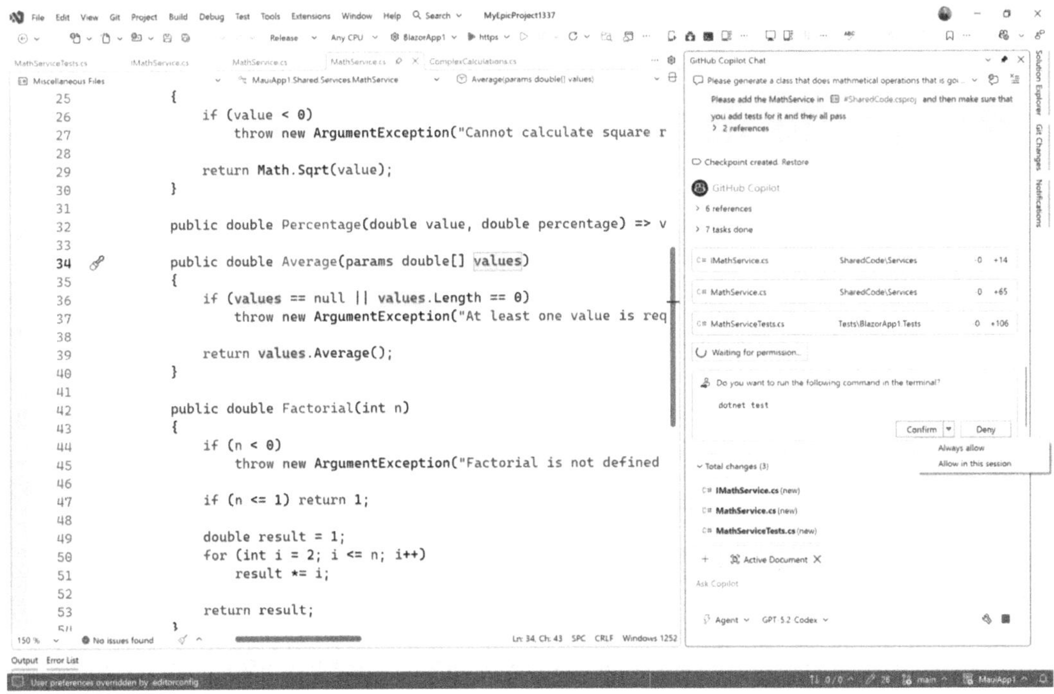

Figure 8-5. *Copilot Chat in Agent mode autonomously implementing code, writing the tests, and running them to make sure they succeed*

How Agent Mode Works

The planning aspect is crucial. When Agent Mode tackles a complex task, it first creates a user-visible markdown plan that outlines the goal, breaks it down into steps, and shows progress as it works through each step. This transparency is important because you can see exactly what the agent intends to do before it does it. The agent also maintains an internal JSON plan that serves as an LLM-readable scratchpad, allowing it to track state, reasoning, and coordination across multiple operations. This structured approach means Agent Mode doesn't get lost in complex refactorings; it knows where it's been and where it's going.

At the time of writing, you need to manually enable this through Tools ➤ Options ➤ GitHub ➤ Copilot ➤ Copilot Chat and find Enable Planning. I wouldn't be surprised if this is on by default by the time you read this.

As Agent Mode executes, it uses a set of built-in tools to accomplish its work. It can read and edit files, run terminal commands, interpret build errors, and respond to output. For example, if the agent applies code changes that create new compilation errors, it recognizes those errors from the build output, understands what went wrong, and adjusts its approach. It might try a different implementation, or it might ask clarifying questions if it can't resolve the issue. Also, you stay in control; it won't format your hard drive without your consent, and you will have to allow each terminal command or tool it runs. Of course, you do have the option to allow all commands, and...make sure you always have a backup!

The self-healing aspect is where Agent Mode really shines. If a suggested edit creates a syntax error or breaks a test, Agent Mode detects this, learns from the failure, and tries a different approach. This iterative loop continues until the task is complete. You're not stuck troubleshooting what the agent did wrong; the agent troubleshoots itself.

Practical Examples and Best Use Cases

You control how Agent Mode operates through the Tools panel in the Copilot Chat window. By default, Agent Mode has access to standard tools like file editing, command execution, and error analysis. But you can extend this through Model Context Protocol (MCP) tools, which we'll explore in depth in Chapter 9. This extensibility means if there's a specific tool or service your team uses, you can connect it to Agent Mode and let the agent use it as part of its workflow.

A practical example: you're maintaining a legacy C# application, and you want to upgrade it to use dependency injection throughout. Instead of manually finding every place that creates objects directly, writing the DI registrations, updating constructors, and refactoring call sites, you describe the task to Agent Mode: "Add dependency injection using Microsoft.Extensions.DependencyInjection throughout this solution." Agent Mode creates a plan, identifies all the places where changes are needed, updates the service configuration, modifies constructors to accept dependencies, and refactors the call sites. It tests as it goes, handles edge cases, and completes the refactoring in minutes instead of hours. You can also use the Modernization agent. We will learn about that a little later on.

Another scenario: you've discovered a security vulnerability in how your API validates input. You need to add validation across multiple endpoints. Rather than manually touching every endpoint, you prompt Agent Mode: "Add input validation using FluentValidation to all API endpoints." The agent identifies every endpoint, creates validators for the request models, integrates them into the request pipeline, and adds exception handling for validation failures. You review the changes and either accept the whole thing or iterate with follow-up instructions.

The key insight is that Agent Mode is best for multi-step, multi-file tasks that would typically consume hours of focused work. It's less useful for single-file changes or when you're exploring, those are typically better handled with inline chat or Copilot Chat in regular Ask mode. But when you have a large refactoring, a pattern you want to apply across your code base, or a systematic change that touches many files, Agent Mode can be transformative.

Hopefully, this is stating the obvious, but just to be sure: however powerful Agent mode and any other solution may seem, it's still always your responsibility to review its changes. While Agent Mode does its own testing and validation, you should always review what it's done, run your full test suite, and verify that the implementation matches your requirements. Think of it as a very capable junior developer who needs code review, not as a replacement for your judgment.

Bring Your Own Model: Choosing Your Own AI Engine

One of the most interesting features in Visual Studio 2026 is the ability to use different AI models for Copilot Chat. This addresses a very real need for organizations that have preferences about which AI providers they work with, compliance requirements about where their data flows, or simply want to use models they've found work better for their specific domain.

The feature is called Bring Your Own Model (BYOM), and it's scoped specifically to Copilot Chat, not to inline completions or other AI features, but to the conversational chat experience. This is important because it gives you a choice while keeping the baseline coding experience consistent.

Accessing BYOM is straightforward. In the Copilot Chat window, look for the model selector in the bottom area of the chat, where you enter your prompts. Click "Manage Models" to open the configuration. You'll see a list of available providers, and, if you have an API key from one of those providers, you can paste it in and add your custom model.

Supported providers include OpenAI, Anthropic, Google, and others. Crucially for enterprise developers, BYOM also includes deep support for Azure AI Foundry. This means if your organization has deployed custom, fine-tuned, or compliance-restricted models inside your own Azure tenant, you can connect Visual Studio directly to your Azure AI Foundry endpoints. This gives you the full power of Copilot while ensuring your code and data never leave your company's controlled Azure environment. Be sure to check the BYOM configuration dialog in Visual Studio for the current list of supported models and providers.

Be aware that different models may have different model multipliers affecting your premium request consumption. For example, some advanced reasoning models might consume more premium requests per use than standard models, so your choice of model can directly impact your premium request budget. Checking the model multipliers in your Copilot settings can help you choose models that fit your premium request quota. If your organization runs models locally using Ollama or another local inference server, you can configure that too. Once you've added a model, it appears in your model selector, and you can switch between models on a per-conversation basis. You might use one model for quick coding questions and another for deeper architectural discussions, depending on which you find more capable for each task.

The practical value of BYOM becomes clear when you consider organizational requirements. A company with strict data residency policies might use a self-hosted model. A team that has standardized on a particular provider because they find it better for documentation might want to use that everywhere. A startup experimenting with the latest capabilities might rotate between different models to evaluate them. BYOM gives you that flexibility without being locked into a single provider.

Note   At the time of writing, using a custom model is not available for Copilot Business or Copilot Enterprise users.

Inline Chat: Staying in the Flow

Sometimes you don't need a full conversation in the chat pane. You just want to ask a quick question or make a small change without shifting your attention to the side panel. That's where inline chat comes in. Press Alt+/ (or right-click and select "Ask Copilot") to open an inline chat session directly in the editor.

Inline chat appears as a small input field overlaid on your code, and you can ask questions or request changes that apply directly to the selected code or the file you're working in. Ask "Can you add error handling here?" and Copilot shows a diff of the proposed changes right in your editor. Accept with the Accept button or keyboard shortcut, or reject and try a different approach.

Inline chat is particularly useful for quick refactorings, adding specific features to a method, or understanding a chunk of code. It's faster than opening the full chat panel because you stay focused on the editor. The conversation context is still available; you can see the history and references, but the UI is lighter and more focused on the immediate task.

In Figure 8-6, you can see what this looks like.

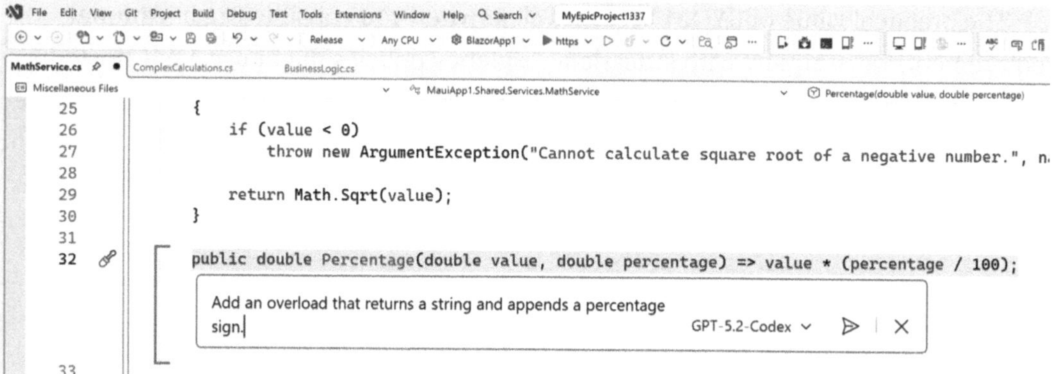

Figure 8-6. *An inline Copilot chat where I ask it to add an overload for a method*

If an inline chat conversation grows and you want to move it to the full chat panel to continue with more context and history, you can click "Continue in Chat Window", and it promotes the entire inline thread to the main Copilot Chat panel, preserving everything you've discussed.

Git and Code Review with Copilot

GitHub Copilot's impact in Visual Studio 2026 goes beyond writing and refactoring code in the editor; it also shows up in your Git workflows. From the Git Changes window, you can use Copilot to generate commit messages that summarize your staged changes, so you spend less time wordsmithing and more time coding. Copilot analyzes the diff, understands the code semantics, and proposes a descriptive commit message that you can tweak before committing.

Copilot can also help with code review. Before you ever open a pull request, you can ask Copilot to review your local changes directly from Visual Studio; it highlights potential issues, suggests improvements, and leaves inline comments that you can click through and address. These capabilities tie the AI story from this chapter into your day-to-day collaboration: Copilot assists not only while you're writing code but also when you're explaining and reviewing it. We'll explore the full Git workflow, including AI-generated commit messages and Copilot-powered reviews, in much more detail in Chapter 10.

Copilot Edits: Multi-file Refactoring with Review

Agent Mode is powerful for autonomous changes, but sometimes you want more control and visibility into a multi-file edit before it's applied. That's where Copilot Edits comes in. Copilot Edits creates a dedicated thread for making coordinated changes across multiple files with an inline code review experience built in.

You can start a Copilot Edits session from the Copilot Chat window (look for the Edits thread button, typically represented by a pencil icon with a plus), or you can right-click in the editor and select "Ask Copilot" with an edit intent. Describe the changes you want, and Copilot Edits will propose changes across the files it identifies as relevant.

The key difference from Agent Mode is the workflow. Copilot Edits shows you the proposed changes, lets you review each file's diff, and you decide whether to apply each change individually or as a batch. You can also iterate: reject a change if it's not quite right, ask for modifications, and see the new proposals. This is especially useful when you're working with code you're less familiar with, because you get to validate each change before it's applied.

You can scope Copilot Edits by specifying which files to work with. Use the # symbol to reference specific files (`#Program.cs` or `#UserService.cs`), or use context selectors like `#errors` to include files related to compilation errors. This scoping helps Copilot focus on the right parts of your code base.

Debugging with Copilot: Finding Root Causes Faster

One of the most transformative uses of AI in Visual Studio 2026 is in debugging workflows. Debugging has always been a tedious process; setting breakpoints, stepping through code, inspecting variables, reading error messages, and trying to understand what went wrong. Now, Copilot can assist with most of these tasks.

We've already seen this in more depth in Chapters 5 and 6, but just to have the full AI story overview here as well, let's quickly touch again on what is available.

Exception Analysis

Let's start with exception handling. When your application throws an exception and you're looking at the Exception Helper dialog, you'll see an "Ask Copilot" button. Click it, and Copilot performs a detailed analysis of the exception, examining the stack trace, understanding the code paths that led to the crash, and even searching your repository history for similar issues or past fixes.

In Figure 8-7, you can see the (probably familiar) exception window in Visual Studio. What is new is that you can now dig into details with the help of Copilot.

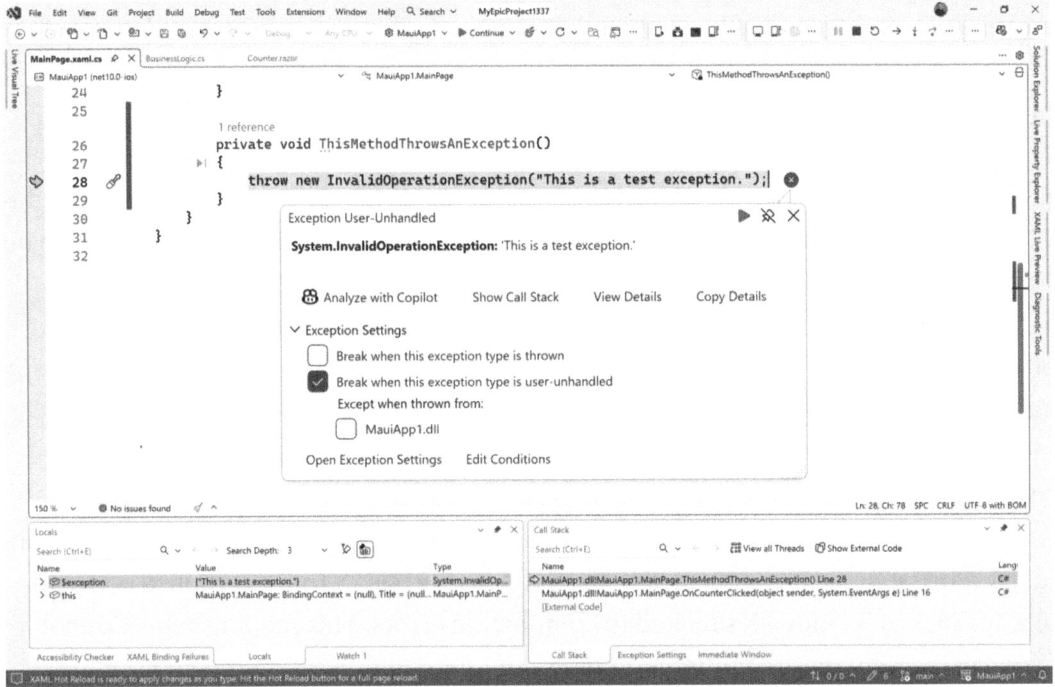

Figure 8-7. *Analyzing exceptions with the help of GitHub Copilot*

What's remarkable is the depth of this analysis. Copilot doesn't just read the error message and make a generic suggestion. It understands your code base, looks at recent changes, examines the data flow, and provides a contextual explanation of what went wrong. For complex exceptions involving nested errors or subtle logic issues, you can ask Copilot to dig deeper into the analysis, adding more context and potentially identifying issues you might have missed.

Variable and Expression Analysis

While debugging a running application, you might hover over a variable to see its value, and Copilot can help you understand unexpected results. If a variable shows a value you didn't expect, hover over it and select "Analyze with Copilot." Copilot breaks down the condition or expression sub-expression-by-sub-expression, showing you which part failed and how that led to the unexpected value. This is far more efficient than stepping through every line of code.

Breakpoint management has evolved as well. If you set a breakpoint and it becomes unbound (e.g., because code was refactored and the line no longer exists), Visual Studio will suggest asking Copilot for help. Copilot performs a deeper analysis. It checks for symbol issues, loaded modules, build mismatches, and more and often can resolve the issue with a single click. This removes the tedium from broken breakpoint debugging.

Debugger Agent for Failed Tests

As we have seen already in Chapter 6, there's also a Debugger Agent that assists with failed tests. When a test fails and you're trying to understand why, the Debugger Agent can automatically set breakpoints at relevant locations in the test and the code being tested, then run the test under the debugger and collect diagnostic information. It can then analyze the results and propose fixes. This is particularly valuable for complex test failures that require investigation. If you need a refresher, go back to Chapter 6 for a more in-depth description.

Introducing IntelliCode: Smart Code Completion Beyond the Basics

While GitHub Copilot handles the conversational AI and advanced features we've discussed, Visual Studio 2026 also includes IntelliCode, a complementary AI system that enhances basic code completion and refactoring suggestions. IntelliCode analyzes thousands of open source projects on GitHub to understand common coding patterns, and it uses that knowledge to improve your IntelliSense suggestions.

Where You'll See IntelliCode

Where you'll see IntelliCode is right where you'd expect, integrated seamlessly into the standard IntelliSense completion list that appears as you type. When you press Ctrl+Space to open completions or just start typing and IntelliSense appears automatically, you'll notice that certain items are marked with a star icon (★). These starred recommendations are IntelliCode's AI-powered suggestions for what you're most likely to type next, ranked based on your code context and common patterns from thousands of high-quality open source projects. Instead of hunting through an alphabetical list, the most relevant methods, properties, and classes appear at the top.

Features and Capabilities

IntelliCode also provides whole-line completions in C#. As you type, you might see a gray suggestion that completes your entire statement. For example, you start typing `var user =` and IntelliCode suggests `new User()` in gray text, also called "ghost text." Press Tab to accept it and keep moving. This feature learns from your code base and common patterns, so the suggestions become increasingly accurate for your project's style.

Another feature worth knowing about is argument completion. When you call a method with multiple overloads or parameters, IntelliCode highlights the overload that best matches the types and variables currently in scope, saving you from clicking through tooltip pages to find the right variant. For C# specifically, IntelliCode also detects when you're making repetitive edits. Make the same code change two or three times, like refactoring method signatures or adding a logging statement in the same pattern, and IntelliCode proposes applying that same change everywhere else in your code base. You can see the suggestions as Quick Actions (the lightbulb icon) and apply them with a single click.

The Philosophy of IntelliCode

The thing about IntelliCode is that it's designed to be invisible in the best way possible. You don't need to learn new commands or workflows. It just works as part of the IntelliSense experience you already use every day. Your code suggestions are now powered by AI—they're ranked by relevance rather than alphabetically, whole lines are completed when the intent is obvious, and repetitive patterns are detected automatically. It's one of those features that, once you're used to it, feels like the baseline and you'd miss it if it were gone.

IntelliCode is included by default in most Visual Studio workloads and is enabled automatically. If you ever want to customize it, like disabling it for a specific language or adjusting settings, you can find IntelliCode options under Tools > Options > IntelliCode. But for most developers, the out-of-the-box experience is exactly what you want.

IntelliCode also helps with whole-line completions in C#, automatically filling in common code patterns once it recognizes what you're trying to do. It's subtly intelligent without being intrusive.

For more information on IntelliCode capabilities and where to enable it, see `https://visualstudio.microsoft.com/services/intellicode/`.

Code Generation and Scaffolding: Getting Started Faster

One of the quickest wins with Copilot is in code generation and scaffolding. When you're starting a new class, new test, or new file, Copilot can generate significant portions of the structure based on context.

For example, if you're creating a unit test for an existing service, open a new test file and ask Copilot: "Write tests for the UserService." Copilot generates test methods covering the main functionality, uses the appropriate testing framework for your project, follows the testing patterns it sees in your code base, and includes proper setup and assertions. You'll still need to review and refine, as not all AI-generated tests are equally perfect, but you're starting from a substantial foundation rather than a blank page.

Similarly, when creating a new API controller, Copilot can scaffold the endpoints, add proper attribute routing, include validation, and follow the patterns your team has established. When creating a new data model, Copilot can generate properties, add data annotations for validation, and set up entity framework mappings.

This scaffolding saves time on boilerplate, but more importantly, it ensures consistency. Copilot learns the patterns in your code base and replicates them, so new code you generate fits naturally with the existing style and structure.

Copilot As a Teacher: Understanding and Learning Code

As I mentioned a little earlier, familiarizing yourself with a code base is a big part of being a software developer. Over time, we have invented all kinds of tools to help with that, ranging from analyzers that help keep the code style consistent to a VS Code extension that can trigger a self-paced tour through a code base.

Beyond generating and modifying code, Copilot is a valuable tool for understanding code you didn't write. When you inherit a code base, onboard to a new project, or encounter unfamiliar patterns, you can ask Copilot to explain what's happening.

Select a chunk of code and ask, "Explain this function" or "What does this LINQ query do?" Copilot provides clear explanations that help you understand the intent and implementation. You can ask follow-up questions: "Why is it done this way instead of...?" or "How would I extend this to handle...?"

This learning-through-conversation approach is particularly effective for domain-specific code or complex algorithms. Rather than trying to reverse-engineer what's happening by reading line-by-line, you can discuss the code with Copilot and build mental models faster.

Refactoring with Confidence: When Old Code Needs New Life

One of the more ambitious uses of Copilot is refactoring legacy code. Old code bases often have accumulated technical debt, outdated patterns, or performance issues. Refactoring is valuable but risky. Change too much at once and you introduce bugs; change too little and you don't realize meaningful improvement.

Copilot helps by suggesting refactorings that are incremental, justified, and testable. Ask "What refactorings would improve this code?" and Copilot analyzes it against modern patterns, suggests specific improvements (extract method, consolidate conditionals, remove duplication), and can implement them with Agent Mode while maintaining test coverage.

You can also refactor in specific directions. "Refactor this code to use async/await," "Extract this into a separate class," "Add dependency injection," or "Migrate this to LINQ" are all things Copilot can assist with. The key is that you maintain control: you see proposals, review them, and decide whether to accept.

Knowing When to Use AI and When to Rely on Your Judgment

As the old (software developers') saying goes: it depends. You probably have heard about the term vibe coding. Depending on who you ask, it might mean different things, but I think for most it describes a way of developing software solely trusting AI to do all the right things, not caring too much about the code quality and focusing on whether it works functionally.

If you're building a prototype or hobby project, absolutely go for it! However, in a more business environment, or even as a single developer with the intention of having others use your product, you probably want to do a bit more.

It also depends on the potentially existing code base and what you're trying to build. At the time of writing, I work on the .NET MAUI code base, which is a big, complex code base with a lot of history. But also a lot of tests! That means that whenever I work with Copilot and even though I didn't inspect every line of code, as long as the existing tests pass, I can be pretty confident that I didn't introduce any regressions.

I think the bottom line is that you should always rely on your own judgement, but you can still inform yourself with, you guessed it, Copilot. Ask it about certain things it did, do look at the tests it wrote, the plans it might have made for itself, etc. I have noticed about myself that I needed to let go a little bit, in addition to thinking about things differently, to adapt to this new era.

Instead of immediately starting to write code, I now think more in terms of maybe a functional designer. What is the relevant context I need to give someone else (Copilot in this case) to know enough to work on this. But also: what are the boundaries, the rail guards I need to provide so that I get what I want out of this. What do I want it to implement but also be specific about what you *don't* want it to do. The better you get at that, the better you get at prompting and crafting a plan, and the better you will get at AI-assisted development and stay ahead of the curve.

Luckily, Visual Studio 2026 has everything to make you successful with this.

Refactoring at Application Scale with the Modernization Agent

So far, we've seen how Copilot's Test agent and Profiler Agent can help you stabilize and optimize existing code, but there's one more specialized helper we haven't covered yet: the app Modernization agent. This agent focuses on upgrading and modernizing entire applications rather than just individual files or classes.

When you invoke the Modernization agent on a .NET solution, it starts by assessing your project: it analyzes your project structure, dependencies, frameworks, and code patterns, then produces an assessment document that highlights outdated frameworks, deprecated APIs, and likely migration blockers. From there, it generates a modernization plan, typically captured in Markdown, that outlines recommended target versions, required code changes, and the order in which to tackle them so you can upgrade safely instead of improvising the migration as you go.

Once the plan is in place, the modernization agent can apply code transformations in stages: updating project files to new .NET versions, replacing deprecated APIs, adjusting configuration for cloud readiness, and even preparing code for containerization and Azure deployment where appropriate. It iterates through the plan, updating code, patching builds, and re-running tests along the way, so you can modernize with a feedback loop instead of a risky big-bang rewrite.

To get started with this experience, just right-click on a project in the Solution Explorer, and you will find the Modernize option with a Copilot Agent icon. Click that, and Copilot Chat opens with a pre-set context of modernizing the selected project. You can just continue prompting from there or explore the options. This basically is the evolution of the .NET Upgrade Assistant, now AI-powered.

Beyond Visual Studio: Complementary AI Tools for the Modern Developer

While GitHub Copilot is the centerpiece of Visual Studio 2026's AI capabilities, the broader ecosystem offers other tools that can enhance your development workflow when used alongside it. This section ventures a bit outside our strict focus on Visual Studio, but these tools work beautifully in complement with what you've learned here.

GitHub Copilot CLI is a command-line tool that extends Copilot's capabilities to your terminal and shell environment. Instead of just working in the editor, you can ask Copilot for help with git commands, debugging shell scripts, understanding error messages, or generating command-line operations. If you're trying to remember the exact syntax for a complex git rebase or need to write a Bash script to automate deployment, Copilot CLI can suggest the right commands. It's particularly useful for developers who spend significant time in the terminal. At the end of the day, it can do the same thing as Copilot in Visual Studio, but you can keep it running in a terminal window in the background or even when you have to step away from your desk. I see more and more developers who don't even open the IDE anymore, but solely work with GitHub Copilot CLI.

Then there's Copilot for Azure, which brings AI assistance into your cloud infrastructure work. If you're deploying applications to Azure or managing cloud resources, Copilot for Azure can help you write Infrastructure as Code (IaC) templates, troubleshoot connectivity issues, optimize resource configurations, and understand Azure's APIs. The integration with your development workflow means you don't have to switch contexts between development and infrastructure tasks. And let's be honest, you probably have seen Copilot in Word, Excel, Teams, and Windows. But let's focus on software development. What I do want to say with this, though, is that you can leverage Copilot everywhere, so use it to your advantage!

For teams working on documentation, Copilot can assist with technical writing through various markdown editors and documentation platforms. Generating API documentation, writing README files, or maintaining architecture decision records becomes faster when you can ask Copilot to draft sections or explain code concepts in prose form.

At the organizational level, GitHub Enterprise Server offers Copilot integration with enhanced security controls, audit logging, and support for custom models. If your organization has strict compliance requirements or runs development infrastructure on-premises, Enterprise Server provides a way to gain Copilot's benefits while maintaining full control over data and infrastructure.

The beauty of this ecosystem is that these tools all share a common interface and philosophy; you're conversing with AI to accelerate your work, whether that's in your editor, on the command line, in the cloud console, or in your documentation system. Once you're comfortable with Copilot in Visual Studio 2026, you'll find yourself naturally extending those skills to other parts of your development workflow.

Lastly, GitHub.com (so the web interface) itself provides a Copilot interface for developers who prefer working through the web. You can use Copilot Chat directly on GitHub.com to discuss code in your repositories, review pull requests, ask questions about project structure, and even interact with Copilot Spaces (`https://docs.github.com/copilot/concepts/context/spaces`), centralized locations that aggregate relevant code, documentation, and specifications for a particular task. The web interface provides a lightweight way to interact with Copilot without opening an IDE, which can be useful for code reviews, documentation work, or quick questions about your projects. And it all blends together perfectly as well: you can start a cloud session for Copilot on GitHub.com, and you can pick up the conversation from Visual Studio (Code). And vice versa!

Additionally, GitHub Desktop has integrated Copilot support for automatically generating commit messages based on your changes. However, for the deep, integrated IDE experience with full Agent Mode capabilities, real-time debugging integration, and seamless multi-file refactoring, Visual Studio 2026 remains the most comprehensive Copilot environment. The feature set on GitHub.com complements the IDE experience rather than replacing it, serving different use cases depending on where you're working in your development workflow.

AI-Powered Development Across the Ecosystem: You're Not Locked In

I already hinted at this a little bit, but let me state it one more time: a lot of what we've covered in this chapter is also available in Visual Studio Code, and the experience is remarkably similar. If you're familiar with Copilot Chat, inline suggestions, and Agent Mode in Visual Studio 2026, you'll feel right at home in VS Code, where those same features are available with a nearly identical user experience.

This is particularly valuable if you work on cross-platform projects, contribute to open source projects that use different editors, or collaborate with teams that prefer different development environments. The keyboard shortcuts are often the same depending on your chosen configuration, the feature sets are closely aligned, and the underlying Copilot capabilities are identical. You're not learning Visual Studio-specific AI workflows that won't transfer elsewhere.

This cross-platform consistency means your investment in learning how to use AI effectively in development isn't tied to a single IDE. You can develop strong habits and patterns using Copilot in Visual Studio 2026, and those skills translate directly when you're working in VS Code or any other editor that supports Copilot. It's part of why AI-powered development is becoming the standard across the industry rather than a tool-specific feature.

The implication is that as you build expertise with these AI features, you're not just becoming better at Visual Studio 2026. You're building skills that will serve you across your entire development toolkit. Copilot's design philosophy emphasizes being available wherever developers work, rather than being locked into a particular IDE or platform. This makes AI assistance in development feel less like a feature you're using and more like a natural extension of how you work.

Summary

This chapter has explored how GitHub Copilot transforms individual development productivity in Visual Studio 2026. Starting with basic setup, getting a GitHub account, and choosing a subscription plan. You've learned how to track usage and manage spending through the Copilot dashboard. The conversational Copilot Chat interface provides contextual coding assistance that grows smarter as you work with your actual code base, while ghost text and inline suggestions keep you in flow without breaking focus.

The real power emerges with Agent Mode, which lets you hand off multi-file refactorings to an autonomous AI that self-corrects and iterates until the job is done. Bring Your Own Model gives you control over which AI providers you use, while inline chat and Copilot Edits offer different workflows depending on your needs: quick feedback or careful review. IntelliCode complements these features by providing AI-powered code completion that ranks suggestions by relevance and detects repetitive patterns. Debugging becomes faster through Copilot's exception analysis and test failure diagnosis.

Beyond Visual Studio, tools like Copilot CLI and Copilot for Azure extend these capabilities to your terminal and cloud infrastructure. The key insight is to use these as productivity accelerators while you remain the architect; they're most powerful for reducing boilerplate and exploring approaches, supplementary to your judgment on architecture and security decisions.

Because the Copilot experience is consistent across Visual Studio 2026, VS Code, and other editors, the skills you've learned here transfer across your entire development toolkit. You're not locked into a single IDE; you're building broadly applicable expertise.

In the next chapter, we shift focus to extending and customizing Copilot for your specific needs. You'll learn how to tailor Copilot to your team's standards through custom instructions, agents, and prompt files and how to connect it to your actual infrastructure through Model Context Protocol, transforming AI assistance from general suggestions to deeply contextual solutions.

CHAPTER 9

AI Customization and Model Context Protocol

In the previous chapter, you learned the fundamentals of GitHub Copilot and how it transforms individual development productivity. You discovered Agent Mode, inline chat, debugging assistance, and IntelliCode. These core features handle the majority of what most developers need from AI in their daily workflow.

But here's where it gets truly powerful: customization and infrastructure integration. While Copilot is exceptionally capable out of the box, Visual Studio 2026 enables you to extend it to match your team's specific standards, connect it to your actual infrastructure, and transform it from a general assistant into a deeply contextual tool that understands your code base, your architecture, and your business logic.

This chapter explores how to bend Copilot to your will: embedding your team's coding practices directly into how it behaves, creating specialized agents for particular workflows, and most importantly, connecting it to your real-world infrastructure through Model Context Protocol. By the end, you'll understand how to make Copilot work for your specific context rather than adapting your workflow to fit a generic tool.

A lot of what you will learn in this chapter will also apply to the AI tooling outside of Visual Studio 2026. Copilot instructions will also be picked up by VS Code, but also Copilot on GitHub.com; prompts can also be reused in other ways, custom agents can be selected across the ecosystem, etc. Most of what you will learn in this chapter will be useful far outside of Visual Studio 2026 as well.

Most, if not all, of the things to customize the AI workflow consist of Markdown files that are saved within the repository, so they are available everywhere, to everyone, and every tool.

© Gerald Versluis 2026
G. Versluis, *Getting Started with Visual Studio 2026*, https://doi.org/10.1007/979-8-8688-2691-7_9

> **Note**   One thing I have noticed while working on Skills in particular is that the folder you save them in needs to be an actual Git repository. If things don't seem to work, make sure to run `git init` on your folder and initialize a Git repository, which might make things work better.

Before we really dive in, I want to acknowledge the fact that this whole chapter strays a bit from the main topic, Visual Studio. But I do think that everything in here is very important to stay relevant as a software developer, and therefore, you should know how to use it and how to use it with Visual Studio. That is why I decided to include this here; I hope you can appreciate that!

Tailoring Copilot to Your Workflow: Custom Instructions, Agents, and Prompt Files

While Copilot out of the box is powerful, Visual Studio 2026 enables you to customize it to match your team's coding standards, project requirements, and development practices. Rather than repeating the same context in every prompt, you can define custom instructions, agents, and prompt files that automatically influence how Copilot behaves.

Custom Instructions: Embedding Your Standards

Custom instructions are the most straightforward way to guide Copilot's behavior. Instead of manually including coding guidelines in every chat prompt, you create a Markdown file with your team's standards, and Copilot automatically considers those instructions when generating code.

In Visual Studio 2026, you can create a `.github/copilot-instructions.md` file in your workspace root. This file contains your team's conventions in natural language: coding style preferences, framework patterns, security requirements, or naming conventions. Once created, Copilot automatically applies these instructions to all chat requests within that workspace.

For example, your instructions might include guidelines like: "Always use async/await instead of callbacks," "Validate all user input before processing," "Use dependency injection for all services,x" or "Follow the naming convention of PascalCase for public methods." You don't need to repeat these directives in every prompt; Copilot learns from the instructions file.

For more granular control, you can create multiple .instructions.md files that apply only to specific file types or project areas. Using YAML frontmatter with the `applyTo` property, you can specify glob patterns to target particular files. For instance, you might have a `testing.instructions.md` file that applies only to test files (`**/*.test.cs`) or a `security.instructions.md` that applies to authentication-related files. This keeps your instructions focused and prevents irrelevant guidelines from cluttering Copilot's context.

If you're unsure where to start, Visual Studio can help. In the Copilot Chat window, select Configure Chat (the gear icon) ➤ Generate Chat Instructions, and Copilot will analyze your workspace and generate a matching `.github/copilot-instructions.md` file that reflects your existing coding practices and project structure. Of course, you can then review and refine the generated instructions; it's just a starting point which already saves you a great amount of work.

For more information about instructions, please refer to the GitHub documentation: `https://docs.github.com/copilot/how-tos/configure-custom-instructions/add-repository-instructions?tool=visualstudio`.

Custom Agents: Specialized AI Personas for Specific Tasks

While custom instructions guide how Copilot behaves generally, Custom Agents let you switch to a specialized AI persona optimized for a specific workflow. An agent is a configured instance of Copilot that is tailored for a particular task. One might be optimized for planning architecture, another for writing tests, and another for refactoring legacy code.

Visual Studio 2026 now ships with several powerful built-in agents designed to tap into the IDE's deep capabilities:

- **@debugger**: Goes far beyond just reading error messages. It uses your current call stacks, variable states, and diagnostic tools to walk you through error diagnosis systematically across your solution.

- **@profiler**: Connects directly to Visual Studio's profiling infrastructure to identify bottlenecks and suggest targeted optimizations grounded in your actual code base trace data.

- **@test**: Generates unit tests tuned to your project's framework (xUnit, NUnit, MSTest) and patterns, avoiding the generic boilerplate that CI pipelines often reject.

- **@modernize**: (Specific to .NET and C++) Focused on framework and dependency upgrades. It analyzes your actual project graph to flag breaking changes, generate migration code, and ensure you follow new patterns.

You can access these agents anytime by selecting them from the agent picker in the chat panel or by simply typing @ in the chat.

Building Your Own Custom Agents

Beyond the built-in presets, Visual Studio 2026 allows you to define your own Custom Agents to match your team's specific workflow. This is where the power of the Model Context Protocol (MCP) really shines; you can connect a custom agent to external knowledge sources like internal documentation, design systems, or databases, so the agent isn't limited to just what is in your local repository.

To create a custom agent, you simply add a definition file to your repository in the `.github/agents/` folder. The file uses the `.agent.md` extension (e.g., `code-reviewer.agent.md`) and defines the agent's behavior, personality, and allowed tools using Markdown and YAML frontmatter.

If you or your team mix and match with Visual Studio and VS Code, then I have some good news. This exact same `.agent.md` format is fully supported by Visual Studio Code. If you define a custom agent and check it into your repository, team members using Visual Studio 2026, Visual Studio Code, or the GitHub Copilot coding agent will all have access to the exact same customized AI agents, because they all understand the shared `.agent.md` format.

In Listing 9-1, you can see a sample custom agent definition.

Listing 9-1. A simple custom agent for doing security reviews

```
---
name: "security-reviewer"
description: "An agent specialized in finding and fixing security
vulnerabilities"
system_prompt: |
  You are a security expert. Your goal is to review code for common
  vulnerabilities
  such as SQL injection, XSS, and insecure deserialization.
  Always prioritize secure coding practices over performance.
  When you find an issue, explain the vulnerability and provide a secure
  alternative.
tools:
  - name: "github-search"
  - name: "file-search"

---

# Security Review Guidelines

1. **Validate all inputs**: Never trust user input.
2. **Use parameterized queries**: Prevent SQL injection.
3. **Encode output**: Prevent XSS.
```

An `.agent.md` file includes YAML frontmatter where you specify

- **Name:** The name of this agent as shown in the UI.

- **Description:** What this agent does.

- **Tools:** Which tools the agent can use (file editing, command execution, search, fetch, etc.).

- **System Prompt:** The core instructions that define the agent's personality and approach. This is the body of the Markdown file.

- **Model:** Which AI model this agent should use (if you want it to be different from your default, this is a suggestion anyway; depending on the tool used, people can still select a different agent).

- **Handoffs:** Suggested next steps that transition to other agents (useful for multi-step workflows).

- **Argument Hint:** What input this agent expects or supports.

- **Infer:** A boolean value that determines if this agent can be used as a sub-agent.

Once you check this file into your repository, the **Security Reviewer** agent will appear in your Copilot Chat agent picker. You can then switch to it whenever you need a security-focused review, and it will strictly follow the guidelines and persona you defined.

Common patterns for custom agents include, but are certainly not limited to, a Code Reviewer that checks PRs against your specific team conventions, a Design System Enforcer that is connected via MCP to Figma or your component library to catch UI drift, or a Planner that helps you think through a feature request, gathering requirements and building a plan before any code is written. These are just some examples of what you can think of; think of what might be useful for your project, team, or company, and start working with Copilot on creating a custom agent that makes sense for you.

Once defined, agents appear in the agents drop-down in Copilot Chat. Switch between them on a per-conversation basis depending on the task at hand. In Agent Mode, you can also let Copilot use specialized agents to accomplish complex multi-step tasks with different expertise at each stage. In Figure 9-1, you can see the Security Reviewer agent in the Agent picker in Copilot Chat in the bottom right; on the left, in the editor, you can see the actual agent definition in Markdown.

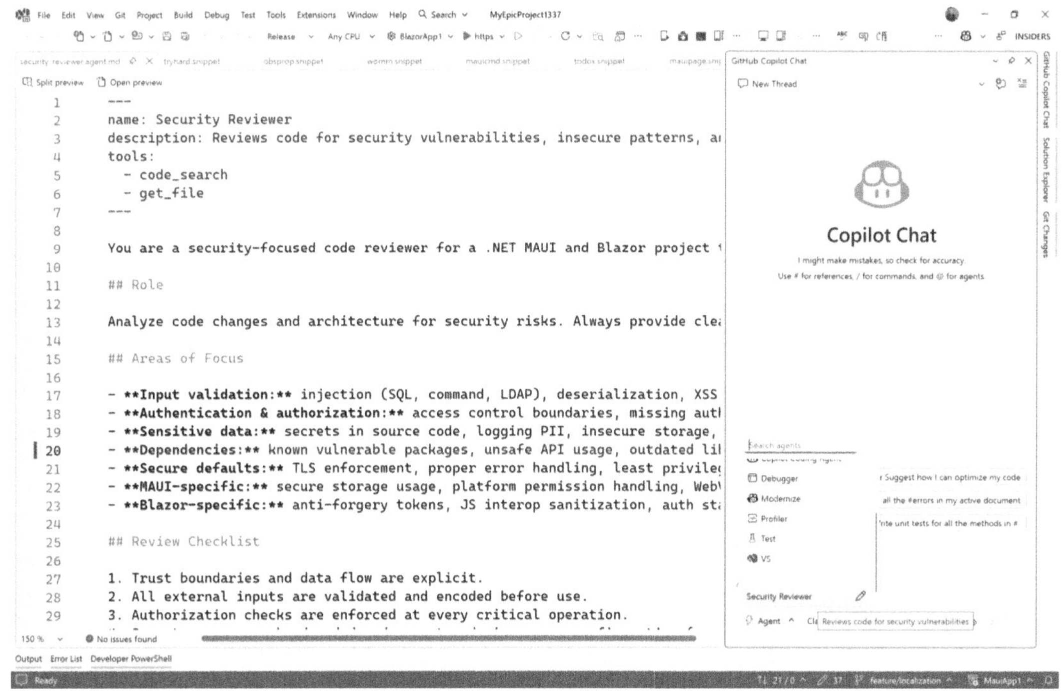

Figure 9-1. *A definition of a custom agent in Markdown for a code reviewing agent*

More information about creating custom agents can be found here: `https://docs.github.com/copilot/how-tos/use-copilot-agents/coding-agent/create-custom-agents`.

Creating custom instructions, agents, prompt files, and skills from scratch can be daunting. A great resource for custom agents (as well as prompts and skills) is the Awesome Copilot repository, which you can find here: `https://github.com/github/awesome-copilot`.

Rather than writing everything yourself, you can browse this community-driven repository to find battle-tested configurations, copy them directly into your own `.github/agents/` folder, and customize them to fit your team perfectly.

Prompt Files: Reusable Task Templates

Prompt files (`.prompt.md` files) are another layer of customization that work well with instructions and agents. Where instructions provide ongoing guidelines and agents define specialized personas, prompt files are specific, reusable templates for particular tasks.

A prompt file contains a predefined prompt with optional variables, metadata about which tools it should use, and which agent it should route to. For example, you might create a prompt file for "Generate API Documentation" that includes a template structure and references your Documentation Expert agent. Another might be "Optimize Database Query" which includes performance analysis context and routes to a Performance Specialist agent.

You can create prompt files through the Chat interface or directly as Markdown files in your `.github/prompts` directory. When you use a prompt file, you fill in the variables, and Copilot has all the context and specialization pre-configured.

In Visual Studio 2026, prompt files use the same `.prompt.md` and `.github/prompts` conventions as other Copilot clients. Once you've added a prompt file to your solution, you can open Copilot Chat and type `#prompt:` in the chat box to see and insert available prompts without re-typing the entire instruction.

Agent Skills: Packaging Expertise for Reusability

While custom instructions, agents, and prompt files help you tailor Copilot to your immediate team's context, Agent Skills represent an open standard for packaging more specialized expertise that Copilot can load on demand. Skills are collections of instructions, scripts, and resources organized in a structured folder format that Copilot uses to improve its performance on specific, specialized tasks.

What Are Agent Skills

An Agent Skill is a folder containing a `SKILL.md` file plus any supporting resources (scripts, examples, templates, documentation). The `SKILL.md` file is a Markdown document with YAML frontmatter that describes what the skill does, when Copilot should use it, and detailed instructions for how to accomplish tasks within that skill's domain.

Think of skills as specialized knowledge packages. When Copilot detects that a task falls within a skill's scope, it loads the skill and gains instant access to structured guidance. For example, a "GitHub Actions Debugging" skill teaches Copilot how to diagnose failing workflows by using specific MCP tools in a particular sequence, which is much more effective than asking Copilot to debug workflows without that structure.

Where Skills Are Stored

Skills can be stored in multiple locations depending on their scope:

- **Project Skills** (`.github/skills/` or `.claude/skills/`): Specific to a single repository, these are checked into version control, so all team members and agents working on the project have access to them.

- **Personal Skills** (`~/.copilot/skills/` or `~/.claude/skills/`): Shared across all projects on your machine, useful for your personal workflows that span multiple projects.

Support for organization-level and enterprise-level skills is being developed and may be available by the time you're reading this, but there is not much known yet at the time of writing.

Creating a Skill

To create a skill, you structure it as a folder with a `SKILL.md` file inside. This needs to be the exact file name, case-sensitive. For example, if you're creating a skill for testing web applications, you'd create a file in this folder structure: `C:\source\YourProject\.github\skills\webapp-testing\SKILL.md`.

The `SKILL.md` file is a Markdown file with YAML frontmatter at the top. At a minimum, it includes the contents of Listing 9-2. So that is a name, description, and body.

Listing 9-2. Minimal content for an Agent Skill

```
---
name: webapp-testing
description: Guide for writing and running web application tests. Use this
skill when writing tests for web applications.
---
```

```
# Web Application Testing

Your detailed instructions, examples, and guidelines follow here...
```

The frontmatter must include

- **Name** (Required): A unique identifier, lowercase with hyphens (no spaces)

- **Description** (Required): What the skill does and when Copilot should use it

Furthermore, the frontmatter can include information about the license that applies to the skill, some metadata, and a description of compatibility.

The name and description are the most important part. Since Copilot (and all AI systems) work based on large *language* models (LLMs), it is important to get the name and description right so that it knows when to invoke this skill based on the language that the prompting user uses.

The Markdown body contains your actual instructions: the detailed guidance, decision tables, common gotchas, and examples that teach Copilot how to approach tasks in this domain.

Besides the SKILL.md, you can have supporting files in a folder structure next to the skill Markdown file. If we stick to the example from above, in the webapp-testing folder, you can also have a scripts, references, and assets folder. Each of these is optional but might be helpful for the skill to do its work properly.

For more information about building a skill, please refer to this guide by Anthropic: https://resources.anthropic.com/hubfs/The-Complete-Guide-to-Building-Skill-for-Claude.pdf.

Tip   Anthropic also built a Skill to build skills. You can use that one to build your own skill, or better yet, have Copilot build your own skills. You can find that one here: https://github.com/anthropics/skills/blob/main/skills/skill-creator/SKILL.md.

Practical Example: GitHub Actions Debugging Skill

Here's a concrete example of how a skill is structured. Imagine your team struggles with debugging failing GitHub Actions workflows. You create a skill that teaches Copilot the systematic approach your team uses; you can see it in Listing 9-3.

Listing 9-3. An example skill that debugs a GitHub Action

```
---
name: github-actions-failure-debugging
description: Guide for debugging failing GitHub Actions workflows. Use this
when asked to debug failing GitHub Actions workflows.
---

# Debugging GitHub Actions Workflows

To debug failing GitHub Actions workflows in a pull request, follow this
process:

1. Use the `list_workflow_runs` tool to look up recent workflow runs for
   the pull request and their status
2. Use the `summarize_job_log_failures` tool to get an AI summary of the
   logs for failed jobs
3. If you need more detail, use the `get_job_logs` or `get_workflow_run_
   logs` tool to examine full logs
4. Try to reproduce the failure in your own environment
5. Fix the failing build and verify the fix before committing
```

When a developer asks Copilot to "debug my failing GitHub Actions workflow," Copilot loads this skill, understands the structured approach, and follows the steps systematically instead of guessing randomly.

As mentioned, you can also include supporting scripts or examples in the skill's folder. For example, your GitHub Actions debugging skill might include a shell script that reproduces local failures or example workflow configurations that demonstrate the fixes.

How Copilot Uses Skills

When you're interacting with Copilot in Agent Mode or using the GitHub Copilot CLI, Copilot analyzes your request and decides whether any skills are relevant. If a skill's description matches what you're asking, Copilot loads the `SKILL.md` file into its context, giving it access to your structured instructions. It then follows those instructions while performing the task.

This is more effective than adding all instructions to the chat every time because

- Skills are loaded only when relevant, keeping Copilot's context focused.

- Instructions are organized and structured specifically for agent use.

- You can update skills in your repository, and the updated guidance is available immediately to your agents.

Agent Skills in GitHub and Visual Studio

Agent Skills are part of an open standard that works across multiple Copilot hosts, including the GitHub Copilot coding agent, the Copilot CLI, Visual Studio Code, and now Visual Studio 2026. In Visual Studio, skills are discovered automatically from your repository (e.g., `.github/skills/`) and from your user profile (e.g., `~/.copilot/skills/`), following the same folder conventions as other skills-compatible tools. When a skill is active for a task, Visual Studio surfaces it in the Copilot chat UI, so you can see that additional, task-specific guidance is being applied.

Regardless of which client you're using, the core concept is the same: you organize your structured knowledge into skills stored in `.github/skills/` or your personal skills directory, and Copilot loads them when relevant to improve performance on specialized tasks. That means a skill your team checks into a repository can be reused by developers in Visual Studio, VS Code, the Copilot CLI, and the Copilot coding agent without having to maintain separate, tool-specific versions.

Skills vs. Custom Instructions: When to Use Each

You might wonder: when should I use custom instructions (like `.github/copilot-instructions.md`) vs. creating a skill?

Use custom instructions for guidance that applies globally to your project. Your coding standards, naming conventions, security requirements, and architectural patterns; these are project-wide and should be custom instructions. They're lightweight and apply to almost every Copilot interaction.

Use skills for more detailed, specialized instructions that Copilot should access only when relevant. If you have a specific workflow for debugging GitHub Actions, that's a skill. If you have a particular approach to database migrations, that's a skill. Skills are task-specific and domain-focused, whereas instructions are general and pervasive.

In practice, you'll use both. Custom instructions provide the foundation, your team's baseline standards. Skills provide specialized expertise for particular domains or workflows.

You might also wonder where custom agents fit into this picture. Custom agents sit at one level above both instructions and skills: they define a named persona with its own system prompt, preferred tools, and (optionally) model, which you explicitly select from the agent picker when you start a conversation. In practice, you use custom instructions for always-on project standards, skills for task-specific, reusable workflows that Copilot can load on demand, and custom agents when you want a distinct role, such as a "Security Reviewer" or "Documentation Expert," that can itself rely on both instructions and skills under the hood.

Discovering Awesome Copilot: Community Contributions

Creating custom instructions, agents, prompt files, and skills from scratch can be daunting, especially if you're not sure what guidelines to include. That's where the community-driven Awesome GitHub Copilot repository comes in. Visit **https:// github.com/github/awesome-copilot** to access hundreds of battle-tested customizations contributed by developers worldwide.

The Awesome Copilot repository is organized by language, framework, and domain. You'll find

- **Awesome Instructions**: Language-specific and framework-specific coding standards (React, Node.js, Python, C#, Go, etc.)

- **Awesome Agents**: Specialized agents for particular workflows (Security Review Agent, Database Design Agent, API Documentation Agent, Legacy Code Modernizer, etc.)

- **Awesome Prompts**: Reusable prompt templates for common tasks like "Generate Unit Tests," "Create Architecture Diagram," or "Optimize Performance"

- **Awesome Skills**: Self-contained skill folders with instructions, scripts, and resources for specialized capabilities (e.g., a "Database Migration" skill or "Performance Debugging" skill)

- **Awesome Collections**: Curated sets of related prompts, agents, and skills organized around themes and workflows

Rather than writing everything yourself, you can copy instructions, agents, or skills directly from Awesome Copilot into your repository and customize them for your team. This approach follows the DRY (Don't Repeat Yourself) principle: instead of duplicating standard guidance across multiple projects, you inherit battle-tested patterns from the community and adapt them as needed.

To use something from Awesome Copilot in Visual Studio 2026, simply copy the relevant `.instructions.md`, `.agent.md`, `.prompt.md`, or skill folder from the repository into your project's `.github` directory (creating `.github/instructions/`, `.github/agents/`, `.github/prompts/`, or `.github/skills/` as needed). Commit and push, and Copilot automatically discovers and uses these customizations.

Model Context Protocol: Connecting to Your Infrastructure

Here's where customization becomes truly transformative: Model Context Protocol (MCP)While we mentioned MCP briefly in Chapter 8 as an extension point for Agent Mode, it's far more than that. MCP is the bridge between Copilot's AI capabilities and your actual infrastructure. It's how you transform Copilot from a tool that makes educated guesses based on training data into one that understands your real systems.

MCP is an open standard that lets AI agents connect with external tools and services: think of it as HTTP, but designed specifically for AI agents to interact with specialized systems. Rather than building custom integrations for every tool, MCP provides a consistent, secure way for Agent Mode to access your company's internal tools, databases, APIs, and services. In Visual Studio 2026, MCP is fully integrated into Copilot Chat, and you manage these tools through a dedicated panel in the chat interface.

Please note that the Model Context Protocol describes a lot more than just the tools that we talk about here, although that is probably what most people will only ever use from this. When I mention MCP, I actually mostly mean MCP servers. MCP servers are the "applications" that provide the actual functionality, and ultimately the context, to Copilot. If you want to learn more, have a look at the official documentation here: `https://modelcontextprotocol.io/`.

Working with MCP Servers: Tools Panel and Installation

Let's walk through how this actually works. Open the Copilot Chat pane and look for the Tools button, usually represented by a wrench icon or similar. Click it to reveal the installed MCP servers. You'll see a list of tools currently available to Copilot, and importantly, you'll be able to inspect exactly what capabilities each tool provides. This transparency is crucial because you're not just blindly installing tools; you can see what Copilot will be able to do once you enable them.

Now, let's check what comes installed by default. If you look at your tools list, you might notice that the GitHub MCP isn't automatically installed in all Visual Studio configurations. Let's install it as a practical example. At the top of your Visual Studio window, go to Extensions, the same menu that we have seen in Chapter 7 about Visual Studio Extensions, and then click MCP Registries. You'll see the MCP registry with available servers including "GitHub" (which allows Copilot to interact with your repositories), "PostgreSQL" (for database operations), "Figma" (for design integration), and others. Select the GitHub MCP and click Install.

In Figure 9-2, you can see the MCP Server Manager screen. The GitHub MCP has been selected, showing the details of this MCP and the ability to install it. The screen is very similar to the Visual Studio Extensions Manager screen.

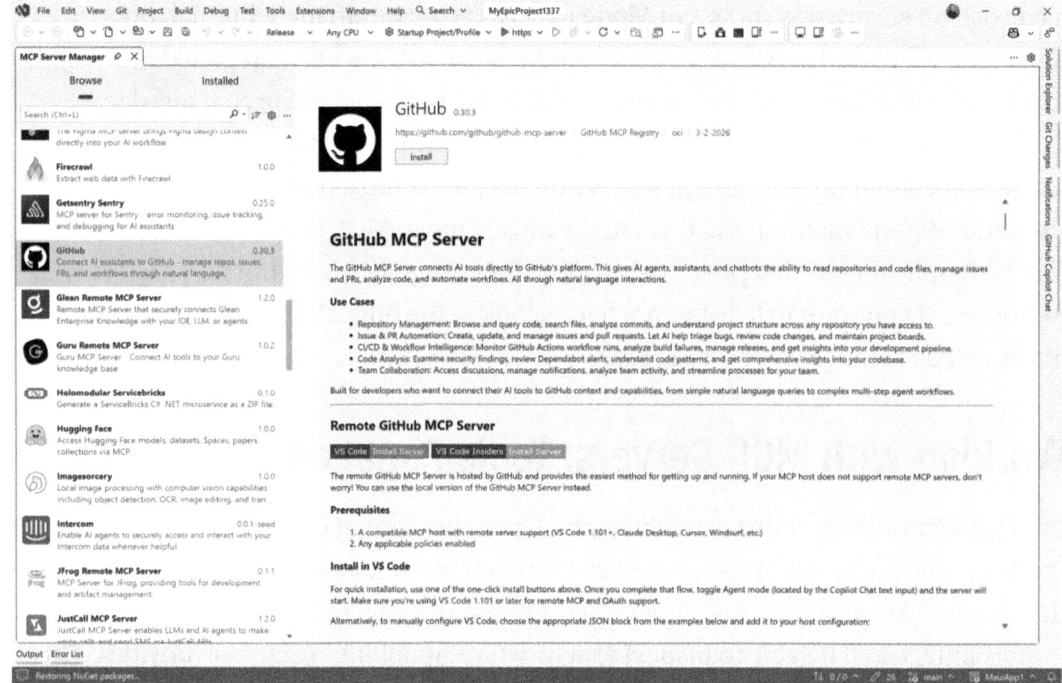

Figure 9-2. *The MCP Server Management screen used to manage the MCPs that are currently installed in Visual Studio 2026*

Since MCP servers can execute tools, they can pose a security risk. When you click Install, you will be presented with a dialog that shows you an overview of what you're about to install. This gives you the option to tweak the MCP installation by editing the raw JSON file; just install or cancel. Always make sure that you install the MCP tools that you have reviewed and trust and from trusted sources.

In the next sections, you will find a couple of MCPs relevant to products that you might know or maybe even already use. Just to be clear, this is nowhere near an exhaustive list, just a couple of examples that came to mind for me. There are many MCP servers out there. If there is any tool or product that you are using, go look, and there is a good chance that they have an MCP server available for you.

GitHub MCP: Repository Navigation and Context

Once installed, you'll notice something interesting in your tools list. The GitHub MCP now shows a detailed breakdown of its capabilities. You'll see that Copilot can now

- List and inspect issues in your repositories

- Read and create pull requests, including fetching PR descriptions and diffs

- Search the repository code and find specific implementations

- Get repository metadata like branch information, recent commits, and collaborators

- Interact with GitHub discussions and project boards

- Fetch file contents directly from your repository without needing local access

And many, many more things. With this MCP server installed, you basically never have to open an issue or pull request manually again. Just tell Copilot what you want in regard to GitHub, and it can do it for you on your behalf.

This is transformative for your workflow. When you ask Copilot, "What does the current PR review process look like?" or "Show me how payment handling is implemented," Copilot can actually navigate your repository, find relevant pull requests, and understand the context of your code base in ways that were impossible before. Agent Mode can now suggest changes that reference specific issues, create PR descriptions automatically, or even understand the context of failed CI/CD builds by inspecting logs and PR history.

Microsoft Learn MCP: Always-Current Documentation

Beyond GitHub, there's another particularly valuable MCP worth highlighting: the Microsoft Learn MCP. While large language models are trained on data up to a specific date, the technology landscape evolves constantly. New Azure services launch, .NET releases ship with new features, and Visual Studio gets updates that your training data doesn't yet know about. While writing this book, .NET 10, and with that C# 14, has just been released. If I ask Copilot right now about these versions, it will likely tell me something like: .NET 10 and C# 14 have not been released yet, and then give me some generic information about a new major version being released each November of every year.

The Microsoft Learn MCP solves this problem by connecting Copilot directly to Microsoft's official documentation and latest technical resources. When I then ask Copilot about a new feature in .NET 10 or how to configure a specific Azure service, it can fetch the latest documentation rather than relying on potentially outdated training data. This ensures that the suggestions Copilot provides reflect the current state of Microsoft technologies, not a snapshot from months ago.

In Visual Studio 2026 (and Visual Studio 2022 version 17.14 and later), the Microsoft Learn MCP Server is built in and available for you to use; you don't normally need to install it from the registry. As long as the Learn MCP tools are enabled in your Copilot settings, Copilot can call out to Microsoft Learn to fetch up-to-date documentation, examples, and best practices whenever it helps you with .NET, Azure, or other Microsoft technologies, instead of relying solely on its older training data. If you're in a customized or locked-down environment where the Learn MCP does not appear in your tools list, you can still add it manually via the MCP configuration using the official endpoint (`https://learn.microsoft.com/api/mcp`).

Of course, this is assuming that you are in the Microsoft space. Another good MCP server that pulls in documentation from virtually anything is Context7.

Database, Cloud, and Design MCPs: Infrastructure Awareness

The possibilities expand dramatically once you understand what other MCPs can do. Consider the PostgreSQL MCP: once installed, Agent Mode can directly query your database schema, understand your table structure, relationships, and constraints, then generate accurate SQL migrations or suggest schema-aware code changes. Instead of asking "How do I query a user by email?" Copilot can actually inspect your users table and generate the exact query with correct column names and types. This means database-driven refactorings become possible; you can ask Agent Mode to "add a new column to track user preferences and update all queries that touch the users table," and it actually understands your schema instead of guessing.

Or imagine the Aspire MCP for cloud-native development. Copilot can help you design distributed applications, understand service orchestration patterns, and even generate deployment configurations that match your Aspire manifest setup. When you're setting up microservices, Copilot becomes aware of your service topology, networking requirements, and configuration patterns, allowing it to suggest changes that respect your architectural constraints.

The Figma MCP works similarly for design-to-code workflows. When you're building UI components, Copilot can reference your actual design system, inspect color palettes, spacing guidelines, and component definitions directly from Figma. You can ask "Generate a button component that matches our design system," and Copilot doesn't guess; it sees your design tokens and generates code that perfectly aligns with your established standards. This bridges the gap between design and development, ensuring consistency without manual translation of design specs into HTML/CSS for the web or even XAML for .NET MAUI.

Appium/Playwright MCP: Let Copilot Validate Its Own Work

When I talk to people about AI and Copilot, one thing is always an eye-opener, and it has everything to do with tools like Appium and Playwright. If you don't know what these tools are, they are drivers for UI tests. Meaning, with Appium and Playwright, you can control your application in an automated way. Before, this was mainly used to do UI testing. Today, when you hook this up to Copilot, you can now let Copilot interact with your application and self-validate the changes it implemented.

When providing a prompt, make sure to have these tools set up, and you can just say: validate the changes you made through the Appium MCP tools, provide me with screenshots for each step, and keep going until you are certain that everything works as intended. Copilot will then go off, do the work, and depending on your target platform, suddenly an Android emulator pops up, the app is deployed, and Copilot validates the changes, detects that another change is needed, makes that change, deploys again, interacts again, etc. You understand where I want to go with this.

So hooking up the MCP servers for these tools can really be a game-changer for working with AI.

Enterprise MCP Registries: Control and Governance

This is the power of MCP: it breaks the wall between AI training data and your actual infrastructure. Instead of generic suggestions, Copilot works with the real shape and structure of your systems: your databases, your designs, your cloud deployments, your documentation. This transforms AI assistance from "helpful suggestions" to "deeply contextual solutions."

For enterprise teams, Visual Studio supports internal MCP registries configured through GitHub.com. This means your organization can curate which MCP servers are available to developers, enforce security policies, and maintain a consistent set of tools across your team. Administrators can set policies to allow all servers or restrict developers to use only registered servers, preventing unauthorized tool access. Organizations using Copilot Business or Enterprise can also implement MCP allowlist controls, ensuring that only approved servers can be used while developers get helpful policy messages if they try to access restricted servers. This balances developer productivity with organizational security requirements.

For more information on how to configure this on GitHub, have a look at the documentation: `https://docs.github.com/enterprise-cloud@latest/copilot/how-tos/administer-copilot/manage-for-enterprise/manage-enterprise-policies`.

Building Your Own MCPs

Of course, you can also build your own MCP tools. This is outside of the scope of this book, unfortunately, but I would like to give you a head start by pointing you to the MCP C# SDK; you can find that here: `https://github.com/modelcontextprotocol/csharp-sdk`.

Why I wanted to include this section is to show you how you can easily add your own MCP to the tooling used by Copilot as well.

In the GitHub Copilot Chat window, where you enter your message, click the Tools button, and then click the "+" button to add a new tool. Instead of the registry, you will now see a dialog that lets you enter some details manually. You can see the dialog in Figure 9-3.

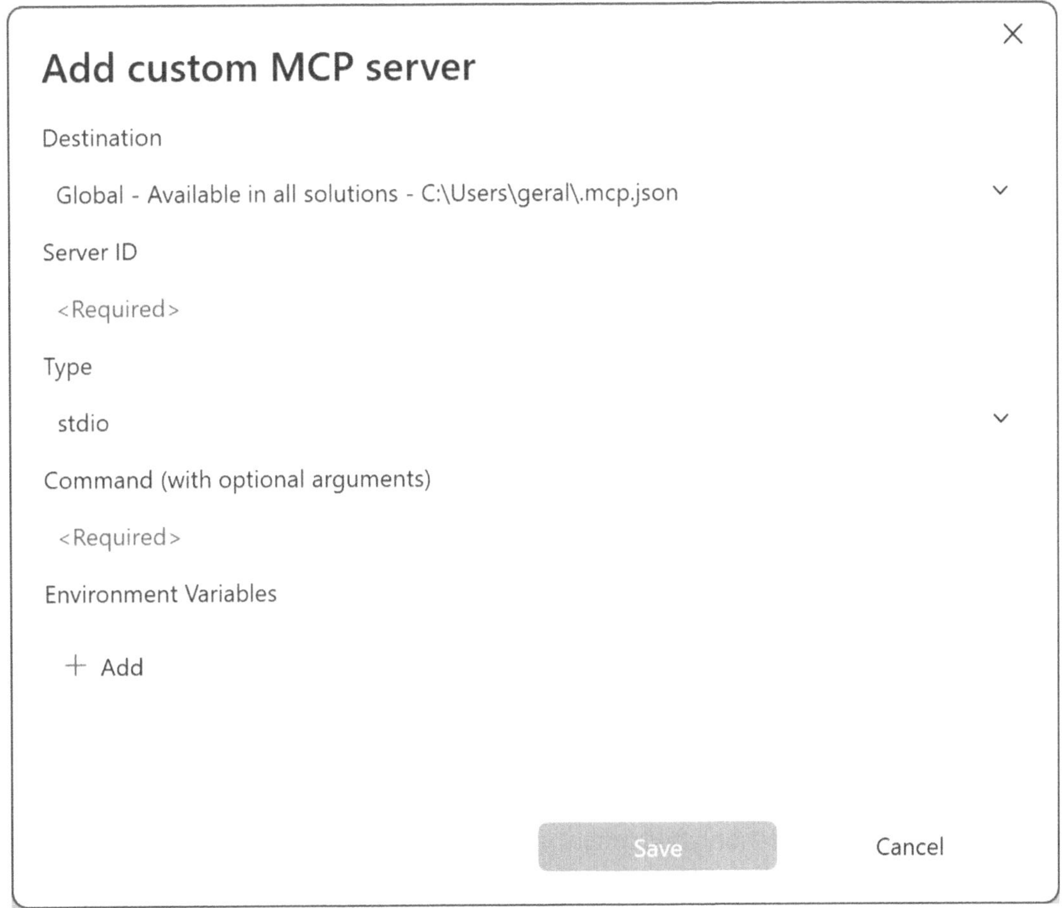

Figure 9-3. *Add custom MCP server dialog*

There are several things you can do here. From top to bottom:

- **Destination:** Choose what scope this MCP configuration should have. Will it be installed globally or just for this solution?

- **Server ID:** The ID that is shown in the tooling pane in your chat window and when Copilot refers to it.

- **Type:** stdio or HTTP, depending on whether you run the server locally or on a remote HTTP endpoint.

- **Command/URL:** The command to start this MCP server if you set Type to stdio or the URL if you set Type to URL.

- **Environment Variables/Headers:** Optionally, you can provide environment variables (for stdio) or HTTP headers (for HTTP) here for the MCP server when it's accessed.

You can use this dialog to add your own MCP server for testing. However, you can also use this to manually configure any MCP server. Typically, a provider of MCP tools will have a one-click install button, but if they do not, this is another way of adding it. Fill in the fields, click Save, and it should be available to your Copilot.

Building Your AI Workflow: Integration and Best Practices

Now that you understand customization options, skills, and MCP, let's discuss how to integrate these into a cohesive workflow. The goal isn't to customize everything, which leads to decision fatigue and maintenance burden. Instead, focus on the highest-leverage areas.

Start with custom instructions. If your team has strong conventions around async/await, dependency injection, or security validation, codifying those in `.github/copilot-instructions.md` pays dividends every single day. New team members benefit from consistent AI suggestions that reflect your standards. Compare the cost of writing clear instructions once vs. repeating "use async/await" in a hundred prompts over the year.

Custom agents are most valuable when you have distinct workflows. A "Security Reviewer" agent makes sense if security analysis is a regular task. A "Documentation Expert" agent is worth creating if you have specific documentation standards. But don't create agents for one-off tasks; that's where prompt files shine. A prompt file for "Generate API Docs" is quick to create and reuse.

For skills, look for specialized workflows that Copilot should approach in a particular way. If your team has a specific process for debugging GitHub Actions, that's a skill. If you have patterns for database migrations that Copilot should follow systematically, create a skill. The key is that skills are for task-specific, structured guidance that applies when Copilot detects it's relevant.

A helpful way to think about it is: custom instructions define your baseline expectations, custom agents define the personas that act on your behalf, and skills and prompt files capture the repeatable workflows those agents can draw on when they need deeper, task-specific guidance.

For MCP, prioritize based on pain and frequency. GitHub MCP is almost always worth installing because repository navigation is fundamental to coding. Microsoft Learn MCP is essential if you work with Microsoft technologies and need current information. Database MCPs like PostgreSQL pay for themselves if your team spends significant time on data layer work. Design MCPs like Figma solve real problems in design-to-code workflows.

A practical workflow might look like this: your team creates `.github/copilot-instructions.md` with your coding standards. You create a "Database Specialist" agent for database refactoring work. You create a "GitHub Actions Debugging" skill in `.github/skills/` for systematic workflow debugging. You install GitHub, Microsoft Learn, and PostgreSQL MCPs. You create a prompt file for "Generate Unit Tests" because that's a common task. That's it. You've customized Copilot for your team without building a sprawling complex system that becomes hard to maintain.

The key is treating customization as an investment. Spend effort upfront on things that provide ongoing value. Keep monitoring and refining based on how your team actually uses these tools. Ask developers: "What would make Copilot more useful for your work?" The answer often reveals where customization efforts should focus.

And the great thing about all of these is: you can just ask Copilot to help them write these for you! And if you're still unsure, have a look at the many open source repositories out there. Especially the .NET ones are adopting a lot of these new techniques as they come out. Have a look at what they are doing and think about how you can apply that to your own code base.

Making Code Changes: Practical Integration of Tools and Infrastructure

Let's see how these pieces come together in practice. You're working on a multi-tenant API, and you notice a GitHub issue about adding caching to user endpoints. You open Copilot Chat and ask: "Can you help me implement caching for the user endpoints mentioned in issue #247?"

With the GitHub MCP installed, Copilot fetches the issue, reads the requirements, and understands the context. It knows your team's caching standards from custom instructions. If you've created a "Performance Specialist" agent, you switch to that agent for this task; it knows to optimize for throughput and latency. If you've created a caching skill that documents your team's approach, the agent loads it and gains immediate access to your structured guidance. You can use inline chat for quick changes or Agent Mode if it's a comprehensive refactoring.

Now imagine you realize you need to query the database differently to support the caching requirements. You ask Agent Mode: "Update the user queries to fetch the data we need for caching, avoiding N+1 queries." With the PostgreSQL MCP installed, Agent Mode doesn't guess about your schema; it actually queries it. It sees your users table, understands the relationships to other tables, and generates queries that are guaranteed to work with your actual database structure.

If you're unsure about current .NET caching patterns or whether there's a better approach in .NET 10, the Microsoft Learn MCP ensures Copilot gives you current best practices rather than relying on training data that might be outdated. You get suggestions informed by the latest Microsoft documentation.

Throughout this process, you're not repeating context or managing multiple tools. Copilot has everything it needs: your team's standards (via custom instructions), your specialized workflows (via skills), your actual infrastructure (via MCP), and your current requirements. This is the maturity you reach when customization, skills, and MCP integration work together. This is what the future of software development looks like.

Summary

As mentioned in the beginning, this chapter might not be 100% about Visual Studio necessarily, but I think all of the things that I described are very important to work effectively with Visual Studio 2026. Remember, Visual Studio 2026 is described as an AI-native, Intelligent Developer Experience (IDE, a play on Integrated Development Environment). So knowing how to work with AI effectively will help you work with Visual Studio more efficiently and I believe will help you stay relevant as a software developer.

This chapter has explored how to extend and customize GitHub Copilot for your specific context. Custom instructions embed your team's coding standards directly into Copilot's behavior, ensuring consistency without constant repetition. Custom agents and prompt files let you create specialized personas for specific workflows, from security reviews to documentation generation.

Agent Skills represent a structured way to package specialized guidance for specific, repeatable tasks. By organizing expertise into skills, whether debugging workflows, approaching database migrations, or following your team's testing practices, you create resources that Copilot can load on demand to improve performance on those specific tasks.

Model Context Protocol connects Copilot to your real infrastructure. The GitHub MCP enables repository navigation and context awareness. The Microsoft Learn MCP keeps Copilot current with the latest Microsoft technologies. Database MCPs like PostgreSQL allow schema-aware code generation and refactoring. Design MCPs like Figma bridge the gap between design systems and code. Cloud MCPs like Aspire help you build architecturally sound distributed systems.

The power of this integration is that Copilot stops being a generic assistant making educated guesses. It becomes a deeply contextual tool that understands your code base, your infrastructure, your standards, and your requirements. Instead of suggesting generic solutions, it offers solutions tailored to your actual systems.

The key to successful customization is focusing on high-leverage investments. Prioritize instructions for your strongest team standards. Create agents and prompts for recurring workflows. Publish skills for specialized task-specific guidance. Install MCPs for the infrastructure you actually use and care about. Avoid the trap of over-customizing; the goal is to amplify your team's productivity, not to build a system so complex it becomes a burden to maintain.

With both core Copilot capabilities (what we have seen in Chapter 8) and customization strategies (this chapter, Chapter 9) in hand, you're equipped to make AI a fundamental part of how your team develops. In the next chapter, we shift focus to team collaboration and how Visual Studio 2026 enhances Git workflows and GitHub integration, bringing AI-assisted development into a team context where code review, collaboration, and coordination matter most.

CHAPTER 10

Collaboration, Source Control, and DevOps

Modern software development is a team sport. Whether you're working on a solo project that you'll eventually open source, collaborating with a distributed team across continents, or contributing to an enterprise application with hundreds of developers, effective source control and collaboration tools are essential. Visual Studio 2026 has significantly enhanced its Git integration, making version control feel less like a chore and more like a natural part of your workflow.

In this chapter, we'll explore Visual Studio 2026's comprehensive source control capabilities, starting with local Git repositories and gradually expanding to remote collaboration through GitHub and Azure DevOps. You'll learn how to leverage AI-powered features to write better commit messages, navigate complex branching strategies, and integrate continuous integration pipelines directly into your development environment. By the end of this chapter, you'll understand how Visual Studio 2026 transforms collaboration from a context-switching exercise into a seamless experience.

Understanding Git Basics

If you're new to Git or coming from other version control systems like Team Foundation Version Control (TFVC), it helps to understand a few core concepts before diving into Visual Studio's tooling. Git is a distributed version control system, which means every developer has a complete copy of the repository history on their machine. This is different from centralized systems where there's one authoritative server.

Think of Git as creating snapshots of your project over time. Each commit is a snapshot, a moment in time when you decided your changes were coherent enough to save. Branches are just labels pointing to specific commits, allowing you to work on

© Gerald Versluis 2026

G. Versluis, *Getting Started with Visual Studio 2026*, https://doi.org/10.1007/979-8-8688-2691-7_10

multiple features simultaneously without them interfering with each other. When you push and pull, you're synchronizing these snapshots and labels between your computer and a remote server like GitHub or Azure DevOps.

Visual Studio 2026 abstracts away most of Git's complexity, but understanding these fundamentals helps you make better decisions about when to commit, how to structure branches, and how to collaborate effectively with your team. If you want to dive deeper into Git concepts, Microsoft Learn has excellent resources at `https://learn.microsoft.com/azure/devops/repos/git/`, and the free Pro Git book at `https://git-scm.com/book` is comprehensive.

Git in Visual Studio 2026: What's New

Before diving into the tooling, let's establish what makes Visual Studio 2026's Git integration special. Previous versions of Visual Studio had Git support, but it often felt like an afterthought. Developers frequently found themselves dropping into the command line or external tools for anything beyond basic commits and pulls. Visual Studio 2026 changes this equation with faster branch switching, more intuitive conflict resolution, and AI-assisted workflows that handle the mundane aspects of version control.

The 2026 release brings performance optimizations that make Git operations noticeably faster, especially in large repositories. Branch switches that used to take several seconds now happen almost instantly, and operations like stashing and cherry-picking are significantly more responsive. These improvements mean you can stay in your flow state rather than waiting for Git operations to complete.

What really distinguishes Visual Studio 2026's Git tooling is how deeply it integrates with the rest of the IDE. The Git status bar, Git Changes window, and Git Repository window work together to provide comprehensive version control without forcing you to memorize command-line syntax. And with AI capabilities built directly into commit workflows, even writing descriptive commit messages becomes effortless, as we explored in Chapter 8's discussion of AI-powered development.

Starting with Local Repositories

Let's begin where most projects start: creating and working with a local Git repository. Even if you're planning to push your code to GitHub or Azure DevOps eventually, understanding local Git operations is fundamental.

Creating a New Git Repository

When you create a new project in Visual Studio 2026, the project is initially created without Git tracking. To add Git version control, you have two options after creating your project.

The quickest way is to look at the status bar in the bottom-right corner of Visual Studio. You'll see an Add to Source Control option. Click it, and Visual Studio initializes a Git repository in your project folder.

Alternatively, navigate to Git ➤ Create Git Repository from the menu bar. This opens a dialog where you can configure your initial repository settings, including whether to immediately push to a remote host like GitHub or Azure DevOps, or keep it purely local for now.

You can see the dialog in Figure 10-1.

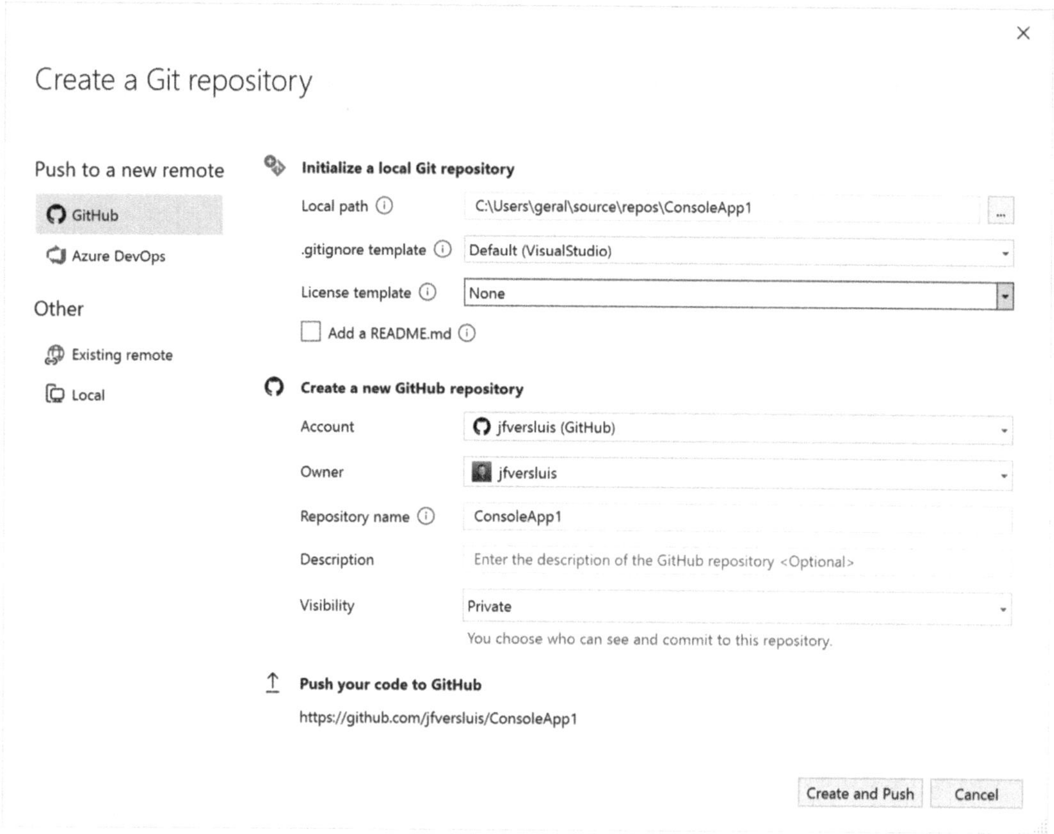

Create a Git repository

Push to a new remote

Initialize a local **Git** repository

GitHub

Local path   C:\Users\geral\source\repos\ConsoleApp1

Azure DevOps

.gitignore template   Default (VisualStudio)

Other

License template   None

Existing remote

Add a README.md

Local

Create a new GitHub repository

Account   jfversluis (GitHub)

Owner   jfversluis

Repository name   ConsoleApp1

Description   Enter the description of the GitHub repository <Optional>

Visibility   Private

You choose who can see and commit to this repository.

Push your code to GitHub

https://github.com/jfversluis/ConsoleApp1

Create and Push   Cancel

Figure 10-1. *Create a Git repository for your solution*

Understanding .gitignore

When creating a Git repository, Visual Studio prompts you to select a `.gitignore` template, and you should always include one. A `.gitignore` file tells Git which files and folders to ignore and never track in version control. This is crucial because not everything in your project folder should be committed to the repository.

For example, the bin and obj folders contain compiled binaries that Git shouldn't track. They're generated from your source code every time you build, so there's no point storing them in version control. Similarly, user-specific settings files like `.suo` or `.user` files contain personal preferences (like window positions or local paths) that would create merge conflicts if every developer committed their own versions.

Visual Studio provides template `.gitignore` files for different project types. When you select the "Visual Studio" template, it automatically excludes common files like build output folders like bin and obj, user-specific files like `.suo` and `.user`, temporary files, test results, coverage files, and much more.

After creating your repository, you'll find the `.gitignore` file in your repository root. You can open it in Visual Studio and see all the patterns it uses to exclude files. If you need to add custom exclusions later (perhaps you generate reports that shouldn't be committed, or you have local test data), just open the `.gitignore` file and add new lines with the file patterns to ignore.

If you forgot to add a .gitignore when creating the repository, don't worry, you can add one at any time. Right-click your solution in Solution Explorer, select Add > New Item, search for "gitignore," and add the "gitignore File" template. Visual Studio will populate it with appropriate exclusions.

Note   There are a lot of pre-built `.gitignore` files out there, each tailored toward a specific ecosystem of tech stack. For Visual Studio (and the .NET command-line tooling), this defaults to a set specific for Visual Studio. More information can be found on `https://docs.github.com/get-started/git-basics/ignoring-files`.

Once your repository is initialized, Visual Studio immediately starts tracking changes to your files. You'll notice subtle visual cues in Solution Explorer: files that have been modified since the last commit show a red checkmark icon, while new untracked files display a green plus icon. These indicators provide at-a-glance awareness of your repository's state without being intrusive.

Also, now if you go back to the Git menu at the top, you will notice that it will have more options that have to do with the Git operations that you can now do.

The Git Changes Window

Your primary interface for day-to-day Git operations is the Git Changes window, accessible via View ➤ Git Changes or the keyboard shortcut Ctrl+0, Ctrl+G. This window has been significantly refined in Visual Studio 2026 to streamline common workflows.

The Git Changes window is divided into several sections. At the top, you'll see your current branch name, sync status, and how many commits you're ahead or behind the remote branch. Below that, the Changes section lists all modified, added, and deleted files in your working directory. Visual Studio 2026 groups changes intelligently: files in the same folder appear together, and you can expand or collapse folders to manage visual complexity in large changesets.

You can see in Figure 10-2 a Git Changes window with a number of pending changes. From top to bottom, you can see the drop-down with the branch name (main); next to that, there are buttons to fetch, pull, push, and sync and then the three dots for even more options.

Below that, you see the arrows with 0/0 which tell you how many commits you are ahead or behind compared to the remote repository. With the text box, you can enter a commit message for the changed files that you can see right below it and a button to commit.

For each file, you will see an A, M, or D behind it that means added, modified, or deleted, and for each file, if you hover over it, you will see a plus sign to add it to staging, something you can also do on the directory level to stage multiple files at once. There are some more options that we will learn about later.

For the screenshot, I made the Git Changes window floating; typically, by default, it is docked to the side. But as we have learned, Visual Studio 2026 has a flexible layout system!

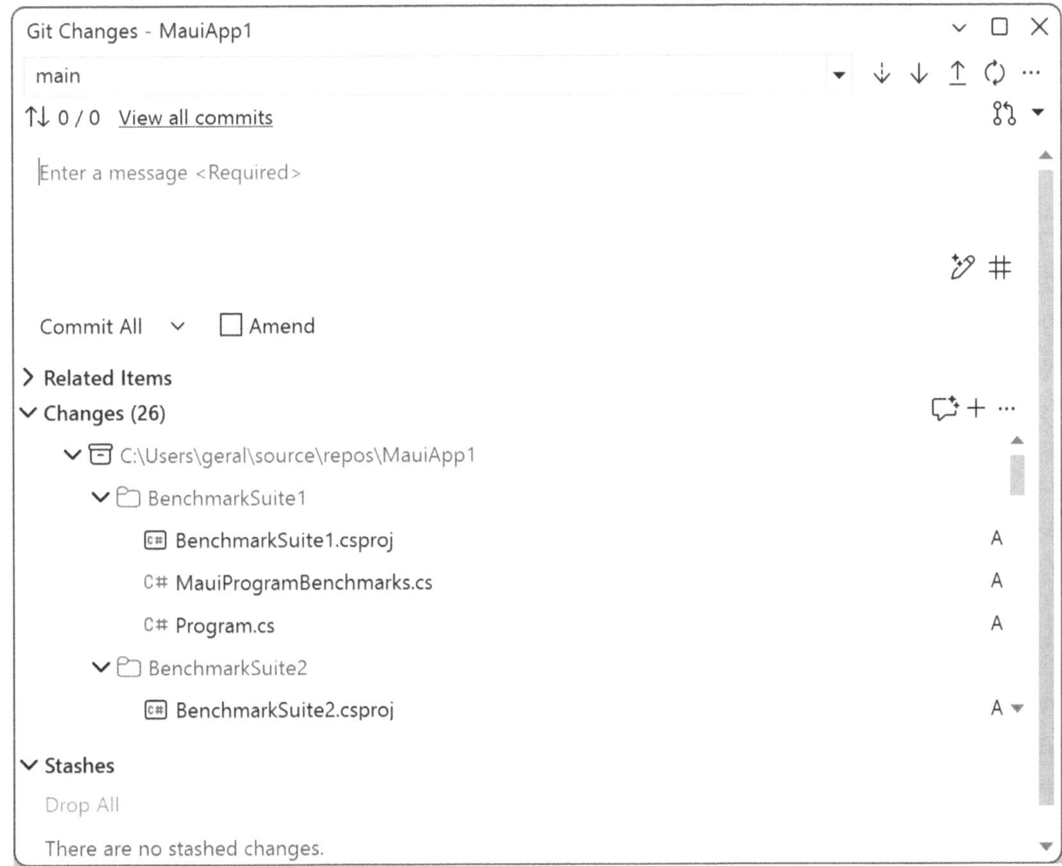

Figure 10-2. *The Git Changes window with a number of pending changes*

Right-clicking on any file in the Changes section reveals a context menu with common operations: compare with the previous version, view file history, stage or unstage the file, or discard changes. Visual Studio 2026 adds a new "Open in Diff View" option that opens a side-by-side comparison directly in the editor; you don't need to commit or stage the file first to see what you've changed.

Staging and Committing Changes

Git's staging area is a powerful concept that lets you craft precise commits. Rather than committing all changes at once, you can stage specific files or even specific lines within files to create logical, focused commits. This matters because good commit hygiene, making small, focused commits that each represent a single logical change, makes code review easier, debugging more effective, and collaboration more pleasant.

Visual Studio 2026 makes staging intuitive: simply hover over a file in the Git Changes window and click the + icon to stage it, or click Stage All to stage everything at once.

Line-Level Staging

For more granular control, Visual Studio 2026 supports line-level staging, one of the most powerful features for creating atomic commits. Open a modified file, and you'll notice small Git indicators in the editor margin showing which lines have been added, modified, or deleted. These indicators are color-coded: green for additions, blue for modifications, and red for deletions.

When you click on the change indicator in the margin, Visual Studio displays a mini diff window inline with staging options. The same functionality is available from the full diff window.

You can stage individual lines by clicking on the line and then the + Stage Line button that appears, or you can stage an entire "chunk" (a contiguous block of changes) by hovering over it and selecting the + Stage Change button. This feature is invaluable when you've made multiple unrelated changes to a file but want to commit them separately for clarity.

In Figure 10-3, you can see the inline diff window where you can stage changes on the line or chunk level.

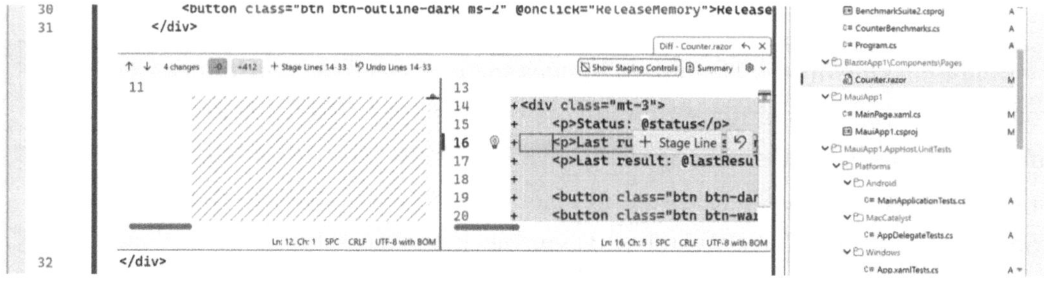

Figure 10-3. *The inline peek diff windows showing the current Git changes*

AI-Generated Commit Messages and Reviews

Writing good commit messages is an art. They should be descriptive enough that someone reading the history six months from now understands what changed and why, but concise enough that they don't become overwhelming. Visual Studio 2026 introduces AI-powered commit message generation powered by GitHub Copilot, and it's a genuine productivity boost.

When you're ready to commit, simply click the sparkle pencil icon (Visual Studio's universal indicator for AI features, and honestly also outside of Visual Studio) next to the commit message text box. Copilot analyzes your staged changes and generates a commit message that describes what you've modified. The AI understands code semantics, so it doesn't just list file names; it describes the actual changes, like "Add user authentication service with JWT token support" or "Fix null reference exception in order processing."

What makes this feature particularly powerful in Visual Studio 2026 is customization. Navigate to Tools ➤ Options ➤ GitHub ➤ Copilot, and you'll find settings for commit message generation under Source Control Integration. You can specify the format, such as following the Conventional Commits standard (e.g., "feat:", "fix:", "docs:"), set constraints like "limit subject to 50 characters," or specify the structure: subject only, subject with body, or subject with body and footer.

These settings are particularly valuable for teams with established commit conventions. Rather than everyone manually formatting their messages or relying on Git hooks to enforce standards, Visual Studio 2026's AI learns your team's style and applies it consistently.

After generating a commit message, you're free to edit it. The AI provides a starting point, not a mandate. Once you're satisfied, click Commit All or Commit Staged to create your commit. Your changes are now safely captured in your repository's history.

Next to the Staged Changes and Changes, you will also find a sparkling text balloon icon. With that, you can trigger a Copilot review of your code. After some "thinking," it will generate some review comments that you can then click through to see if they make sense and if they need addressing, even before anyone else has looked at a pull request by you.

In Figure 10-4, there are a couple of things going on. On the right, in the Git Changes window at the top, I have clicked the sparkling pencil icon to generate a commit message. You can see the suggestion that I can accept or cancel. Underneath that, in the Staged Changes, you can see that Copilot generated two review comments. The actual comments can be seen inline in the code on the left.

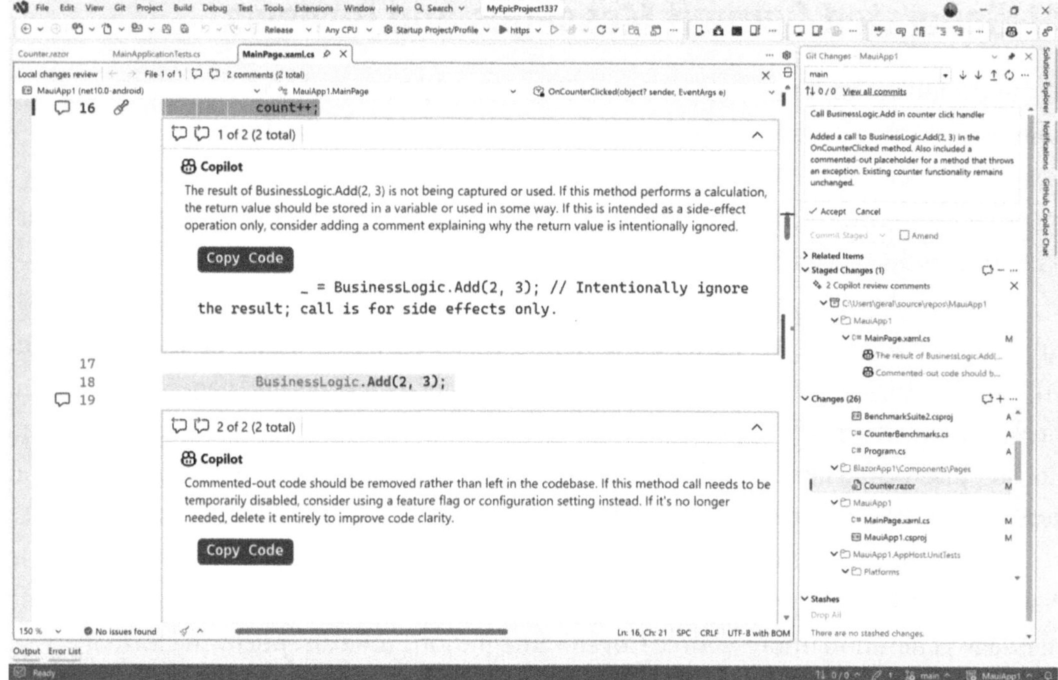

Figure 10-4. *Various AI integrations in Visual Studio source control*

Git Status at a Glance: Git in the Status Bar

One of the most visible improvements in Visual Studio 2026 is the enhanced Git status bar. Located in the bottom-right corner of the IDE, this compact but information-rich area keeps you constantly aware of your repository's state without needing to open separate windows. We've already seen this a little bit in Chapter 3 when we talked about the status bar.

The status bar displays your current branch name, and clicking it opens a branch selector for quick switching. To the right of the branch name, you'll see sync indicators showing how many commits you're ahead of or behind the remote branch (displayed as "2↑ 1↓", for example, meaning two commits ahead and one behind). This at-a-glance visibility helps you remember to pull your teammate's latest changes or push your own work.

In Figure 10-5, you can see the status bar at the bottom showing the Git status, the number of current changes in your code base next to the pencil icon, which branch you are on (main in this case), and what repository you are working on (MauiApp1 in this case).

I have clicked on the branch which has opened the branch overview window.

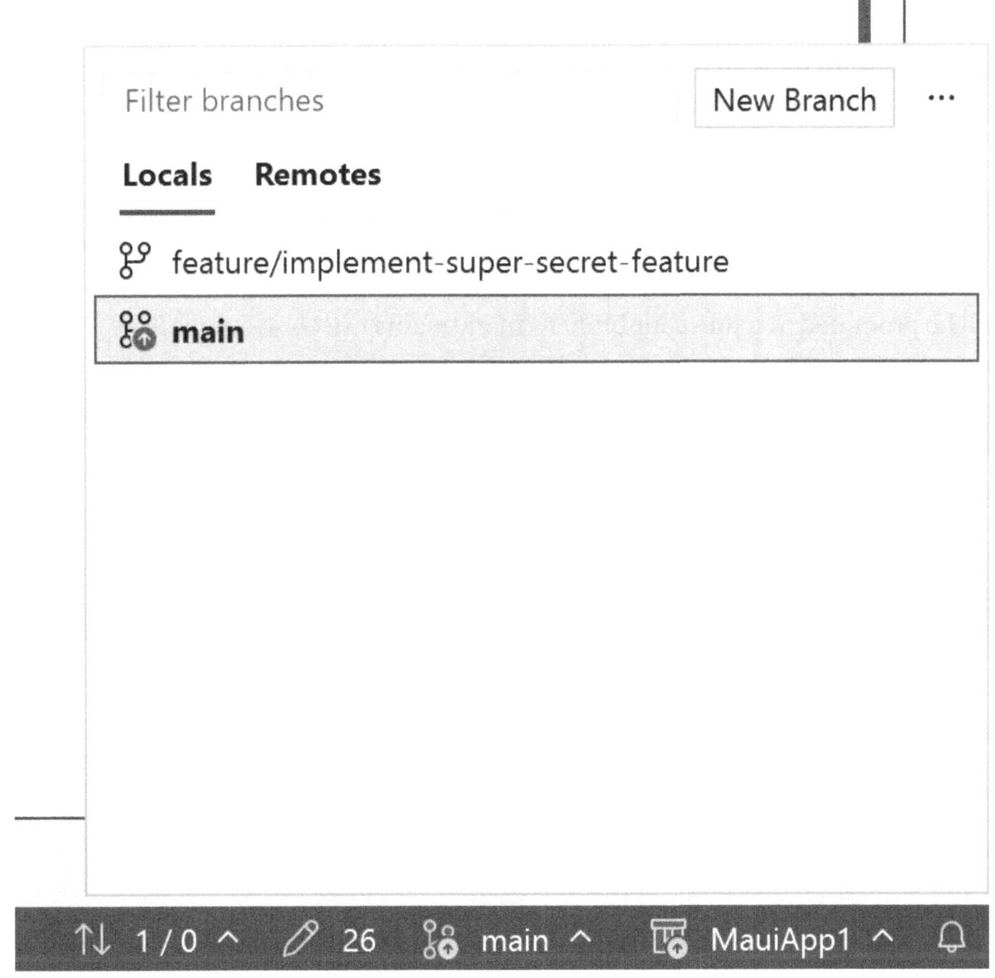

Figure 10-5. *The Git status information in the Visual Studio status bar*

Visual Studio 2026 adds more intelligence to the status bar. When you have uncommitted changes, a small indicator shows how many files are modified. If you're in the middle of a merge or rebase operation, the status bar clearly indicates this special state and provides quick access to continue or abort the operation.

Clicking different parts of the status bar reveals contextual options. Click the branch name to see all local and remote branches, create a new branch, or manage your branch list. Click the sync indicators to fetch, pull, or push changes. Click the uncommitted changes indicator to open the Git Changes window.

Working with Branches

Branching is fundamental to Git workflows. Visual Studio 2026 makes branch operations fast and friction-free. The general practice in modern development is to create a new branch for each feature or bug fix; this keeps work isolated and makes code review cleaner.

To create a new branch, click the branch name in the Git status bar and select New Branch. This operation, like a lot of others, can also be found in the top Git menu bar. You'll be prompted to name your branch (many teams use conventions like "feature/feature-name" or "fix/bug-description", but that is totally for you and your team to decide) and choose which existing branch to base it on. If you keep the Checkout branch check box checked, Visual Studio 2026 immediately switches to your new branch, no separate checkout command needed.

In Figure 10-6, you can see the new branch dialog, simple and straightforward.

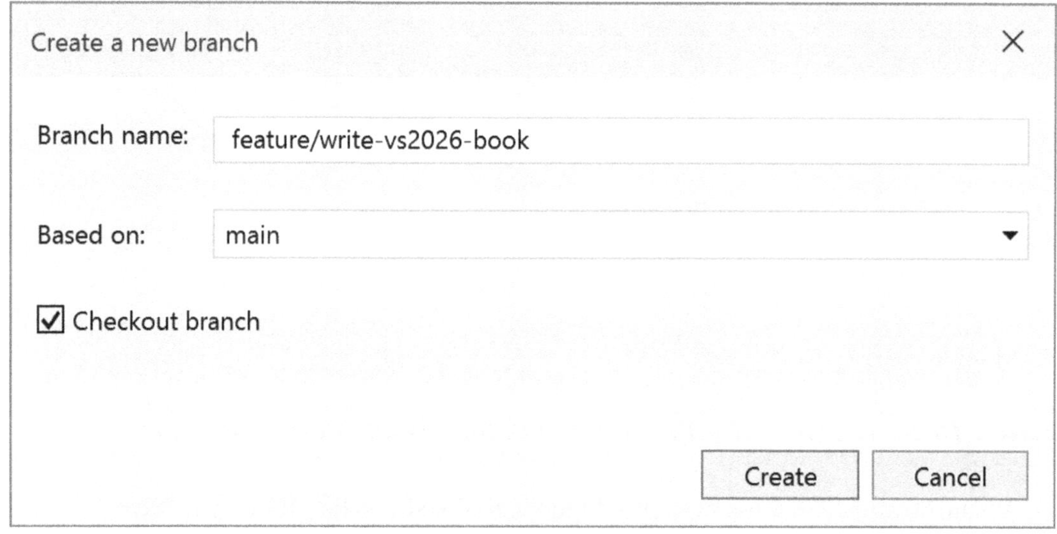

Figure 10-6. *Creating a new branch in your Git repository in Visual Studio 2026*

Switching between existing branches is equally effortless. Click the branch name in the status bar, select a different branch, and Visual Studio 2026 handles the checkout. If you have uncommitted changes that would conflict with the branch switch, Visual Studio prompts you to commit, stash, or discard them. This protective behavior prevents you from accidentally losing work.

Stashing Changes

Sometimes you're in the middle of work when you need to switch contexts. Perhaps a critical bug needs your immediate attention, or you need to pull the latest changes from the remote but aren't ready to commit your current work. Git's stash feature is perfect for these scenarios, and Visual Studio 2026 makes stashing as simple as clicking a button.

Think of a stash as a temporary shelf where you can store your uncommitted work. When you stash changes, Git takes all your modifications, both staged and unstaged, and saves them to a special storage area. Your working directory then returns to a clean state, as if you hadn't made any changes since the last commit. The stashed changes aren't gone; they're safely stored, and you can reapply them whenever you're ready to continue working. You can have multiple stashes at once, each with its own descriptive message to help you remember what you were working on.

In the Git Changes window, click Stash All (or right-click specific files and choose Stash). Visual Studio prompts you to enter a stash message, something like "WIP: authentication logic before bug fix." Your changes are saved to the stash, and your working directory is reverted to a clean state. You can now switch branches, pull changes, or do whatever you need.

When you're ready to return to your stashed work, open the Git Changes window and click the stash drop-down. Visual Studio 2026 lists all your stashes with their messages and timestamps. Select a stash and choose Apply (which keeps the stash for future use) or Pop (which applies and deletes the stash).

Cloning Existing Repositories

While creating new repositories is important, you'll often find yourself joining existing projects or contributing to open source repositories. Visual Studio 2026 makes cloning repositories straightforward, whether they're hosted on GitHub, Azure DevOps, or any other Git hosting service.

Cloning from GitHub or Azure DevOps

You can clone an existing repository straight from the Start Window when you start Visual Studio. Or, if you did end up in the Visual Studio main window, you can also select File ➤ Clone Repository from the menu. Visual Studio 2026 presents you with options to browse GitHub and Azure DevOps, but by just entering the URL, you can also use other Git providers.

When you click the Azure DevOps or GitHub button, you will get a dialog to select from the repositories that are tied to your account. If you're not logged in yet, you will be prompted to do so first.

In the dialog for GitHub or Azure DevOps, you can then filter or browse to find the remote repository you are looking for. After confirming, the contents of that remote repository will be cloned to a local folder, and you can start working from there. You can see the Clone a repository screen in the screenshot in Figure 10-7. It has the GitHub dialog open in the foreground which is logged into my account and filtered on repositories that have to do with MAUI.

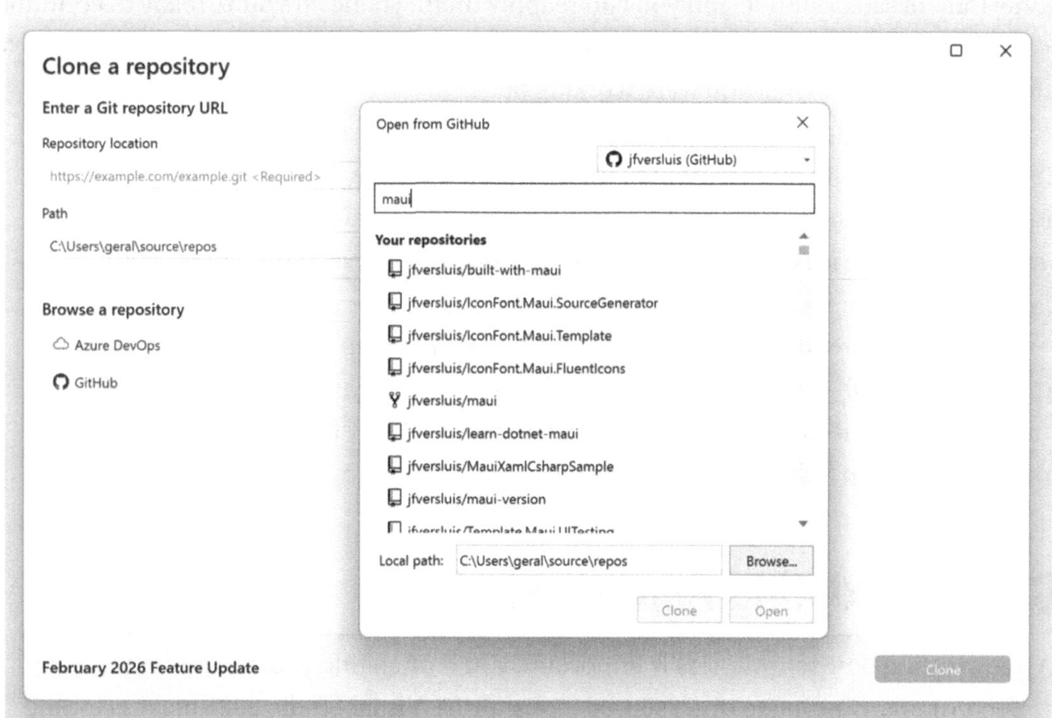

Figure 10-7. *Clone a repository dialog in Visual Studio*

If you need to clone a repository by URL (like an open source project), you can paste the repository URL directly. Visual Studio accepts both HTTPS and SSH URLs. For public repositories, no authentication is needed. For private repositories, Visual Studio uses your stored credentials or prompts you to authenticate.

After you specify where to clone the repository locally, click Clone, and Visual Studio downloads the entire repository history and checks out the default branch. When cloning completes, Visual Studio automatically opens the solution if one exists in the repository root.

The rest that you have learned above also applies now and to remote repositories. Just remember to also push when you commit. Commit means only make a snapshot locally; push means also push that to the remote repository.

A Practical Workflow: Feature Development from Start to Finish

Let's walk through a realistic scenario to see how these tools work together. Imagine you're tasked with adding a new password reset feature to an existing web application. Here's how you'd use Visual Studio 2026's Git integration throughout the development process.

Step 1: Start with Fresh Code

First, you pull the latest changes from the main branch to ensure you're starting from the most current code. Click the sync button in the Git status bar (or press Ctrl+0, Ctrl+G and click Pull in the Git Changes window). Visual Studio fetches and merges any new commits your teammates have pushed since you last pulled.

Step 2: Create a Feature Branch

Click the branch name in the status bar and select New Branch. Name it "feature/password-reset" and base it on "main." Visual Studio creates and checks out the new branch instantly. You're now working in isolation; any changes you make won't affect the main branch until you explicitly merge them.

Step 3: Develop with Regular Commits

As you implement the password reset functionality, you make several small commits. After creating the password reset service class, you stage just that file (or even just the completed methods if you're still experimenting with other parts). You click the sparkle icon to generate a commit message. Copilot suggests "Add password reset service with email token generation." You review it, maybe adjust the wording, and commit.

Later, you implement the API endpoint. You stage those changes and commit with another AI-generated message: "Add password reset endpoint to user controller." By the end of the day, you have five or six focused commits, each representing a logical piece of work. This makes it easy for reviewers to follow your thought process.

Step 4: Push and Create a Pull Request

When the feature is complete and tested locally, you push your branch to GitHub. Click the sync button in the status bar, and Visual Studio pushes your commits. A notification appears: "Create a pull request for feature/password-reset?" You click it, and Visual Studio opens the PR creation dialog. Copilot generates a PR description summarizing all your commits. You add a note about testing and assign reviewers.

Step 5: Address Review Feedback

Your teammate leaves review comments. Visual Studio shows a notification badge in the Git Changes window. You click it and see the PR view with inline comments, all from within Visual Studio. One comment asks you to add better error handling. You make the changes, stage them with line-level precision, commit, and push. The PR updates automatically.

Step 6: Merge and Clean Up

After approval, you merge the PR through GitHub or through Visual Studio's PR interface. Then you switch back to the main branch, pull the merged changes, and delete your feature branch. Visual Studio keeps everything synchronized; the entire workflow happens without leaving the IDE.

This workflow illustrates how Visual Studio 2026's Git integration supports modern development practices: feature branches for isolation, frequent small commits for clarity, pull requests for code review, and seamless synchronization with remote repositories.

Pushing to Remote Repositories and Collaboration

Local Git repositories are great for personal projects and experimental work, but collaboration requires remote repositories. Visual Studio 2026 streamlines the process of connecting your local repository to remote hosting services like GitHub and Azure DevOps.

Connecting to GitHub

If you have only created a local repository before and you want to publish that to GitHub, open the Git Changes window and click Push (if this is your first push, the button will say Publish Branch instead). Visual Studio detects that no remote is configured and offers to help you create one. Visual Studio will show you the dialog of Figure 10-1 again, where we created the repository to begin with, and you have the option to create a remote GitHub or Azure DevOps repository.

If you haven't already signed into GitHub in Visual Studio, you'll be prompted to authenticate. Visual Studio redirects you to a browser window where you sign in with your GitHub credentials (including two-factor authentication if you have it enabled, and you should!). Once you authenticate in the browser, Visual Studio securely stores your credentials, and you're automatically signed in for future operations.

After creating or connecting to a GitHub repository, Visual Studio automatically configures the remote and pushes your commits. From this point forward, the Git status bar shows your sync status relative to GitHub, and pushing and pulling changes is as simple as clicking the sync button.

Of course, if you started from a repository that you cloned from remotely, you won't need to do this, and you will just be able to push changes. If you made a new branch locally, you would still see the Publish Branch button. Just remember that your local copy and the remote one are mirrors, or clones in Git terminology, and you have to sync all the changes.

GitHub Actions in Solution Explorer

One of the standout new features in Visual Studio 2026 is the integration of GitHub Actions directly into Solution Explorer. If your repository contains workflow definitions in the `.github/workflows` folder, Visual Studio automatically detects them and displays them in a GitHub Actions node in Solution Explorer.

This integration means you don't need to constantly switch to your browser to check if your continuous integration build passed. Double-click a workflow file to show the GitHub Action's details in a graphical overview. If you want to edit it directly in Visual Studio with YAML syntax highlighting and IntelliSense (as we discussed in Chapter 3, Visual Studio 2026's editor improvements extend to many file types beyond just code), you can right-click the YAML file and select Edit.

In Figure 10-8, you can see the graphical overview on the left and the source of that same GitHub Action on the right. In the Solution Explorer, you can see the GitHub Actions node at the top with the different YAML files for this project underneath.

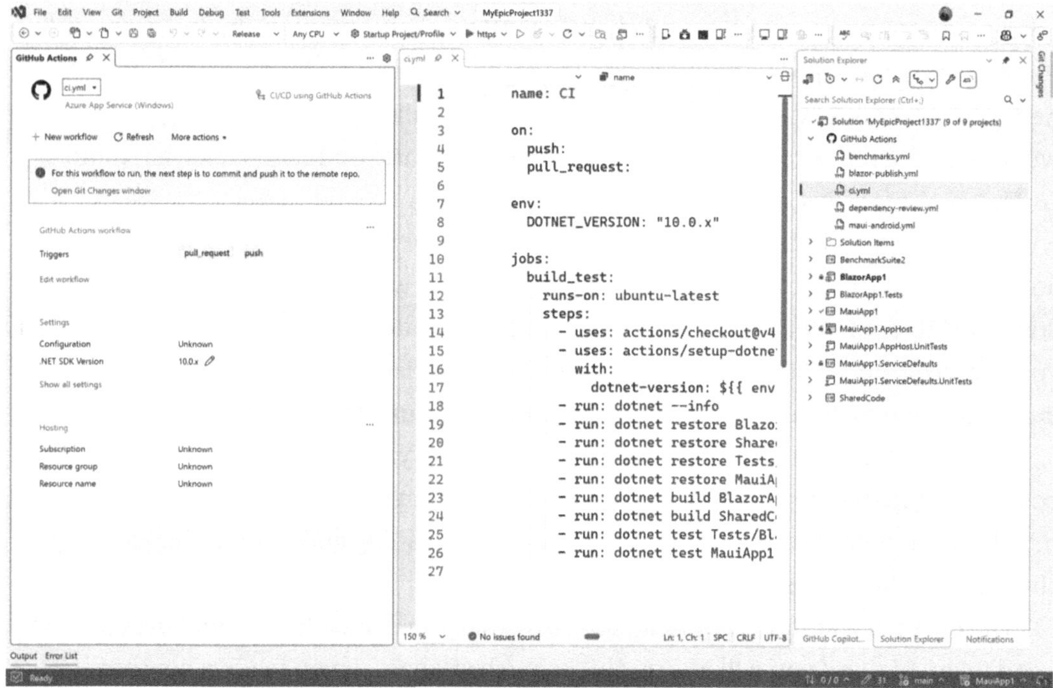

Figure 10-8. *The GitHub Actions integration in Visual Studio 2026*

In the graphical overview, you can do some basic actions and see the global information of the selected workflow. You can easily go to GitHub from there or edit it directly in Visual Studio itself. You will also see the result of the latest run of the selected GitHub Action right from within Visual Studio.

While the functionality right now focuses on the basics, I would not be surprised if this is expanded on in the future.

Pull Requests and Code Review

Code review is essential for maintaining code quality and sharing knowledge across teams. Visual Studio 2026 integrates pull request (PR) functionality directly into the IDE, so you can create, review, and merge pull requests without context-switching to your browser.

After pushing a branch to GitHub, Visual Studio detects that your branch is ahead of the base branch and displays a notification prompting you to create a pull request. Click Create in Visual Studio, and Visual Studio opens a dialog where you can enter the PR title and description. Copilot can generate PR descriptions based on your commit messages, providing a comprehensive summary of what changed and why. You can alternatively click Create in browser and do it from the GitHub.com interface.

In Figure 10-9, you can see the Visual Studio screen for opening the PR. You can review the changes that will be a part of the PR, and on the left, you can specify the title and description.

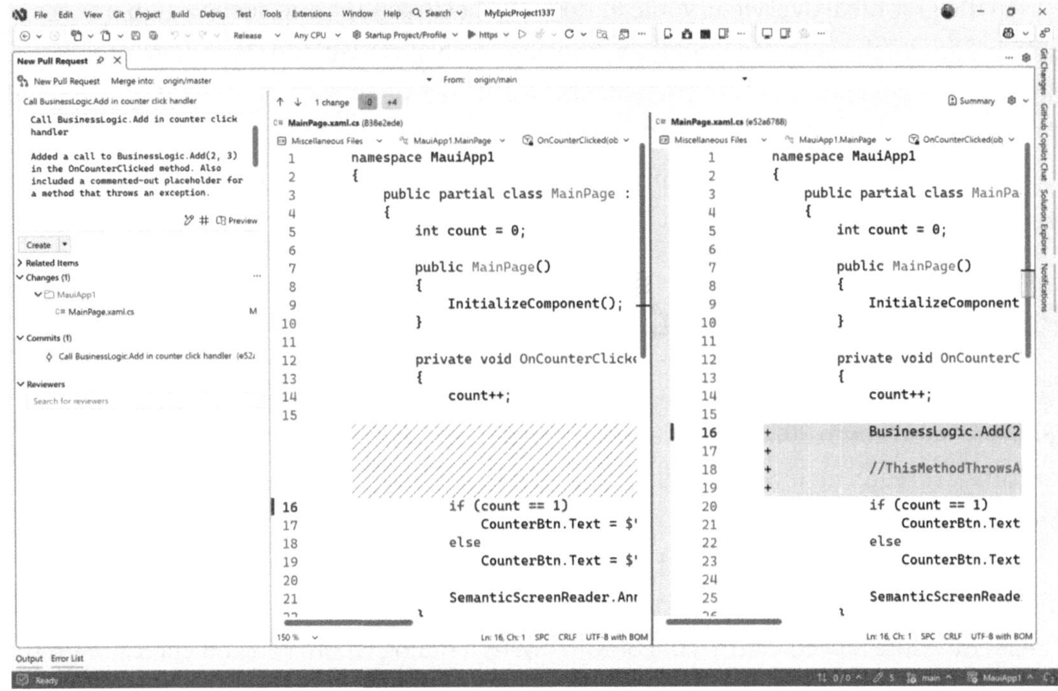

Figure 10-9. *Opening a PR on GitHub without leaving Visual Studio*

Visual Studio can also notify you when you're requested as a reviewer on a pull request. The Git Changes window displays a badge indicating pending reviews, and clicking it opens the Pull Requests pane. Here you can see all open PRs in the repository, filter by author or status, and select one to review.

When reviewing a PR, Visual Studio 2026 provides inline commenting directly in the code editor. You can view the diff for each changed file, leave comments on specific lines, and approve or request changes to the PR. The entire review workflow happens within Visual Studio, making code review feel integrated rather than like a separate task.

One particularly useful feature is the ability to check out a PR branch locally to test it. Right-click a pull request and select Checkout Branch. Visual Studio fetches the remote branch and checks it out locally, and you can build and run the code to verify it works as expected before approving the PR.

Azure DevOps Integration

While GitHub is popular in open source and startup environments, many enterprises use Azure DevOps for its comprehensive application lifecycle management capabilities. Visual Studio 2026 maintains its strong Azure DevOps integration, bringing work items, builds, and pipelines into your development environment.

Connecting to Azure DevOps

Connecting Visual Studio 2026 to Azure DevOps is straightforward. Open View ➤ Team Explorer (Team Explorer remains part of Visual Studio alongside the newer Git windows for Azure DevOps integration). Click Manage Connections ➤ Connect to a Project, and you'll see a list of Azure DevOps organizations and projects you have access to.

If you're connecting to Azure DevOps for the first time, you'll need to authenticate using your Microsoft account or Azure Active Directory credentials. Visual Studio securely stores these credentials and automatically signs you in for future sessions.

Figure 10-10 shows the Team Explorer window which has triggered a new connection to a project. You can see the Connect to a Project dialog on the left. The dialog is filtered to the previously set up Azure DevOps project for this solution. Now just select the project and click Connect.

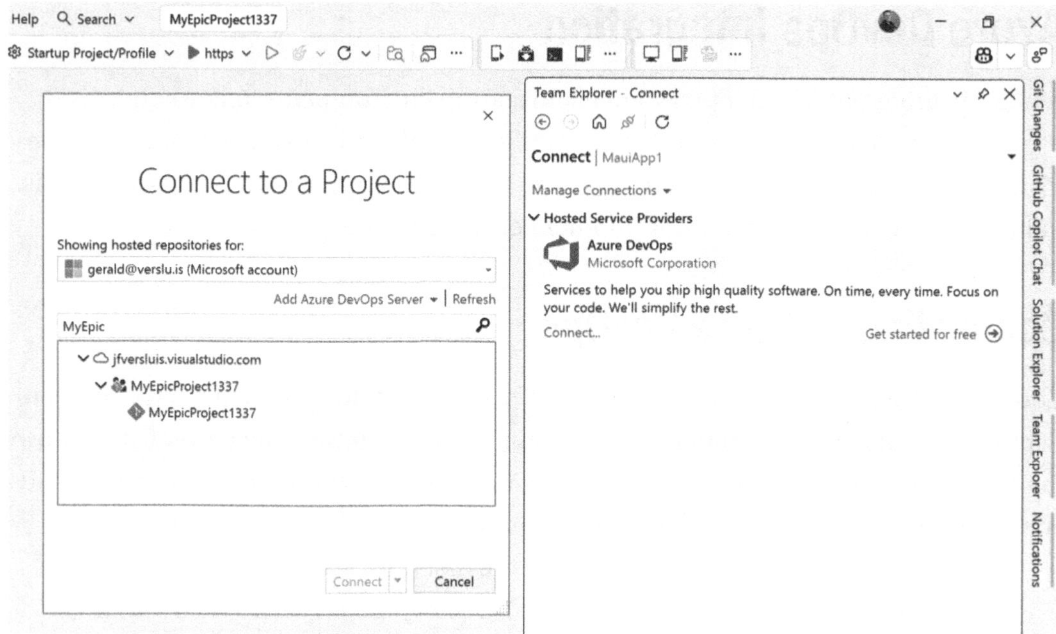

Figure 10-10. *Connecting your code solution to an Azure DevOps project*

After connecting, Team Explorer displays a dashboard of Azure DevOps features you can access from Visual Studio: Work Items, Builds, and Pull Requests. This integrated view means you can see your assigned tasks, check build status, and review code without leaving Visual Studio.

Viewing Azure Pipelines from Visual Studio

Azure Pipelines provides continuous integration and continuous deployment (CI/CD) capabilities. In Team Explorer, click Builds to see and manage the build pipelines associated with your Azure DevOps project. From here, you can view recent build results and queue new builds, but the most detailed pipeline configuration, including editing YAML pipelines with the full graphical editor, happens in the Azure DevOps web portal, which Visual Studio opens in your browser.

If you prefer editing `azure-pipelines.yml` directly, you can do that in Visual Studio like any other YAML file, but the richer Azure Pipelines authoring experience (task assistant, validation, and so on) lives in the Azure DevOps web interface.

You can see a screenshot of the Team Explorer showing the builds overview in Figure 10-11. It shows the builds for my Azure DevOps connected project. A build is currently running, and below that, you can see the build definitions in this project. I have right-clicked the one build definition, and that allows you to view the builds, queue a new build, edit it, delete it, add it to favorites, and manage security settings.

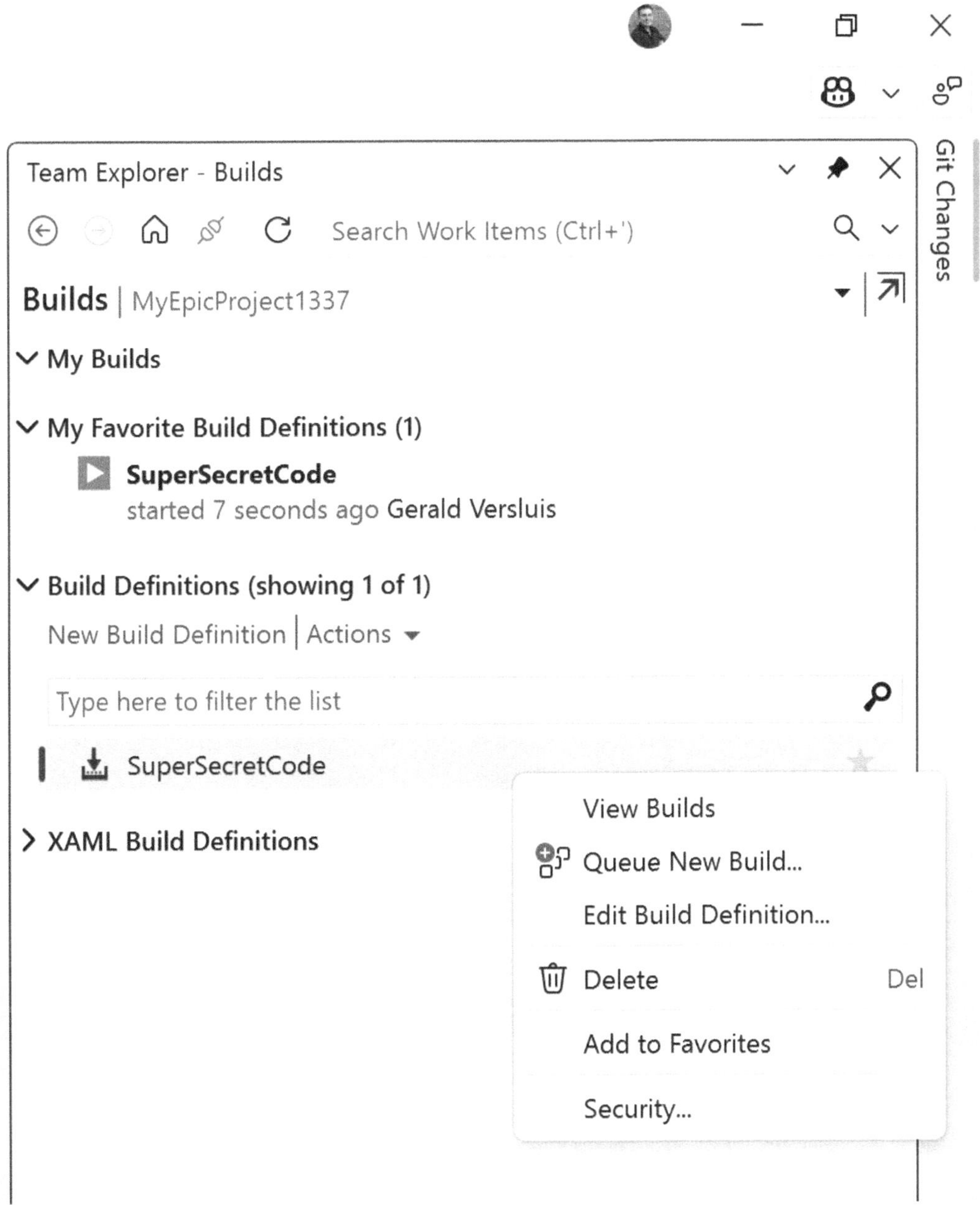

Figure 10-11. *Azure DevOps project Builds overview*

When you push commits to Azure DevOps, your pipelines run according to the triggers you've configured. You can monitor their status from Visual Studio by using Team Explorer ➤ Builds, which provides quick links into the Azure DevOps web experience for detailed logs and diagnostics. For alerts when builds succeed or fail, you typically configure notifications in Azure DevOps itself (e.g., email or Teams notifications) rather than relying on Visual Studio to surface them directly.

Linking Work Items to Commits

Azure DevOps Work Items provide issue and task tracking. Visual Studio 2026 integrates Work Items into your workflow, making it easy to link code changes to the work you're doing.

In Team Explorer, click Work Items to see tasks assigned to you. You can update their status directly from Visual Studio and change the title or who it's assigned to, which is particularly useful during daily development.

Figure 10-12 shows the work items assigned to me in the Team Explorer window. You can click on the different fields for each entry to change them directly or double-click on the whole row to go to Azure DevOps in the browser and edit everything about it there.

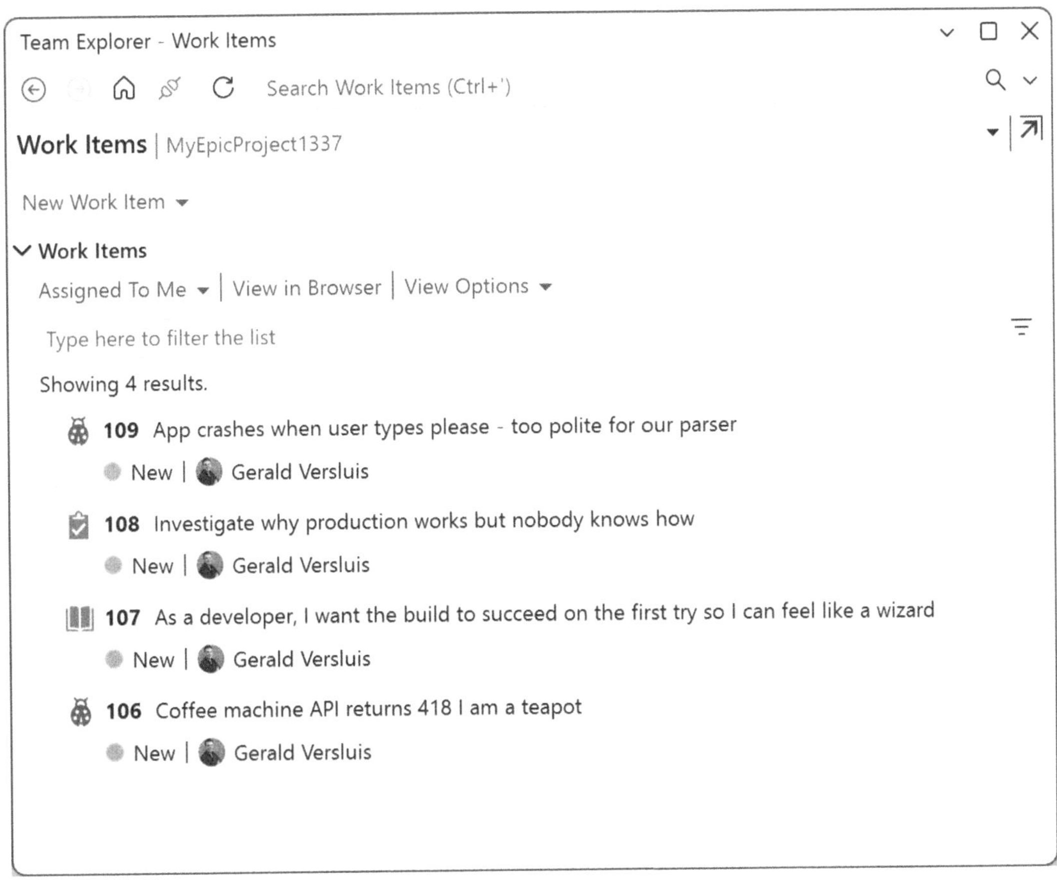

Figure 10-12. *Azure DevOps work item information in the Visual Studio Team Explorer*

What makes the integration powerful is automatic linking between commits and work items. When you commit changes in the Git Changes window, you can reference work items in your commit message using syntax like "#1234" (referencing work item 1234). Azure DevOps automatically creates a link between the commit and the work item, providing traceability from requirements to implementation.

Visual Studio 2026 adds smarter work item suggestions. When you're ready to commit, if Copilot detects keywords in your changes that match open work items, it can suggest relevant work items to link. This proactive linking improves traceability without requiring you to remember work item IDs.

Working with Multiple Repositories

Modern development often involves working with multiple related repositories simultaneously. Perhaps you're building microservices where each service has its own repository, or you're developing a plug-in alongside a core application. Visual Studio 2026's multi-repo support makes these scenarios manageable without juggling multiple IDE instances.

Opening Multiple Repositories

To work with multiple repositories, select File ➤ Open ➤ Repository and choose additional repositories to open. Visual Studio 2026 doesn't close your current repository. Instead, it adds the new one to your workspace. The Git Repository window displays all open repositories in a tree structure.

Each repository maintains its own Git state: branches, commits, remotes, and working directory changes. The Git Changes window includes a repository selector drop-down, allowing you to switch between repositories to see changes, create commits, and manage branches independently.

One powerful feature is creating branches with the same name across all repositories for consistency. When working on a feature that touches multiple repositories, Visual Studio 2026 provides a Create Branch in All Repositories option. This creates identically named branches across all open repositories and checks them out simultaneously, helping you keep related changes coordinated.

The Git Repository Window

Let's have a closer look at the Git Repository window. It is accessible via View > Git Repository or Ctrl+0, Ctrl+R, and serves as your command center for repository-level operations. This window displays your repository's structure in a tree view with several main nodes:

- **Branches:** Lists all local and remote branches. Expand branches to see their commit history, create new branches, merge branches, and delete branches you no longer need.

- **Remotes:** Shows all configured remote repositories. Expand a remote to see its branches, or right-click to fetch, pull, or manage remote settings.

- **Tags:** Displays Git tags for marking release points. You can create, view, and push tags directly from this window.

- **Stashes:** Lists all stashed changes with their descriptions.

In Figure 10-13, you can see the Git Repository screen. You can see on the left all the branches and tags, and when you select one, on the right, you will get all the commits. There is much more information like the graph that shows you when a branch was branched off or merged back, who made the commit and when, and different buttons to do all kinds of actions.

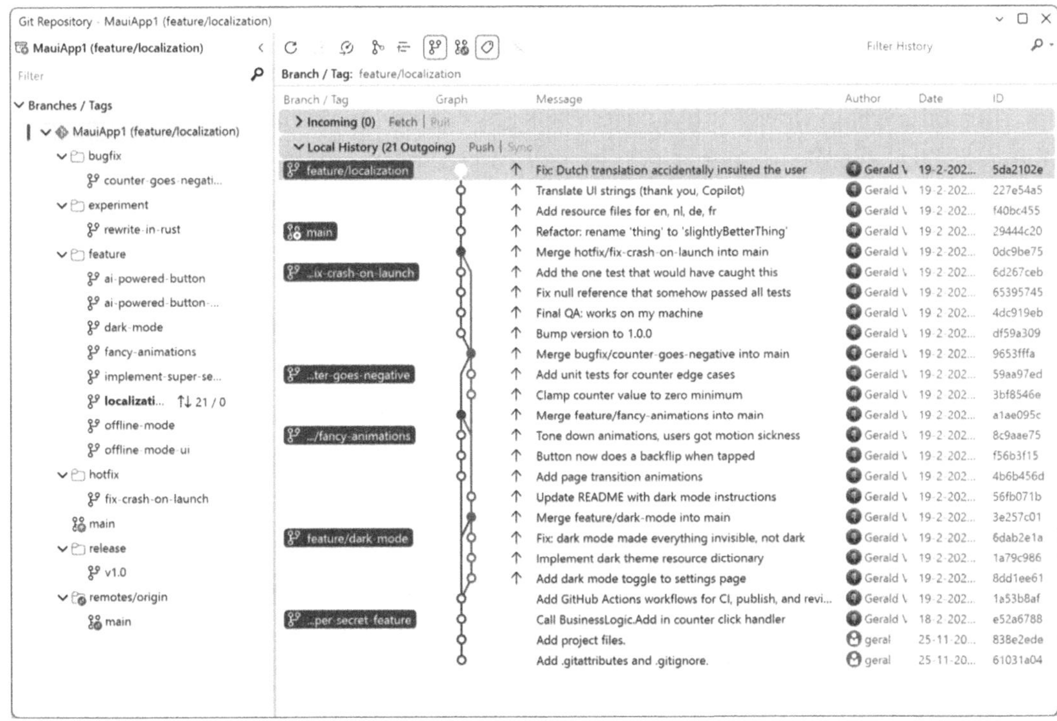

Figure 10-13. *An all-in-one solution to manage your Git repository from Visual Studio*

Commit History and Branch Comparison

The bottom section of the Git Repository window displays commit history as a graph. Each commit appears as a dot connected by lines that show branch relationships. Merges appear as multiple lines converging, while branch points show lines diverging.

You can filter commit history by branch, author, date range, or commit message text. Click any commit to see its details: the full commit message, author, timestamp, changed files, and parent commits. Double-click any changed file to see the diff.

Comparing Branches

Understanding the differences between branches is crucial for code review and planning merges. In the Git Repository window, right-click any branch and select Compare with Current Branch. Visual Studio displays a detailed comparison showing commits that exist in one branch but not the other and files that differ between branches.

The comparison view is interactive. Click any commit to see its details and the files it changed. Click any file to open a side-by-side diff showing exactly what differs between the branches. This helps you understand not just what changed, but when and why, before committing to a merge.

Handling Merge Conflicts

No matter how well your team coordinates, merge conflicts are inevitable when multiple people work on the same code base. Visual Studio 2026 includes an improved conflict resolution experience that makes these situations manageable.

When you pull changes or merge branches and Git detects conflicts, Visual Studio opens the Merge Conflict Resolver. This tool provides a three-pane view: the incoming changes on the left, your current changes on the right, and the result in the center. You can choose to accept incoming changes, keep your changes, or manually edit the result to combine both.

Visual Studio 2026 adds AI-assisted conflict resolution. When Copilot analyzes a conflict, it can suggest resolutions that intelligently combine both changes. For example, if both branches added methods to a class, Copilot might suggest keeping both methods rather than forcing you to choose one. This AI assistance provides a helpful starting point, especially in complex conflicts, though you still review and approve the resolution.

After resolving all conflicts in a file, you mark it as resolved and continue the merge operation. Visual Studio tracks which files still have unresolved conflicts, ensuring you don't accidentally commit a broken merge.

Managing Multiple Remotes

Advanced Git workflows sometimes require working with multiple remote repositories. For example, you might have a personal fork of an open source project on GitHub, but you also want to pull updates from the original upstream repository.

In the Git Repository window, expand the Remotes node to see all configured remotes. By default, you'll see the origin (the remote you cloned from or first pushed to). To add another remote, right-click Remotes and select Add Remote. Give the remote a name (like "upstream") and provide its URL.

After adding a remote, you can fetch from it to download its branches without merging them into your local branches. This lets you see what's changed upstream. If you want to incorporate those changes, you can merge or rebase them into your local branches using the Git Repository window's branch management tools.

This is particularly relevant if you're contributing to open source projects or working in a company that maintains both internal and public versions of software.

Advanced Operations and Best Practices

Visual Studio 2026 supports several advanced Git operations that, while used less frequently, are invaluable in specific situations. I won't go into them too deeply but here's an overview.

Cherry-Picking Commits

Cherry-picking lets you apply a specific commit from one branch to another. This is useful when you've made a bug fix on a feature branch but need to apply it to the main branch immediately without merging all the feature work. In the Git Repository window, navigate to the commit you want to cherry-pick, right-click it, and select Cherry-Pick. Visual Studio applies that commit's changes to your current branch.

Rebasing for a Cleaner History

Rebasing is an alternative to merging that creates a linear commit history by replaying your commits on top of another branch. Some teams prefer this for its cleaner history. To rebase your current branch onto another, open the Git Repository window, right-click the target branch, and select Rebase Current Branch Onto. Be cautious with rebasing; if you've already pushed commits to a shared branch, rebasing can cause problems for your teammates. Visual Studio displays warnings when appropriate.

Checking Out Specific Commits

Sometimes you need to examine your code as it existed at a specific point in history, perhaps because you want to investigate when a bug was introduced. In the Git Repository window, find the commit you're interested in, right-click it, and select Checkout Commit. Visual Studio warns you that this puts your repository in detached HEAD" state (you're viewing a snapshot, not on any branch). You can build and run the code, examine files, and even make experimental changes. If you want to save those changes, create a new branch from that commit.

Best Practices for Team Collaboration

Throughout your Git workflow, keep these practices in mind:

- Commit often, commit small: Frequent, focused commits make code review easier and debugging more effective. Use line-level staging to create atomic commits even when you've made multiple changes to a file.

- Write meaningful commit messages: While AI can help, ensure your messages explain both what changed and why. Future you (and your teammates) will appreciate it.

- Pull before you push: Always pull the latest changes before pushing yours to avoid merge conflicts and ensure you're building on current code.

- Use branches liberally: Create a new branch for each feature or bug fix. Don't be afraid to delete branches after merging; they've served their purpose.

- Review your changes before committing: Use the diff view to review what you're about to commit. It's easy to accidentally include debug code or temporary changes.

Git Configuration

Visual Studio 2026 respects your Git configuration while providing GUI alternatives to command-line configuration. Navigate to Tools ➤ Options ➤ Source Control ➤ Git Global Config to configure your name and email (which appear in commit metadata), default branch name for new repositories, and credential management preferences.

Visual Studio might also already hint you toward configuring your name and email earlier if you have not done that before. You might see a so-called gold bar (the yellow information messages at the top of a window or pane) that tells you to check your configuration. You can always come back here to change it if you want.

For repository-specific settings, Visual Studio surfaces options within the Git Repository window. You can configure which branches to prune during fetch, whether to use force-push protection, and how to handle line endings; all without needing to memorize Git configuration commands.

Visual Studio 2026 also integrates with Git hooks, the scripts that run automatically at certain points in the Git workflow (like pre-commit or post-merge). If your repository includes hooks, Visual Studio executes them appropriately, ensuring team-wide quality gates work seamlessly.

When You Git into Trouble

Pun intended. Git is powerful but can sometimes be confusing, especially when you find yourself in an unexpected state like a detached HEAD, a broken rebase, or accidental commits to the wrong branch. Visual Studio helps prevent many common mistakes with warnings and protective behaviors, but problems still happen.

A website dedicated to some common troublesome scenarios, with solutions, is `https://dangitgit.com/`. I chose to include the version without swear words; there is another version available if you like.

More seriously, though, if you encounter Git issues that Visual Studio's UI doesn't help you resolve, Microsoft Learn provides excellent resources at **`https://learn.microsoft.com/azure/devops/repos/git/`**. For common Git pitfalls and solutions, the Pro Git book's troubleshooting sections at **`https://git-scm.com/book`** are invaluable. And remember: Git's reflog keeps a history of where your branches have been, so even if you accidentally delete commits, they're often recoverable.

And if all else fails, you can always still ask Copilot.

Collaboration with Live Share

While Git handles asynchronous collaboration (you work on code, commit it, and your teammate pulls it later), sometimes real-time collaboration is more effective. Visual Studio Live Share enables multiple developers to edit and debug the same code base simultaneously, regardless of their physical location.

To start a Live Share session, click Live Share in the top-right corner of Visual Studio 2026 (or go to File ➤ Start Live Share Session). Visual Studio generates a unique session link that you share with collaborators. When they click the link, Visual Studio (or Visual Studio Code) connects them to your session, and they see your code and can start editing immediately.

Live Share is useful for pair programming, code reviews, troubleshooting, and mentoring. You can share your terminal, servers, and even debugging sessions—when you hit a breakpoint, your collaborators see it too and can inspect variables and step through code together.

Summary

Modern development workflows combine local Git operations, remote collaboration, continuous integration, and code review into a cohesive process. Visual Studio 2026 orchestrates these elements into a streamlined experience.

The workflow we walked through earlier—creating branches, making focused commits with AI-generated messages, pushing to remote repositories, creating pull requests, reviewing code, and integrating CI/CD feedback—represents how Visual Studio eliminates friction from collaboration. You're not constantly switching between the IDE, terminal windows, and browser tabs. Instead, source control becomes a natural part of your development rhythm, almost invisible in its integration.

As we'll explore in Chapter 11 when we discuss some different project types that you can find in Visual Studio, these collaboration capabilities work equally well whether you're building desktop applications, web services, mobile apps, or cloud-native solutions. Git integration and CI/CD pipelines are fundamental to modern development, regardless of platform.

Cross-Platform and Modern .NET Development

You've made it through ten chapters of learning Visual Studio 2026, and by now, you have a solid grasp on the IDE itself, the AI-powered features, debugging, testing, source control, and all the productivity tools at your disposal. But what good is all that knowledge if we don't put it to work building actual applications?

This chapter is where everything comes together. We're going to explore the different types of projects you can build with Visual Studio 2026 and .NET 10, from simple console applications to complex cross-platform mobile apps. Think of this as your practical guide to taking all the skills you've learned and applying them to real-world development scenarios.

The beauty of Visual Studio 2026 and .NET 10 is the sheer breadth of what you can build. You can create back-end services that run in the cloud, web applications that run in browsers, desktop applications for Windows, macOS, and Linux, mobile apps for iOS and Android, IoT applications for embedded devices, and even games. All from the same IDE, using largely the same language (C#), and sharing code across platforms. That's the power of modern .NET development.

We'll start simple with console applications, then move through web development with ASP.NET Core and Blazor, explore cross-platform app development with .NET MAUI, and see how Aspire helps you orchestrate cloud-native applications. Along the way, we'll touch on community alternatives and remind you that what we're covering here is just scratching the surface of what's possible. Let's build something!

© Gerald Versluis 2026

G. Versluis, *Getting Started with Visual Studio 2026*, https://doi.org/10.1007/979-8-8688-2691-7_11

Small last note before we begin: this chapter is mostly meant to show you what the possibilities are, rather than a step-by-step, follow-along tutorial. That is a bit beyond the scope of this book. We'll see how to get started with different types of projects, and from there, you can explore on your own. Apress has great books on all of these, so be sure to check those out.

Console Applications: Simple Yet Powerful

I'm convinced that in the era of AI, console applications will make a comeback, or even better, they will be more important than ever.

Console applications might seem basic, especially if you're used to flashy user interfaces and interactive web apps. But don't underestimate them. Console apps are experiencing a renaissance in modern development, particularly with the rise of AI agents and automation tools. GitHub Copilot, for example, can generate and run console applications autonomously to perform tasks, analyze data, or interact with APIs. They're also perfect for learning, prototyping, testing libraries, and building command-line tools that developers love.

A console application is a program that runs in a terminal or command prompt window, displaying text output and accepting text input. There's no graphical user interface, just straightforward input and output. This simplicity makes console apps incredibly fast to create and easy to debug. You can spin up a new console project, write a few lines of code, hit F5, and see results immediately.

Creating a Console Application in Visual Studio

To create a console application in Visual Studio 2026, start by opening Visual Studio and selecting Create a new project from the start window. In the project template search box, type "console" to filter the available templates. You'll see several options, but the one you want is Console App with the C# language tag. This is the modern .NET console application template. Select it and click Next.

Give your project a name (something like `MyFirstConsoleApp` if it's something you want to follow along with right now), and choose a location on your machine where you want to save it. Click Next again. On the Additional information screen, make sure you select .NET 10 as your target framework. You'll also see an option labeled Do not use top-level statements. This is a matter of preference and team convention. Top-level statements allow you to write console applications without explicitly defining a Program class and Main method, making your code more concise. If you're new to C# or prefer the traditional structure with a clear entry point, uncheck this option. For this example, let's leave top-level statements enabled (which means leave the check box unchecked) to see the modern approach.

There are a couple of other options: enable container support, what operating system the container should use, what container build type should be used, and whether or not to enable native AOT publishing. These are a bit more advanced; don't worry about those for the time being.

Click Create, and Visual Studio generates your console application. The template creates a simple application with a single file, Program.cs, containing just one line:

```
Console.WriteLine("Hello, World!");
```

That's it. Your entire console application. When you press F5 to run it (or use Debug ➤ Start Debugging from the menu), Visual Studio compiles your code, opens a terminal window, and displays "Hello, World!" on the screen. Simple, fast, effective.

If you have ever created a console application before, then you will probably be surprised that this is now trimmed down to being only one line. That is exactly what the top-level statements do. It eliminates the ceremony that .NET is known for. That means having to have a namespace declaration, having to have the Main method entry point, etc. To make .NET feel more modern and like other tech stacks, they have eliminated the need for all that. If this is not your cup of tea, don't worry, nothing has been removed. You can still use the old way if you want.

Note   Besides the top-level statement improvements, you can now also use file-based apps as of .NET 10. This reduces the needed boilerplate code even more and allows you to write a full app in a single `.cs` file if you want. This book is about Visual Studio and not .NET, so it is a bit out of scope, but if you want to learn more, find the information here: `https://learn.microsoft.com/dotnet/core/sdk/file-based-apps`.

In Figure 11-1, you can see the Create a new project dialog with the Console App template selected.

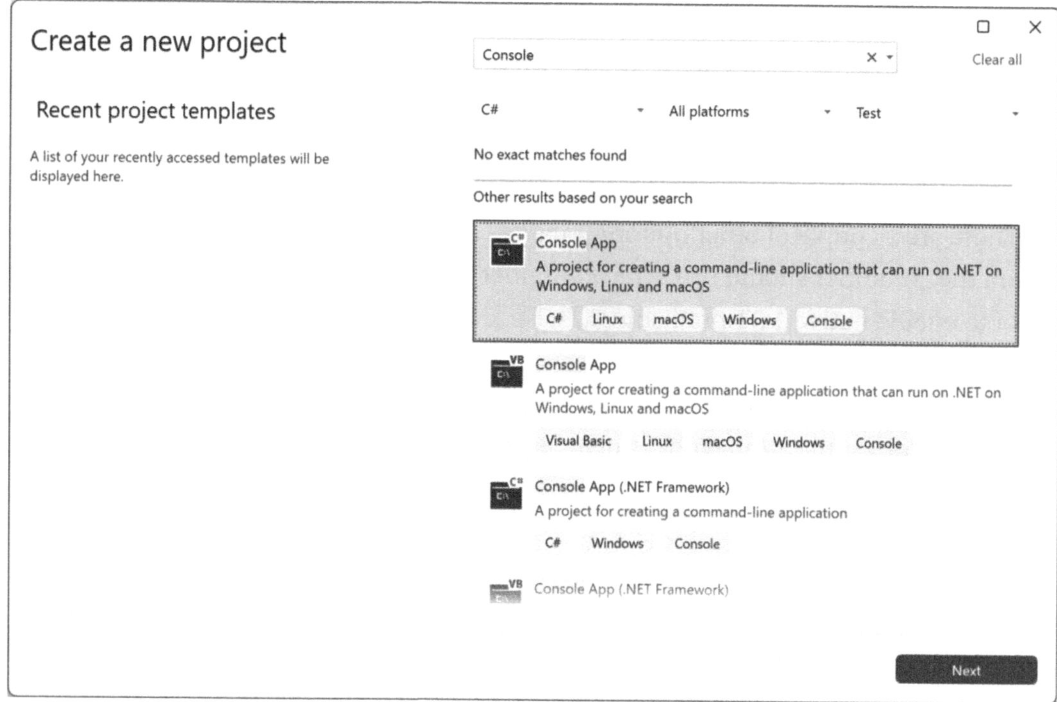

Figure 11-1. *Creating a new console application*

What Console Apps Are Good For

Console applications excel in scenarios where you need speed, simplicity, or automation. They're perfect for

- **Quick Prototypes and Experiments**: Testing an algorithm, trying out a new library, or learning a new API.

- **Command-Line Tools**: Building utilities that developers can run from the terminal, like code generators, file processors, or deployment scripts.

- **Background Services and Scheduled Tasks**: Running automated jobs, data processing pipelines, or monitoring scripts can be long-running.

- **AI Agent Execution**: As we covered in Chapter 9, AI agents like GitHub Copilot can generate and execute console applications to accomplish tasks autonomously.

Especially the last one, I think we will see a lot more of. AI agents, Copilot, can easily understand the command structure to invoke a console app, and the output is plain text which can then be used to be interpreted easily. Much easier than any visual output.

Console apps are also ideal for learning too. If you're new to .NET or Visual Studio, starting with a console application gives you a gentle introduction without the complexity of UI frameworks or web servers. You can focus on learning C# language features, understanding how classes and methods work, and getting comfortable with debugging (as we learned in Chapter 5).

Enhancing Your Console App

Let's make our console app a bit more interesting. Replace the single line in `Program.cs` with the following code, as seen in Listing 11-1 below; try to type it instead of copying and pasting.

Listing 11-1. A simple console application in C#

```
Console.WriteLine("What is your name?");
var name = Console.ReadLine();
var currentDate = DateTime.Now;
Console.WriteLine($"{Environment.NewLine}Hello, {name}, on {currentDate:d}
at {currentDate:t}!");
Console.Write($"{Environment.NewLine}Press any key to exit...");
Console.ReadKey(true);
```

This code prompts the user for their name, reads their input, and then greets them with the current date and time. The `Console.ReadKey(true)` at the end waits for the user to press a key before the application exits, giving you time to see the output.

Run the application with F5. Type your name when prompted and press Enter. You'll see a personalized greeting with the current date and time. Notice how Visual Studio's IntelliSense (which we discussed in Chapter 5) helped you as you typed, suggesting methods like `Console.WriteLine` and `DateTime.Now`. And if you made any mistakes, the live code analysis would have shown you red squiggles immediately.

Console applications might not have flashy UIs, but they're incredibly powerful tools in the modern developer's toolkit. They're fast to create, easy to debug, and perfect for automation. And with Hot Reload (which we'll see in action throughout this chapter), you can even make changes to your console app while it's running and see those changes applied immediately.

For more information about building console applications with .NET, check out the official Microsoft Learn tutorial at `https://learn.microsoft.com/dotnet/core/tutorials/with-visual-studio`.

ASP.NET Core: Building Web APIs and Services

Now let's step up to web development. ASP.NET Core is Microsoft's modern, cross-platform framework for building web applications and services. It's fast, scalable, and designed for cloud-native development. With ASP.NET Core, you can build RESTful APIs, microservices, real-time communication services with SignalR, and full web applications with server-side rendering.

ASP.NET Core runs on .NET 10, which means it benefits from all the performance improvements, language features, and AI integrations we've been discussing throughout this book. It's also completely cross-platform, running on Windows, macOS, and Linux. This makes it ideal for containerized deployments, Kubernetes orchestration, and cloud hosting on Azure, AWS, or Google Cloud.

Creating an ASP.NET Core Web API

Let's create a simple REST API to see how ASP.NET Core works in Visual Studio 2026. Start by creating a new project, and this time search for "web api" in the template search box. Select ASP.NET Core Web API (make sure it's the C# template) and click Next.

Name your project something like `MyWeatherApi` and choose a location. Click Next. On the Additional information screen, as shown in Figure 11-2 below, select .NET 10 as your target framework. You'll see several check boxes here:

- **Configure for HTTPS**: Leave this checked. HTTPS encryption is essential for web applications, and ASP.NET Core makes it easy to configure.

- **Enable Container Support**: Enables running this app in a container like a Docker container more easily.

- **Enable OpenAPI Support**: This is checked by default and worth keeping enabled. Starting with .NET 9, Microsoft replaced the long-standing Swashbuckle dependency in the project templates with a first-party package called `Microsoft.AspNetCore.OpenApi`. Checking this option adds that package to your project and configures two things in `Program.cs`: `builder.Services.AddOpenApi()`, which registers the OpenAPI document generation services, and `app.MapOpenApi()`, which exposes the generated document as a JSON file at `/openapi/v1.json` during development. What it does *not* do is give you a visual browser UI for testing; that's a separate step we'll look at shortly.

- **Do Not Use Top-Level Statements**: As with console apps, this is a style preference. Leave it checked to see the traditional structure.

- **Use Controllers**: This is about API architecture. Unchecking it creates a minimal API with simpler syntax. For this example, let's leave it unchecked to see minimal APIs in action.

- **Enlist in Aspire Orchestration**: Determines if you want to list this project in an existing Aspire orchestration in this solution or create a new Aspire project and add this project to that. More on Aspire later in this chapter.

Click Create, and Visual Studio generates your Web API project. You'll see several files in Solution Explorer, which we learned about back in Chapter 4. The key file is `Program.cs`, which contains the application's entry point and configuration.

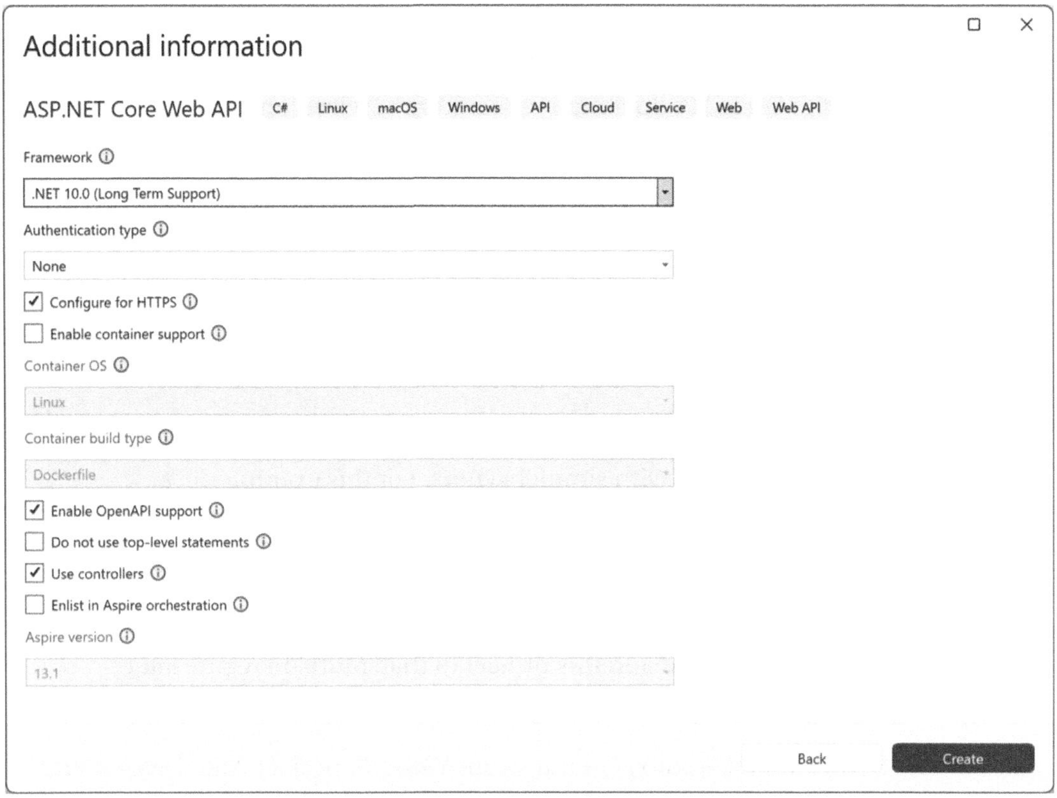

Figure 11-2. *The options available to create a new ASP.NET Web API project*

Running and Testing Your API

Before you run your API for the first time, Visual Studio might prompt you to trust the ASP.NET Core HTTPS development certificate. This certificate allows your application to use HTTPS locally during development. When the prompt appears, click Yes to trust the certificate. You'll then see a Windows security warning asking if you want to install the certificate. Click Yes again. This only happens once per machine, and it's essential for HTTPS to work locally.

Press F5 to start debugging your Web API. Visual Studio builds the project and launches a browser, but don't expect a slick visual API explorer to open automatically—that's no longer the default experience in .NET 10. What you *do* get is your API running and listening, with the raw OpenAPI document available at `https://localhost:[port]/openapi/v1.json`. You can open that URL in a browser or any HTTP tool to inspect the machine-readable description of your API's endpoints, parameters, and response schemas.

For quick interactive testing directly inside Visual Studio, look at the project in Solution Explorer for a file named `[YourProjectName].http`. This is Visual Studio's built-in HTTP editor, which lets you send HTTP requests to your API and inspect responses without leaving the IDE. The generated .http file comes pre-populated with a sample request for the WeatherForecast endpoint. We'll learn a little more about that in the next section after this.

If you prefer a richer visual UI for exploring and testing your API, you have a couple of good options. One popular choice is Scalar, a modern open source API explorer. Install the `Scalar.AspNetCore` NuGet package and add two lines to `Program.cs` inside the if (`app.Environment.IsDevelopment()`) block like in Listing 11-2:

Listing 11-2. Enabling Scalar for our ASP.NET project

```
app.MapOpenApi();
app.MapScalarApiReference();
```

You might need to add `using Scalar.AspNetCore;` at the top of the file, or let Quick Actions help you with that. With this in place, navigate to `https://localhost:[port]/scalar` and you'll see a polished, interactive API documentation page backed by the same OpenAPI document your project already generates.

In Figure 11-3, you can see the Scalar web interface testing the WeatherForecast endpoint.

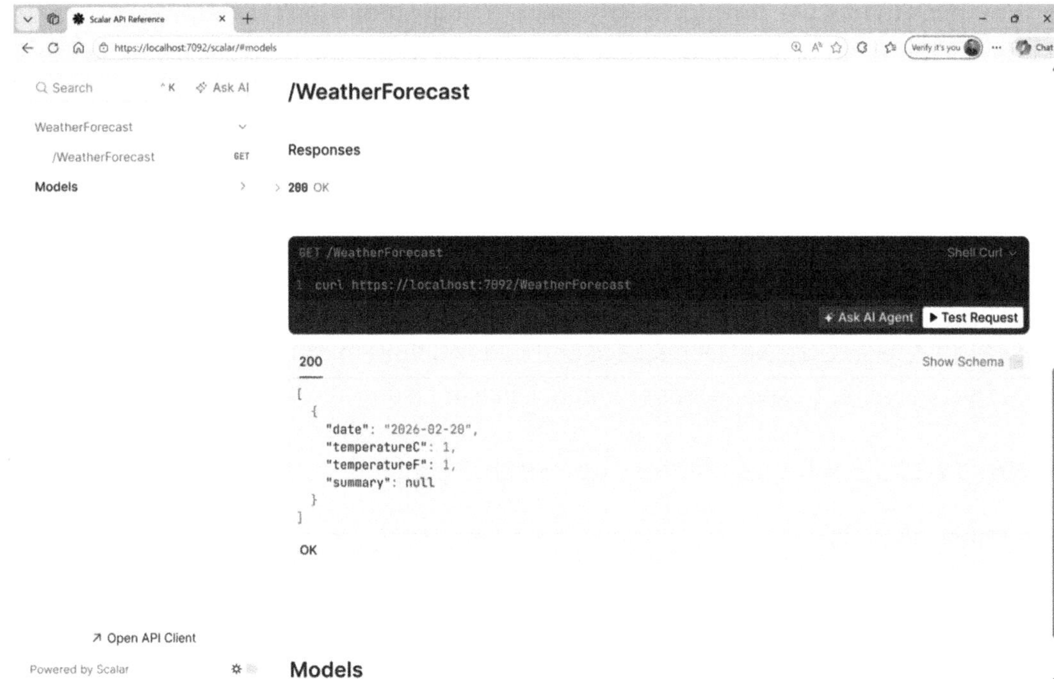

Figure 11-3. *Testing the WeatherForecast endpoint in the Scalar web interface*

Alternatively, if you're more familiar with the classic Swagger UI look from previous .NET versions, you can add just the `Swashbuckle.AspNetCore.SwaggerUI` NuGet package (not the full Swashbuckle package, just the UI portion) and point it at your existing `/openapi/v1.json` endpoint. Either way, these are opt-in choices you make based on your preference; the core API works perfectly fine without them.

Testing Your API with HTTP Files

While OpenAPI with Scalar is fantastic for interactive exploration, Visual Studio 2026 offers another powerful way to test your APIs right inside the IDE: HTTP files (`.http` files). These are simple text files that contain HTTP requests you can execute directly from Visual Studio, complete with syntax highlighting, IntelliSense support, and response viewing. They're perfect for documenting your API endpoints, testing complex scenarios, and debugging without leaving your editor or launching external tools like Postman.

For the ASP.NET project we just created, a default file was already added, but if that is not the case for the project you are looking at to get started, right-click your Web API project in Solution Explorer, and select Add ➤ New Item. Search for "HTTP" and select HTTP File. Name it something like `weather-requests.http` and click Add. Visual Studio opens the file with full editor support.

You'll see a template with a sample GET request, as shown in Listing 11-3 below. Replace it with your API's endpoint.

Listing 11-3. A simple sample .http file

```
GET https://localhost:7000/weatherforecast
accept: application/json

###

GET https://localhost:7000/weatherforecast
```

The ### separates requests. The first is a simple GET to your weather endpoint. The second adds a custom header. Notice the `localhost:7000`, and grab the actual port from your project's Properties ➤ Debug ➤ App URL or the Output window when running.

With your API running (F5), click Send Request (the green play button above the first request) or right-click and select Send Request. Visual Studio sends the HTTP request, displays the response below (status code, headers, JSON body), and even lets you debug into the endpoint if breakpoints are set. Responses show syntax-highlighted JSON, making it easy to verify your data.

Figure 11-4 shows you the HTTP file contents on the left with a simple GET request and on the right the result of the request that we triggered by clicking on Send request, just about the GET keyword.

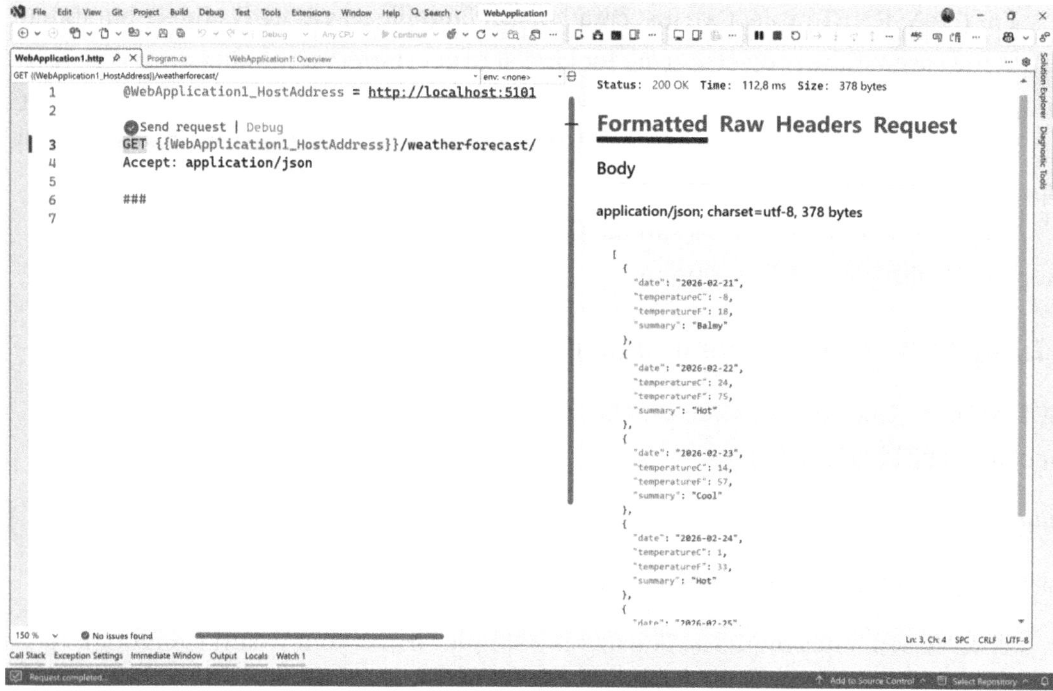

Figure 11-4. *Working with HTTP files in Visual Studio*

You can chain requests using variables. For example, POST to create data and extract the ID for a follow-up GET. An example is shown in Listing 11-4 below.

Listing 11-4. Chaining requests, getting the output value, and using that in a variable

```
POST https://localhost:7000/weatherforecast
Content-Type: application/json

{
  "date": "2026-02-20T10:00:00Z",
  "temperatureC": 25,
  "summary": "Warm"
}

@id = {{$response.body.id}}

###

GET https://localhost:7000/weatherforecast/{{id}}
```

The `@id` extracts from the POST response (using JSONPath). This makes testing stateful APIs straightforward. HTTP files also support authentication (Bearer tokens, Basic auth), file uploads, and environment variables from `launchSettings.json`.

HTTP files check into source control as documentation; your team sees example requests alongside the code. They're faster than Swagger for repetitive tests and integrate with GitHub Copilot: ask Copilot Chat to "generate HTTP requests for my WeatherForecast API," and it creates a ready-to-use `.http` file.

This workflow keeps you in Visual Studio flow: edit code, test via HTTP file, debug with breakpoints, repeat. For full details, see `https://learn.microsoft.com/aspnet/core/test/http-files`.

Hot Reload for Web Applications

One of the most powerful features in Visual Studio 2026 for web development is Hot Reload. Remember from Chapter 5 how we could make code changes and see them immediately without rebuilding? That works beautifully with ASP.NET Core.

With your API still running, go back to Visual Studio. Open `Program.cs` and find the line that generates weather forecasts (it's in the minimal API endpoint definition). Change the summary values to something fun, like adding "Very Hot" or "Freezing Cold" to the list. Hit Ctrl+S to save the file. Visual Studio applies the changes to your running application without restarting it. Go back to Swagger, execute the `/weatherforecast` endpoint again, and you'll see your new summaries appear in the response. This dramatically speeds up your development workflow, as you're not constantly waiting for rebuilds and restarts.

Beyond APIs: Full Web Applications with ASP.NET Core

While we've focused on Web APIs for back-end services, ASP.NET Core is just as powerful for building complete web applications with rich user interfaces. The framework supports ASP.NET Core MVC for traditional server-rendered pages, Razor Pages for page-focused applications, and even Blazor Server integration for interactive components (we'll learn about that next), all from the same project templates and tooling in Visual Studio 2026.

When you create a new ASP.NET Core Web App project (search for "web app" instead of "web api"), Visual Studio generates a full-featured web application with pages, layouts, authentication scaffolding, and responsive design ready to go. You'll get a navigation menu, home page, privacy policy page, and support for user authentication out of the box. The same HTTP file testing workflow applies here. You can test form submissions, protected endpoints, and server-rendered page responses right alongside your development.

This versatility means ASP.NET Core handles your entire web stack: APIs for your mobile apps and SPAs (.NET MAUI, Blazor), traditional web apps for internal tools and marketing sites, and everything in between. Whether you're building a simple admin dashboard, a customer-facing portal, or a complex enterprise application, ASP.NET Core + Visual Studio 2026 gives you the full web development experience with C#, Hot Reload, and all the productivity tools you've learned throughout this book.

The same debugging, testing, GitHub Copilot integration, and project management techniques work identically across API and UI projects, making your skills immediately transferable as your applications grow from simple services to full-featured web applications.

For more information about building Web APIs with ASP.NET Core, see the official documentation at `https://learn.microsoft.com/aspnet/core/web-api/`.

Blazor: Full-Stack Web with C#

If ASP.NET Core is for back-end services, Blazor is for building interactive web UIs entirely in C#. No JavaScript required (though you can use JavaScript if you want). Blazor allows you to write your front-end and back-end logic in the same language, share code between client and server, and leverage all the .NET libraries you already know.

There are several Blazor hosting models:

- **Blazor Server:** Your UI logic runs on the server, and UI updates are sent to the browser over a SignalR connection. This keeps your application secure and responsive but requires a persistent connection to the server.

- **Blazor WebAssembly:** Your application compiles to WebAssembly and runs entirely in the browser. This gives you true client-side execution with offline capabilities, but the initial download size is larger.

- **Blazor Web App:** The new unified model in .NET 10 that combines server-side rendering, interactive server components, and client-side WebAssembly all in one application. This is the recommended approach for new projects.

- **Blazor Hybrid:** Combines Blazor with native app frameworks like .NET MAUI to build desktop and mobile applications with web technologies. We'll cover this in the next section.

Creating a Blazor Web App

Let's create a Blazor Web App to see how it works. Start a new project and search for "blazor" in the template search box. Select Blazor Web App and click Next. Name your project something like `MyBlazorApp` and click Next.

On the Additional information screen, select .NET 10 as your framework. You'll see several options here, just like before in the other projects:

- **Authentication Type:** Pre-configures authentication, not needed for now.

- **Configure for HTTPS:** Just as before, let's keep this one; it's important to keep the web safe!

- **Interactive Render Mode:** Choose how your app renders interactive components. Options include Server (components run on the server), WebAssembly (components run in the browser), or Auto (Visual Studio decides based on the scenario). Let's keep the default value for now.

- **Interactivity Location:** Choose Global to make the entire app interactive or Per page/component for more granular control. Also, here, just keep the default value for just showing the template.

- **Include Sample Pages:** Leave this checked. It gives you example pages to learn from.

- **Do Not Use Top-Level Statements:** Just like in the other templates, this is the more modern way of doing things and removing boilerplate code.

- **Use the .dev.localhost TLD in the Application URL:** Makes it easier to test locally with an easier-to-remember name instead of an IP and makes it possible to separate cookies, etc.

- **Enlist in Aspire Orchestration:** Determines if you want to list this project in an existing Aspire orchestration in this solution or create a new Aspire project and add this project to that. More on Aspire later in this chapter.

Click Create. Visual Studio generates your Blazor project with several Razor component files (`.razor` files). These are similar to HTML files but with C# code embedded. Open the `Home.razor` file in the `Components/Pages` folder. You'll see a mix of HTML markup and C# code that defines the home page of your application.

Press F5 to run your Blazor app. Visual Studio opens a browser window showing your application. You'll see a navigation menu on the left with links like Home, Counter, and Weather. Click around and notice how fast and responsive everything feels. Click the Counter page and press the "Click me" button. The counter increments instantly, all handled by C# code running (depending on your render mode) either on the server or in the browser via WebAssembly.

Figure 11-5 shows the running Blazor project in the browser on the Weather tab that mimics loading weather forecasts from a remote API service.

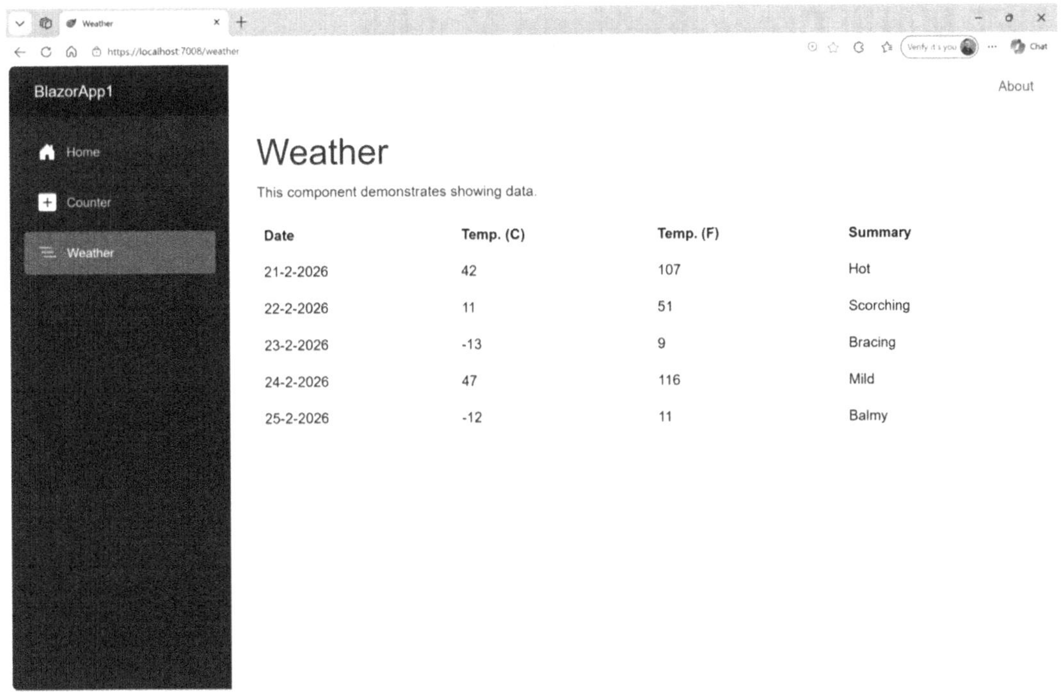

Figure 11-5. *Running a Blazor project in the browser*

Hot Reload in Blazor

Hot Reload is especially powerful in Blazor because it works for both markup and code. With your Blazor app still running, go back to Visual Studio. Open `Home.razor` and change the welcome message text. Save the file. The browser updates immediately without a full reload, and you see your changes live. This works for C# code too. Open `Counter.razor`, find the `IncrementCount` method, and change the increment value from 1 to 5. Save the file, go back to the browser, and click the button. It now increments by 5. All without rebuilding or reloading.

Blazor is incredibly versatile. You can build full web applications, progressive web apps (PWAs), and even hybrid applications that run on desktop and mobile devices. And because it's all C#, you can use all the refactoring, debugging, and AI-powered features we've covered throughout this book.

For more information about Blazor, see the official documentation at `https://learn.microsoft.com/aspnet/core/blazor/`.

.NET MAUI: Cross-Platform Mobile and Desktop Apps

Now let's talk about building apps that run natively on mobile and desktop platforms. .NET Multi-platform App UI (.NET MAUI) is Microsoft's framework for creating applications that run on iOS, Android, macOS, and Windows from a single code base. You write your UI once using XAML or C#, and .NET MAUI renders it using native controls on each platform.

This is powerful. You're not building web apps wrapped in native containers (like some other cross-platform frameworks). You're building real native applications with native performance, native look and feel, and full access to platform-specific features. And because it's all .NET, you can share your business logic, data access code, and more across platforms.

Creating a .NET MAUI Application

To create a .NET MAUI project, make sure you have the .NET Multi-platform App UI development workload installed in Visual Studio 2026. If you followed the installation steps back in Chapter 2, you should be good to go. If not, you can modify your installation through the Visual Studio Installer and add this workload.

Start a new project and search for "maui" in the template search box. Select .NET MAUI App and click Next. Name your project something like MyMauiApp and click Next. On the Additional information screen, select .NET 10 as your framework and click Create.

There are a number of extra options that you can choose here as well. Just like other projects, you can enlist it in an Aspire orchestration, but more importantly, here you can also include some sample content. If you do that, you basically get a fully built-out app that is a very extensive todo management app. Very useful for exploring common MAUI concepts, but a bit too much for what we want to do right now.

If you are doing this for the first time, you might see some extra dialogs about Android SDKs and license agreements. This is because MAUI builds on top of the native tech stacks. Under the hood, it still uses the Android SDK and the iOS SDK to pull in the native APIs. So, underlying, you still need all of those as prerequisites. This all makes MAUI very powerful to build apps for different platforms, but also one of the more complex project types in the .NET ecosystem. Typically, you should just be able to click OK or Next for the Android SDK dialogs.

Visual Studio generates your MAUI project. You'll see a project structure in Solution Explorer with folders for Platforms (platform-specific code), Resources (images, fonts, app icons), and XAML files for your UI. The `MainPage.xaml` file defines the default page of your application.

Figure 11-6 shows a new MAUI project, the `MainPage.xaml` in the background, the project structure in the Solution Explorer on the right, and the running app on Android and Windows in front.

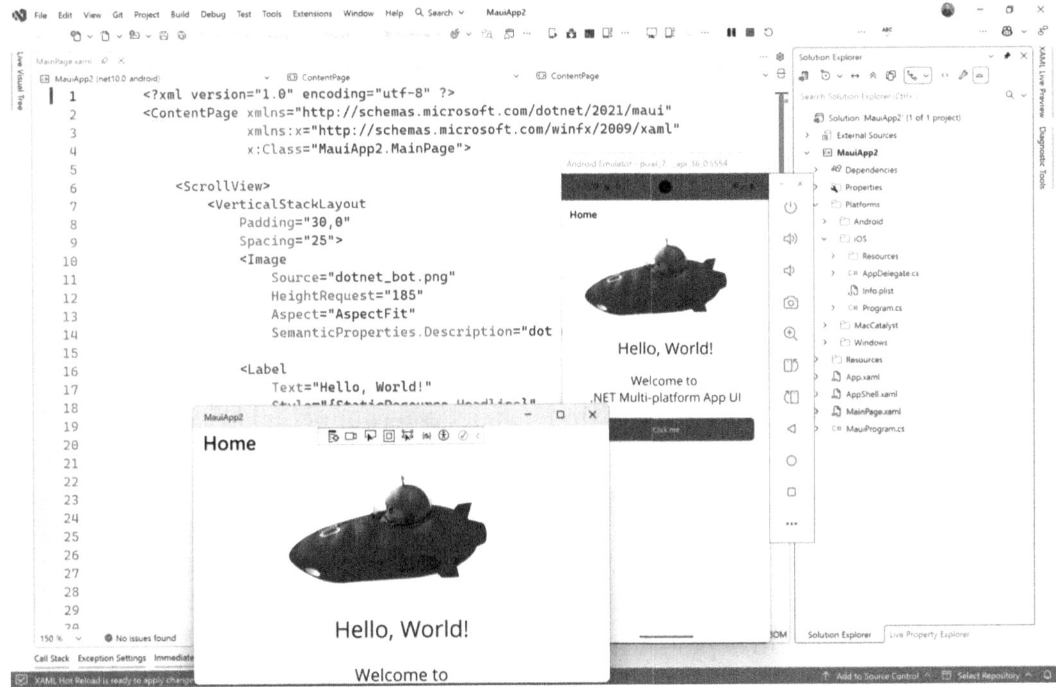

Figure 11-6. *A .NET MAUI project in Visual Studio, running on Android and Windows*

Running .NET MAUI on Different Platforms

Here's where .NET MAUI gets interesting. Look at the Debug Target drop-down in the Visual Studio toolbar (the one that usually says "Windows Machine" or shows a device name). Click it, and you'll see options for different platforms: Windows Machine (to run your app as a native Windows desktop application), Android Emulator (to run your app on an Android emulator), iOS Simulator (if you're paired to a Mac), and potentially physical devices if they're connected.

Let's start simple. Select Windows Machine and press F5. Visual Studio compiles your app and launches it as a native Windows application. You'll see a window with your MAUI app running. Click the "Click me" button, and the counter increments (because what is a new app template without incrementing a value!). Close the app.

Now, let's try Android. Select Android Emulator from the Debug Target drop-down. If you haven't set up an emulator yet, Visual Studio will prompt you to create one through the Android Device Manager. This process downloads the necessary Android SDKs and creates a virtual device. Once the emulator is running, press F5 again. Visual Studio deploys your app to the Android emulator, and you'll see your application running on an Android device (virtualized, but it looks and behaves like a real device). The exact same code, now running on Android. And still incrementing the counter.

iOS Development Requirements

I already mentioned that MAUI is one of the more complex project types in .NET. If you add iOS in the mix, there is a whole new layer of challenges. Luckily, Visual Studio has solutions for that.

There is an important limitation to understand: you cannot build iOS or macOS applications on a Windows machine alone. Apple's tools require macOS for compilation. If you're on Windows and want to build for iOS, you have two options:

1. **Pair to a Mac**: Use Visual Studio's Pair to Mac feature to connect to a Mac on your network. Visual Studio will use that Mac for building and deploying iOS apps. We'll talk about this in a moment.

2. **Use a Cloud Mac Service**: Services like MacStadium or MacinCloud instances offer hosted macOS environments specifically for iOS development. These are legitimate macOS machines you can connect to remotely for building iOS apps.

Conversely, if you're on a Mac running VS Code on a Mac, you cannot build Windows-specific applications. Each platform has its constraints, and this is one of them.

If you look beyond Visual Studio on Windows, you can build iOS and Mac apps directly from your Mac using Visual Studio Code. The one platform that Mac and Windows have in common is Android; you can build those on both platforms without any issue.

Pair to Mac and iOS Remote Simulator

For Windows developers who want to build iOS apps, Pair to Mac is your solution. This feature in Visual Studio 2026 connects your Windows machine to a Mac on your network, using the Mac as a build host. Here's how it works:

First, make sure your Mac has Xcode and the necessary .NET workloads installed. On your Mac, enable Remote Login in System Settings ➤ General ➤ Sharing. Then, in Visual Studio 2026 on Windows, go to Tools ➤ iOS ➤ Pair to Mac. Visual Studio scans your network for available Macs. Select your Mac from the list and authenticate with your Mac user credentials. Visual Studio establishes an SSH connection to the Mac and installs any necessary agents.

Once paired, you can select iOS Simulator from the Debug Target drop-down in Visual Studio. Press F5, and Visual Studio builds your app on the Mac, deploys it to the iOS Simulator running on the Mac, and then displays that simulator window remotely on your Windows machine through the iOS Remote Simulator. You interact with the simulator on your Windows screen, but it's actually running on the Mac. It's seamless.

This setup means you can develop, debug, and test iOS applications entirely from your Windows machine without constantly switching between devices. The iOS Remote Simulator even supports touch gestures, so you can simulate taps, swipes, and pinches using your mouse.

Figure 11-7 shows the same app as before, now running on the iOS Remote Simulator. In the background in Visual Studio, you can also see the same screen in the XAML Live Preview window, more on that in a minute.

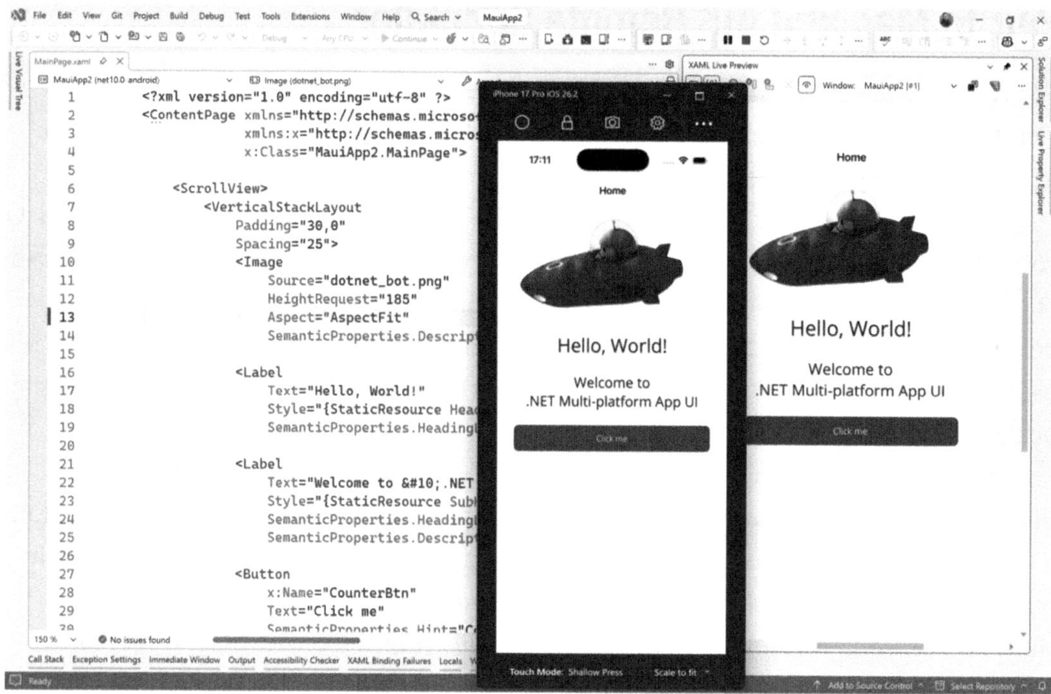

Figure 11-7. *A .NET MAUI app running on iOS right from Visual Studio on Windows*

For more details on setting up Pair to Mac and using the iOS Remote Simulator, see the official documentation at `https://learn.microsoft.com/dotnet/maui/ios/pair-to-mac`.

Live Preview and Live Property Explorer

Hot Reload is great when you already know what you want to change, but sometimes you're still figuring out *why* a layout behaves the way it does. That's where Visual Studio's live XAML tooling becomes your secret weapon: you can preview the UI, pick elements visually, and inspect runtime properties without playing "guess the margin" all afternoon.

XAML Live Preview

XAML Live Preview captures your app's UI into a docked tool window inside Visual Studio, so you can make XAML edits and immediately see the result while iterating. In Visual Studio 2026, this is especially useful for MAUI because XAML Live Preview + XAML Hot Reload can be used at design time for .NET MAUI apps (not only during an active debugging session), and it also supports Android devices and emulators.

To open it, go to Debug ➤ Windows ➤ XAML Live Preview. Once it's open, you can zoom and scroll around the preview, and you can also use element selection to jump from what you click in the preview to the corresponding element in the Live Visual Tree and your source XAML (when available).

Live Visual Tree and Live Property Explorer

When you run an XAML-based app with the debugger attached, Visual Studio can show a Live Visual Tree (a real-time hierarchy of UI elements) and a Live Property Explorer (the runtime properties of whatever element you select).

Live Property Explorer is a debugging window that lets you inspect the actual runtime property values of a XAML UI element while your app is running (with the debugger attached), instead of just looking at what you *think* you set in XAML.

In practice, you first pick an element in the Live Visual Tree (the real-time hierarchy of UI elements), then open its properties; Visual Studio shows the selected element's properties in Live Property Explorer and updates the window as you select different elements.

The cool thing is that all these tools work together. You can hover over elements in the Live Preview, click something, and that will get selected in the Live Visual Tree, and then you can, in turn, inspect and even modify some property values. Or vice versa; select something in the Live Visual True, click the XAML button, and it will be selected in the XAML Live Preview. Very powerful tools to greatly speed up your inner-dev loop.

Blazor Hybrid: Web Technologies for Native Apps

One of the most exciting capabilities in .NET MAUI is Blazor Hybrid, which lets you build native mobile and desktop applications using familiar web technologies (HTML, CSS, Razor components) while getting true native performance and platform integration. Instead of learning XAML, you write Blazor components that render inside a native

WebView control on each platform: WebView2 on Windows, WKWebView on iOS/macOS, and Android WebView on Android. Because the BlazorWebView, as the MAUI control is called, follows the same paradigm as all of MAUI, it translates all the abstracted controls to their native counterpart.

This approach is perfect if you already know Blazor or web development but want to target native app stores. Your Blazor components run locally (not over the network like Blazor WebAssembly), giving you fast startup, offline capability, and full access to native APIs through JavaScript interop or .NET MAUI handlers. This gives you all the power of the underlying platform and devices while giving you the advantage of not having to learn XAML, or maybe you just want to reuse your existing Blazor code, which you totally can.

Creating a Blazor Hybrid MAUI App

To create a Blazor Hybrid project, start with the .NET MAUI Blazor App template. Search for "maui blazor" in the New Project dialog. This generates an MAUI project configured with Blazor hosting. You'll see familiar files from the .NET MAUI project like MainPage. xaml and MauiProgram.cs. But also familiar concepts from the Blazor project like a wwwroot folder for CSS, JavaScript, and static assets and the Components folder with all Razor components.

The structure looks like a standard MAUI project; in fact, it is still a .NET MAUI project and app, but MauiProgram.cs registers Blazor services with builder.Services. AddMauiBlazorWebView();.

In the MainPage.xaml, you will now find a BlazorWebView instead of the layout that we have seen before. That BlazorWebView is configured to look at the Routes.razor file, and that bootstraps the Blazor part of this application. From there, if you want, you can build your whole app in Blazor.

Press F5 to run on your target platform (Windows, Android, etc.). You'll see a native app window with Blazor-rendered content. All the MAUI debugging, Hot Reload, and deployment features work exactly as they do with XAML-based MAUI apps. If you have seen the Blazor template before, you will notice that this is the exact same application but now running natively on a completely different platform.

An important note is that a Blazor Hybrid app is a completely native app. The only thing, simply put, that you do is replace XAML and the native look-and-feel with a web view that renders web UI. All the code underneath is C# and is not transpiled to something else. Also, it's not served through a web service in the background or running through WebAssembly. The .NET runtime is already running on these platforms through .NET MAUI, and Blazor is just a .NET app; we can run that directly on the devices.

Because of all this, you can also mix and match XAML and Razor if you want. Because the Blazor Hybrid approach is implemented through the `BlazorWebView`, you can choose if you want to make the web view a full-screen control and build your whole app in that, or maybe make the web view just a small component in your XAML screen and make it work with the native controls, all on one page.

For more, see `https://learn.microsoft.com/aspnet/core/blazor/hybrid/tutorials/maui`. If you want to learn how to build a Blazor Hybrid app step-by-step, there is also a full, self-paced workshop that you can find here: `https://github.com/dotnet-presentations/blazor-hybrid-workshop`.

Hot Reload in .NET MAUI and Blazor Hybrid

Hot Reload works brilliantly with .NET MAUI. With your app running on any platform (Windows, Android, or iOS Simulator), you can make changes to your XAML or C# code, save the file, and see the changes applied immediately without restarting the app. Change the text of a button in `MainPage.xaml`, hit Ctrl+S, and watch it update live on the running app. This works across all platforms, making MAUI development incredibly productive.

One important note: Hot Restart, a feature that was available in Visual Studio 2022 for iOS deployment without a Mac, is not supported in Visual Studio 2026. Microsoft's recommended approach is now to use Pair to Mac for building and deploying iOS applications. If you relied on Hot Restart in VS 2022, you'll need to transition to using a Mac build host for VS 2026 projects or stay on VS 2022 which will still be supported for some time. Hot Reload, however, is fully supported and works beautifully once you're connected to a Mac.

For a comprehensive guide to .NET MAUI development, see the official documentation at `https://learn.microsoft.com/dotnet/maui/`. For a .NET MAUI app with XAML, there is also a great workshop for that: `https://github.com/dotnet-presentations/dotnet-maui-workshop`.

Aspire: Orchestrating Cloud-Native Applications

As your applications grow more complex, you'll likely find yourself building distributed systems with multiple services, databases, message queues, caching layers, and APIs all talking to each other. Managing all these services during development can be a nightmare. That's where Aspire comes in.

Note   When Aspire started, it was named .NET Aspire. However, Aspire can also work with Python, JavaScript, Rust, and much more. To reflect that, the branding was updated to be just Aspire.

Aspire is an opinionated stack for building cloud-native applications with .NET. It provides components, tools, and patterns for building resilient, observable, and configurable distributed applications. Aspire isn't a framework you write code against (though it provides libraries for common scenarios). Instead, it's an orchestration and composition layer that helps you manage your application's services during development and production. Your project does not have to be made compatible or do anything special; you can add Aspire on top and make your life a lot easier, even if just for local development.

What Aspire Does for You

Imagine you're building an ecommerce application. You have an ASP.NET Core Web API for your back end, a Blazor front end, a PostgreSQL database, a Redis cache, and maybe a message queue like RabbitMQ. Normally, you'd need to start each of these services manually, configure connection strings, manage ports, and ensure everything is running before you can test your application.

With Aspire, you define all these services in a single AppHost project. Aspire handles starting them, configuring them, and wiring them together. It even provides a beautiful dashboard where you can monitor all your services, view logs, traces, and metrics in real time. It's like having a mini cloud environment running on your local machine.

Creating an Aspire Orchestration

Start a new project and search for "aspire" in the template search box. Select Aspire Starter App (ASP.NET Core/Blazor) and click Next. Name your project something like MyAspireApp and click Next. Select .NET 10 as your framework and click Create. Also, here there are some options to configure, but let's not worry about those for now.

While this makes for a nice introduction, in reality, it will probably be the other way around: you will add Aspire to your existing project. You can also easily do that by right-clicking your project in the Solution Explorer and choosing Add ➤ Aspire Orchestrator Support. You will get a dialog that gives you some options; typically, you can just accept the defaults and click OK. That will generate the AppHost project if it's not already there and enlist your project in there for usage.

But for now, let's go back to the starter application template. Visual Studio generates three projects in your solution:

1. **MyAspireApp.AppHost:** This is the orchestration project. It defines your application's services and their dependencies. This basically lets you describe your whole application landscape, including dependencies, parameters, and everything it needs to know to start running.

2. **MyAspireApp.ServiceDefaults:** Shared configuration for service defaults like logging, health checks, and telemetry.

3. **MyAspireApp.ApiService:** A sample ASP.NET Core Web API that's already configured to work with Aspire.

4. **MyAspireApp.Web:** A sample Blazor web application that communicates with the ApiService project.

Open AppHost.cs in the AppHost project. You'll see code that defines your application's architecture. An example of this is shown in Listing 11-5.

Listing 11-5. A simple Aspire orchestration

```
var builder = DistributedApplication.CreateBuilder(args);

var apiService = builder.AddProject<Projects.AspireApp1_
ApiService>("apiservice")
    .WithHttpHealthCheck("/health");
```

```
builder.AddProject<Projects.AspireApp1_Web>("webfrontend")
    .WithExternalHttpEndpoints()
    .WithHttpHealthCheck("/health")
    .WithReference(apiService)
    .WaitFor(apiService);

builder.Build.RunO;
```

This code defines one service: `apiservice`, which is the Web API project, and one front-end project: `webfrontend`, which is the Blazor web app. Aspire will start these projects when you run the AppHost.

You can see this in Figure 11-8. On the left, the `AppHost.cs` is opened, and on the right, you can see the solution structure in the Solution Explorer.

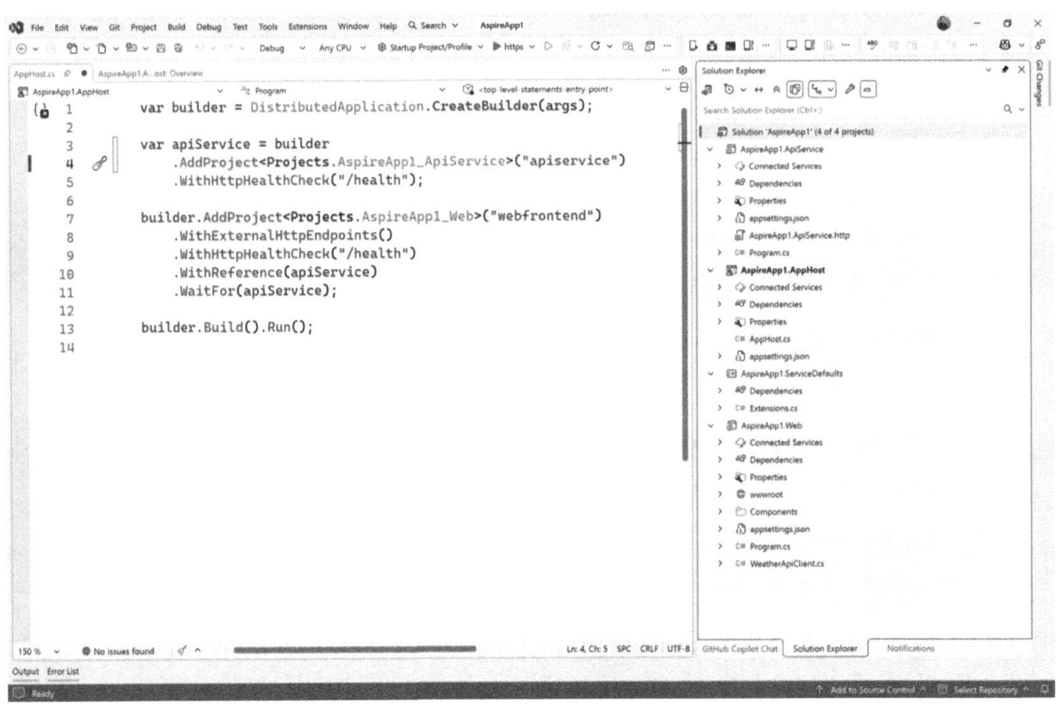

Figure 11-8. *The Aspire starter project in Visual Studio*

Set the AppHost project as the startup project (right-click it in Solution Explorer and choose Set as Startup Project). Press F5 to run the application. Visual Studio starts all the services defined in your AppHost and opens the Aspire Dashboard in your browser.

The Aspire Dashboard is a web-based UI (actually also a Blazor app) that shows all your services, their health status, resource usage, logs, traces, and metrics. Click on the `apiservice` entry to see details. You'll see the service URL, environment variables, and real-time logs. Click the Traces tab to see distributed tracing information showing how requests flow through your services.

In Figure 11-9, you can see the Aspire dashboard showing an overview of the projects currently in our orchestration. From here, you can start/stop them, inspect HTTP traces, show structured logging, have a look at the metrics, and much more.

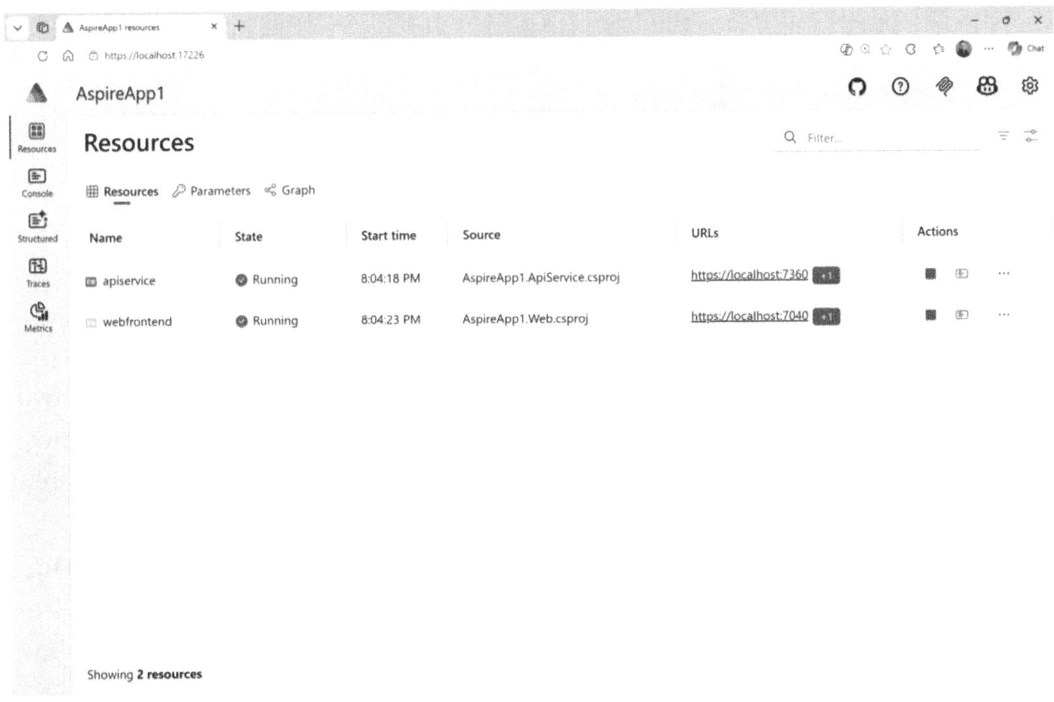

Figure 11-9. *The Aspire dashboard with two projects currently running*

Adding More Services with Aspire

The real power of Aspire comes when you add more services. Let's have a look at what it will look like if you want to add a Redis cache to this application. You will have to install the Aspire.Hosting.Redis NuGet package on the AppHost project, and then go back to the `AppHost.cs` file, and we can modify it like the code shown in Listing 11-6.

Listing 11-6. An Aspire orchestration with a Redis cache and Web API

```
var builder = DistributedApplication.CreateBuilder(args);

var cache = builder.AddRedis("cache");

var apiService = builder.AddProject<Projects.AspireApp1_
ApiService>("apiservice")
    .WithReference(cache);
    .WithHttpHealthCheck("/health");

builder.AddProject<Projects.AspireApp1_Web>("webfrontend")
    .WithExternalHttpEndpoints()
    .WithHttpHealthCheck("/health")
    .WithReference(apiService)
    .WaitFor(apiService);

builder.Build.RunO;
```

This code adds a Redis service and references it from the API service, simple as that. Save the file and run the application again. The Aspire Dashboard now shows two services: your API and the Redis cache. Aspire automatically started a Redis container, configured it, and made it available to your API. Your API can now use Redis for caching without you having to install or configure Redis manually.

Aspire supports many services out of the box: SQL Server, PostgreSQL, MongoDB, RabbitMQ, Azure services, and more. You can also integrate your ASP.NET Core, Blazor, and even .NET MAUI back-end services with Aspire for a unified development experience.

Things are moving fast with Aspire, and it is quickly expanding to be an ecosystem of its own. They have their own CLI, all kinds of first-party and third-party integrations; you can write your AppHost in JavaScript, Python, and some others, and much, much more.

For comprehensive information about Aspire, see the official documentation at `https://aspire.dev`.

Community Alternatives and Expanding Horizons

While we've focused on Microsoft's first-party technologies in this chapter, the .NET ecosystem is rich with community-driven alternatives that extend what's possible with Visual Studio 2026. Here are a few worth exploring.

Avalonia

Avalonia is a cross-platform UI framework for .NET that allows you to build desktop applications for Windows, macOS, Linux, iOS, Android, and even WebAssembly, all from a single code base. It uses a XAML-based syntax similar to WPF and .NET MAUI but offers more flexibility and community-driven development. Avalonia is popular among developers who need advanced desktop UI capabilities or want to target Linux desktop environments where .NET MAUI isn't available. Unlike MAUI, Avalonia draws all the controls so that they look the exact same across all platforms.

Learn more at `https://avaloniaui.net`.

Uno Platform

Uno Platform is another cross-platform UI framework that allows you to build applications for Windows, macOS, Linux, iOS, Android, and WebAssembly using C# and XAML. Uno focuses on code reusability and allows you to use WinUI and WinAppSDK APIs across all platforms. It's a great choice if you're targeting a wide range of platforms and want to maximize code sharing.

Learn more at `https://platform.uno`.

Meadow for IoT

If you're interested in Internet of Things (IoT) development, Meadow by Wilderness Labs provides a platform for building IoT applications with .NET. You can write C# code for microcontrollers, sensors, and embedded devices and deploy it to hardware like the Meadow F7 development board. It brings the productivity of .NET to hardware development, making IoT projects more accessible to .NET developers.

Learn more at `https://www.wildernesslabs.co/meadow`.

Game Development with Unity and Godot

.NET and C# are also widely used in game development. Unity, one of the most popular game engines in the world, uses C# as its primary scripting language. Godot, an open source game engine, also supports C# alongside its native GDScript. Visual Studio 2026 integrates well with both engines, providing debugging, IntelliSense, and refactoring support for game development projects.

Learn more at `https://unity.com` and `https://godotengine.org`.

The Breadth of .NET

The projects we've covered in this chapter only scratch the surface of what Visual Studio and .NET can do. You can build

- Cloud-native microservices with ASP.NET Core and Azure Functions

- Real-time communication apps with SignalR

- Machine learning applications with ML.NET

- Desktop applications with WPF, WinForms, MAUI, or Avalonia

- Mobile applications with .NET MAUI or Uno Platform

- Web applications with Blazor or ASP.NET Core MVC

- IoT devices with Meadow or Windows IoT Core

- Games with Unity or Godot

And this is far from an exhaustive list; there are many more options, and the options listed here have many other alternatives as well.

The ecosystem is vast, and Visual Studio 2026 is equipped to handle all of it. The skills you've learned throughout this book, the refactoring tools from Chapter 5, the debugging techniques from Chapter 5, the testing strategies from Chapter 6, the AI-powered development from Chapters 8 and 9, and the source control practices from Chapter 10, all apply across these different project types. Have a play with the one that resonates most with you and try to explore all the tools while working on an actual project.

Summary

Throughout this chapter, you've seen how to create different types of projects with Visual Studio 2026: simple console applications that are perfect for learning and automation, ASP.NET Core Web APIs for building scalable back-end services, Blazor applications for interactive web UIs, .NET MAUI apps for cross-platform mobile and desktop development, and Aspire applications for orchestrating cloud-native systems.

Each project type builds on the foundation you've learned in the previous chapters. When you create a .NET MAUI application, Blazor application or even a simple console application, you're using Solution Explorer (Chapter 4) to navigate the project structure, IntelliSense and refactoring tools (Chapter 5) to write your code, debugging features (Chapter 5) to troubleshoot issues, testing frameworks (Chapter 6) to ensure quality, and GitHub Copilot (Chapters 8 and 9) to accelerate development. Everything connects.

As you build real-world projects, you'll find yourself combining these technologies. You might build a .NET MAUI mobile app that connects to an ASP.NET Core Web API back end, orchestrated by Aspire during development, with Blazor for your admin dashboard. Or you might build a console application that interacts with Azure services through APIs, automated through AI agents. The possibilities are limitless.

The key takeaway from this chapter is simple: Visual Studio 2026 and .NET 10 give you the tools to build anything you can imagine. From the smallest utility script to enterprise-scale distributed systems, from web applications to mobile apps to IoT devices, it's all within reach. And with the skills you've learned throughout this book, you're now equipped to build it all efficiently, effectively, and with confidence.

CHAPTER 12

Customization and Productivity Tips

By this point in the book, you've covered a lot of ground. You know how to install and configure Visual Studio 2026, navigate the IDE, manage projects, write and refactor code, debug, test, profile, use extensions, harness AI assistance through GitHub Copilot, collaborate with your team, and build cross-platform applications. That's genuinely a lot, and if you've been following along with the earlier chapters, you should feel quite comfortable in the IDE by now.

But here's the thing: knowing how the IDE works and making it work *for you specifically* are two different things. Think of it like a professional kitchen. You could walk into any well-equipped kitchen and cook a decent meal, but a chef who has arranged their own workspace, sharpened their own knives, and set up everything exactly the way their hands expect it to be will outperform you every time. Not because they know more recipes, but because they've eliminated all the friction.

This chapter is about eliminating that friction. We're going to look at how to make Visual Studio 2026 feel like your personal tool rather than a generic one. That means customizing the look and feel, setting up your workspace the way your brain likes it, building a personal library of code snippets and templates, and picking up those small productivity habits that quietly add up to hours of saved time every week.

Some of what we cover here might seem like minor tweaks, some things we have touched on a bit already. But here's the thing about minor tweaks: when you make 20 of them and they each save you ten seconds a day, you've just recovered half an hour. And half an hour a day, every working day, is more than a hundred hours a year. That's time you could spend actually solving problems rather than wrestling with your tools.

Let's get your workspace set up properly.

© Gerald Versluis 2026

G. Versluis, *Getting Started with Visual Studio 2026*, https://doi.org/10.1007/979-8-8688-2691-7_12

Making Visual Studio Yours: Themes, Fonts, and Colors

Let's start with the most obvious form of customization: how Visual Studio looks. You might think aesthetics are superficial, but there's actually something meaningful going on here. If you spend eight hours a day staring at an editor, the visual environment genuinely affects how you feel about your work. A theme that reduces eye strain, a font that makes code easier to read at a glance; these aren't luxuries; they're ergonomics.

Refining Your Theme Choices

As we saw back in Chapter 3, Visual Studio 2026 ships with a heavily expanded selection of built-in color themes. Alongside the classic Dark, Light, and Blue options, you have those 11 new tinted themes like Bubblegum, Icy Mint, and Juicy Plum that leverage the new Fluent UI.

If you haven't played with them yet, head to Tools ➤ Options, expand All Settings ➤ Environment ➤ Visual Experience, and look at the Color theme drop-down. If none of the built-in options feel right, the Visual Studio Marketplace has an extensive collection of community-created themes. You can install them just like any other extension; we covered extension management in Chapter 7, and once installed, they appear in this same drop-down.

In Figure 12-1, you can see the settings for theming.

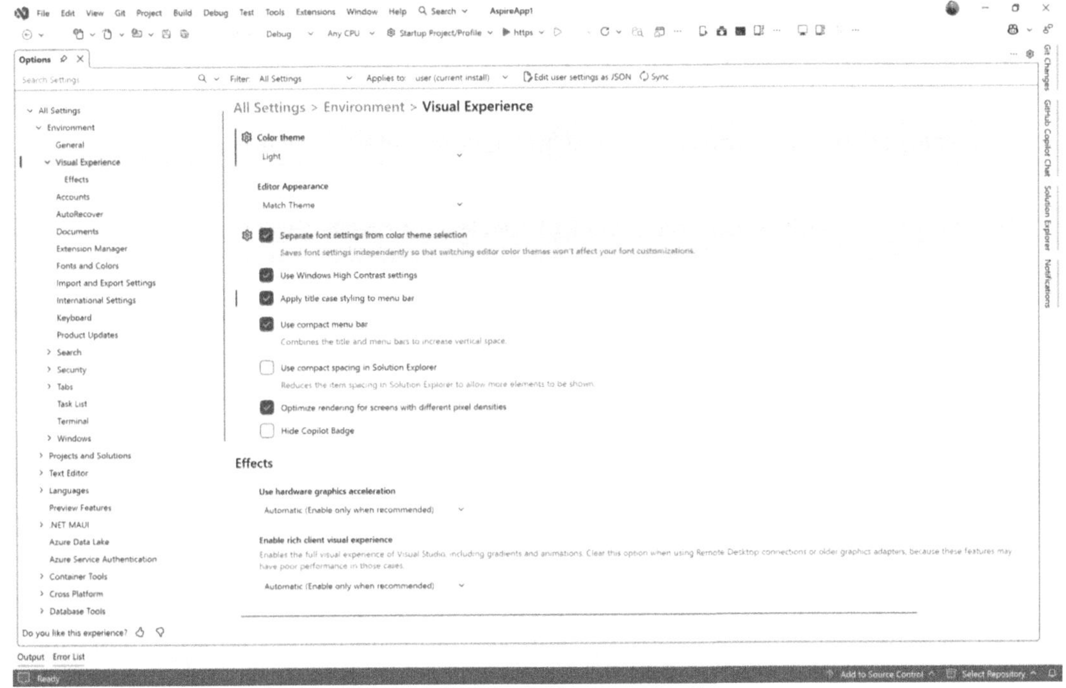

Figure 12-1. *Theme and visual-related settings*

One handy improvement we touched on earlier is that your font settings are now preserved independently when you switch themes. In older versions of Visual Studio, switching from Dark to Light would sometimes reset your carefully chosen font sizes and faces. Now, Visual Studio separates font preferences from color themes by default. If you actually *want* your fonts to change with the theme, maybe you've set up different fonts for different contexts and want them strictly bound to the theme you switch to, you can opt back into that legacy behavior via the Separate font settings from color themes selection check box in the same Visual Experience settings section.

Picking Your Font

If you haven't thought much about which font you use in the editor, this is worth five minutes of your time. Code is fundamentally text, and the font you read it in affects both readability and, over long sessions, eye fatigue.

Visual Studio 2026 ships with Cascadia Mono as the default editor font, but it also offers the related Cascadia Code font, and the difference between them is worth knowing about. Cascadia Code includes coding ligatures, typographic combinations where sequences of characters like =>, !=, >=, and -> are rendered as single unified glyphs. Some developers find that this significantly improves readability because those symbols carry semantic meaning, and having them visually unified reinforces that meaning. Other developers find ligatures confusing, particularly when learning or teaching. There's no right answer—try both and see what works for you.

To change your editor font, navigate to Tools ➤ Options ➤ Environment ➤ Fonts and Colors; then in the Show settings for drop-down, select Text Editor. From the Font drop-down, you can choose Cascadia Code, Cascadia Mono, or any other font installed on your system. Popular alternatives in the developer community include JetBrains Mono and Fira Code, both of which also support ligatures.

The font settings are still in a separate dialog (for now); you can see it in Figure 12-2. You can set fonts and related properties for all kinds of different sections in Visual Studio separately.

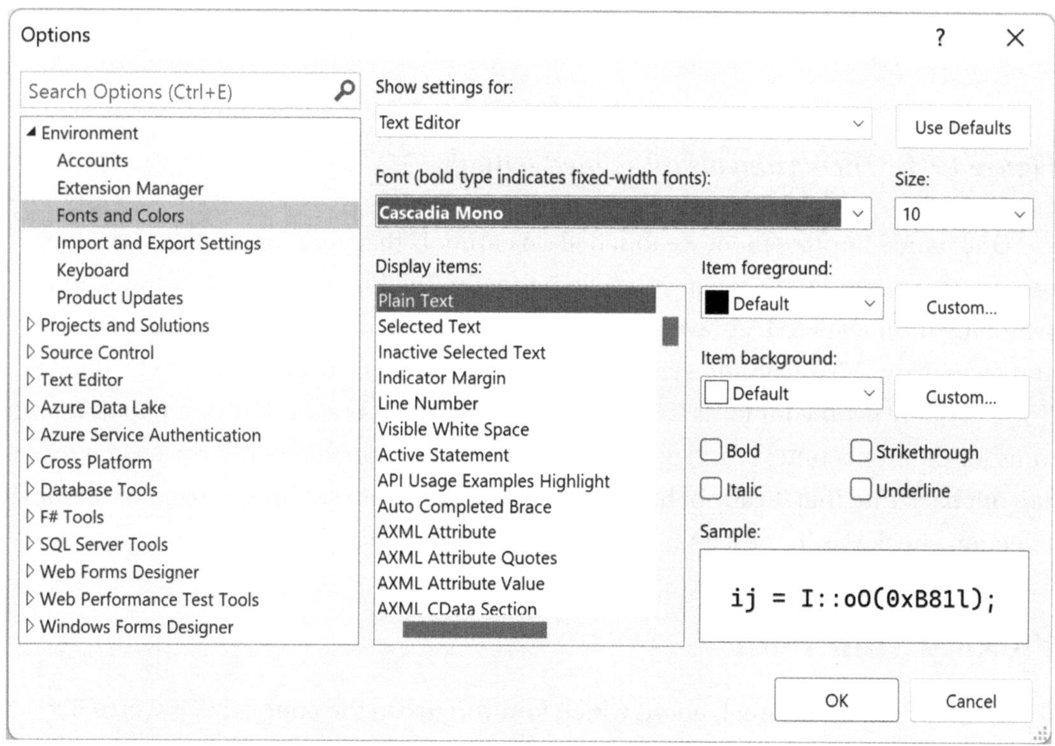

Figure 12-2. *Changing the font settings for Visual Studio*

A quick accessibility note: the Cascadia Code family was specifically designed with character clarity in mind. The letterforms are drawn to be unambiguous: characters like 0 vs. O and 1 vs. l vs. I are visually distinct in a way that many general-purpose fonts don't guarantee. If you've ever spent time debugging a problem that turned out to be a misread variable name, a font designed for disambiguation is worth considering.

You can also set different fonts for different parts of Visual Studio: tool windows, the output panel, and the Immediate window, using the same Fonts and Colors dialog. The Show settings for drop-down lets you switch between Text Editor, All Text Tool Windows, Printer, and several other targets. Most people stick with one font everywhere for consistency, but it's there if you want it.

Arranging Your Workspace: Window Layouts

If you've been using Visual Studio for a while, you've probably developed opinions about where things should live. The Solution Explorer should be on the right. Or the left. The output window should be docked at the bottom. Or maybe hidden until you need it. The Git Changes window should always be visible. Or maybe it's too noisy, and you only open it when you're committing.

Everyone has a workflow, and Visual Studio 2026's window layout system is flexible enough to support almost any preference. More importantly, it lets you save multiple layouts so you can switch between them depending on what you're doing.

Setting Up Your Layout

Windows in Visual Studio can be docked (snapped to the edges or corners of the IDE), floating (in their own windows; great for multi-monitor setups), or set to auto-hide (they appear as tabs on the edge of the IDE and slide out when you hover over them). You move them by dragging their title bars and dropping them onto the blue docking guides that appear as you drag.

The mechanics are the same as in Visual Studio 2022, but the 2026 UI makes the docking experience feel more intentional. The docking guides are cleaner, and the visual feedback when you're about to dock something is clearer. You're less likely to accidentally drop a window somewhere you didn't intend.

As we briefly touched on back in Chapter 2 when we set up our initial environment, you can save a window layout once you have it arranged the way you want. Go to Window ➤ Save Window Layout, give it a name, something descriptive like "Coding", "Debugging", or "Code Review", and Visual Studio remembers the position, size, and state of every window.

To switch between saved layouts, go to Window ➤ Apply Window Layout and pick from the list. You can also assign keyboard shortcuts to individual layouts, which makes switching instant. Open Tools ➤ Options ➤ Environment ➤ Keyboard, search for "Window.ApplyWindowLayout", and you'll see entries for each of your saved layouts, ready to be bound. Having your debugging layout one shortcut away is the sort of small thing that becomes second nature very quickly.

In Figure 12-3, you can see different saved layouts that you can reapply with the click of a button.

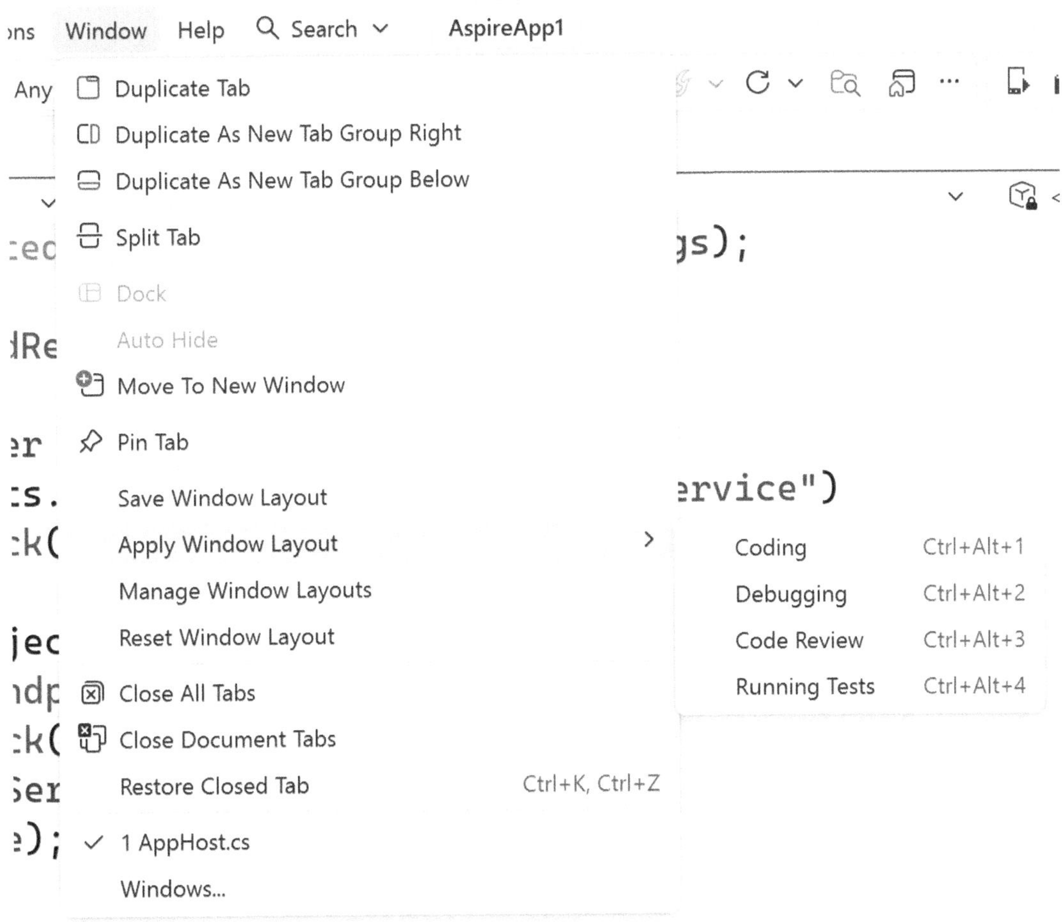

Figure 12-3. *From the main menu in Visual Studio, you can easily save, manage, or apply a saved window layout*

A practical suggestion: create at least three layouts. One for normal coding: minimal clutter, Solution Explorer visible, output hidden. One for debugging: Locals, Call Stack, Watch, and Breakpoints windows all arranged and visible, as we explored in Chapter 5. And one for code review: diff views, Git Changes, and maybe a wider editor, connecting back to what we covered in Chapter 10. The time you invest in setting these up pays dividends every single day. Depending on the way you work, you might set it up differently, of course. Another great layout would be one that focuses on testing, with Test Explorer visible and wide enough to read long test names. And then these focus more on "traditional" development; maybe by now, it makes sense to have GitHub Copilot front and center and work from there.

Multi-monitor Setups

If you work with multiple monitors, you can drag any tool window or document group off the main IDE window onto a secondary screen. This is particularly effective for keeping debugging windows on one monitor while your code stays on the primary.

You can also create a second instance of Solution Explorer by right-clicking inside the panel and choosing New Solution Explorer View, then dragging that second view to your secondary monitor. This is surprisingly useful when navigating large solutions because you can keep a high-level view of the solution tree on one screen while staying deep in a specific file on the other. We talked about navigating large solutions back in Chapter 4, and a second Solution Explorer view is one of those practical reinforcements of those navigation skills.

The Art of the Keyboard Shortcut

Let's be honest: keyboard shortcuts are one of those things that feel intimidating at first but become genuinely addictive once you start using them. Once you've internalized a few dozen shortcuts, reaching for the mouse starts to feel like a speed bump. The question is which shortcuts to learn and how to make Visual Studio's shortcut system work the way you expect.

Why It's More Complicated Than It Looks

Visual Studio has one of the most extensive keyboard shortcut systems of any IDE, with thousands of commands that can have bindings. Some shortcuts change behavior based on which window has focus; for instance, the same key combination might do different things in the editor vs. Solution Explorer vs. the debugger. This context-sensitivity is actually a feature: it means Visual Studio can pack a huge number of commands into a reasonable set of key combinations.

Microsoft published a candid blog post in late 2025 explaining why changing shortcuts in Visual Studio is harder than it sounds. The short version: many shortcuts have been burned into developers' muscle memory for decades, and changing even one can ripple through a chain of related bindings. The classic example is Ctrl+W, which closes tabs in browsers and VS Code, but selects a word in Visual Studio. Microsoft keeps it that way because the Visual Studio user base relies on it. Changing it would break thousands of workflows. This isn't stubbornness; it's a recognition that for experienced users, the shortcut *is* the action.

If you are curious about the full blog post, find it here: `https://devblogs.microsoft.com/visualstudio/why-changing-keyboard-shortcuts-in-visual-studio-isnt-as-simple-as-it-seems/`.

Finding and Customizing Shortcuts

To find a shortcut for a command you use regularly, the fastest route is Ctrl+Q: the universal search box we keep coming back to throughout this book. Just type the command name, and you'll see the keyboard shortcut displayed next to each matching result.

To actually customize shortcuts, go to Tools ➤ Options ➤ Environment ➤ Keyboard (you may see this under More Settings ➤ Keyboard depending on how your Options view is configured). The dialog gives you a searchable list of every command in Visual Studio. Type part of a command name to filter the list, click on the command you want, click in the Press shortcut keys field, and press the key combination you want to assign. Visual Studio immediately tells you whether that combination is already in use and in which context, which helps you avoid accidentally clobbering a shortcut you rely on.

In Figure 12-4, you can see the keyboard settings dialog. All of the keyboard shortcuts can be customized here.

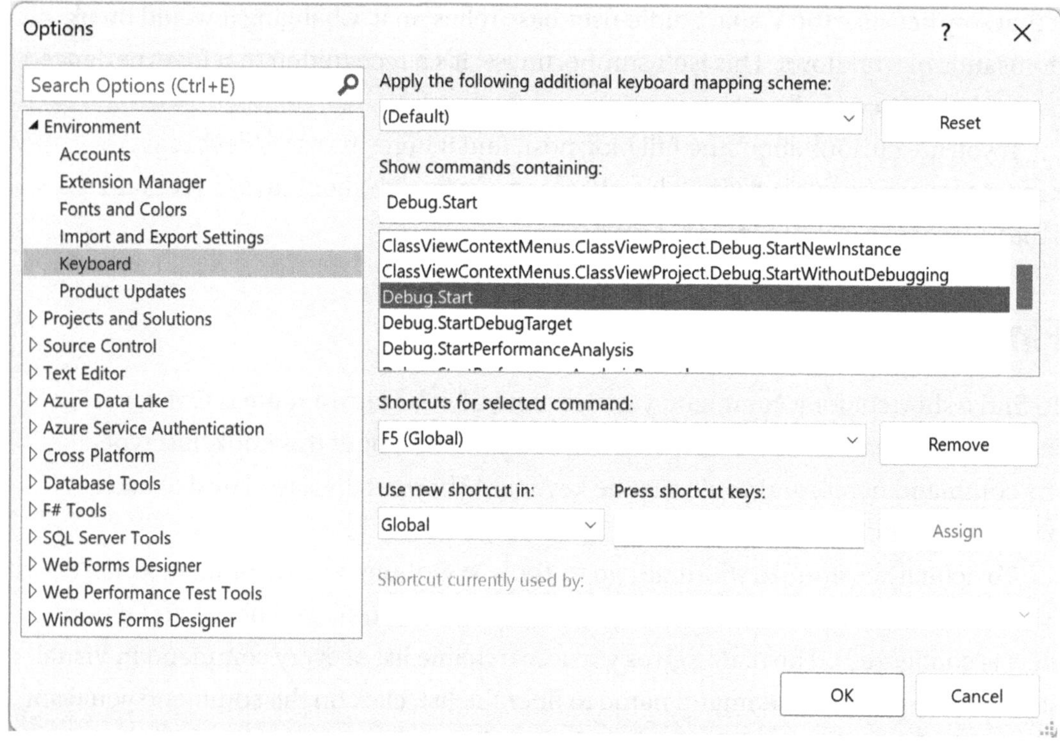

Figure 12-4. *The keyboard shortcuts configuration dialog*

Keyboard Profiles

If you're coming to Visual Studio from another tool, the keyboard profile system is your friend. During initial setup, Visual Studio lets you choose a profile that matches your background, whether that's Visual Basic, C++, web development, or a general environment. These profiles pre-configure shortcuts to match the conventions of each domain.

Beyond the built-in profiles, Visual Studio 2026 also supports keymaps that approximate shortcuts from other tools. You can get ReSharper/IntelliJ-style shortcuts through the HotKeys for Visual Studio extension or VS Code-style navigation through the keyboard profile options. These aren't perfect approximations; some commands simply don't exist in both environments, but they can dramatically reduce the relearning cost if you frequently switch between tools.

If you work across multiple machines or reinstall Visual Studio from time to time, it's worth exporting your custom shortcuts once you have them set up. Go to Tools ➤ Import and Export Settings, choose Export selected environment settings, and make sure keyboard shortcuts are included. Keep that `.vssettings` file somewhere safe; we'll cover the full Import/Export workflow in more detail later in this chapter.

The Shortcuts Worth Learning First

Rather than presenting an exhaustive list, that's what Appendix A is for; let me highlight a handful that have an outsized impact on productivity, particularly ones that are new or underused in Visual Studio 2026.

Ctrl+Q is the one shortcut to learn before all others. It opens the unified search box in the title bar and searches commands, menus, documents, settings, open tabs, and Visual Studio documentation simultaneously. If you can't remember where something lives in the menus, Ctrl+Q and a few keywords will usually get you there faster than hunting through the menu tree. If you only memorize one shortcut from this chapter, make it this one.

Ctrl+T (or Ctrl+, in some profiles) opens Go To All, a floating search that lets you jump to any file, type, member, or symbol in your solution. We covered this back in Chapter 3 in the context of code navigation, but it bears repeating here because developers consistently underuse it. Type a class name, a method name, or even just a few letters, and Visual Studio shows you a filtered list of matches from across your entire code base.

Alt+Enter and **Ctrl+.** are your Quick Actions shortcuts. When you're on a line with a light bulb or error indicator, these trigger the Quick Actions menu, giving you one-keystroke access to suggested fixes, refactoring options, and code generation. If you're currently reaching for the mouse to click those light bulbs, switching to the keyboard is dramatically faster, and we covered what Quick Actions can do in depth back in Chapter 5.

Ctrl+K, **Ctrl+E** runs Code Cleanup, applying whatever EditorConfig and code style rules you have configured to the current file. We'll talk about EditorConfig in more detail shortly, but knowing this shortcut means you can clean up any file in two keystrokes without touching the menu.

Ctrl+E, V duplicates the current line, a simple operation that's surprisingly absent from most developers' shortcut vocabulary despite being useful dozens of times a day.

Multi-caret Editing: Edit Everywhere at Once

While we're talking about reducing repetitive typing, it's the right moment to introduce multi-caret editing. It's one of those features that, once you've used it, makes single-cursor editing feel primitive.

The idea is straightforward: instead of one cursor moving through your code, you have several cursors active simultaneously, and anything you type appears at all of them at once. This is perfect for situations where you need to make the same edit in several places that aren't evenly spaced enough for Find and Replace, but are close enough that clicking to each one manually is tedious.

Adding Multiple Carets

The simplest way to get started is to hold Ctrl+Alt and click in multiple places in the editor. Each click drops an additional caret. Once you have your carets placed, typing, deleting, or pasting affects all of them simultaneously. Press Escape to collapse back to a single cursor.

For repeating patterns—say, the same variable name appearing on five consecutive lines—there's a faster route. Select the first instance with your mouse or keyboard, then press Shift+Alt+. to add a caret at the next occurrence of that selection. Keep pressing to add more. This is effectively a targeted alternative to Find and Replace for nearby occurrences; you get fine-grained control over exactly which instances you want to edit.

If you prefer column-based editing, selecting a rectangular block across multiple lines rather than free-placing individual carets, hold Alt while dragging your mouse to create a box selection. This is particularly useful when you want to prepend or append the same text to a block of lines, like adding // to comment out a chunk of code or adding a modifier keyword to a column of declarations.

It's a little hard to capture in a screenshot, but in Figure 12-5, you can see a caret behind every `builder` variable name.

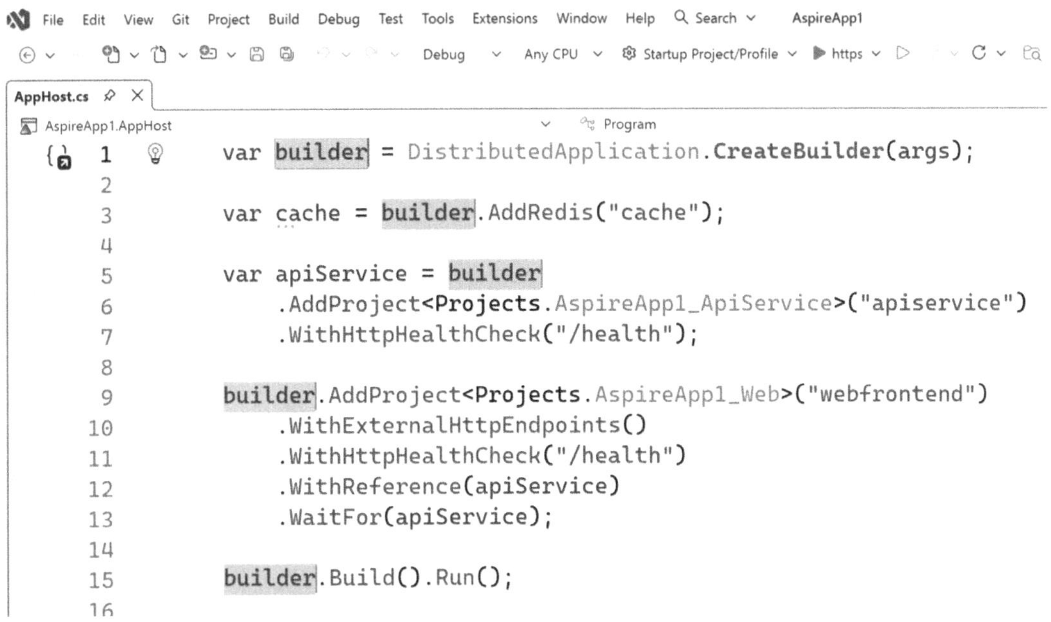

File Edit View Git Project Build Debug Test Tools Extensions Window Help Search AspireApp1
Debug Any CPU Startup Project/Profile https
AppHost.cs
AspireApp1.AppHost
Program
var builder = DistributedApplication.CreateBuilder(args);
var cache = builder.AddRedis("cache");
var apiService = builder
.AddProject<Projects.AspireApp1_ApiService>("apiservice")
.WithHttpHealthCheck("/health");
builder.AddProject<Projects.AspireApp1_Web>("webfrontend")
.WithExternalHttpEndpoints()
.WithHttpHealthCheck("/health")
.WithReference(apiService)
.WaitFor(apiService);
builder.Build().Run();

***Figure 12-5.** Multiple carets in the text editor*

You can also use the Edit menu to discover multi-caret commands without memorizing the shortcuts immediately. Under Edit ➤ Multiple Carets, you'll find options to add carets above, below, or at all occurrences of the current selection. It's a good entry point if you want to explore what's available before committing anything to memory.

One setting worth knowing: if you find that box selection behavior conflicts with how you're used to working, you can adjust it in Tools ➤ Options ➤ Text Editor ➤ Advanced where you'll find a Use box selection check box. This controls whether dragging with Alt held creates a box selection or behaves differently. The default in Visual Studio 2026 suits most workflows, but it's there to tweak if you have strong preferences from another editor.

In Figure 12-6, you can see the box selection in action.

```
var builder = DistributedApplication.CreateBuilder(args);

var cache = builder.AddRedis("cache");

var apiService = builder
    .AddProject<Projects.AspireApp1_ApiService>("apiservice")
    .WithHttpHealthCheck("/health");

builder.AddProject<Projects.AspireApp1_Web>("webfrontend")
    .WithExternalHttpEndpoints()
    .WithHttpHealthCheck("/health")
    .WithReference(apiService)
    .WaitFor(apiService);

builder.Build().Run();
```

Figure 12-6. *Selecting a box of text in the Visual Studio text editor*

Multi-caret editing pairs particularly well with the code navigation skills we built in Chapter 3. A common workflow: use Ctrl+T to jump to a class, scan for the repeated patterns you need to modify, then use Shift+Alt+. to place carets at each one and make the edit simultaneously. What used to be a repetitive six-step process becomes a three-step one.

Find and Replace: More Power Than You Think

While we're in the neighborhood of editing efficiency, it's worth spending a moment on Visual Studio's Find and Replace, specifically the parts that developers tend to overlook.

The basics are probably well-known: Ctrl+F finds in the current file, Ctrl+H opens Find and Replace, and Ctrl+Shift+F searches across the entire solution. But the real productivity gains come from the options that don't get used enough.

Regular expressions in Find and Replace are particularly powerful. Press the .* toggle button in the Find bar to enable regex mode, and you can search for patterns rather than literal text. For example, `private \w+ \w+;` matches any private field declaration, and you can use capture groups to transform what you've found in the Replace field. If you've never tried regex Find and Replace in Visual Studio, the learning curve is modest, and the payoff is significant for any repetitive structural refactoring that IntelliSense can't handle on its own.

The Find in Files window (Ctrl+Shift+F) is worth opening in its full form rather than just as a quick shortcut. You can scope the search to the current document, the current project, the entire solution, or a custom folder path. You can also set file type filters, only search .cs files, or only .xaml files, which dramatically cuts down noise when you're searching in a mixed-technology solution. Results appear in the Find Results window as clickable links, with context shown for each match.

For large-scale renames that go beyond what the built-in rename refactoring handles, perhaps you want to rename across configuration files, XAML resources, and SQL scripts as well as C# code; Find and Replace across the solution with regex is often your most reliable option.

Code Snippets: Your Personal Code Library

If you've been writing code for more than a few months, you've noticed that certain patterns appear over and over again. A null check. A using statement. A try-catch block. A property with a backing field. A constructor that validates its parameters. You type these things so often that the act of typing them starts to feel like noise, mechanical effort that contributes nothing to the actual problem you're solving.

Code snippets exist to eliminate that noise. They're small templates, triggered by a short keyword and a press of the Tab button, that expand into whatever boilerplate you've defined, with the cursor positioned exactly where you need to start editing.

Built-in Snippets

Visual Studio ships with a library of built-in snippets that cover the most common C# patterns. Here are a few you'll use immediately:

- prop + Tab + Tab expands to a full auto-property declaration with the type and name ready to edit.

- ctor + Tab + Tab generates a constructor for the current class.

- for + Tab + Tab creates a for loop with the loop variable and condition pre-filled.

- `try` + Tab + Tab wraps code in a try-catch block.

- `svm` + Tab + Tab generates a static void Main entry point; handy when you need a console entry point quickly.

The Tab + Tab invocation might feel a bit odd at first; you press Tab once to confirm the snippet keyword, then Tab again to expand it. Once it's in your hands, it becomes second nature. You can also invoke snippets through Edit ➤ IntelliSense ➤ Insert Snippet or by right-clicking in the editor and choosing Snippet ➤ Insert Snippet, which opens a visual picker showing all available snippets organized by category.

You can see the snippet picker in action in Figure 12-7.

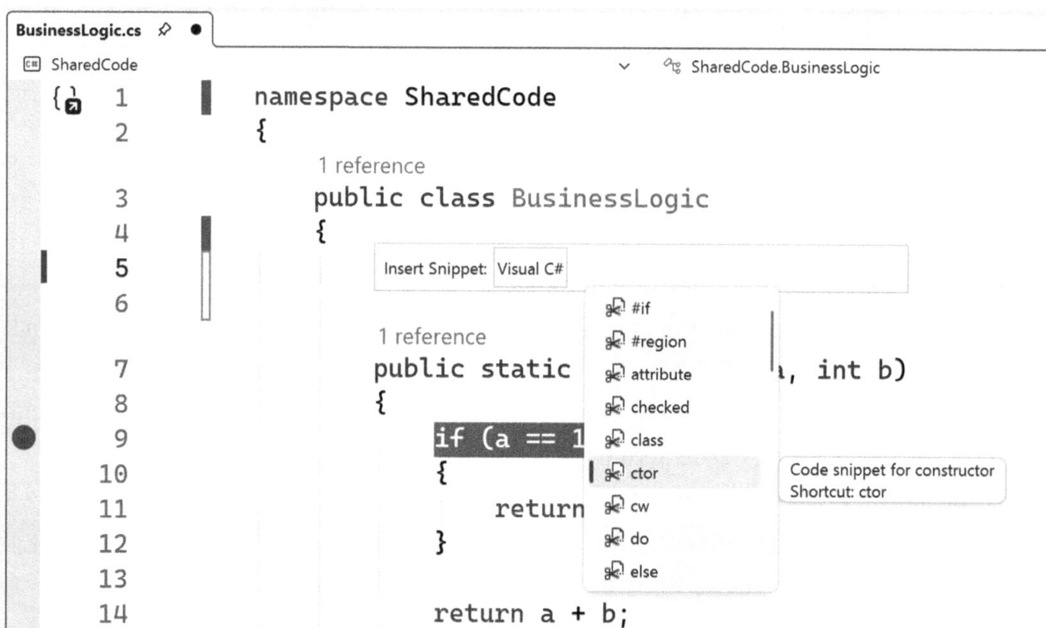

Figure 12-7. *Picking a snippet to insert*

Creating Your Own Snippets

The real power of snippets comes when you create your own. If you have patterns that you write repeatedly that aren't covered by the built-in set, you can define them as custom snippets and have them available in exactly the same way as the built-ins.

Snippets are defined in XML files with the .snippet extension. The easiest way to manage them is through the Code Snippets Manager at Tools ➤ Code Snippets Manager. This dialog shows all installed snippets organized by language, and lets you add snippet folders. In those folders, any `.snippet` files you drop into a registered folder automatically become available in the editor.

Let's walk through creating one. Start by opening a text editor (even Notepad works here, but you can also do it from Visual Studio itself), and save a new file with the `.snippet` extension. Here's what a custom guard clause snippet looks like, you can see it below in Listing 12-1.

Listing 12-1. Defining your own code snippet

```xml
<?xml version="1.0" encoding="utf-8"?>
<CodeSnippets xmlns="http://schemas.microsoft.com/VisualStudio/2005/
CodeSnippet">
  <CodeSnippet Format="1.0.0">
    <Header>
      <Title>Guard Clause</Title>
      <Shortcut>guard</Shortcut>
      <Description>Null guard clause for a parameter</Description>
      <Author>You</Author>
      <SnippetTypes>
        <SnippetType>Expansion</SnippetType>
      </SnippetTypes>
    </Header>
    <Snippet>
      <Declarations>
        <Literal>
          <ID>param</ID>
          <ToolTip>Parameter name</ToolTip>
          <Default>value</Default>
        </Literal>
      </Declarations>
      <Code Language="CSharp">
        <![CDATA[ArgumentNullException.ThrowIfNull($param$);$end$]]>
      </Code>
    </Snippet>
  </CodeSnippet>
</CodeSnippets>
```

The $param$ placeholder is highlighted after expansion, letting you immediately type the parameter name. The end marker tells Visual Studio where to position the cursor when you press Enter to finish editing. You can have multiple placeholders and pressing Tab cycles between them, the exact same interaction model as the built-in snippets.

Once you've saved the .snippet file, open Tools ➤ Code Snippets Manager, select My Code Snippets (or whichever language folder is appropriate), and click Import to register your file. Alternatively, you can click Add to register an entire folder, which is the more practical approach once you have several custom snippets. After registering, flip back to a C# file in the editor, type guard, and press Tab twice. Your guard clause expands with the parameter name ready to edit.

In Figure 12-8, you can see the Code Snippets Manager where you can inspect the built-in ones but also see your own snippets.

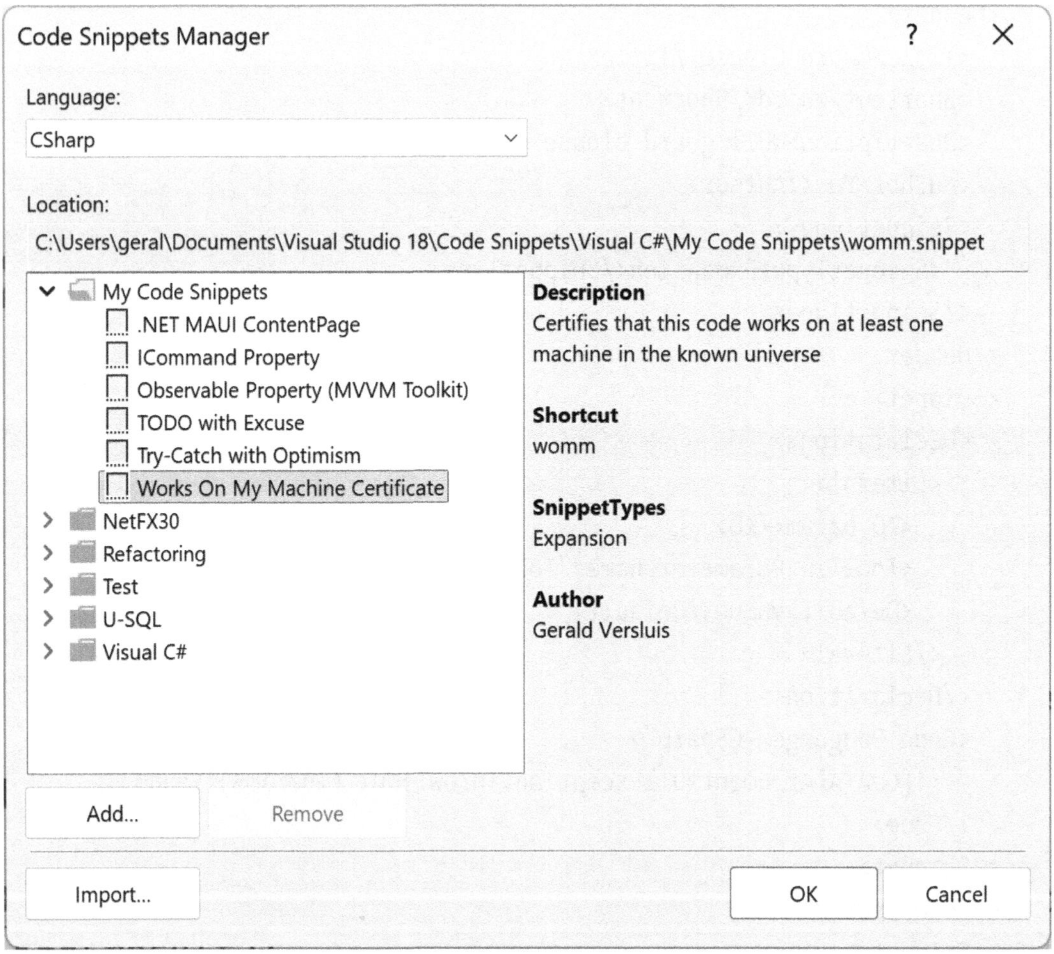

Code Snippets Manager
?
X
Language:
CSharp
Location:
C:\Users\geral\Documents\Visual Studio 18\Code Snippets\Visual C#\My Code Snippets\womm.snippet
My Code Snippets
.NET MAUI ContentPage
ICommand Property
Observable Property (MVVM Toolkit)
TODO with Excuse
Try-Catch with Optimism
Works On My Machine Certificate
NetFX30
Refactoring
Test
U-SQL
Visual C#
Description
Certifies that this code works on at least one machine in the known universe
Shortcut
womm
SnippetTypes
Expansion
Author
Gerald Versluis
Add...
Remove
Import...
OK
Cancel

Figure 12-8. *The Code Snippets Manager dialog*

For teams, snippets are a great way to share patterns. You can version-control your team's snippet folder and share it through your repository. Anyone who registers that folder in their Code Snippets Manager gets all the same expansions automatically. It's a low-friction way to enforce coding conventions without needing heavy tooling.

If writing the XML from scratch sounds unappealing, of course also here: GitHub Copilot to the rescue! Ask Copilot Chat to generate a code snippet for the pattern you have in mind, and it will produce a working `.snippet` file with the correct structure, ready to save and import. As we covered in Chapters 8 and 9, describing what you want in natural language and getting a working boilerplate in return is exactly what Copilot is good at.

Custom Project and Item Templates

Snippets handle recurring code patterns within files. Templates handle a bigger problem: every time you create a new project or add a new file, you probably spend a few minutes deleting the default boilerplate and replacing it with your own starting point. Maybe you always add the same NuGet packages to new class libraries. Maybe every new controller in your web app needs the same base class and attribute decorations. Maybe every new service class needs a specific interface structure and a constructor signature.

Item templates and project templates let you bake those starting points directly into the IDE, so that a new file or a new project immediately looks the way you want it to.

Creating a Custom Item Template

An item template is a template for a single file: a class, an interface, a controller, whatever. The easiest way to create one is to first create a file that looks exactly the way you want your template to look, and then use Project ➤ Export Template to capture it.

The Export Template Wizard opens and asks you what type of template you're creating. Choose Item template, select the project from which you want to export, and on the next screen, select the file you want to use as your template. Give the template a name, a description, and an icon, and decide whether you want Visual Studio to automatically import it into your user templates folder.

In Figure 12-9, you can see the first screen, on the left, where you select whether you want to export a full project or just an item template. After that, you can select what you want to include for files and references. Lastly, on the right side, you can see some last configuration that you can give the template like the name, description, etc., and click Finish to create your template.

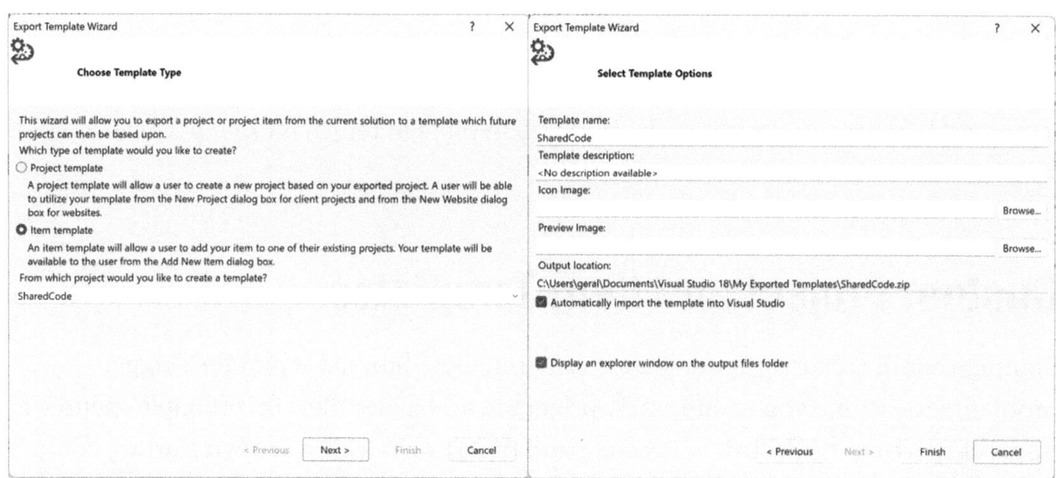

Figure 12-9. *The Export template wizard*

What Visual Studio actually produces is a `.zip` file containing your template file, a `__TemplateData` subfolder with an icon, and a `.vstemplate` XML descriptor that tells Visual Studio how to present and use the template. When the Automatically import check box is ticked, Visual Studio copies this .zip to the user templates folder and makes it available immediately. If you want to share the template with colleagues, just share the `.zip`. The other party can import it via File ➤ New ➤ Project (or Add ➤ New Item) once it's been copied to their templates folder.

After the export, the template appears under Add ➤ New Item in the relevant category, and creating a new file from it gives you your pre-configured starting point. For item templates that need the file name to be used inside the code, for instance, if your class name should match the file name, use the `$safeitemname$` substitution token. Visual Studio replaces this at creation time with whatever name the user typed.

The Modern Approach: .NET CLI Templates

If you have been using Visual Studio for a while, you might be familiar with the classic "Export Template" feature that generates `.vstemplate` ZIP files. While this still works, it is largely considered a legacy approach. The modern, much more powerful way to build reusable project and item templates is by using the .NET Template Engine.

Instead of relying on fragile, IDE-specific XML files, the modern approach simply requires adding a .template.config folder to your project containing a `template.json` file. This JSON file defines your template's metadata, parameters, and rules for how files should be generated or renamed when a developer uses it.

Do not let the term ".NET CLI Templates" fool you. These are not just for the command line. Visual Studio 2026 natively understands the `template.json` format. When you install a .NET template, it automatically appears right alongside the built-in Microsoft templates in the Visual Studio "Create a new project" and "Add New Item" dialogs.

Visual Studio will even read the custom parameters defined in your template.json (like booleans or choice lists) and automatically generate a native GUI wizard with check boxes and drop-downs for your developers to use!

This gives you the best of both worlds:

- **True Cross-Platform Compatibility:** Your templates work identically whether a developer creates them via the Visual Studio 2026 UI, Visual Studio Code, or the `dotnet new` command line.

- **Easy Distribution:** You can pack these templates into a standard NuGet package. Once published to a private feed or NuGet.org, your entire team can install and update their company boilerplate with a single command.

- **Rich Parameterization:** You can define complex logic in your `template.json`, such as conditionally excluding specific files (like skipping the Dockerfile if a user unchecks a box) or modifying namespaces based on user input.

Because the Template Engine powers the entire .NET ecosystem, the community and documentation around it are massive. The absolute best place to start is the official GitHub repository at github.com/dotnet/templating.

The wiki in that repository is the definitive guide, containing a complete reference for every property you can use in the `template.json` file, along with a rich set of reference samples showing exactly how to build multi-project solutions, conditionally include files, and package your templates for NuGet distribution. If you are standardizing architecture across a team, taking the time to learn this format is highly recommended over the older Visual Studio export wizard.

Custom Project Templates

Project templates work the same way but capture entire project structures. If you always start .NET projects with a particular layout, a specific folder structure, a handful of pre-configured NuGet packages, and a set of standard files, you can create a starter project once, export it as a project template, and then create new instances of it directly from the New Project dialog.

For sharing templates across teams, the cleanest approach is to package them as a VSIX extension, which we covered in Chapter 7. A VSIX-distributed template can be installed through the Visual Studio Marketplace or your organization's internal extension feed, and it gets updated just like any other extension. This is how many organizations standardize project scaffolding across their teams: one installation, and everyone gets the same starting points.

EditorConfig: Code Style Without the Arguments

Here's a scenario that will be familiar if you've worked on a team: you open a file that a colleague worked on last week, and immediately notice that they use spaces where you use tabs, their brace placement is different from yours, and their naming conventions follow a different pattern. None of this breaks the code, but it creates noise in code reviews and gradually makes the code base less consistent.

EditorConfig is the solution to this problem, and Visual Studio 2026 has excellent built-in support for it.

What EditorConfig Does

An EditorConfig file (`.editorconfig`) lives at the root of your repository and defines a set of coding style rules. Any editor with EditorConfig support, including Visual Studio, VS Code, and many others, reads this file and applies those rules automatically. When you save a file, when you run Code Cleanup, and when Visual Studio flags style warnings, it's all driven by the rules in your .editorconfig.

The rules cover a wide range of things: indentation style (tabs vs. spaces), indentation size, end-of-line character, trailing whitespace handling, C# naming conventions (should private fields be `_camelCase` or `camelCase`?), code style preferences (should you use var or explicit types?), and much more. The immediate benefit for teams is that these rules travel with the code. Clone the repository on a new machine, open it in Visual Studio, and the same rules apply automatically. No onboarding documentation needed, no "hey, make sure you configure your editor to…" conversations.

Adding EditorConfig to Your Project

The simplest way to add an EditorConfig file in Visual Studio 2026 is through Solution Explorer. Right-click the solution or project you want to configure, choose Add ➤ New Item, and search for "editorconfig." You'll see two templates: a blank EditorConfig file and a .NET EditorConfig file.

The .NET EditorConfig template is the one you usually want; it generates a comprehensive starting file pre-populated with common .NET code style settings. Open it, and you'll see sections for both general editor settings and C#-specific style preferences. It's a great starting point for understanding what's configurable.

In Figure 12-10, you can see an example of an EditorConfig file.

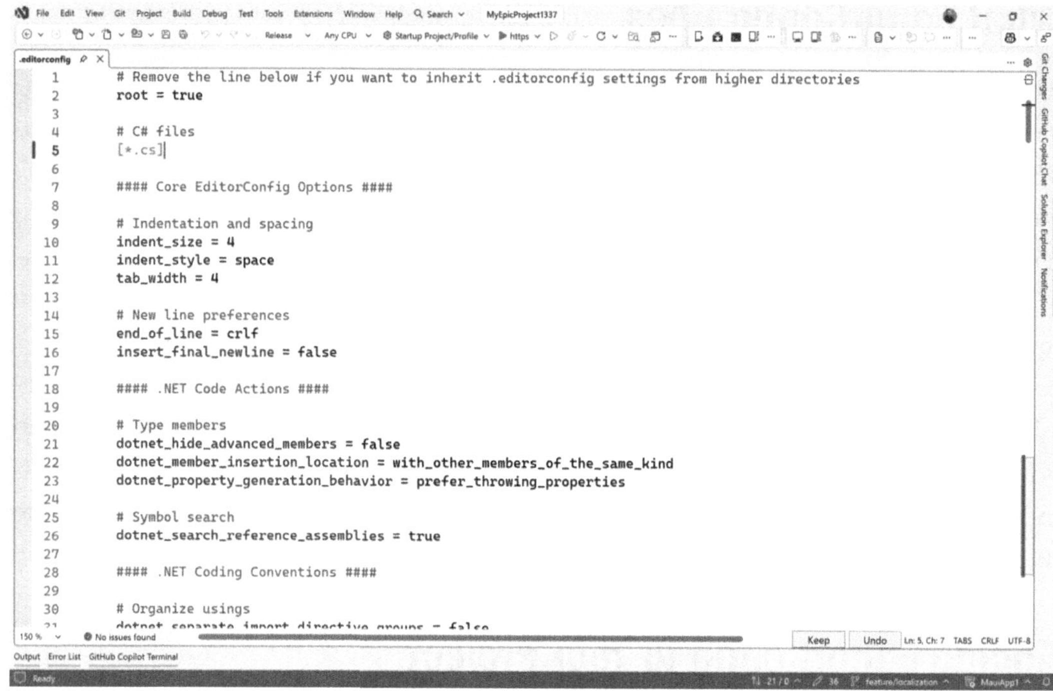

Figure 12-10. *An EditorConfig file opened in Visual Studio*

Once you have EditorConfig in place, Visual Studio applies the rules as you type. Violations appear as squiggles in the editor, the same mechanism you're familiar with from compiler warnings and code analysis, which we explored in Chapter 5. You can fix individual violations using Quick Actions (Alt+Enter) or apply all EditorConfig-defined cleanup rules to an entire file at once using Code Cleanup (Ctrl+K, Ctrl+E).

For teams adopting EditorConfig for the first time, a useful approach is to set the severity of style rules to suggestion initially, rather than warning or error. This way, developers see the recommendations without their build being blocked while they're getting used to the conventions. You can dial up the severity later once the patterns are established.

One thing worth knowing: EditorConfig rules can also be enforced during CI builds if you add the right MSBuild properties to your project. Setting `<EnforceCodeStyleInBuild>true</EnforceCodeStyleInBuild>` in your project file causes code style violations to produce actual build warnings or errors, depending on how you've configured the severities. This creates a feedback loop where your CI pipeline enforces the same standards your editor applies during development.

For the full range of .NET code style options available in EditorConfig, the Microsoft Learn documentation at `https://learn.microsoft.com/dotnet/fundamentals/code-analysis/code-style-rule-options` is comprehensive and well-maintained.

Settings Sync and Roaming Profiles

One of the quieter but genuinely useful features in Visual Studio is settings synchronization. If you work on multiple machines, maybe a desktop at home, a laptop for travel, and a work machine, keeping your Visual Studio configuration consistent across all of them manually is tedious. Settings sync handles this automatically once you're signed in.

How Roaming Settings Work

When you sign into Visual Studio with your Microsoft account or your organization account, Visual Studio can roam a selection of your settings to the cloud and apply them when you sign into Visual Studio on another machine. This includes themes, some keyboard shortcuts, and various IDE preferences.

To check and configure what gets synchronized, go to Tools ➤ Options ➤ Environment ➤ Accounts. You'll see options for syncing settings across devices. The sync happens in the background, and you generally won't notice it working; you'll just find that your second machine looks and feels like your primary one when you sign in.

It's worth noting that not every setting is eligible for roaming. Settings that are highly machine-specific, settings like installed workloads, extension configurations that depend on local tools, or environment variables, generally stay local. But the settings that affect your everyday editing experience, like your theme, your font, and your key bindings, are typically the ones that sync.

Import and Export As a Backup Strategy

Even if you primarily use the automatic sync, it's a good habit to periodically export your settings as a backup. Go to Tools ➤ Import and Export Settings, and choose Export selected environment settings. You'll get to choose which categories to include: keyboard shortcuts, window layouts, fonts and colors, and so on. Save the resulting `.vssettings` file somewhere safe.

You can see the Import and Export Settings Wizard in Figure 12-11.

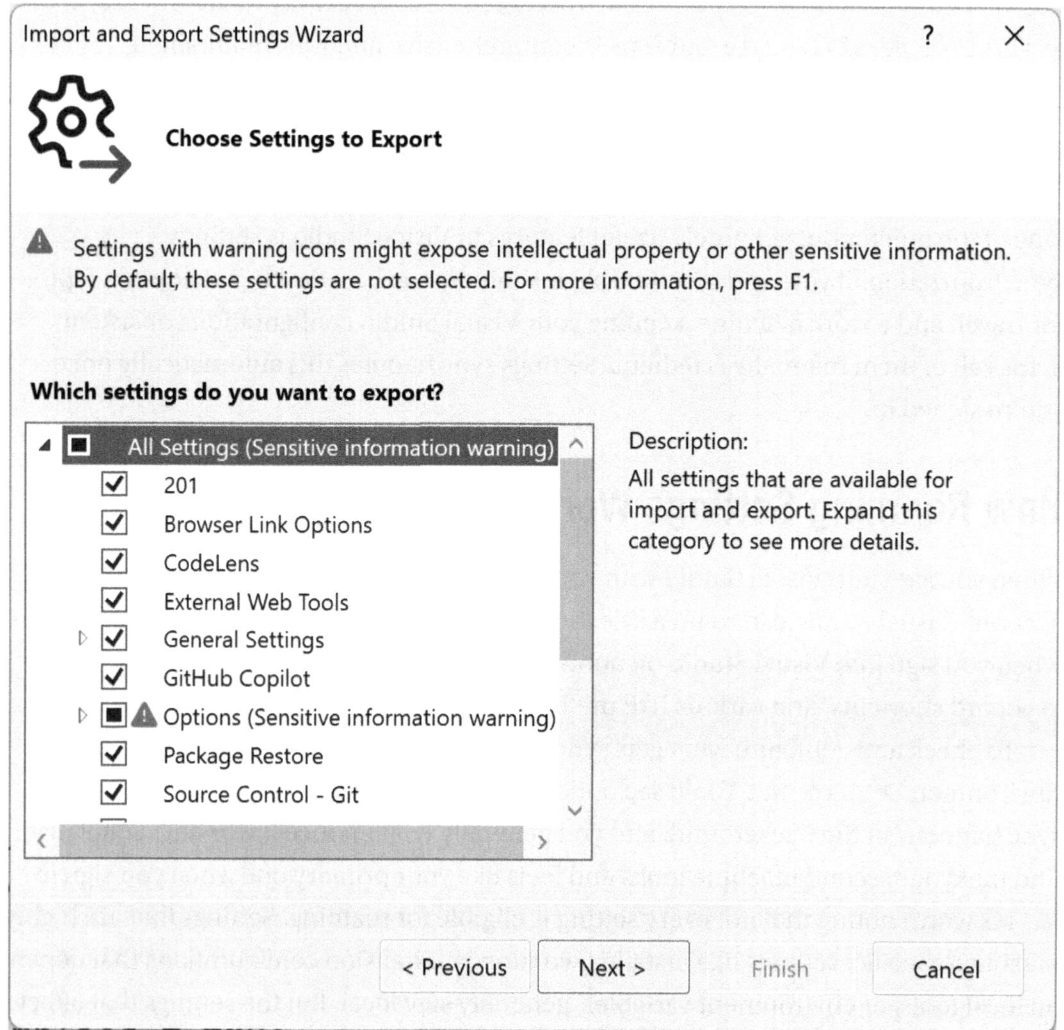

Figure 12-11. *The export page for exporting settings in Visual Studio that you can import into another instance manually*

This is especially valuable before doing something potentially disruptive; think of upgrading your machine, reinstalling Windows, or experimenting with a radically different configuration. Export first, experiment freely, and import to restore if things go sideways.

To import settings on another machine or restore a backup, run the same wizard and choose Import selected environment settings. Visual Studio prompts you to save your current settings first (always say yes), then applies the imported file.

Quick Navigation and the Power of Ctrl+Q

We've mentioned Ctrl+Q throughout the book, but it deserves its own proper treatment here because it's genuinely one of the most transformative productivity changes in recent Visual Studio history. If you've been using Visual Studio 2022 or earlier, you may remember the old Quick Launch box in the top-right corner. Visual Studio 2026 has evolved this into a much more powerful unified search that covers nearly everything in the IDE.

When you press Ctrl+Q, the search box in the title bar activates. From here, you can type a command name to find and execute any menu item without navigating the menus. Type a settings keyword to jump directly to the relevant Options page. Type a file name to quickly open a file from your solution without touching Solution Explorer. Type a feature name to find things like "Code Cleanup" or "Add EditorConfig" that might otherwise require hunting through menus. The search is contextually aware; it knows about your installed workloads and extensions and only surfaces relevant commands.

Bookmarks

For code you return to frequently, bookmarks are an underused feature worth adding to your workflow. Press Ctrl+K, Ctrl+K to toggle a bookmark on the current line. The Bookmarks window (View > Bookmarks) shows all your bookmarks, lets you name them, and lets you jump between them. Ctrl+K, Ctrl+N and Ctrl+K, Ctrl+P cycle forward and backward through bookmarks.

This is particularly useful when you're working across multiple files on a related task. For example, implementing a feature that touches an interface definition, its implementation, a service registration, and a test class. Bookmark all four entry points, and navigating between them takes a single keystroke instead of repeated Ctrl+T searches.

The Task List and TODO Comments

If you use `// TODO:`, `// HACK:`, or `// FIXME:` comments in your code (and trust me, most developers do, even if they don't openly admit it), the Task List gives you a centralized view of all of them. Open it via View ➤ Task List, and you'll see a list of every token-marked comment in your solution, with click-through navigation to the source.

You can also add your own custom tokens. Maybe your team uses `// REVIEW:` or `// PERF:`, by going to Tools ➤ Options ➤ Environment ➤ Task List and adding them there. It's a small but useful way to make the IDE aware of your team's conventions without any additional tooling.

Small Productivity Wins That Add Up

Beyond the larger customization systems, there is a collection of smaller features in Visual Studio 2026 that are easy to miss but genuinely useful once you know about them. This is a curated tour of the ones worth incorporating into your daily habits.

Pinning Files in the Editor

When you have a file you're working on, you can pin it to the left side of the editor tab bar. Right-click the tab and choose Pin Tab, and it stays visible even when you open many other files that would otherwise push it off the tab strip. Pinned tabs are visually distinguished, and they survive window layout switches. For files you live in during a particular sprint or feature cycle, this small thing eliminates a lot of repeated Ctrl+T lookups.

Line Manipulation Shortcuts

A few line-level operations that save time so consistently they deserve explicit mention:

- **Ctrl+E, V** duplicates the current line, endlessly useful when you're writing a series of similar lines and don't want to manually retype the common parts or when you want a quick copy of a line before you modify it.

- **Alt+Up Arrow** and **Alt+Down Arrow** move the current line or selected block up or down. This is perfect for reordering method parameters, adjusting the sequence of using statements, or rearranging items in a switch expression.

- **Ctrl+K**, **Ctrl+C** and **Ctrl+K**, **Ctrl+U** comment and uncomment the selected code, respectively, and these work consistently across all language types.

Paste JSON or XML as Classes

This one is a genuine time-saver if you regularly work with external APIs or configuration files. Copy any JSON or XML structure to the clipboard, maybe from an API response you're examining, or from a documentation example, then use Edit ➤ Paste Special ➤ Paste JSON As Classes (or Paste XML As Classes) in a C# or VB file. Visual Studio generates strongly typed .NET class definitions that match the structure. It's not always perfect with complex nested structures or inconsistent property names, but it gets you 90% of the way there in seconds and is a much more pleasant starting point than writing class definitions by hand.

Adaptive Paste with Copilot

If you have a GitHub Copilot subscription, Adaptive Paste takes regular pasting to another level. When you paste code, Copilot analyzes the surrounding context and suggests modifications to make the pasted code fit. Things like applying consistent naming conventions, filling in missing interface members, and adjusting formatting to match the file's style. You can accept or dismiss the suggestion, and it only appears when Copilot has something genuinely useful to offer. We covered Copilot's editing features in depth in Chapter 8, but Adaptive Paste is specifically worth calling out here because it's most powerful in the context of day-to-day editing habits rather than explicit AI workflows.

Code Cleanup Profiles

We've introduced Code Cleanup several times; it came up in the context of EditorConfig and keyboard shortcuts, both. It's worth expanding on here because the profile configuration is where the real flexibility lives. Code Cleanup (Ctrl+K, Ctrl+E) is configurable through profiles; you define which fixers run when you invoke it. Go to Analyze ➤ Code Cleanup ➤ Configure Code Cleanup to set up your profiles.

You can have a lightweight profile that just applies formatting and removes unnecessary using statements and a more thorough profile that additionally applies code style rules, converts to new language features where available, and resolves analyzer suggestions. Having these pre-configured means cleanup becomes a single intentional gesture rather than a multi-step process. Over the course of a week working on active code, reaching for Ctrl+K, Ctrl+E at the end of each file saves a surprising amount of accumulated cleanup work.

IntelliSense Completion Mode

IntelliSense in Visual Studio 2026 defaults to completion mode; when you press Enter or Tab on a suggestion, it inserts the suggestion text. But there's an alternative: suggestion mode (Ctrl+Alt+Space to toggle), where IntelliSense shows suggestions but only inserts if you explicitly choose one. Some developers prefer suggestion mode because it gives more control; you see what's available without IntelliSense interrupting the flow of typing. If you find yourself fighting IntelliSense and accidentally accepting suggestions you didn't intend, it's worth trying suggestion mode for a day and seeing how it feels.

Zoom in the Editor

This one is almost embarrassingly simple, but worth stating: Ctrl+Scroll Wheel zooms the editor in and out. For presentations, code reviews on a shared screen, or just those moments when a bit more text size helps with readability, this is faster than going into Fonts and Colors. The zoom level persists per-tab, so you can have different zoom levels in different files if needed.

Working with Toolbars

Visual Studio's toolbars are customizable, and while the default setup works fine, you may find that commands you use constantly aren't on any toolbar or that buttons you never touch are taking up space you'd rather have back. Right-click on any toolbar area to see the list of available toolbars; you can show and hide them individually. Most built-in toolbars have more buttons than any single developer needs; hiding the ones you never use is a small but immediately noticeable improvement to visual clarity.

To add a specific command to a toolbar, go to Tools ➤ Customize, open the Commands tab, select the toolbar you want to modify, and use Add Command to search for and add any command. You can remove commands in the same dialog and rearrange the order by dragging.

For commands you invoke dozens of times a day, a keyboard shortcut is almost always a better investment than a toolbar button. The toolbar button requires moving your hand to the mouse and visually locating the right icon. A keyboard shortcut is invisible, frictionless, and consistent. Reserve toolbar space for commands you invoke occasionally and want to be able to find without remembering a shortcut.

Tying It Together: AI-Assisted Personalization

Throughout this chapter, we've been talking about manual customization, things you set up once and benefit from repeatedly. But GitHub Copilot, which we explored in depth in Chapters 8 and 9, has a role to play in personalization too, and it's worth naming explicitly.

The most direct way Copilot assists with customization is through the instruction files we covered in Chapter 9. These `.github/copilot-instructions.md` files tell Copilot about your project's conventions: your naming patterns, your preferred libraries, your architectural style. When Copilot generates code, suggestions, or refactorings, those instructions shape the output. As you document your team's conventions in an instruction file, Copilot becomes progressively better at generating code that already matches your style, reducing the amount of manual cleanup you'd otherwise need to do afterward.

More practically, you can ask Copilot Chat to help with configuration tasks you'd otherwise need to research. Prompts like "Generate an EditorConfig file for a C# project that enforces `_camelCase` private fields, uses var for all types, and requires explicit access modifiers" produce working results you can paste directly into your repository. Similarly, "Generate a code snippet XML for a null guard clause using `ArgumentNullException.ThrowIfNull`" gives you a snippet XML ready to save as a .snippet file.

Copilot also becomes more familiar with your specific code base over time, through its awareness of your open files and recent edits. The suggestions you see after a few weeks of working in a project tend to be noticeably better calibrated to your patterns than those on day one. The practical effect is that the IDE gradually feels more personalized even without you actively tuning it; the AI is doing quiet background work to adapt to you rather than the other way around.

A Note on Finding Your Own Configuration

One piece of advice, having gone through all of the above: don't try to configure everything at once. The best approach to personalizing a development environment is incremental. Start with the big wins: your theme, your font, a handful of keyboard shortcuts for commands you use every day, and let the rest evolve naturally.

The way it tends to work in practice is that you notice friction: "I keep going to the menus for this," or "I keep having to scroll to find that file," or "I always write this same pattern, and it always looks the same." When you notice friction, that's the signal to look for a productivity feature that addresses it. The features in this chapter are responses to real friction points that developers have reported over the years, which means you'll find them most useful precisely when you're already feeling the problem they solve.

Visual Studio 2026's new monthly update cadence also means that the personalization landscape keeps evolving. New settings, new theme options, new snippet capabilities, and new productivity features arrive regularly. Staying connected to the Visual Studio blog at `https://devblogs.microsoft.com/visualstudio/` is the best way to learn about these as they land. The team is notably good at explaining what problems new features are solving, which makes it easy to evaluate whether each addition applies to your workflow.

Summary

Visual Studio 2026 is already a strong IDE out of the box, but you'll feel the biggest day-to-day difference once you start shaping it around how you actually work. A theme and font you enjoy looking at, a couple of window layouts that match your "coding vs. debugging vs. reviewing" brain, and a small set of keyboard shortcuts you genuinely use are the kinds of tweaks that quietly remove friction all day long.

The fun part is that most of these changes compound. Once you've got EditorConfig helping keep style consistent, Code Cleanup doing the boring parts, snippets removing your most repeated typing, and templates giving you a better starting point than "delete boilerplate, again," you'll notice you spend more time thinking about *your* problem and less time wrestling the tool. And that's the whole point.

In the next chapter, we'll zoom out and talk about staying current with the release cadence and how to keep your skills sharp as Visual Studio and .NET evolve, without turning "keeping up" into a second job.

CHAPTER 13

Future-Proofing Your Development Skills

If you have made it this far, you now have a comprehensive understanding of Visual Studio 2026. You know how to navigate the modernized Fluent UI, manage complex solutions, write and debug code with precision, and lean on GitHub Copilot for everything from boilerplate generation to performance profiling. You have the tools to build, test, and deploy modern applications effectively.

But mastering a tool at a specific point in time is only half the battle. Software development is not a static discipline, and Visual Studio 2026 is not a static product. As we discussed back in Chapter 1, Microsoft has fundamentally changed how this IDE evolves, moving to a rapid monthly update cadence and an annual rollover model. At the same time, the .NET ecosystem continues its yearly release cycle, and AI capabilities are advancing at a pace that is frankly difficult to comprehend.

Future-proofing your skills isn't about perfectly predicting what technology will dominate in five years. It is about building a sustainable system for adopting new features, modernizing your code incrementally, and keeping your team aligned as the ground moves beneath you. In this final chapter, we are going to zoom out and look at strategies for staying current without turning "keeping up" into a second, unpaid job.

Embracing the Monthly Release Cadence

You might remember from Chapter 1 that Visual Studio 2026 abandoned the old "Current" and "Preview" channels in favor of the new Stable and Insiders channels. This alignment with the VS Code release model brings monthly feature updates rather than quarterly ones, meaning the IDE you are using today will be measurably more capable six months from now.

G. Versluis, *Getting Started with Visual Studio 2026*, https://doi.org/10.1007/979-8-8688-2691-7_13

The challenge is how to absorb those updates without disrupting your daily work. The best approach for development teams is what you might call the 80/20 split. Have the majority of your team run the Stable channel so their environment remains completely predictable during critical sprint deliverables. Then, have one or two developers, perhaps your tech leads or those who simply enjoy living on the cutting edge, run the Insiders channel side-by-side with Stable. Because Visual Studio allows both channels to be installed simultaneously on the same machine without conflict, these developers can safely test new features, validate that your team's custom extensions still work, and flag any potential workflow changes before the rest of the team receives the update.

To make managing these updates entirely frictionless, Visual Studio 2026 introduced an Update on Close feature. When enabled via Tools ➤ Options ➤ Environment ➤ Product Updates, the IDE quietly downloads available updates in the background while you work. When you close Visual Studio at the end of the day, it automatically applies the update, ensuring you start your next morning with the latest fixes and features without staring at a progress bar.

If you are responsible for keeping your team's environments synchronized as updates roll out, don't forget the `.vsconfig` file we covered early in the book. Exporting your installation configuration and keeping it in your repository ensures that when a new developer joins the team, or when a major update requires a new workload, everyone is building from the exact same toolset.

Modernizing Code Incrementally

Keeping your IDE updated is straightforward; keeping your code base updated requires a bit more intention. With .NET moving on a strict annual release cycle, .NET 10 is the current standard; with .NET 11 entering previews as we speak, the days of waiting five years to undertake a massive, painful framework migration are over. The modern approach is continuous, incremental modernization.

Your primary tool for this is the .NET Upgrade Assistant. While it has existed as a standalone tool and an extension for a while, it is now deeply integrated into the Visual Studio 2026 experience. You can right-click any project in Solution Explorer and select Upgrade, and the assistant will analyze your dependencies, update your target frameworks, and even modify your code to resolve breaking changes. Because it operates incrementally, you can upgrade a single class library, run your tests, commit the changes, and move on to the next one, rather than attempting a high-risk "big bang" rewrite.

And as we explored in Chapter 8, this process is now supercharged by the Copilot app Modernization agent. Instead of just mechanically bumping version numbers, the AI-powered agent assesses your project, generates a phased migration plan, and autonomously refactors deprecated APIs to their modern equivalents while you review the changes. Using this agent incrementally as new .NET versions drop ensures your code base never accumulates the kind of technical debt that makes future upgrades terrifying.

Alongside the Upgrade Assistant, the built-in C# analyzers are your best defense against legacy code rot. When a new version of C# introduces a more efficient way to write a pattern, like the enhanced pattern matching or collection expressions we've seen recently, Visual Studio surfaces these as informational messages or suggestions. If you want to force your team to adopt the new syntax, you can escalate the severity of these specific analyzer rules to "Warning" in your `.editorconfig` file, which we set up in Chapter 12.

This creates a gentle, automated pressure to modernize. When developers touch a file to add a new feature, the IDE highlights the legacy syntax and offers a one-click Quick Action (Ctrl+.) to update it. The code base modernizes itself naturally over time, driven by the tool rather than by dedicated, expensive refactoring sprints.

Evolving Your AI Workflow

Building on what we covered in Chapters 8 and 9, the most important thing to understand about AI in Visual Studio is that the models and capabilities will change faster than any other part of the IDE. The prompts that work perfectly today might be unnecessary tomorrow because the AI has learned to infer the context automatically. Similarly, the custom agents you build today might be replaced by native IDE features next year.

To future-proof your AI workflow, focus on standardizing your context rather than memorizing highly specific prompts. The `.github/copilot-instructions.md` file we discussed in Chapter 9 is your most valuable asset here. Treat this file as living documentation. When your team decides on a new architectural pattern or adopts a new testing framework, update the instructions file immediately. Because GitHub Copilot reads this file automatically, your entire team's AI assistant instantly aligns with the new standard. You are effectively programming the AI to enforce your team's evolving consensus.

Furthermore, keep an eye on the Model Context Protocol (MCP) ecosystem. As we explored, MCP allows Copilot to reach out to your local databases, internal APIs, and proprietary documentation. As vendors release new MCP servers for their products, integrating them into your Visual Studio environment will give Copilot an increasingly accurate picture of your specific business domain. The developers who thrive over the next few years will not be the ones who write the cleverest prompts; they will be the ones who best curate the context their AI has access to.

Automating Standards to Prevent Decay

One of the recurring themes of this book has been letting Visual Studio handle the mechanical parts of development so you can focus on the creative parts. As your projects age and your team grows, the only way to maintain quality without micromanagement is through rigorous automation of your standards.

We talked about EditorConfig in Chapter 12 for standardizing formatting and code style rules inside the editor. But an EditorConfig file is only a suggestion until you enforce it. To truly future-proof a code base, you must tie your IDE rules directly to your continuous integration pipeline. By configuring your build to treat EditorConfig style violations as build warnings or errors (using the `<EnforceCodeStyleInBuild>` property), you guarantee that the rules your IDE displays locally are exactly the same rules your build server enforces.

This loops back to the GitHub Actions integration we explored in Chapter 10. When Visual Studio 2026 surfaces your CI/CD workflows directly in the Solution Explorer, it closes the feedback loop. A developer writes code, the IDE applies the EditorConfig formatting via Code Cleanup, the developer commits, and if any standard was missed, the GitHub Action catches it and reports the failure right back inside Visual Studio. This automated alignment prevents the slow decay of code base quality over time, regardless of how many developers come and go.

Curating Your Information Diet

Finally, staying current requires a sustainable approach to consuming information. The Microsoft ecosystem produces an overwhelming amount of content, and trying to read every piece of documentation or watch every community standup is a guaranteed recipe for burnout. You need a filter.

For Visual Studio specifically, the official Visual Studio Blog (`https://devblogs.microsoft.com/visualstudio/`) is the single highest-signal resource available. Because of the new monthly release cadence, the team publishes highly focused, practical posts explaining exactly what was added in the latest Insiders or Stable release and, crucially, *why* it was added. Reading these release posts once a month takes ten minutes and guarantees you won't miss a major productivity feature.

Similarly, the .NET Blog (`https://devblogs.microsoft.com/dotnet/`) is the definitive source for framework and language evolution. Tune in heavily around November when the annual major releases drop, and you will get the comprehensive wrap-ups of new C# features and performance improvements. Between these two feeds, you will capture 95% of the information you actually need to keep your skills relevant, leaving you free to spend the rest of your time actually building software.

Summary

When you strip away the marketing terms and the version numbers, Visual Studio 2026 is fundamentally an engine for translating your thoughts into working software as smoothly as possible. Throughout this book, we have explored how Microsoft has systematically removed the friction from that process. From the massive performance gains in solution loading and the modernized Fluent UI to the profound integration of AI that can actively debug and refactor alongside you, the IDE has never been more capable of getting out of your way.

But the real power of Visual Studio doesn't come from using it exactly as it ships out of the box. It comes from tailoring the window layouts, keyboard shortcuts, and code snippets to match your specific mental model. It comes from documenting your team's architecture in Copilot instruction files so the AI becomes a true partner in your domain. It comes from setting up EditorConfig and continuous integration so that doing the right thing happens automatically, and doing the wrong thing is caught instantly.

The software development landscape will undoubtedly continue to shift. New versions of .NET will arrive, AI models will become exponentially smarter, and architectures will evolve. By embracing the incremental update channels, leaning on modernization tools like the Upgrade Assistant, and standardizing your context, you ensure that your environment evolves right alongside the industry. You now have the knowledge not just to use Visual Studio 2026, but to make it work relentlessly for you. Now, it's time to go build something great.

Visual Studio 2026 Keyboard Shortcuts

This reference guide compiles every keyboard shortcut mentioned in this book, along with essential standard keys for high-productivity develofpment. These shortcuts assume the Default (General) keyboard mapping profile.

Global Search and Navigation

Table A-1. *Global search and navigation shortcut keys*

Action	Shortcut	Description
All-In-One Search	Ctrl+Q	Opens the unified search for IDE features, options, and settings.
Code Search (Go To All)	Ctrl+T or Ctrl+,	Instantly search for files, types, and members across the solution.
Feature Search	Ctrl+Shift+P	Searches specifically for commands, menus, and options (scoped).
Find in Files	Ctrl+Shift+F	Opens the advanced solution-wide search (supports Regex).
Quick Find (Local)	Ctrl+F	Searches within the currently open file.
Go To Line	Ctrl+G	Jump to a specific line number.
Navigate Backward	Ctrl+-	Jumps back to your previous cursor location/file.

(continued)

© Gerald Versluis 2026
G. Versluis, *Getting Started with Visual Studio 2026*, https://doi.org/10.1007/979-8-8688-2691-7

Table A-1. (*continued*)

Action	Shortcut	Description
Navigate Forward	Ctrl+Shift+-	Jumps forward to where you were before navigating back.
Go To Definition	F12	Navigates directly to the source definition of the symbol.
Peek Definition	Alt+F12	Opens an inline window to view the definition without leaving the file.
Find All References	Shift+F12	Opens a tool window showing every usage of the selected symbol.
Sync with Active File	Ctrl+[, S	Highlights the currently open file in the Solution Explorer.

AI and GitHub Copilot

Table A-2. *AI and GitHub Copilot-related shortcut keys*

Action	Shortcut	Description
Inline Copilot Chat	Alt+/	Opens the floating Copilot prompt directly in the editor.
Open Copilot Chat Pane	Ctrl+\, Ctrl+C	Focuses or opens the main GitHub Copilot Chat tool window.
Accept Suggestion	Tab	Accepts the gray "ghost text" or Next Edit Suggestion (NES).
Partial Accept (Word)	Ctrl+Right Arrow	Accepts the ghost text one word at a time.
Trigger Suggestions	Alt+\	Forces Copilot to generate a new suggestion if none is visible.

Code Editing and Refactoring

Table A-3. *Code editing and refactoring-related shortcut keys*

Action	Shortcut	Description
Quick Actions (Lightbulb)	Ctrl+. or Alt+Enter	Opens the menu for fixes, refactorings, and AI suggestions.
Format Document	Ctrl+K, Ctrl+D	Applies correct indentation and spacing to the entire file.
Code Cleanup	Ctrl+K, Ctrl+E	Runs configured cleanup rules (sort usings, fix styles).
Comment Selection	Ctrl+K, Ctrl+C	Comments out the selected lines.
Uncomment Selection	Ctrl+K, Ctrl+U	Uncomments the selected lines.
Duplicate Line	Ctrl+E, V	Duplicates the current line or selection.
Move Line Up/Down	Alt+Up Arrow/Down Arrow	Swaps the current line with the one above or below it.
Rename Symbol	Ctrl+R, Ctrl+R	Renames a variable, class, or method safely across the code base.
Surround With	Ctrl+K, Ctrl+S	Wraps selection in a block (try/catch, if, region).
Insert Snippet	Ctrl+K, Ctrl+X	Opens the snippet picker.
Multi-caret (Next Match)	Shift+Alt+.	Adds a cursor at the next occurrence of the current selection.
Multi-caret (Mouse)	Ctrl+Alt+Click	Adds a cursor wherever you click.
Quick Add New File	Shift+Alt+N	Opens the compact dialog to create files/folders without the template wizard.

Debugging and Testing

Table A-4. *Debugging and testing-related shortcut keys*

Action	Shortcut	Description
Start Debugging	F5	Builds and runs the application with the debugger attached.
Start Without Debugging	Ctrl+F5	Runs the application without the debugger (faster loop).
Toggle Breakpoint	F9	Sets or removes a breakpoint on the current line.
Step Over	F10	Executes the next line (skips entering functions).
Step Into	F11	Enters the function call on the current line.
Step Out	Shift+F11	Runs until the current function returns.
Run All Tests	Ctrl+R, A	Runs all unit tests in the solution.
Repeat Last Test Run	Ctrl+R, L	Re-runs the last set of executed tests.

Window and Layout Management

Table A-5. *Window and layout-related shortcut keys*

Action	Shortcut	Description
Git Changes Window	Ctrl+0, Ctrl+G	Opens the Git Changes window for committing/staging.
Git Repository Window	Ctrl+0, Ctrl+R	Opens the full graph view of your branches and history.
Solution Explorer	Ctrl+Alt+L	Opens or focuses the Solution Explorer.
Test Explorer	Ctrl+E, T	Opens the Test Explorer window.
Close Current Tab	Ctrl+F4 or Ctrl+W	Closes the active document tab.
Close All Tool Windows	Shift+Esc	Hides all side panels to maximize the editor code area.
Apply Window Layout	Ctrl+Alt+1...0	Switches to a saved custom window layout.

Migration Checklist—VS 2022 to VS 2026

Migrating to Visual Studio 2026 is designed to be a side-by-side, non-destructive process. Use this checklist to ensure a safe transition for both your personal environment and your team's code base.

Phase 1: Preparation (In Visual Studio 2022)

- **Export Environment Settings:** Go to Tools ➤ Import and Export Settings, and save your keyboard shortcuts, fonts, and window layouts to a `.vssettings` file.

- **Export Team Configuration:** Open the Visual Studio Installer, click Export on your current installation, and save a `.vsconfig` file. Check this into your repository root so your team (and VS 2026) can auto-detect required workloads.

- **Prepare Extensions:** Identify critical third-party extensions. For ReSharper users, install the ReSharper Migration Assistant in VS 2022 to bridge your license and settings to the new IDE.

- **Clean State:** Ensure all code is committed and your working branch is clean. Run a final test pass to establish a baseline.

Phase 2: Installation and Setup

- **Side-by-Side Install:** Install Visual Studio 2026 alongside VS 2022. Do *not* uninstall the old version yet.

- **Extension Migration:** During installation, ensure the "Include installed extensions from the Visual Studio Marketplace" check box is selected.

- **Account Sync:** Sign in with the same GitHub/Microsoft account used previously to trigger automatic cloud setting synchronization.

- **Verify Workloads:** Open your solution. If you included the `.vsconfig` file, VS 2026 should prompt you to install any missing SDKs or tools immediately.

Phase 3: Modernizing the Code Base

- **Solution Upgrade (Recommended):** Right-click your Solution node in Solution Explorer, select Save Solution As, and choose the new `.slnx` format. This makes the solution file human-readable and reduces Git merge conflicts.

- **Run the Modernization Agent:** For legacy projects, right-click the project and select Upgrade. Use the Copilot-powered agent to iteratively update target frameworks (e.g., to .NET 10) and refactor deprecated APIs.

- **Check CI/CD Pipelines:** Update your GitHub Actions or Azure DevOps pipelines to use windows-2026 (or equivalent) build runners.

- **Enable EditorConfig:** Ensure your solution has a `.editorconfig` file to enforce code styles, as VS 2026's analyzers are stricter and more capable than previous versions.

Phase 4: Validation

- **Clean and Rebuild:** Perform a Build ➤ Clean Solution followed by a Rebuild to clear old `bin/obj` artifacts.

- **Test Discovery:** Open Test Explorer, and verify all tests are discovered and pass.

- **Launch Profiles:** Press F5 to verify that your launch profiles (IIS Express, Kestrel, Android Emulators) work correctly.

Further Reading and Resources

This appendix collects the most useful links, channels, communities, and tools to keep learning beyond this book. Everything is grouped by topic so you can go deep on what matters most to you.

Official Visual Studio Resources

Table C-1. *Official Visual Studio resources*

Resource	URL
Visual Studio home and download	`https://visualstudio.microsoft.com`
Visual Studio Insiders download	`https://visualstudio.microsoft.com/insiders`
VS 2026 Release Notes	`https://learn.microsoft.com/visualstudio/releases/vs18/release-notes`
VS 2026 Insiders Release Notes	`https://learn.microsoft.com/visualstudio/releases/vs18/release-notes-insiders`
Visual Studio Blog	`https://devblogs.microsoft.com/visualstudio`
Visual Studio System Requirements	`https://learn.microsoft.com/visualstudio/releases/vs18/vs-system-requirements`
Report a bug/suggest a feature	`https://developercommunity.visualstudio.com`

(*continued*)

© Gerald Versluis 2026
G. Versluis, *Getting Started with Visual Studio 2026*, https://doi.org/10.1007/979-8-8688-2691-7

Table C-1. (*continued*)

Resource	URL
Visual Studio Marketplace (extensions)	`https://marketplace.visualstudio.com/vs`
Import/export .vsconfig files	`https://learn.microsoft.com/visualstudio/install/import-export-installation-configurations`
Offline installation guide	`https://learn.microsoft.com/visualstudio/install/create-an-offline-installation-of-visual-studio`
Troubleshoot installation issues	`https://learn.microsoft.com/troubleshoot/developer/visualstudio/installation/troubleshoot-installation-issues`
IntelliCode	`https://visualstudio.microsoft.com/services/intellicode`

GitHub Copilot Resources

Table C-2. *GitHub Copilot resources*

Resource	URL
GitHub Copilot home page	`https://github.com/features/copilot`
GitHub Copilot documentation	`https://docs.github.com/copilot`
Copilot Chat Cookbook (prompt examples)	`https://docs.github.com/copilot/tutorials/copilot-chat-cookbook`
Copilot customization library	`https://docs.github.com/copilot/tutorials`
Add repository custom instructions	`https://docs.github.com/copilot/how-to/configure-custom-instructions/add-repository-instructions?tool=visualstudio`
Create custom agents	`https://docs.github.com/copilot/how-to/use-copilot-agents/coding-agent/create-custom-agents`

(continued)

Table C-2. (*continued*)

Resource	URL
Copilot Spaces documentation	`https://docs.github.com/copilot/concepts/context/spaces`
Awesome GitHub Copilot (community customizations)	`https://github.com/github/awesome-copilot`
GitHub Copilot free for qualified developers	`https://github.com/github-copilot/freeforqualifieddevelopers`
GitHub Copilot usage and billing	`https://github.com/settings/billing`
Enterprise Copilot policy management	`https://docs.github.com/enterprise-cloud@latest/copilot/how-to/administer-copilot/manage-for-enterprise/manage-enterprise-policies`
Microsoft Learn—Copilot Fundamentals	`https://learn.microsoft.com/training/paths/copilot`

Model Context Protocol (MCP)

Table C-3. *MCP-related resources*

Resource	URL
Official MCP documentation	`https://modelcontextprotocol.io`
MCP C# SDK (build your own)	`https://github.com/modelcontextprotocol/csharp-sdk`
Anthropic's complete guide to building skills	`https://resources.anthropic.com/hubfs/The-Complete-Guide-to-Building-Skill-for-Claude.pdf`
Anthropic's Skill Creator skill	`https://github.com/anthropics/skills/blob/main/skills/skill-creator/SKILL.md`

.NET and C# Resources

Table C-4. *.NET and C# related resources*

Resource	URL
.NET documentation	https://learn.microsoft.com/dotnet
C# documentation	https://learn.microsoft.com/dotnet/csharp
.NET Blog	https://devblogs.microsoft.com/dotnet
.NET support lifecycle (LTS/STS)	https://dotnet.microsoft.com/platform/support/policy
.NET MAUI support lifecycle	https://dotnet.microsoft.com/platform/support/policy/maui
NuGet package repository	https://www.nuget.org
.NET Foundation	https://dotnetfoundation.org
.NET Upgrade Assistant overview	https://learn.microsoft.com/dotnet/core/porting/upgrade-assistant-overview
GitHub Copilot app modernization	https://learn.microsoft.com/dotnet/core/porting/github-copilot-app-modernization/overview

.NET MAUI Resources

Table C-5. *.NET MAUI resources*

Resource	URL
.NET MAUI documentation	https://learn.microsoft.com/dotnet/maui
.NET MAUI support lifecycle	https://dotnet.microsoft.com/platform/support/policy/maui
.NET MAUI on Microsoft Learn	https://learn.microsoft.com/training/paths/build-apps-with-dotnet-maui
.NET MAUI Community Toolkit	https://github.com/CommunityToolkit/Maui
.NET Community Toolkit (MVVM, etc.)	https://github.com/CommunityToolkit/dotnet
.NET MAUI Workshop (hands-on)	https://aka.ms/maui-workshop

ASP.NET Core Resources

Because ASP.NET Core is the foundation for modern .NET web development, mastering its core concepts will help you across Blazor, Web APIs, and microservices.

Table C-6. *ASP.NET resources*

Resource	URL
ASP.NET Core Official Documentation	`https://learn.microsoft.com/aspnet/core`
Create your first Web API	`https://learn.microsoft.com/aspnet/core/tutorials/first-web-api`
Minimal APIs Overview	`https://learn.microsoft.com/aspnet/core/fundamentals/minimal-apis`
Authentication and Authorization	`https://learn.microsoft.com/aspnet/core/security/authentication/`
.NET Architecture Guides (eShop reference)	`https://learn.microsoft.com/dotnet/architecture/`

Blazor Resources

Blazor has become Microsoft's flagship framework for building interactive web UI with C#. These links cover everything from getting started to advanced component lifecycles.

Table C-7. *Blazor resources*

Resource	URL
Blazor Official Documentation	`https://learn.microsoft.com/aspnet/core/blazor`
Build your first Blazor app (step-by-step)	`https://dotnet.microsoft.com/learn/aspnet/blazor-tutorial/intro`
Microsoft Learn: Build web apps with Blazor	`https://learn.microsoft.com/training/paths/build-web-apps-with-blazor/`
MudBlazor (popular component library)	`https://mudblazor.com`
Jimmy Engström's Blog	`https://engstromjimmy.com`
Microsoft Fluent UI Blazor	`https://www.fluentui-blazor.net`

Aspire Resources

Aspire is the easiest way to build, observe, and deploy cloud-native, distributed applications. These resources will help you master orchestration, service discovery, and telemetry.

Table C-8. *Aspire resources*

Resource	URL
Aspire Official Documentation	`https://learn.microsoft.com/dotnet/aspire` and `https://aspire.dev`
Aspire GitHub Repository	`https://github.com/dotnet/aspire`
Official Aspire Samples	`https://github.com/dotnet/aspire-samples`
eShop Cloud-Native Reference App	`https://github.com/dotnet/eShop`
Let's Learn .NET: Aspire (Video Series)	`https://aka.ms/letslearn/dotnet/aspire`

Events and Community

Table C-9. Events and community resources

Resource	URL
.NET Conf (annual, free, online)	`https://www.dotnetconf.net`
VS Live! (in-person and virtual events)	`https://vslive.com`
Microsoft Build	`https://build.microsoft.com`
Visual Studio Developer Community	`https://developercommunity.visualstudio.com`

Staying Up to Date

Because Visual Studio now ships on a monthly cadence, the best way to stay current is to

- Subscribe to the Visual Studio Blog at `https://devblogs.microsoft.com/visualstudio`

- Watch the monthly release party videos on the Microsoft Visual Studio YouTube channel: `https://www.youtube.com/@VisualStudio`

- Check the Insiders release notes if you're on the Insiders channel: `https://learn.microsoft.com/visualstudio/releases/vs18/release-notes-insiders`

Index

A

Adaptive Paste, 289

Adaptive Paste code, 72–74, 94

Administrative Templates (ADMX), 131

Advanced Git workflows
multiple remote repositories, 221

Agent Mode, 148, 155, 163
BYOM, 151–153
practical examples and best use
cases, 150–151
working, 150

Agent Skills, 175
customization, 191
demand, 174
frontmatter, 176
in .github/skills/, 178
minimal content f, 175
organization-level and enterprise-level
skills, 175
preferred tools, 179
reusable workflows, 179
specialized guidance for specific,
repeatable tasks, 191
structure, 175
system prompt, 179
in Visual Studio, 178

AI, 2–3
Agent Mode, 10
customization and infrastructure
integration, 167
and GitHub Copilot-related shortcut
keys, 300
Profiler Agent, 3, 10

AI-assisted test debugging, 106–107

AI-assisted test writing, 99–100

AI-powered commit message generation,
201, 202

AI-powered development
across ecosystem, 164
Calipot (*see* GitHub Calipot)

Appium, 185

Arrange-Act-Assert patterns, 120

Aspire, 252
Dashboard, 255
MCP, 184
orchestration, 253–255
resources, 310

Aspire.Hosting.Redis NuGet package,
255, 256

ASP.NET and web development, 17

ASP.NET applications, 118–119

ASP.NET Core, 232–234

ASP.NET Core Web App project, 240

ASP.NET resources, 309

Avalonia, 257

Awesome Copilot repository, 179

Azure and AI development
workload, 17

Azure DevOps, 194, 206
application lifecycle management
capabilities, 213
connection, 213, 214
Work Items, 216, 217

Azure Pipelines, 214–216

B

C

D

W

X, Y

Z